Founder of Tannoy

The
TANNOY
Story

JULIAN ALDERTON

First published 2004
Re-Published 2019 by
Guy R. Fountain Ltd
PO Box 1559
Guildford
GU1 9AA

isbn: 978-1-78972-169-0

© Julian Alderton

Photos and Drawings supplied by
Michael Fountain

The
TANNOY
Story

JULIAN ALDERTON

This book is sold subject to the condition that it shall not be re-sold, lent, hired out or otherwise circulated in any binding or cover other than that in which it is published and without a similar condition being imposed upon the subsequent purchaser without the express consent of the author and publisher.

Printed and bound by
Knaphill Printing Company Ltd
16 Lower Guildford Road
Knaphill
Woking
Surrey
GU21 2EG

PREFACE

The Aldertons and the Fountains were close friends and neighbours in West Norwood, South East London in the 1920s and their friendship and that of their children endured for years.

Julian, the younger son of Douglas and Kathleen Alderton, has always had a keen interest in the history of communication and thus, when he renewed contact with me some years ago with a view to putting this remarkable piece of history into print, I was only too keen to co-operate.

Having worked with my father, Guy Fountain, from 1946 to 1967 and having always maintained subsequent contact with all the old employees wherever possible, it was a pleasure and a challenge to provide all that I could by way of my own experiences and to facilitate access to the many ex-employees who were able to be interviewed by Julian in their later years. Sadly few remain from that exciting era and the opportunity to reminisce diminishes year by year.

This story however, is a true record of those days of pioneering, innovation and invention and, whilst it might appeal more to those of us who can still recall those days it is, nevertheless, an important record of much that has led to modern society and technology for Tannoy was undoubtedly the inspiration for the whole of the public address industry.

Michael H. Fountain,
Guildford, Surrey.

February, 2003.

*Left:
Transverse current
Microphone Type 400.
From a 1937 Tannoy
Brochure*

*Right:
Moving Coil
Microphone Type 410.
From a 1937 Tannoy
Brochure*

CONTENTS

PREFACE	By Michael H. Fountian	5
INTRODUCTION		9
ACKNOWLEDGEMENTS		12
CHAPTER 1	WHY IT STARTED – AND HOW	15
CHAPTER 2	GUY IS INTRODUCED TO SOUND AMPLIFIERS	29
CHAPTER 3	EARLY PROGRESS IN PUBLIC ADDRESS	37
CHAPTER 4	SWINGS AND ROUNDABOUTS	59
CHAPTER 5	THE DEVELOPMENT OF TANNOY IN THE LATE 1930s	73
CHAPTER 6	TANNOY'S INVOLVEMENT WITH THE R.A.F.	85
CHAPTER 7	THE POWER MICROPHONE	97
CHAPTER 8	1939–1945	117
CHAPTER 9	THE RABBIT WARREN	129
CHAPTER 10	THE END OF THE BEGINNING	139
CHAPTER 11	ADMINISTRATION 1947–1950	163
CHAPTER 12	THE DUAL CONCENTRIC LOUDSPEAKER	181
CHAPTER 13	GUY BACK AT THE HELM	197
CHAPTER 14	GUY STILL AT THE HELM	219
CHAPTER 15	THE HARMAN YEARS	237
CHAPTER 16	TANNOY TODAY	251
EPILOGUE		253
BIBLIOGRAPHY		258
INDEX		259

WHAT ARE WATTS?

SO much confusion exists regarding the output rating of power amplifiers in relation to their efficiency, that it is felt that some notes on the subject will prove of value.

Owing to the lack of standardisation, it is quite possible that the output of a particular amplifier could be stated as 10 watts, 15 watts or even 50 watts. The first figure of 10 watts is taken at less than 5%, harmonic distortion (usually known as undistorted output), the second is maximum speech output, and the third, anode dissipation.

Audibility.

The function of a correctly designed amplifying system is to give natural reproduction of speech and music over a given area, or throughout a certain building. There are other factors besides 'output watts' which determine the audibility given by an equipment under any particular circumstances.

1. The efficiency of the loudspeaker affects the acoustic output. An efficient loudspeaker used with a small amplifier may give twice the volume of sound obtainable from an inefficient loudspeaker used with an amplifier having double the 'watts' output.

2. The quality or 'naturalness' of the reproduced sound is of far greater importance than mere volume. The 'watts output' of an amplifier has no relation to this feature. The frequency characteristic is usually the only other point quoted. A characteristic that is stated to be linear from 50—10,000 cycles implies that any frequency between these limits is equally amplified. The amplitude characteristic is even more important. An amplifier is said to have a linear amplitude characteristic if an increase in input ratio gives the same increase in output ratio.

3. The correct design and matching of the complete system from microphone or pick-up to amplifier and loudspeaker is also of primary importance.
"TANNOY" engineers have realised the importance of these considerations, and know that it is often possible to economise in the size of the amplifier and subsequent running costs.

The advice of "TANNOY" experts and a test of the equipment under actual conditions, are the best methods of choosing suitable sound amplifiers.

Taken from a 1936 Tannoy brochure

INTRODUCTION

Since the industrial revolution the names of a few entrepreneurs or of the companies they created have become so closely associated with ideas, inventions or products that they have become words which are now in common use. Amelia Bloomer, James Thomas Brudenell the 7th Earl of Cardigan, Charles Mackintosh, and Arthur the 1st Duke of Wellington, gave their names to articles of clothing. John McAdam is remembered by a road surface and John Montagu the 4th Earl of Sandwich preceded McDonald on the snacks scene. However, company names which have become universally accepted as definitive terms are few, but notable among these are Thermos, Hoover and, of course, Tannoy.

Public address systems, of whatever make, are very often referred to as 'the tannoy' and in offices and factories throughout the country requests for personnel to be paged are so often answered by the sentence, "I'll call him on the tannoy". Such is the fame of Guy Fountain's brainchild that the word, 'tannoy' is an entry in the Oxford Dictionary:

> **Tannoy**: /tænoi/ *n. proper.* a type of public address system.

In an article in *Wireless World* of 13th November, 1936 entitled 'Early P.A. Sound Amplification in the Ancient World', C. Eric Dust wrote:

> "Convincing evidence of early apparatus to amplify the human voice is plentiful in all parts of the world. The use by the Greeks of amphorae to amplify the voices of actors in stage plays is interesting as it shows that they possessed a not inconsiderable knowledge of acoustics. A number of jars, [two-handled and with narrow necks and bases], were placed at various positions around the stage and they were partly filled with liquid until they were tuned to the voice frequency desired. The voice was amplified by the sympathetic resonance of the jars. It is probable that some similar method was used at Delphi and at other homes of the Oracles. . . . In these cases the amphorae were probably used to add an unearthly atmosphere to the pronouncements of the Seers as well as to amplify their words."

The TANNOY Story

Greek history records that on many occasions the Oracles addressed large audiences. [Audiences so great that, almost certainly, they could not have heard their words without some form of acoustic assistance. This principle was further developed in the mid 19th Century by the German scientist, Hermann von Helmholtz, a pioneer of both optics and acoustics. His resonating vessels became known as Helmholtz Resonators.]
The article continues:

> "It has been suggested that the ancient Egyptians understood how to construct their temples and theatres so that the voices were actually amplified and not absorbed as is so often the case in modern buildings. Perhaps the Egyptians learned this art from the natural whispering galleries which are to be found in many parts of the world. Incidentally, these galleries must often have been used by sentinels to warn their people of the approach of enemies and one can readily imagine the ordered alarm of some hill village occasioned by the hollow roar of warning from the amplified voice of the lonely outpost perhaps two or three miles away."

[In later years these galleries were reproduced, deliberately or otherwise, in the construction of buildings, notably the whispering gallery in Sir Christopher Wren's St. Paul's Cathedral.]

> "Anterior to the Greek and Egyptian P.A. was the use of the drum. While this does not amplify the voice it is undoubtedly a method of public address, and a very effective one at that. The cunningly devised tree trunk body of the African drum addresses vast numbers of people at much greater distances than would be possible with our up-to-date equipment. He who has heard the lokali can never forget its mysterious throb and all who know Africa will testify to its efficiency Detailed information is sent and understood, but only by the natives, never the white man.
> "The 'Moose' call of the North American Indians is possibly the ancestor of the modern megaphone, in this case the human voice is used, the hunter imitating the cry of a moose which is amplified and made directional by the horn. The quality of reproduction is presumably good as it is said that any moose within hearing will answer the call. These instances will be sufficient to prove that amplifying equipment is not new by some thousands of years. It only remains for some intrepid explorer to find the fossilised remains of a prehistoric thermionic valve in the Gobi Desert to prove that we have actually made little advance since the stone age. As, however, this discovery has yet to be made, we can still pride ourselves on being such clever fellows as to have devised our modern sound amplifying equipment."

More recently the Autexophone, which was invented by Sir Charles Parsons and developed by *His Masters' Voice*, used pneumatic power to amplify sound in which the movement of the diaphragm of a gramophone soundbox was used to modulate the airflow from a turbine.

The idea for this book came to me one evening in the 1980s when I was making one of my customary visits to the Vintage Wireless Museum in Dulwich and, in the course of a typical conversation with Gerry Wells, its curator, I asked

Introduction

Gerry if he would restore my Tannoy wireless set and the conversation drifted around to the Tannoy company and its creator, Guy Fountain. Gerry had known Guy Fountain quite well and he recalled many amusing anecdotes about Guy's unusual, erratic behaviour and the ensuing interchange of stories led to a most amusing evening; we sat at Gerry's kitchen table, drinking numerous mugs of tea and I suggested to Gerry that the story should be recorded and the decision to do so was made that evening. Thus the seed was sown.

Gerry Wells volunteered to feed me with technical information and he gave me unrestricted access to his library of technical books and journals but it was soon apparent that we needed much more intimate knowledge before I could make a start. I therefore set about searching for Michael Fountain with whom I had lost contact since about 1965. This took me nearly three years but I eventually ran him to ground. Michael rose to the bait and very soon he had introduced me to several of his father's former employees; particularly 'Stan' Livingstone, Bill Preedy, Norman Robottom, Dennis Terrett and George Wheeler. He also introduced me to Guy's sisters-in-law, Dilys Fountain and Doris Virgo and to John Gilbert who had been a close friend of Guy Fountain and who had recorded much useful information in his articles in the technical and musical press.

As the project progressed, fitfully to start with as I was still, regrettably, numbered amongst the ranks of the gainfully employed, Michael's enthusiasm gained pace. There followed several visits to the site of the original factories in West Norwood, to a later Tannoy office at High Wycombe, to numerous individuals with tales to tell and to sites of several Tannoy installations including, most importantly, the Palace of Westminster. I also visited the *Newark Aircraft Museum*, the *Army Signals Museum*, the *Bluebell Railway Museum*, and the *Chalkpits Museum* and I made many visits to the *Vintage Wireless Museum*. Most recently I visited the Tannoy factory in Coatbridge, near Glasgow.

With the help of all these contacts the project progressed and is now, at last, complete. I do hope that there are readers who will enjoy reading this story as much as I have enjoyed writing it.

Julian F Alderton
Pear Tree Cottage
Outwood
Surrey

February 2003

ACKNOWLEDGEMENTS

I would never have been able to complete this work in such detail without the help of many people. I am particularly grateful to Michael Fountain who has given unstintingly of his time and energy by locating many former Tannoy employees and introducing them to me and by arranging many interviews. He has also given me much information about his father, his family and the Tannoy company which was his father's creation.

I am also deeply indebted to the late T.B. 'Stanley' Livingstone whose clear memory of many events relating to Tannoy and of the company's many great achievements has made the compilation of this book possible. His patience and helpful information given so willingly and so wittily, almost to the day of his tragic death, have made the task so enjoyable.

I am much indebted to the late George Wheeler, the company's first General Manager, to Dennis Terrett who was with the company from 1951 to 1978 and was at one time Systems Engineering Manager and then Chief Engineer, to Bill Preedy, the second General Manager who was with the company from 1947 to 1974, to Norman Robottom, a mainstay of the hire department from 1932 to 1957 and to the late John C.G. Gilbert, a contributor to various music related journals. Their considerable help in amassing much detail and for their many anecdotes about Guy Fountain and his company is very much appreciated.

I am particularly grateful to the Tannoy Company for their support and for willingly agreeing to back the publication of this book I am especially grateful to Isobel McEwan who found many of illustrations among the company's archives and who oiled many wheels for me. I also wish to thank Henny Groenendijk, the former Managing Director who agreed to offer support on behalf of the company and to Anders Fauerskov, who assumed the position of Managing Director following the recent acquisition of the company by T.C. Electronic of Denmark, for confirming Henny Groenendijk's decision.

I also wish to thank Bozi Mohacek for processing some of the illustrations and

Acknowledgements

Stephanie Bartlett and my elder son, Nick Alderton, for their help in designing the cover. I am also greatly indebted to the following who made such important contributions to the work:

Chris Bisaillion	'VE3 CBK' (Ontario) Authority on military radio equipment.
David Bissett-Powell	Managing Director of Martin Audio, formerly Export Director of Tannoy.
Dennis Cunningham	Westminster Sound Systems formerly part of Tannoy.
Michael C. Doughty	Chairman and Managing Director, Stentor Music Co. Ltd.
Dilys Fountain	Sister-in-Law to Guy Fountain.
Michael Fountain	Former Tannoy Managing Director.
R.C. Gilbert	Former Royal Artillery Gunner.
William. J. Haines	Former Tannoy Manager.
Jonathan Hill	Wireless Historian.
T.B., (Stanley), Livingstone	Former Tannoy Manager.
Ernest Marsden	Former Tannoy Employee.
Edmund Newton, M.B.E	Westminster Sound Systems, formerly with Tannoy.
Derek Pipe	Former Chief Engineer, Tannoy.
E.A.H.W. (Bill) Preedy	Former General Manager of Tannoy, 1947 - 1974.
Norman Robottom	Former Tannoy Hire Dept. employee, 1932 - 1957.
Thomas Singfield	Aviation Photographer and Writer
Dennis Terrett	Systems Engineering Manager and Chief Engineer.
Doris Virgo	Sister to Elsie Fountain.
Gerald Wells	Curator, The Vintage Wireless Museum.
George Wheeler	The first Tannoy General Manager, 1929 - 1947.
Adrian Wilkins	Directorate of Engineering, Trinity House.
Claude Yates	Former Tannoy Manager.
Bluebell Railway Museum	Horsted Keynes.
Chalk Pits Museum	Amberley.
Newark Air Museum	Newark.
Vintage Wireless Museum	Dulwich.

Finally, my most grateful thanks must go to Doug Jeffrey, Marketing Manager, and Tim Lount, Communications Manager, for their tireless help and support in providing information about Tannoy.

*West Norwood, London SE7
early site locations*

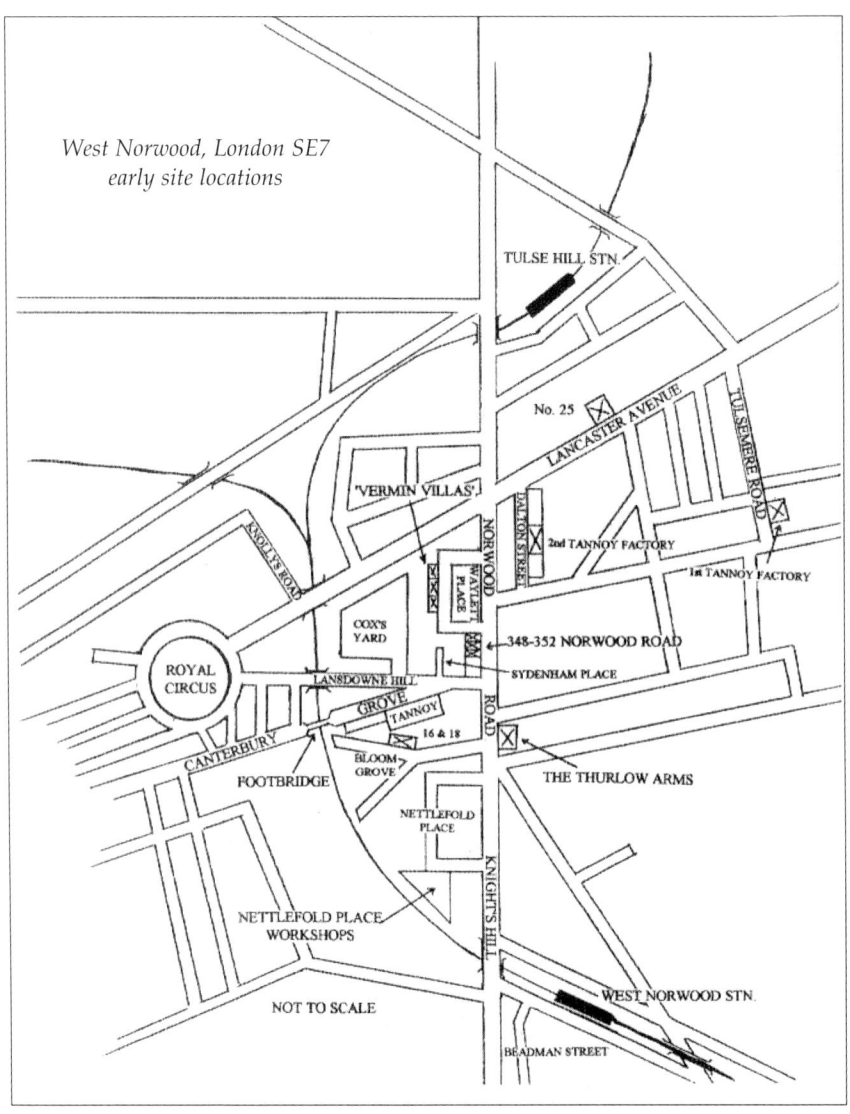

CHAPTER ONE

WHY IT STARTED AND HOW

The history of the Tannoy company is essentially the story of one man, its founder, Guy Fountain, but although he was indisputably the company's creator and the driving force behind its development, there were many others who were deeply involved and without whom the company would never have progressed in the way in which it did nor, without their influence, would the name of Tannoy have become the household word that it is today. This is the story of Guy Fountain and the company which was his brainchild, but it is necessarily also the story of his family, his friends, his employees and, to some extent, his adversaries.

Before embarking upon the story of Guy Fountain, it is necessary to explore his background in order to establish what were the driving forces behind him and how his will to succeed was nurtured.

Rupert Guy Fountain was born in Selby, Yorkshire, on 26th November 1898, the youngest of four children of Richard and Mary Fountain. Richard was a silversmith and jeweller employed by *Dysons*, a firm of jewellers with a shop at 24, Lower Briggate, Leeds and it is probable that he travelled the twenty miles each day from Selby by train and walked the short distance from Leeds City station. *Dysons'* shop was very well known, not only in Leeds, but throughout the country; perhaps even throughout much of the world, because the Dyson family never allowed the premises, nor the style of much of the stock, to be altered in the interests of modernisation, so the shop remained substantially as it was when it was first opened right up to itsclosure in 1990. It is interesting to note that the building also had a time ball on its roof, similar to that which is still in operation at the Royal Observatory in Greenwich, and which, like its counterpart on the observatory roof, was raised each day to the top of its mast and then lowered to the bottom at 1 pm precisely.

When Guy was still young, Richard was involved in an accident in which he sustained a severe head injury and had to have a metal plate inserted into his skull. He was unable to continue working and the burden of bringing up the four children, Arthur, Queenie, Lulu and Guy, fell upon Mary; a difficult task which she accepted with characteristic stoicism and determination in conditions of some hardship and with little money.

Mary was the daughter of Henry Oldcorn, who is known to have been a handsome man with great charm from whom she inherited much of her character and strength. He was an artistic man with an interest in antique furniture, a subject on which he was very knowledgeable. He was also an accomplished musician and wood carver and it has been said that some of his carvings are still to be found in the Church at Brougham, about a mile to the south east of Penrith. His family had been well known for several generations for their artistic ability and for their creativity, and these qualities were passed on in some measure through Mary to the young Guy. Henry Oldcorn had died young, leaving a large family to be brought up on a very limited income and the lessons which Mary learned from her mother in these difficult times were evidently of considerable value to her in later life when she had to face similar circumstances.

In bringing up the younger children Mary enrolled the help of her elder son, Arthur, some seven years older than Guy, and Arthur assumed the role of the family 'prop', a responsibility which he took very seriously and this created friction between him and his younger brother; friction which remained between them to some extent throughout their lives. However, there is no doubt that Mary was the dominant influence in shaping the character and personality of the young Guy and that he inherited also from her his determination to succeed.

Little is now known of Guy's childhood and schooldays but it is believed that it was not a very happy time for him. He was often the object of teasing and the butt of many gibes, particularly about his name, Rupert, which he did not like. He was frequently referred to at school as 'Loopy Rupy', and for this reason he later insisted on reversing the order of his names so that he could become known as Guy.

As a young man Guy came to London to serve in the army in the Great War and he enlisted in the Army Service Corps which, in recognition of its fine performance in that war, was granted a Royal Warrant by King George V in November 1918 and became the Royal Army Service Corps. During his war service Guy became friendly with a fellow soldier, Walter Portwine, and he was often invited to spend leaves with Walter and his family. Guy was a very likeable and handsome young man and Walter's parents, John and Emma Portwine, welcomed him as a visitor to their home, 'The Firs', on Sydenham Hill, South East London, and they enjoyed his company. For Guy, their kindness and hospitality were undoubtedly enhanced by the presence of Walter's five sisters, Constance, Marjorie, Elsie, Doris and Joyce, and it was not long before he became attracted to Doris, whom he courted for some time. He was also, at this time, the proud owner of a motorcycle and he would go away for a day or two to visit his relatives, particularly his brother Arthur who was by then married to Dylis and living with her family in Leytonstone. Dylis recalled that he would appear unexpectedly on his travels, enjoy a meal, a bath and a night's rest, and then ride off; until the next time.

John Portwine had started his working life in the family business of butchers with a wholesale meat warehouse and retail shops in South London. In time he had expanded the business until, at about the turn of the century, he owned several shops and used a number of horse-drawn wagons to transport supplies of meat to his shops and to make deliveries to his customers. He developed an interest in motor cars and was an early motorist, holding driving licence No. 4. He was friendly with a skilled mechanical engineer, John Weller and he provided the financial backing for Weller's engineering business in a little back street off Norwood Road called Thomas Place.[1] In 1902, Weller and Portwine made the *Weller* car there and a goods-carrying vehicle which they called the 'Auto Carrier'. This little truck had a flat bed over the two front wheels, with the driver's seat perched high behind, over the single rear wheel. This 'Auto Carrier' was quite successful and they supplied other retailers with similar vehicles and, in 1907, the company became *Auto Carriers Ltd.*, a name which was abbreviated to *A.C.* for their cars. In 1911 they decided that the future of this company lay in the production of private cars rather than with commercial vehicles, so they established another factory at Thames Ditton which they named the *A.C. Car Company Ltd.* John Portwine never flaunted his money, he was a devout Baptist who worshipped at Chatsworth Road Baptist Church and although he made a lot of money during the war when his factory was building military vehicles including the first, Mark I tanks, he would not touch any of that money, he gave it all to Missionaries.

After the Great War, John Portwine established Walter and Guy as partners in business at *Lancaster Motors*. The garage was in Norwood Road, West Norwood, near to the junction of Lancaster Road, (which was later re-named Lancaster Avenue to avoid confusion with Lancaster Road in South Norwood), and from this it took its name, *The Lancaster Motor Company*.[2] This partnership lasted only two or three years and it was probably Guy's dominant character which created a breach between himself and Walter. Another likely factor in the termination of Guy's association with Walter Portwine was Guy's lack of independence when employed under John Portwine and John Portwine's determination to maintain some element of control over how the garage was run. Guy wanted his own way and could not get it. Following the departure of Guy from *Lancaster Motors*, Walter Portwine continued to run the business under the guidance of his father.

However, it was in this garage that Guy's early ideas were fostered. John Portwine often visited Walter and Guy at the garage and sometimes took with him his youngest daughter, Joyce, who was still at school and she would occasionally prepare meals for her brother and Guy. They had beds at the garage so that, if they had to work late, they could sleep on the premises. It was also about this time that Guy's interest in Doris waned and his attention was drawn to her elder sister, Elsie, to whom he soon became engaged. This shift in his affection upset Doris very considerably and shortly before her death, some 70 years later, she admitted to the author that she had borne him some resentment for the remainder of her life. Guy and Elsie were married on 18th July 1922 at Christ Church, Gipsy Hill, a Church which was unfortunately destroyed by fire on 18th August 1982 and which has been replaced by a building which can reasonably be described as a hideous, modern monstrosity. But the 'Trendies' who love modern ecclesiastical architecture probably think it is wonderful.

These were, of course, still the early days of motoring being little more than thirty years since the first motor cars had spluttered falteringly out onto the public highways, and there was obviously a great future for the motor industry. But Guy already had other ideas as his interest in the newer technology of wireless communication was growing rapidly. Wireless telegraphy had become an established means of communication, accelerated in its development by the needs of the services during the war, and many amateurs had made for themselves simple crystal sets so that they could listen to the signals in Morse code which were transmitted throughout Europe and much of the rest of the World. But occasionally the sound of the human voice could be heard in their earphones and the hobby quickly gathered a wider following.

At this stage of the development of wireless communication, the early 1920s, Britain lagged behind several other countries, notably Russia, America and Holland, which had already established public transmitting stations and were regularly broadcasting both speech and music, but in Britain considerable constraints were imposed by the Post Office, which was the licensing authority.

During the Great War a total ban had been imposed on the use of wireless transmitting equipment and this ban was not lifted until 1919, but even then

Why It Started And How

only calibration signals and wireless telegraphy, using the Morse code, were permitted. It was under these restrictions that the *Marconi Company*, the leaders in the development of wireless telegraphy and wireless telephony in Britain, had to operate and conduct their pioneering work in broadcasting. This work was carried out by the Experimental Section of their Design Department in their factory at Chelmsford and, on 23rd February, 1920, they began their experimental transmissions of speech and music on a regular basis, transmitting two programmes daily, each lasting 30 minutes, at 350 metres on the medium wave band. On 15th June, in association with the *Daily Mail*, they broadcast a recital by Dame Nellie Melba, a recital which aroused the interest of the public and did a great deal to further the development of broadcasting. However, in November of that year the Post Office imposed a ban on these transmissions following complaints that they interfered with other communications which were deemed to be of greater importance.

This ban caused much indignation among the growing band of amateur wireless listeners and a petition was raised by 63 wireless societies which eventually resulted in the Post Office relenting and granting the *Marconi Company* a licence to include 15 minutes of telephony in their regular weekly telegraphy transmissions for amateurs. This licence was granted towards the end of 1921, but the company managed to extend the duration of their broadcasts to rather more than half an hour each week by taking advantage of the compulsory breaks in which they had to listen for instructions to stop if more important communications needed to be transmitted and received.

These broadcasts, the first regular service in the British Isles, started on 14th February, 1922, from a wooden hut at Writtle, using a 250 watts transmitter powered by a petrol driven generator and using the call sign '2MT', under the leadership of Captain P.P. Eckersley who played records and sang to his enthusiastic audience of 'listeners in'. These transmissions lasted from 7 pm to 7.25 pm and from 7.35 pm to approximately 8.05 pm and included the required breaks in which to listen for 'more important' communications. Later in 1922 the Post Office issued licences to three other transmitters, one of which was another *Marconi* transmitter, the almost legendary '2LO', which was installed in Marconi House, at the junction of The Aldwych and The Strand, and it was in this manner that the broadcasting industry in Great Britain was born. But Britain had much progress to make before it could catch up with other countries for, in 1914 a concert had been broadcast from a transmitter in Moscow and in 1916 the *American Radio and Research Corporation* had started regular twice weekly broadcasts of concerts. Nearer to home, Radio 'P.C.G.G.' in Holland commenced transmissions of music in April 1920 which were heard by many enthusiasts in England.

The TANNOY Story

But Peter Eckersley's broadcasts progressed and soon became more frequent, more professional and, of course, of longer duration and, in December, 1922, he was taken to Magnet House, in Kingsway, to meet a Mr. John Reith who had been appointed General Manager of the *British Broadcasting Company*. The *B.B.Co.*'s Chief Executive was in a tiny office which Eckersley[3] described as little more than a cupboard, with the rest of the staff, numbering about 15, working in the connecting office. Peter Eckersley recounted that he felt that he would like to work for Mr. Reith although he had learned that a Chief Engineer had already been appointed from *Marconi*'s Head Office. But in January 1923 he was told that the man who had been offered the job had turned it down and he was advised to apply for it. He did so and in February he was appointed to the position of Chief Engineer to the *B.B.Co.* – a title which was somewhat more grandiose than the job for he was, in fact, the only engineer, with a total staff of four. The British Broadcasting Company had started its regular broadcasts of entertainment programmes from Marconi House on 14th November 1922 although it was not until 18th January, 1923 that it received its first licence from the Post Office and, in April 1923, the company, with its studios and transmitter, was moved to a wing of the Institution of Electrical Engineers' building at Savoy Hill. Peter Eckersley remained with the B.B.C. until the summer of 1929 when John Reith, a strict moralist and disciplinarian, sought his resignation when he was about to become the guilty party in a divorce case.

The broadcast by Dame Nellie Melba from *Marconi*'s factory in Chelmsford had made a considerable impact upon the imagination of the British public but another lady with great foresight and deep imagination gave the public, and the *B.B.Co.*, unexpected encouragement in their enthusiasm for their new art form. Beatrice Harrison, one of four extremely talented musical sisters, was regarded for most of the first half of the 20th Century as the greatest cellist in Europe, possibly in the World, and she had discovered that a nightingale was stimulated by the sound of her cello when, on a warm Spring evening in 1923, she had played it in her garden at Foyle Riding, near Oxted, and the bird had added its beautiful song as an accompaniment to her cello. She was deeply moved by this experience and felt that she should be able to share her pleasure with the widest possible audience and she devoted much time and effort to persuading the *B.B.Co.* to allow her to broadcast a recital from her garden. Eventually, with much reluctance on the part of Reith, she was allowed to attempt such a broadcast and in the Spring of 1924 the complicated apparatus of the time was set up in her garden and, with *B.B.Co.* engineers and their equipment, she started playing each evening in the hope of attracting the nightingale again. After many evenings without result, the nightingale was once again triggered into song and accompanied her cello. Quickly the engineers arranged for the programme to be interrupted and the first of many outside broadcasts of *The Cello and the Nightingale* was transmitted late on the evening of 19th May, 1924. This performance was repeated each year for 12 years until the Harrison sisters moved house and it was also broadcast, on at least one ocasion, on the *B.B.C. Empire Service* and was heard by listeners all over the World, including New Zealand where it drew some very favourable comments. In the course of a radio interview many years later, in 1955, Miss Harrison recalled a meeting with King George V when he had told her, "You have done what I have not yet been able to do. You have encircled the Empire with the song of the nightingale and your cello".[4] This successfully proved the value of the new broadcasting industry.

In those pioneer days of broadcasting most receivers were simple crystal sets, often home made, consisting of an aerial coil, either tapped or with a tuning condenser, and a crystal rectifier or 'detector'. A pair of high impedance earphones would be connected to these wireless sets and when the little spring electrode called the 'catswhisker' had been adjusted to find a 'sensitive spot' on the crystal, a faint, but usually very clear signal could be heard. However, the sound was very feeble and it was necessary for silence to be maintained in the room for the listener to hear the programme undisturbed, the cause of many family arguments.

Guy followed the trend of many technically minded young men of those days and made several of these crystal sets and, also following the trend, he made them in the most convenient containers, old cigar boxes. But early in the 1920s thermionic valve detectors were becoming more readily available following the invention of the diode valve by Dr. J.A. Fleming[5] in 1904 and the triode valve by Lee de Forest in 1906. This was improved by H.J. Round who made the so-called 'soft' triode valve in 1913 with a filament made of platinum coated with both barium oxide and calcium oxide, the grid was a fine nickel wire and the anode was a nickel tube. Further improvements were made in America by Irving Langmuir who managed to produce a near perfect vacuum in 1913 which led to the first 'hard' valve in 1915. French military scientists produced a successful triode valve which was used by both French and British units for wireless communication during the first months of the Great War and British manufacturers soon made an equivalent valve which was known as the 'R' Type. In 1915, R.C. Clinker, of the British Thompson-Houston Company, made Britain's first successful commercial high-vacuum triode valve although production of the 'R' type valve continued well into the 1920s.

So, by the early 1920s, more and more amateur wireless enthusiasts were beginning to understand the function of the valve and were building valve receivers. In these early valves it was necessary for the cathode filament to be heated to a high temperature in order to achieve the necessary emission of electrons and this was usually done by means of a six volt accumulator which was connected to the filaments which were nominally rated at 5.5 volts. These early valves were by no means standardised, and although many of them operated on other voltages varying from 3.5 volts to 22 volts, 6 volt valves were, perhaps, the more usual.[6] By the early 1920s many of the intermediate voltages had been abandoned and valve filaments were usually either 2 volts, 4 volts or 6 volts. These valves, which later became known as bright emitter valves, also required a substantial current to maintain the necessary temperature so that the accumulators had to be re-charged frequently, a job which was carried out either by the local wireless shop or, quite often, by the nearest garage.

Many garages were situated where mains electricity was already available and in those areas where the supply was direct current, it was only necessary to connect the accumulators to the mains through a variable resistance or rheostat, or through a barretter,[7] or through a bank of carbon filament lamps, to reduce the voltage to that which was required to charge the accumulators. Some establishments had no electricity supply and they had to use petrol driven generators, but most, particularly those in large towns, had an alternating current mains supply which, of course, had to be rectified to produce the direct current necessary for charging accumulators. This was usually done by means of rotary converters, which were inefficient, or by using circuits containing mercury-arc rectifiers, which were expensive. However the principle of the electrolytic rectifier was already established and it was probably with one of these that Guy and his brother-in-law, Walter, charged the accumulators for the wireless sets as well as for the motor cars of West Norwood.

Guy soon began to think of other ideas and he experimented with various metals in his attempts to improve the performance of the electrolytic rectifiers then in use and, in the early 1920s a reasonably satisfactory electrolytic rectifier was available which had a positive electrode made of tantalum and a negative electrode of an alloy of lead, these being immersed in a fluid electrolyte which comprised a dilute solution of the same sulphuric acid which was contained in accumulators, but with added ferrous sulphate. The tantalum was both expensive and difficult to work with because the sheets of tantalum were very brittle and it is believed that Guy experimented with tantalum in powder form, deposited on ebonite rods. He also tried using aluminium and lead alloys and he often talked of "Tantalum-Alloy" rectifiers though it is doubtful if any of his experiments produced better results than were obtained using tantalum and lead alloy as the electrodes, but it is on record that he achieved the first sales of Tantalum/Lead alloy rectifiers in 1927, a year after he started making them.

Why It Started And How

But Guy's interests were moving more towards the wireless sets themselves and he spent much of his spare time at home making receivers. With the knowledge he had gained with his battery chargers he believed that he could develop mains operated receivers and he often talked of his ideal of 'Wireless from the mains'. He made several valve wireless sets for his own use and friends were so impressed by their performances that they asked him to make sets for them, and it was in this way that he progressed into the serious business of constructing wireless receivers.[8]

Having broken away from Walter Portwine and the Lancaster Motor Company in about 1925, he started his own business, initially in Tulsemere Road, West Norwood. He gave it the name of the *Tulsemere Manufacturing Company* although in that year it was also referred to as *Guy R. Fountain Ltd.*, a name which was not registered until 1928. It was not long, however, before Guy's expanding company outgrew these premises and he had to look for a larger building.

In late 1926 he found new premises, again over lock-up garages, in Dalton Street, a little back-street running parallel to Norwood Road, which leads off Lancaster Avenue. In this factory he made wireless sets, (both crystal and valve sets), and battery chargers. He also started making battery eliminators. These were very popular pieces of equipment well into the 1930s as a means of operating battery wireless sets from mains electricity. Guy became interested in this line of development following further experiments with the design of rectifiers. In his 'Tantalum-Alloy' rectifiers the life of the electrodes was shortened by corrosion caused by immersion in the acid electrolyte, so he changed to dry rectifiers, which he bought from the *Westinghouse Brake and Saxby Signal Company*, in which an electric current passes effectively only in one direction between two dissimilar metals and it was with these dry rectifiers that the company was able to progress along its self designated path towards the objective of 'Wireless from the mains'. It was also in 1926 that the company first exhibited at the Radio exhibition at Olympia. Elsie's youngest sister, Joyce, was still occasionally involved with the company and she sometimes worked at Dalton Street when he was still making crystal sets and on one occasion Guy took her to Selfridges to see a television demonstration by John Logie Baird.

These metal rectifiers also made possible the further development of the battery eliminator but it was necessary for Guy to obtain a licence from *Westinghouse* to use their rectifiers in his equipment. His eliminators incorporated a mains transformer and a metal rectifier, with choke coils and condensers to smooth the ripples in the direct current produced and their output was usually 120 volts for the high tension and 2 volts low tension to charge the accumulator. This was done because the provision of a smoothing circuit to prevent a loud mains hum from being heard in the earphones or the loudspeaker via the valve filaments was costly, so battery eliminators were usually then fitted with a changeover switch so that the unsmoothed low tension circuit could be switched to charge the accumulator while the set was not in use. By this time, the early valves with their numerous filament voltages were being replaced by dull-emitter valves which worked satisfactorily at a lower temperature and which generally had 2 volts filaments. These battery eliminators represented an intermediate step towards Guy Fountain's goal of making 'wireless from the mains' a realistic possibility for the public.

He was probably something of a pioneer in this respect, looking to the future of entirely mains operated wireless sets, for valves could only be operated with a direct current supply to the filaments and this necessitated the use of an accumulator. Indirectly heated valves had been made in America in 1923 but the type which was eventually adopted was developed in 1924 and patented in 1926 by E. Yeoman Robinson of *Metropolitan-Vickers* and which became readily available in the following year. In this type of valve the cathode was a tiny tube with a heater filament inside it so that alternating current could be used to heat it without producing any noticeable hum; the first 'mains' valve.

However, Guy had not entirely abandoned his 'Tantalum' rectifiers for, in the *Wireless World* of 30th March, 1927, there was an article about the development of the tantalum rectifier by the Tannoy company which stated:

A.C. MAINS, L.T. SUPPLY.

The recent adoption of tantalum for the construction of the electrodes of the electrolytic rectifier has, to some extent, re-established this form of rectifier for use in circuits where a comparatively heavy current is handled at low potential. For battery charging, therefore, this form of rectifier possesses certain merits over other types as it is inexpensive to build, running costs are low while the temperature rise of the solution is much less than in the case of the Nodon rectifier.

This form of tantalum rectifier has been developed by the Tulsemere Manufacturing Company, Tulsemere Road, West Norwood, London, S.E. 27 and is marketed under the name of the Tannoy Supply Unit.

The outfit is compact, being enclosed in a hinged box measuring 4" by 5" by 5" when the lid is closed. Contained in the case is the power transformer and the electrolytic cell built in a celluloid box closely resembling in appearance a small accumulator, together with a panel carrying a changeover switch, while on the outside of the box is an ammeter reading to 500 milliamps. Full wave rectification is provided, the electrolytic cell being fitted with two tantalum electrodes. This form of rectifier makes use of a solution of ferrous sulphate in dilute sulphuric acid and consequently care must be taken not to upset the electrolytic cell for the exterior appearance does not suggest that the interior contains spillable acid. A celluloid ventilating tube is brought out through the switch panel and, except for this, the electrolytic cell is completely sealed.

On test it was found that a charging rate of 0.5 ampere was obtained when the rectifier was connected up to a six volt battery, a four volt battery charged at 0.6 and a two volt cell at 0.75 ampere. As an inexpensive source of L.T. supply from an alternating current mains this unit will be found to give satisfactory service'.

(These figures are open to some doubt if, as stated, the ammeter read only to 500 m.A. although an external ammeter may have been used for these tests).

Following the move to Dalton Street, the Tulsemere Manufacturing Company was formally registered as 'Guy R. Fountain Limited' on 10th March, 1932 and the registration documents state that the company then owned the trademark, 'TANNOY'. With a small staff of workers it progressed steadily with the design and manufacture of better and more powerful wireless sets for use on mains electricity and it also continued to improve the quality of its battery chargers and eliminators. Trade shows and exhibitions specifically for the growing wireless industry were mounted and Guy's little company exhibited at these using 'WIRELESS FROM THE MAINS' as its theme; a theme which featured very prominently in the early publicity material issued by the company.

Another article in *Wireless World*, dated 13th April, 1930, stated:

'The Tulsemere Manufacturing Company, 1-7 Dalton Street, has for long specialised in the production of mains units of all types in which the electrolytic type of rectifier is incorporated. To these has now been added a range of units fitted with the Westinghouse metal rectifiers.

On 31st. December, 1930, the A.C. Mains Unit, CP2 was mentioned as being a high tension eliminator and trickle charger which measures $9^{1/2}$" by $5^{1/8}$" by $3^{3/4}$" and therefore fits into the battery space of the majority of portable receivers.

It was at about this time that Guy and Elsie settled into a large, semi-detached house at 25, Lancaster Avenue, which they rented from John Portwine, and during these years of the development of his company they became the proud parents of a family of three: Jeanne, who was born on 4th May, 1923, Michael on 2nd April, 1927 and David on 27th September, 1929. Guy had a wooden aircraft propeller in the Lancaster Avenue house and he used to joke with his guests by 'shooting a line' about his service in the Royal Flying Corps. He had never, of course, served in the R.F.C.

By this time Guy's parents had left Yorkshire, presumably to be nearer to their children, most of whom were living in the south of England, and they had moved to Biggin Hill, Kent, where they lived in a house called 'The Castle' which was situated in line with the end of one of the runways of theR.A.F. station, so near that on one occasion, when a pilot misjudged his approach, his aircraft removed one of their chimney-pots.

Some years later, in 1943, Guy and Elsie moved into another house which they rented from John Portwine: Tudor Lodge, 112 College Road, Dulwich, which had previously been called 'Three Gates', one of which was a lytch gate.

John Portwine had lived there until he let it to Guy and Elsie. The house had been built for John Portwine in 1924 and this date can still be seen in the hopper heads. Guy calculated that this house was directly above the tunnel which takes the railway between Sydenham Hill and Penge East stations. When John Portwine died, Elsie inherited this house from him and, after her death, Guy had to buy it from her estate[9]. John Portwine owned and built a number of properties in the South of England, notably at Pilgrims Way in West Humble, near Dorking and in Birchington, Kent, where he spent his remaining years.

As the company progressed through the 1920s it also became apparent to Guy that its name, 'The Tulsemere Manufacturing Company', was much too cumbersome and that a short, catchy name should be adopted as a trademark to project the image of the expanding company. There were already many makers of wireless sets with names which could easily be remembered and instantly recognised such as *Pye*, *Ekco*, *Marconi* and *Philips*. There were, of course, others which were less readily understood such as *Gecophone*, being the wireless manufacturing arm of *G.E.C.*, and *Burndept*, a company which made extremely fine and powerful sets, the name being derived from the name of its founder, Witt Burnham, and from the location of the factory in Deptford. So Guy devoted a great deal of thought in his attempts to devise a simple, easily remembered name for his company and its products and eventually, in 1926, he thought of the idea of going back to where he had started, with rectifiers, and by juggling the words 'tantalum' and 'alloy' he formed the name 'TANNOY'.

The author's parents, Douglas and Kathleen Alderton, were close friends of Guy and Elsie Fountain and were then living in a flat at 79, Tulsemere Road, near to Guy's workshop. In later years Douglas often told of the time in about 1926 when Guy had asked his help in the task of devising a suitable, catchy word to adopt as a trademark for his company. Guy had asked him to spend an evening with him in a public house in West Norwood to discuss the problem. They thought back to Guy's early experiments with electrolytic rectifiers and they considered the tantalum and the lead alloys which he had used as electrodes and together they had together come up with the name of 'Tannoy' but it is now, regrettably, no longer possible either to confirm or dispute this account of events.

Why It Started And How

CHAPTER NOTES

1   Thomas Place is of interest for, as will be seen later in this account, it was to be renamed 'Waylett Place', where Guy Fountain established parts of the Tannoy factory and invested in some old cottages.

2   There is still, (October, 2000), a filling station on the site. This is next to the *Co-operative* shop which was built on the site of a pair of large, four-storey semi-detached houses, Nos 294 and 296 Norwood Road, which were owned by the author's paternal grandfather. No. 294, 'Rosemount', was the Alderton family home where the author's father was brought up and the other was let to Francis Bartlett, the author's maternal grandfather. There were no less than 20 children in these two families and it was almost inevitable that there would be at least one union in marriage between these families.

3   'The Power behind the Microphone', P.P. Eckersley, published by the Scientific Book Club, c. 1941.

4   The 'Cello and the Nightingale', by Beatrice Harrison. Published by Murray, 1985.

5   Dr. Fleming was then Scientific Adviser to the *Marconi Company*. His patent is dated 16th November 1904.

6   In researching this detail the author has found records of valves which were available in 1928 with more than 20 different filament voltages ranging from 1 volt to 22 volts. It must be remembered that early valve wireless sets incorporated a rheostat to vary the filament voltage and that some sets had separate rheostats for each valve.

7   A resistance device which reduced the voltage and also maintained a constant current in the circuit.

8   *The M.O. Valve Co. Ltd.* had produced their first indirectly heated, A.C. mains valve, type KL1, in June, 1926. It went on sale in January, 1927. It is on record, however, that *Read and Morris* introduced a 4-valve mains receiver in March, 1925 which was, they claimed, 'The first mains set in the world'. It was essentially a battery receiver but it derived both its H.T., L.T. and grid bias supplies from the mains by means of a built-in mains unit. The first A.C. mains receiver in which the power supply from the mains was combined with the circuit was made in 1926 by *Gambrell Brothers* of London, SW 8.

9   There is no No. 114 in College Road because the three plots, 112, 114 and 116 were used to build the two houses, 112 and 116. The name of No. 112 was changed to Tudor Lodge in 1943.

Sound Amplifying Equipment

THE general utility of sound amplifying equipment has resulted in its widespread use in the catering and amusement industries.

Public services and commercial undertakings are now realising its value and each day sees new applications of amplifying equipment to commercial use.

Comparatively recently, it has been proved that sound amplifiers can be used to increase efficiency in Works and Offices. 'Call systems' ensure that contact can be made with any member of the Staff in any part of the premises in a matter of a few seconds.

The provision of suitable music in factories increases production and lessens sub-conscious fatigue, particularly in the case of operatives engaged on repetition work.

Regular uses of Sound equipment include :—

Advertising,	Municipal Buildings and Parks
Aerodromes and Airlines,	Night Clubs,
Amusement Arcades,	Offices,
Bands,	Pageants,
Bathing Pools and Swimming Baths,	Police and Crowd Control, etc.,
Cafés,	Political Parties,
Canteens and Clubs,	Publicity,
Cinemas,	Rinks,
Cathedrals and Churches,	Railways,
Dance Halls,	Schools,
Engineering,	Scout Groups,
Exhibitions,	Seaside Resorts,
Factories,	Showrooms,
Fire Brigades,	Sight-seeing Tours,
Fun Fairs,	Sports Grounds,
Garages,	Stadiums,
Hotels,	Theatres,
Hospitals,	Tournaments,
Holiday Camps,	Tours.
Lecture Halls,	

The ever-increasing demand for "TANNOY" equipment has resulted in the production of amplifiers suitable for all purposes, which, under correct conditions, are capable of virtually perfect reproduction of speech and music "TANNOY" have been manufacturing amplifying equipment since 1927, and can claim to be one of the pioneers of this class of engineering. They are now the largest firm in the country specialising solely in sound amplifying equipment.

The choice of suitable equipment for any particular purpose is a matter for the specialist, and the "TANNOY" staff of experts are always ready to advise. Some idea of the factors governing the suitability of equipment will be found overleaf.

Taken from a 1936 Tannoy brochure

CHAPTER TWO

GUY IS INTRODUCED TO SOUND AMPLIFIERS

Guy Fountain was a very curious man, not only in the sense that he was a mystery to others – that he was difficult to understand – but also because he was intensely inquisitive and always needed to get to the bottom of things; to probe endlessly into the most minute details of anything which puzzled him, particularly things mechanical or electrical, until he was entirely satisfied that he completely understood that which had mystified him.

If he bought a new household gadget, and there were frequent innovations in the times under consideration, or a new car, or a new toy for his children, he would play about with it almost endlessly to ensure that he knew all that there was to know about it and that he had investigated its full potential and the limits of its performance before, perhaps reluctantly, putting it away or returning it to its rightful owner.

As an illustration of this, one Christmas in the mid 1930s, at a time when many children in the British Isles were happily playing with their new sets of 'Hornby' Gauge '0' model trains, Guy felt that he had to be different; that he had to go one better, so he bought an elaborate and rather expensive set of electric toy trains for his sons, Michael and David, made by an American company, *Lionel Lines*. The layout was set up in the basement of the Lancaster Avenue house and for a very long time the operation of the trains was closely supervised by Guy while Michael and David, together with the author whose family was visiting for Christmas, hardly managed to get a look-in. The frustration experienced by these three small boys, particularly Michael and David, eagerly hoping to get their hands on such a wonderful new toy, was disturbing to say the least, but until Guy had satisfied himself that the boys were completely capable of running the trains without undue risk of damage and, what is probably more to the point, until he had explored to the full the potential of the trains, they were allowed only to stand aside and watch. It was a rather long time before Michael and David gained the freedom to play with their new trains, but not before they had been told repeatedly, 'Don't tread on the track!'.

He was much the same at work if a new or unusual piece of equipment came into the factory or if a new product were under test. He would seldom allow others freedom to conduct their trials without frequent interference. It was as if he were under the influence of some unseen force, some mysterious and irresistible compulsion, to probe into every last detail of the object under examination until his intense curiosity had been completely satisfied. He would often spend, or perhaps waste, many hours on his detailed investigations into what seemed to others to be the most trivial of matters. There were, of course, many occasions when this was merely so much time wasted, but there were other times when this almost child-like curiosity of his led on to the most important developments; and so it was with the introduction of the first Tannoy sound amplifiers.

In about 1927 a train of events was set in motion which was to alter completely the course of the development of Guy's company. This was not, of course, known or recognised at the time and it is unlikely that Guy Fountain would even have admitted much of it later, but it is quite probable that the company would not have become as large and as successful as it did, nor would its name have become so widely recognised and accepted as a household word, without the intervention of these events. By this time, the company was firmly established as a manufacturer of battery chargers, battery eliminators and 'radios' as they were then beginning to become known. Guy had come to realise that his growing little company needed more technical strength and that he had to have a capable assistant to handle the engineering developments to enable him to devote more of his time and energy to the expansion of the company, so he advertised in the *Wireless World* for an assistant. This advertisement was seen by a young and enthusiastic wireless engineer called George Wheeler whose first job had been with *Modern Wireless*. He had also worked for *Burndept Wireless Ltd*. until Alfred and Witt Burnham were forced into receivership in June 1927. *Burndept* had been very well known for the quality of its wireless sets, the *Burndept* having being regarded by many as the 'Rolls Royce' of the wireless industry, a reputation later earned by Harry Roberts' company, *Roberts Radio*. George Wheeler recounted the occasion as follows:

> "I'd done my matric and 18 months or so of my inter B.Sc. and I answered an advertisement in *Modern Wireless* which turned out to be a job with Scott Taggart's magazine, *Modern*

Guy Is Introduced To Sound Amplifiers

Wireless. I went there at about 17 years of age with a head too big for my boots. When I look back, I almost blush at what I used to do, and they sacked me. If I'd been in their position I should have done the same. All the senior people were on about £2 or £2.2.0d. per page because they wrote up the details of their developments. Over two months I wrote articles which they could not turn down because they were good articles and I drew about £50 on top of my salary. There were those who were very upset about this and I used to ring up companies such as *Burne-Jones* and announce myself as 'Mr. Wheeler of *Modern Wireless*'. (I was still a young kid of 17 years of age), 'Would you send me a Model . . .?', because they used to give us the equipment for testing and writing up. Well, Mr. Scott-Taggart soon got rid of me, he was not going to have that, and out I came."

George Wheeler's interest in wireless communication had been stimulated in about 1921 while he was still at school when he and his father had built a three-valve set to listen to the Sunday afternoon music broadcasts from station 'P.C.G.G.', which had been started in the Hague, Holland, by Hans Idzerda in order to promote sales of his company's crystal sets. From 15th June, 1920, 'P.C.G.G.' broadcast regular programmes of music on Sunday afternoons and on Monday and Thursday evenings and such was the enterprise of this company that the announcements, in Dutch, were repeated in both French and English.

The Wheelers' set had a pair of *S.G. Brown* earphones which they sometimes took off the headband and placed in two pudding bowls on the table to act as primitive, but quite effective loudspeakers, so that the family could listen in to the music while they took their afternoon tea. Indeed, it was on this set that the Wheeler family heard the famous broadcast by Dame Nellie Melba from the *Marconi Company*'s station in New Street, Chelmsford.

On reading Guy's advertisement, George Wheeler telephoned him to ask for an interview, explaining that he could not attend during working hours as he would not be permitted to leave his work. By this time he was working for the *Telephone Manufacturing Company Ltd.*, following brief periods with *Brown Brothers Wholesale* and with *Johnson and Phillips*. He asked if he could come after work, in the early evening, and it was arranged that he would go to the Dalton Street factory to meet Guy on a Friday evening at six o'clock.

On the appointed day, George made his way by train to Tulse Hill station which was only a few minutes walk from Dalton Street. On arriving at Dalton Street he was immediately put off by the dingy and shabby appearance of the factory and by its tiny size. He stopped in the street for a few minutes, taking in the miserable surroundings and then, instead of going in for the interview, he walked past. When he looked back he decided that he could not possibly work in such a place; that nobody in his right mind would want to do so, and he walked back to Tulse Hill station to take the next train home. However, when he enquired at the station he was told that the next train which would take him home was not for about an hour, so he changed his mind, coming to the conclusion that if he was going to have to wait an hour for the train, he might just as well spend the time at the interview.

When he returned to the works he found that everyone had gone except for Guy Fountain, so they had a talk about the job for a while and Guy showed George around the workshop. Eventually he offered George the job at £3 per week. George felt unable to make a decision at the time and asked if he could come again with his father. This was agreed and the following afternoon, after work, George's father brought him over to Dalton Street on his 'Indian' motorcycle and sidecar, talked to Guy and then said that they would consider the offer over the weekend and let him know of their decision on the following Monday. George recalled that the only instrument which he saw as he walked around the factory with his father was a side-band voltmeter which had a period of about 25 seconds. They discussed the offer on the Sunday and George's father advised him to take the job. He said that having seen the place, and having found the factory in such a dreadful state, he felt that George could not possibly make it any worse; only better, and so it was that he telephoned Guy again on the Monday and agreed to take the job. He started with a wage of £3-5-0d. per week and, in addition to Guy and himself, there were just five youths on the staff. When interviewed shortly before his death, George Wheeler was not able to remember in which year he joined Tannoy although he thought that it had been 1928 or 1929. However, he did recall the fact that he was unable to invite Guy to his 21st Birthday as he had lied about his age at his interview. His 21st Birthday was in 1928 so it seems almost certain that George Wheeler joined the company in 1928.

Within a very short space of time, George Wheeler realised that the design of Guy Fountain's battery chargers and, more particularly, his battery eliminators, left much to be desired and he found it necessary to spend a good deal of time in his early days with the company re-designing these pieces of equipment to make them safer and more efficient. He also found that the factory was very poorly equipped with instruments and test meters and he had his work cut out convincing Guy that they needed much better equipment and persuading him to spend the necessary money to obtain it.

While George had been with *Burndept*, one of the directors had returned from America where he had acquired an extremely powerful Rice-Kellogg amplifier[1] and loudspeaker unit which they did not fully understand at the time. But when he heard this, it sparked off George's interest in amplifiers and he built one of his own, probably from a *Wireless World* design, with three LS5A valves, powered by a 400 volts high tension supply and giving, he claimed,

Guy Is Introduced To Sound Amplifiers

about 30 watts output. He connected this to a *Woodruff* Pick-up, one of the best then available in spite of the very high mass of the moving components, which had been modified in accordance with *B.B.C.* recommendations and which he mounted on a *Garrard* spring driven turntable and, after hearing a lecture by Dr. Niel McLachlan,[2] he had mounted a big, moving-coil loudspeaker on a 4ft. baffle board. It was not long before word got about and George started receiving invitations to take this equipment to clubs and to local functions to save the cost of hiring bands for dances and, being a member of the Charlton Cricket Club, he was asked if he would bring his amplifier to the Woolwich Town Hall to play records at the club's annual dance while the band took a break.

When he asked Guy for permission to leave early on the day so that he could set up his equipment for the dance, Guy's curiosity was aroused. He asked him what he was going to do and, typically, he wanted to know all about it. George told him that he was going to take his amplifier and some gramophone records to Woolwich Town Hall for the Charlton Cricket Club dance and that he was going to play the records during the interval. Guy replied that it all seemed rather interesting and could he come along as well? This was agreed and George left work an hour or so early and a friend of his picked him up in his car and took him and all his equipment to Woolwich. But George's girl friend had to go to the dance by bus as there was no room left for her in the little car.

When they arrived at the Town Hall, an hour or so before the dance was due to start, George Wheeler set up his equipment and switched it on. Immediately a fuse blew and out went all the lights! George hunted around and eventually found the fuse-box in the basement, re-wired the fuse and switched on again, with the same result. Again he replaced the fuse-wire and switched on his amplifier, and again the fuse blew, so he took off the cover of the amplifier to look for a fault but he could find nothing wrong so, once again, he re-wired the fuse and switched on, but again the fuse blew.

By this time the members of the cricket club and their guests were beginning to arrive for the dance, including Guy, immaculate in evening dress, and an announcement was made that George Wheeler would be playing records through his amplifier during the interval, an announcement which caused him considerable embarrassment. His frantic attempts to trace the fault, aided by the ever more curious Guy, were not successful and eventually he had to admit defeat; there would be no gramophone records during the band's interval. By this time, Guy's curiosity was aroused to the point at which he could contain himself no longer, but realising that there was nothing that they could do that evening, he suggested to George that he put all the equipment into his car so he could take it to the factory on the following morning and give it all a thorough check.[3]

The TANNOY Story

So the next day, on Sunday morning, they set up George's amplifier, turntable and loudspeaker in the Dalton Street Factory and, with some misgivings, switched on. To their amazement and relief, after the valves had warmed up, it worked perfectly and Guy was immediately impressed by its excellent performance; he had heard nothing like it before and, as usual, he could not bring himself to leave it alone. He just had to keep on and on trying it with one record after another to hear just how much sound it could produce, and at what quality. They then mounted the loudspeaker on a large wooden partition to increase the size of the baffle and tried again and it sounded absolutely marvellous. Guy played it on and on, so fascinated was he with its seemingly immense power, power that he had not experienced before – a portent, perhaps, of the power which he himself sought in life. His fascination was probably enhanced by his artistic enjoyment of the music, engendered by this characteristic inheritance from his grandfather.

After a while, Guy suggested that they should try to find out just how far the amplifier could be heard, so they carried the loudspeaker up onto the factory roof and Guy then told George to keep on playing records while he walked along the road to find out how far away from the factory it could be heard. George did as he was asked and Guy walked for some considerable distance along Lancaster Avenue. Eventually, Guy returned to the factory, his inquisitiveness satisfied, and they realised that they could do no more with it just then so they took all the equipment back to George's home.

A few days later, the landlord of a nearby public House, the Thurlow Arms, which is nearly a quarter of a mile along Norwood Road, near St. Luke's Church, visited the factory and asked to speak to the proprietor. He told Guy that he had heard the music from the amplifier and thought that it would be a good idea to be able to play gramophone records with similar equipment in his pub. It is not too difficult to imagine his interest in those days when public address equipment and electronic amplifiers were little known. Under George's supervision another amplifier was built in the factory and within a few days it was delivered to the Thurlow Arms and installed in the saloon bar. The landlord was then able to play records for the entertainment of his customers, unaware of the fact that he was blazing a trail for future publicans to follow; unaware of the fact that he was almost certainly the first to install in licensed premises any form of electronically reproduced music. There are, of course, those who would wish that he had also been the last, but that is another matter.

It was from these humble beginnings that Guy Fountain's company took its first steps into the serious business of making amplifiers, steps which would lead it into the manufacture of public address equipment and sound reinforce-

Guy Is Introduced To Sound Amplifiers

ment systems on the grandest of scales, for use throughout the British Isles and much of the World. These same steps would very soon establish the company as the universally acknowledged leaders of the industry, rapidly overtaking the pioneers of public address in Great Britain, *Standard Telephones and Cables Ltd.*, formerly *Western Electric Ltd.*

It is interesting to look back on those events of more than seventy years ago and to reflect on the thought that had the young George Wheeler, then about twenty years of age, not changed his mind and returned to attend his interview with Guy Fountain, the company would not have taken that critical turn in its development and it might never have become involved in sound amplification instead of radio. By the same token, had Guy's natural curiosity not been so typically aroused and his imagination so fired by the performance of George's amplifier, their involuntary demonstration of its power and capabilities to the landlord of the Thurlow Arms would not have taken place and so, in all probability, the company would not have moved into the business of sound equipment at all; in all probability it would have become one of the many radio manufacturers which, within a few years, failed.

CHAPTER NOTES

1   This was designed by Chester Rice and Edward Kellogg of the *American General Electric Company* who had also, incidentally, exhibited a successful moving-coil loudspeaker at the 1925 Spring convention of the American Institute of Electrical Engineers in St. Louis. These became commercially available in Britain in 1926.

2   It is almost certain that this was the Dr. McLachlan who was then employed in the Research Department of the *Marconi Company*. He is said to have been a brilliant mathematician and to have written a book on the design of loudspeakers which was the definitive manual on the subject at that time.

3   In researching the events at Woolwich Town Hall the incident was recounted to Gerry Wells, the curator of the Vintage Wireless Museum who commented, "Of course the fuses blew, Woolwich Town Hall was on a d.c. supply in those days". This has subsequently been found to be true, but only partially true for, in later years, George Wheeler remembered that when Tannoy Rentals were again asked to supply an amplifier to the Town Hall, they found that only a part of the building was supplied by its own d.c. generator.

MR. TANNOY——A Story WITH words!

A politician tried to speak,
It really seemed absurd;
Without P.A. his voice was weak,
No one heard a word.

"TANNOY" is the largest organisation in Great Britain specialising SOLELY in Sound Equipment.

CONSULT THEM on the use of sound.

LOUDSPEAKER SOUND SYSTEMS designed, manufactured, installed and maintained.

AND REMEMBER! you don't necessarily have to lay out Capital!

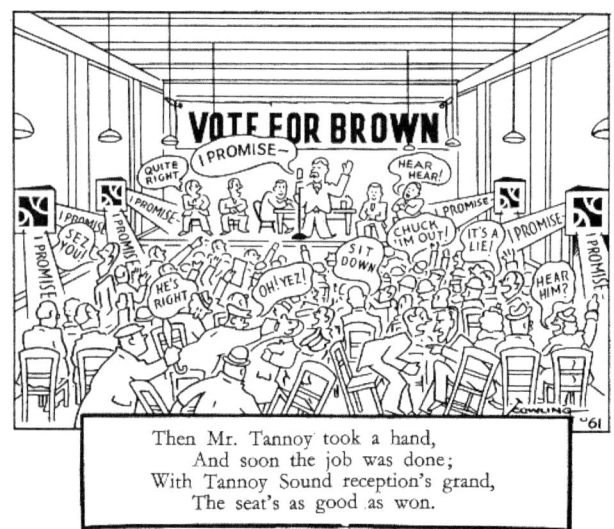

Then Mr. Tannoy took a hand,
And soon the job was done;
With Tannoy Sound reception's grand,
The seat's as good as won.

\TANNOY/
THE SOUND PEOPLE
GUY R. FOUNTAIN LTD.
CANTERBURY GROVE, S.E.27 AND BRANCHES
'Phone: GIPsy Hill 1131

CHAPTER THREE

EARLY PROGRESS IN PUBLIC ADDRESS

Not long after the episode at Woolwich Town Hall and the consequent sale of an amplifier to the Thurlow Arms, the company was again asked to supply amplifying equipment, this time for an outside event. A gentleman who lived in what George Wheeler described as a spacious house at Pebble Coombe, just at the top of Pebblehill Road, near Dorking, was planning a garden party. He had taken an interest in the new technology and wished to impress his guests by using an amplifier to play gramophone records and make announcements during the party. At such a function the music would usually have been provided by a band or even a small orchestra, but any announcements would have had to be shouted above the voices of the guests, possibly with the aid of a megaphone. Approaches were made to Tannoy and it was decided to use George's amplifier, so they bought a microphone and three horn loudspeakers to go with it and George took all this equipment to Pebble Coombe and arranged it to the best of his ability in the garden. The event was a complete success and it represented two firsts for Tannoy: not only was it their first outside event, but it was also the first occasion on which the company hired out equipment; a service which was destined to become a very substantial part of Tannoy's operation, eventually becoming a separate company, Tannoy Rentals Ltd. This point in thecompany's history can also be said to have marked the beginning of the way in which Tannoy later developed into 'Products' and 'Systems Engineering' in which the installation of public address amplifiers very gradually became separated from their manufacture. This eventually became an important distinction, but more of this later.

Following these early successes, Guy decided to diversify the company's

The TANNOY Story

activities by adding public address amplifiers to its established range of wireless sets and battery eliminators although this was not achieved until about 1930 for, in the catalogue for the 1930 National Radio Exhibition which was staged at Olympia from 19th to 27th September, the company, listed as "Tannoy Products, (Formerly Tulsemere Mfg. Co.)", occupied Stand 111 and the following products are listed in the show catalogue:

TANNOY	"All Electric" Radio Receivers.
TANNOY	Radiogramophone incorporating all electric equipment and moving coil loudspeaker.
TANNOY	H.T. and L.T. mains units, (separate and combined), special mains units for portable and transportable receivers.
TANNOY	Components for home construction of Mains Units.
TANNOY	Chokes, Mains Transformers, rectifiers and all electric equipment including mains operated moving coil loudspeakers.

This last should have been listed as 'mains energised' loudspeakers.

It seems strange that the show catalogue gives no more details of the radiograms, nor any details of the radios which Tannoy were then making. Advertisements in the trade journals during the previous year had featured the following:-

Tannoy	2-valve radio model R2 priced at 10 gns.
Tannoy	3-valve radio model R3 priced at 19 gns.
Tannoy	4-valve console radio model R4 priced at 39 gns.
Tannoy	Senior radiogram priced at 60 gns. in a mahogany cabinet or at 55 gns. in an oak cabinet.
Tannoy	Junior radiogram, sometimes called the Standard radiogram, priced at 45 gns.
Tannoy	Junior radiogram, battery model, priced at 35 gns. (Presumably this had a clockwork turntable).

It is interesting to note the emphasis on 'moving coil' loudspeakers for, at the time, moving iron loudspeakers were more usually used.[1] It is also of interest that, in common with many manufacturers of radio equipment at the time, Tannoy offered for sale components for the home construction of their mains units, for these were the days when many amateur constructors made their own wireless sets and accessories. However, there is no mention in the show catalogue of Tannoy amplifiers so, although these were probably under development, amplifiers were not then considered to be of prime importance. What is more significant, however, is that as early as 1930, Tannoy were among the dozen or so radio manufacturers showing radiogramophones at the exhibition. This was at the time when well known companies such as *Ekco* and *Ultra* were still offering wireless sets with separate loudspeakers, usually of the moving-iron type. Incidentally, at about the same time the Tannoy two-valve wireless sets were being sold with a separate, moving iron loudspeaker made in Austria by *Triotron*[2].

Guy Fountain undoubtedly took advantage of the fact that not far from the West Norwood factory lived a gentleman called Paul Voigt who had worked on electrical and reproduction systems for the *Edison Bell company*. He agreed to help Guy Fountain to develop his lead in sound reproduction techniques in return for which Tannoy manufactured equipment to Voigt's designs, probably principally his loudspeakers.

Through the early 1930s Tannoy continued to seek markets for its developing sound equipment business and it was clear at this stage that the company was becoming more orientated towards industrial and commercial applications and less obviously aimed at the domestic market although a very early contract which was won covered both fields. This was for the installation of radio receivers and amplifiers in a radio relay company in South Wales. Radio relay was first tried in Holland, it is believed by a Mr. Bauling, and systems were installed there, in France and in several other continental countries. The purpose of radio relay was to overcome the distortion experienced in early wireless broadcasting resulting from interference between transmitters operating on adjacent frequencies, and to eliminate the tendency of long-wave stations to 'fade' in certain areas, notably in Newcaste-on-Tyne. The first, simple relay service was established in Hythe, Kent by the owner of an electrical shop but the first well organised, commercial radio relay stations were established in Newcastle-on-Tyne and in Burnley, Hull, Nottingham, St. Peter's (near Ramsgate), Swansea and in various areas in South Wales, usually using the telephone network as their distribution lines. In modern times, reception of V.H.F. and U.H.F. signals is sometimes limited to 'line-of-sight' and homes situated in deep valleys, in some instances whole villages, have to build aerial installations on tall masts or nearby hilltops with signal amplifiers to enhance their radio and television reception. This was often the case in the early days of wireless entertainment, so relay companies were formed to serve such communities and to ensure that they were able to enjoy programmes which would otherwise have been denied them. The term which eventually became almost universally applied to these schemes was, 'rediffusion', a name devised by P.P. Eckersley who, following his removal from the B.B.C., founded the *Rediffusion Company*.

In 1930 or 1931 Tannoy won a contract to supply just such a relay service, Kenfig Hill and District Radio Relays, South Wales, with two radio receivers and two 100 watts amplifiers to distribute programmes to residents in the nearby valley community situated about 4 miles north of Porthcawl. Their publicity claimed that it was :

'. . . one of the largest and most powerful privately owned in the country, providing a perfect single and dual programme of British and Continental radio entertainment.'

The TANNOY Story

The subscription rates for their services were 1/- per week for the single programme and 1/6d. per week for two programmes. It is also probably true that many families in communities such as this could not afford wireless sets and the relay companies gave them access to B.B.C. and to continental programmes at an affordable fee. The continental programme would probably have been Radio Luxembourg. This contract was quite an achievement for the company but, in Guy's mind, it suffered a serious disadvantage in that it was not heard 'loud and clear' over great distances, nor did it offer him the opportunity to emblazon the name 'TANNOY' in huge letters in public places. This did not at all satisfy his ego.

George Wheeler has said that in 1929, soon after he joined the company, he started work on the design of a loudspeaker capable of handling an output of 500 watts. It has also been said that Tannoy introduced its first 15" mains energised loudspeaker in 1930 which was shown at the National Radio Exhibition at the Olympia from 19th to 27th September, 1930. However, subsequent information has revealed that this may not have been true for more recent information suggests that the first Tannoy-made loudspeaker did not appear until about 1933, prior to which all loudspeakers are said to have been bought in.[3] What is very much more likely to be true is that George Wheeler, in his work to improve the reliability and more importantly the safety of Tannoy's battery eliminators, was responsible for the design and, in 1930, the introduction of the type 16 CH and type HL 8 Mains Units which were first advertised in *Wireless World* in April of that year.

Following discussions between Guy and the *Westinghouse Brake and Saxby Signal Co.* then at 82, York Road, King's Cross, regarding the relative merits of metal rectifiers and the tantalum electrolytic rectifiers which he favoured, these mains units were the first to incorporate *Westinghouse* metal rectifiers. (Tannoy had, however, used *Westinghouse* metal rectifiers before this, for the 1930 Tannoy wireless set in the author's collection incorporates such a rectifier). The tantalum rectifiers had 8 or 12 tantalum rod electrodes and a similar number of lead ones in an electrolyte consisting of ferrous sulphate and dilute sulphuric acid.

These mains units were followed in December by type CP 2 which comprised both a high tension eliminator and a trickle charger which could recharge the low tension accumulator when the set was not in use. In December 1930, reference is made to the H.T. eliminator and trickle charger which fits into the H.T. battery space of the majority of portable sets and this may well have been the type CP 2. January 1931 saw the introduction of the GB 1, also a combined mains unit which, in addition to a high tension supply and a trickle charger, also provided a small negative voltage for grid bias. This represented another step forward in Guy's quest for 'Wireless from the mains', for it enabled battery wireless sets to be operated without either high tension or grid bias batteries and without the need to make frequent visits to a radio shop or garage to have the accumulator charged. Thus, by using Tannoy battery eliminators, more and more battery wireless sets were operated from mains electricity although Tannoy and other manufacturers had by then been making mains wireless sets for some time and, surprisingly enough, at a time when George Wheeler was devoting so much time and effort to improving such a primitive piece of equipment, the company was also introducing a comparatively sophisticated item, their first Radiogram, the Tannoy 'Senior', which was featured at the 1930 Radio Exhibition.

At about the same time, a development took place in the manufacture of transformers, coils and chokes for, during the 1920s these had been supplied by the *Keston Manufacturing Co. Ltd.*, a company which was founded in 1919 by W.B. (Bill) Kirsting at 69a Park Hall Road, not far from the Tannoy works. Bill Kirsting and his son, known as 'Chum' Kirsting, were acknowledged experts in the design and manufacture of transformers but, in common with many people at the time, they were a little sensitive about the German sound of their name, so they called their company Keston. They were a great help to Guy Fountain in passing on to him and to his company much of their knowledge and expertise and they supplied transformers to Guy with the name 'Tannoy' boldly printed on them, a point on which Guy typically insisted, notwithstanding the fact that such components were seldom seen as they were usually hidden inside the cabinet of the radio. By the end of the decade an almost inevitable difference of opinion arose between Guy and the Kirstings, probably over prices, and Guy established his own coil winding section. Bill Haines took over the responsibility for coil winding when he joined the company in 1933 and he recalled that he had a booklet which came from the suppliers of the core stampings which showed the sizes and the number of core stampings which were needed to cope with various powers to be transformed and he used this as his reference point at which to start the designs (the manner of Bill Haines' recruitment to the company is recounted later in this chapter).

In various articles in the *Wireless World* it is possible to follow the progress of the company not only in the production of mains units but also in the manufacture of radiograms. In April, 1930, for example, it was reported that the Tulsemere Manufacturing Company:

> Specialised in mains units of all types which used the electrolytic type of rectifier.

The TANNOY Story

However, in September of that year an article recorded that:

> Many so-called radiograms offered to the public do not justify this title; they are essentially electrically reproducing gramophones in which the radio section is a subsidiary part capable of receiving only one or two powerful, local stations. This criticism cannot be levelled at the Tannoy radiogramophone, for the radio side includes an efficient H.F. (High frequency) stage which provides a range and variety of broadcast reception capable of rivalling the best library of gramophone records...
>
> We have heard this instrument in operation at the works of Tannoy Products and there can be no doubt that the performance justifies the care displayed in the design of the circuit...
>
> The excellence of the gramophone reproduction is in no small measure due to the steady running of the Paillard induction motor and the small background noise consequent upon the absence of brushes. This radiogram is available in oak at 55 guineas or in walnut or mahogany at 65 guineas.

This was then about half the price of a small, family car! The *Paillard* induction motor was probably a feature of *Garrard* turntables which were usually fitted to these radiograms. These early Tannoy radiograms were enclosed in cabinets which were made for the company by 'Camco', the *Carrington Manufacturing Co. Ltd*. Camco were originally at West Norwood, just behind the *Telephone Manufacturing Company*'s factory, but they moved to premises just behind the Swan & Sugar Loaf public house at South Croydon.[4] They made particularly fine, elegant cabinets for radiograms which sold well to the 'nouveau aristocracy' and they also had showrooms at 24, Hatton Garden, E.C.1. In the first of the above references, (April 1930), Tannoy is still referred to as 'The Tulsemere Manufacturing Company' while, some five months later, (September 1930), it is given the name of 'Tannoy Products'.

While Tannoy was developing radiograms and still producing mains units, the company was devoting more and more attention to the production of public address amplifiers. By 1931 a compact portable public address system, developed by George Wheeler from the designs which he had used at Woolwich Town Hall, the Thurlow Arms and Pebble Coombe, was in production, but more sophisticated amplifiers were being designed. George was experimenting with amplifier design and he made an amplifier with 6 battery triode valves wired together as one valve for the output stage. This idea was not very successful but it does show that he was striving to achieve greater and greater output from his early amplifier designs.

Although Tannoy could rightly claim to be among the leading companies in Great Britain in the manufacture of public address amplifiers, they

Early Progress In Public Address

were by no means the first. It is on record that *Western Electric* gave the first demonstration of public address equipment in Britain at the Radio Exhibition in the Horticultural Hall in 1922 and they also installed an amplifier for the Empire Exhibition in 1924 which was used by His Majesty King George V at the opening ceremony.

However Tannoy's radiograms still captured more attention than their amplifiers for, in a review published in the *Wireless World* on 25th March, 1931, the magazine is very complimentary about the Tannoy Senior model Radiogram which, it records:

> ... incorporates a stroboscopic speed indicator which is fitted as a permanent fixture to the turntable which is driven by a Paillard induction motor. An unusual refinement is noticed in the record cleaning brush mounted on the pick-up arm. This radiogram also features an automatic stop and is available in an oak cabinet at 55 guineas, or in mahogany, at 10 guineas extra.

Although stroboscopes were available throughout most of the 1930s in the form of cardboard discs which could be placed on top of the record being played to check the speed of the turntable, and although they were incorporated in the turntables of studio equipment, it was not until many years later that stroboscopes were incorporated in the turntables of commercial 'Hi-fi' equipment and it is interesting to record that Tannoy was among the first with this innovation, some thirty years ahead of other manufacturers. The record cleaning brush was also copied, many years later, with the introduction of accessories such as the 'Dust Bug' soon after the first vinyl, 'long playing' records became available.

Also in 1931, the company was making a compact table model radiogram in two cabinets, one being the radio, gramophone and amplifier and the other being a separate loudspeaker in a matching cabinet. It has the appearance of a very practical, though somewhat basic piece of equipment, but it's appearance is slightly marred by a large, porcelain fuseholder on the deck just behind the turntable. Archives now held by the Tannoy company label this as the 'Original Music Centre', a boast which seems quite justified. There was also a large gramophone reproducer which was featured in Tannoy advertisements by August, 1931. This had twin turntables and a loudspeaker in a separate cabinet and was priced: 'from £60'.

On 17th February, 1932, again complimenting the Tannoy 'Senior' radiogram, the *Wireless World* states:

> Until recently the radio side of even expensive radiogramophones has been rather neglected and many models have incorporated simple receivers of a type suited for no more than local reception. The demand for better radio equipment has coincided with the growth in popularity of the superheterodyne and so it is not surprising that many of the latest and most up-to-date radiogramophones are fitted with this type of receiver. 6 valves are employed in the Tannoy 1932 superhet.

The TANNOY Story

The company was registered as 'Guy R. Fountain Limited' on 10th March, 1932 with its registered office in Dalton Street and with a capital of 1,000 ordinary shares of £1 each. The company was the registered owner of the trademark, 'Tannoy'. Of the 1,000 shares, 998 were held by Guy Fountain and the remaining two were held by the company's solicitors, Percy Hammond and Graham Maw. Later, in 1936, the company's capital was increased to £10,500 when the *Crofthill Investment Trust* took up 17% of the £6,000 worth of ordinary shares and 44% of the preference shares. Their holding was diluted in May 1938 when the company's capital was further increased to £20,000, (£6,000 in ordinary shares and £14,000 in preference shares). In 1938 the *Banque Belge pour l'Etranger (Overseas) Ltd.* invested in the company to the extent of £6,500 in preference shares and, in 1940, a further £9,500 (this will be covered in Chapter 7). Following the initial investments in 1932 the company really started to accelerate its progress, but the premises in Dalton Street were far from ideal. For example, it had a spiral staircase leading down to what was euphemistically called 'The Stores', making it difficult to manhandle large items of equipment between floors.[5]

There were other problems which the company had to face during the Dalton Street days, in addition to purely technical problems. There was, for a time, an accountant, who was thought to have sold equipment and pocketed the money and on one occasion it is said that a customer brought some equipment back saying that it was not what he wanted. The accountant offered to repay the man by cheque but, it is alleged, he did not do so. In time, a summons was issued to Guy Fountain for payment of the money and the accountant is said to have attended court pretending that he was Fountain. He was fined but the story continues that he failed to pay the fine within the 10 days allowed by the court. The outcome of this episode is not recorded but, if there is any truth in it, it must have caused Guy considerable embarrassment.

In 1932, work was going on to develop more powerful amplifiers and in August of that year a 250 watts amplifier was introduced. In the following year a powerful battery amplifier and gramophone console were fitted in a large motor van, sponsored by the *Daily Mirror*, which toured the holiday resorts publicising the *Daily Mirror* to increase their circulation. They achieved this by employing a team of eight attractive young ladies, attired in the fashionable games dresses of the time, who demonstrated keep fit exercises to music and with a commentary played through loudspeakers mounted on the roof of the coach which was purpose built by *Garner Motors Ltd*. This promotion, which was called 'The Daily Mirror Eight', continued each summer until the outbreak of war in 1939, touring holiday resorts throughout England, Scotland and Wales during the holiday seasons. It was very important that the preparation of this coach was completed on time and at Easter, 1933, the factory was kept working on Good Friday and Guy bought all the staff a 2d. Walls ice cream as a reward for their labours! Although the words, DAILY MIRROR EIGHT were very prominent on the sides of the coach in which the girls travelled and which served as their dressing room, the Tannoy logo was even more prominent, together with the company's address in West Norwood, on and around the loudspeakers. More importantly to Guy, the front of the van carried the words: 'TANNOY, THE SOUND PEOPLE' in very large letters. A year or so later the van was replaced by another *Garner* vehicle, this time with Tannoy even more blatantly displayed and, in August 1935 a new *Leyland* coach was similarly equipped with DAILY MIRROR EIGHT written on the sides and with the upper circle of a figure '8' encircling a round window. However, the Tannoy logo was again even more prominent on the front of the vehicle and on the loudspeakers which were fixed on its roof where they were not only more obvious to see but where, by their very nature, they attracted much attention. This vehicle served the promotion for three or four years. The girls involved the spectators in their displays as much as possible by leading them in mildly athletic games, often using a large, brightly coloured ball.

At this time, the *Daily Mirror* and the *Daily Sketch* were the two most popular tabloid newspapers and each had its strategy for increasing its circulation. The *Daily Sketch* ran similar tours with six hulking males, very handsome young men of course, who demonstrated lifesaving methods from the beaches in the Australian style with a rope wound on a drum on the beach. They tried to steal the thunder from the *Daily Mirror* by following their tour very closely, sometimes even appearing in the same town and, occasionally staying at the same hotel, an arrangement which suggested endless possibilities. The manager of the DAILY MIRROR EIGHT tour, who was usually the newspaper's circulation manager, was absolutely terrified that there might be any scandal and the girls were ordered not to have anything whatsoever to do with the *Daily Sketch* life saving team; they were warned that they would be fired on the spot if they were found to have any sort of liaison with 'those awful *Daily Sketch* lifesavers'. However, at each venue the coach had a board placed in front of it naming the next destination so that when they left, all the young lads on their annual holidays could follow the coach in their little two-seat sports cars, waving at the girls in their coach and trying by signs to make dates. So the girls were ordered not to have anything to do with anyone; the only people they were allowed to associate with were the staff; a wonderful situation for the Tannoy team.

The *Daily Mirror* published a spread the day before each appearance, telling readers where the girls would be on the next day and each day they took photographs of the show and rushed these back to London to prepare a special edition for that town on the following day, thus substantially increasing their circulation. There was an added benefit, however, for the shows increased circulation throughout the country, not just locally, and people even used to write to the *Daily Mirror* during the winter and ask when the team would be appearing at Scarborough, or at Bournemouth, or wherever, so that they could book their holidays to coincide with the appearance of the show. Such was the following of the Daily Mirror Eight.

On a technical note, the Tannoy personnel had something of a problem because their valve amplifiers consumed a considerable amount of power, much of it being lost in the inefficiency of the rotary converter, and they had to make arrangements in each town to have the batteries re-charged overnight. In spite of this, Norman Robottom can remember no incidents of major technical problems although they did have frequent difficulties when sand penetrated the rotary converter or the gramophone motor.

Norman Robottom, who was the Tannoy engineer involved with most of these annual shows, had joined the company in 1932 and the story behind his recruitment is quite significant. He had been brought up in Clapham where his father enjoyed a rare privilege in those days, a company flat, however humble it was. His father was a messenger with the Bank of England, always to be seen resplendent in top hat and tail coat, conveying documents around the City for the bank. This position warranted company accommodation and the family had a flat over the Midland Bank at Clapham Junction, on a corner of what Norman Robottom jokingly referred to as a rather delightful road called Abyssinia Road where there were often fights, bare knuckle fights, on Saturday nights when the beer was flowing in the local pubs; a rather frightening experience for the family. As a young boy Norman had a fine treble voice and his father decided that he would like Norman to have his voice trained so that he could become a choirboy in a local Church, so he found a tutor at Wandsworth Common where Norman took lessons each week. Unknown to the family, this tutor was a personal friend of Mr. Stanley Roper who was the organist of the Chapel Royal at St. James's Palace and Roper wrote to the tutor one day and advised him of two vacancies in their choir and had he anyone suitable? So Norman, then approaching his eighth birthday, and another boy attended auditions at St. James's Palace. There were about fifty applicants and Norman was one of the two lads who were accepted. When he arrived home his parents asked how he got on and he told them that he thought that he had been accepted and that the Lord Chamberlain would like to see them at St. James's Palace on the following morning! They were astounded.

In gaining acceptance into the choir, for which he had to wear a fine, Tudor style uniform, Norman also won a choral scholarship to the City of London School at Blackfriars. It was not a particularly happy time for him for this was a school for the sons of 'gentlemen' and he had won a scholarship, so his parents did not pay, resulting in some bullying. To add to this, much jealousy arose from the fact that the choristers were not subjected to any punishment after school because they had to attend choir practice each evening at St. James's Palace.

Whilst he was in the choir, he attended many royal and society occasions, augmenting the choir at St. Margaret's Church. Each Sunday when the Royal Family were at home, they used to sing at the service at St. James's Palace and then march across the park to Buckingham Palace and sing again there. He sang at Princess Margaret's Christening and, when she married, he wrote to her to say that he had sung at her Christening so how about a ticket for the wedding? He did not receive the desired reply. He also sang in Canterbury Cathedral for the enthronement of Dr. Fisher as the Archbishop of Canterbury.

However, he had to leave when his voice broke and it was then that he went on to Wandsworth Technical Institute where he studied electronics and where he met a classmate called Ronnie Rackham. By the time he went to Wandsworth Technical Institute the family were living at Beckenham and each day, on his train journey, he saw the new Tannoy factory with its two tall masts as he travelled through West Norwood. So when the careers master asked him where he wanted to go from there he answered, 'There's a company called Tannoy which is not too far from where I live, I would not mind going there.' So it was arranged that he would go to the Tannoy factory where he was interviewed by George Wheeler and was taken on almost immediately. After about a month he was again approached by George Wheeler who asked him if he knew anybody else who might be interested in joining Tannoy and Norman mentioned Ron Rackham, saying that he lived nearby in West Norwood. 'Oh, send him down', said Wheeler, and that is how Ronald H. Rackham came to join Tannoy.[6] He started in the winding shop, winding transformer coils.

In his first job at Tannoy Norman Robottom was given two bricks and told to rub them together to form a powder of brick dust which was then used to polish the brass studs of the stud fader potentiometers.

Norman Robottom was employed by Tannoy from 1933 to 1958 and, much to Guy Fountain's annoyance, stayed with the company just long enough to get his gold watch. He spent most of his time in the hire department and was appointed to accompany many of the 'Daily Mirror Eight' tours as the engineer in charge of the equipment and, some 65 years later when recounting the sheer joy of accompanying these delectable young beauties said, 'Well, I suppose somebody had to do it!' He recalled several amusing incidents. One of these involved another member of the Tannoy team, Michael Quick, regarded by many as something of a nutter because he got up to some very amusing antics. On occasions, if he lost any of his tools in the factory, he would offer a cash prize to anyone who could find them for him. During the Daily Mirror Eight tours, the Tannoy personnel were occasionally invited to local functions and, on one occasion, 'Mickey' Quick was among those who were entertained to lunch by the Mayor at one of their venues. During the lunch he was heard to say rather loudly, 'I'm having a jolly good time on this tour, with all these lovely girls, you know, but of course, I don't read the *Mirror*, I only buy the *Daily Sketch* – hey, who's kicking me?'

Returning to the development of the company during the early 1930s, another significant contract which was awarded to the company in January, 1932 was for the installation of Tannoy public address equipment by the largest of the four railway companies, the *London, Midland and Scottish Railway Company*, for the announcement of train arrivals and departures at Blackpool station, a popular and busy holiday resort. This installation was important because it proved to be a very successful experiment and the *L.M.S.* awarded Tannoy a similar contract for New Street Station, Birmingham later that year and at London's St. Pancras station. The *London, Midland and Scottish Railway Company* became one of Tannoy's more important contracts for Tannoy amplifiers were eventually installed in nearly all of the *L.M.S.* stations and, also in 1936, the *London and North Eastern Railway Company* followed their example with an installation at Liverpool Street Station.

It was at about this time that a difference of opinion started to develop between George Wheeler and Guy, a difference which was to simmer for many years. Guy always insisted on having his own way at the factory where his attitude seemed to be based on the premise, 'There are three ways of doing the job, the right way, the wrong way and MY way.' So everything had to be done HIS way, regardless of engineering requirements and George Wheeler often said that the engineering side of Tannoy developed 'in spite of Guy Fountain'. At the time of these events it had become clear that some amplifiers needed to be mounted on steel racks instead of in the woodencabinets which Guy favoured, and when George went to the *L.M.S. Railway Company* to negotiate with them they said that they did not want equipment in wooden cases, specifying that it had to be readily accessible for maintenance and therefore mounted on racks. George told Guy what he had been told by the *L.M.S.* but he just would not listen; he said that they would have to try to swing *L.M.S.* to cabinets, so George had to tell him that Tannoy would not get the order if the amplifiers were not mounted in racks. At that time Tannoy had no facilities for making racks so,

Above : The Tulsemere Manufacturing Company's first premises in Tulsemere Road 1927

Below : Second premises in Dalton Street 1930

Above : Guy Fountain at his desk in the Dalton Street Factory 1930

Right, above and below : original 1931 Music Centre or Compact System

Above: The author's two-valve Tannoy Wireless Set with its Triotron loudspeaker. Douglas Alderton bought this set from Guy Fountain in 1930 and sold it to neighbours in 1934. They used it throughout the Second World War. In 1945 they gave it back to the author

Above : 250 watts Tannoy Amplifier in a wooden case at the Dalton Street Factory early 1930s

Below : The first use of Tannoy Public Address Equipment by a Railway company Blackpool 1932

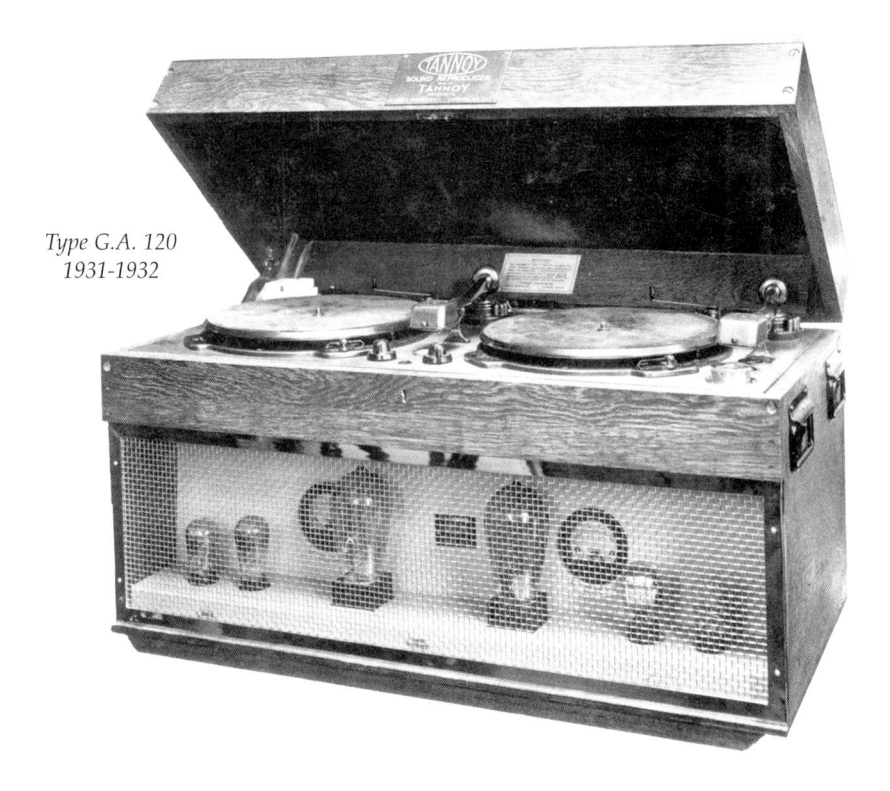

*Showman's Twin
Turntable
Dalton Street
1931-1932*

*Type G.A. 120
1931-1932*

*1935 Schools Radiogram
with 12 watts output*

Guy R Fountain and 'Freddy' March, the Duke of Richmond and Gordon at the opening of the purpose-built Tannoy factory at Canterbury Grove, West norwood, London in 1934

The opening ceremony 1934

*A toast to the Company.
The duke of Richmond is on the left and Guy R Fountain on the right.
The lady in the centre is almost certainly The Countess of March*

Above : outside Wrendal House, Tannoy Manchester, 1935

Below : 1932 battery-powered Public Address System for Bertram Mills Circus. Probably a Raleigh 3-Wheel Van

A Second transportable Public Address System in a Raleigh van 1933

Above: c 1935

Below: c 1934

At Bertram Mills Circus, Olympia 1934-5. Note the related adverts (left and right) which read 'Decca Brunswick records used exclusively at the circus'. Nevertheless, on this stand alone the word 'Tannoy' appears no less than 21 times.

Tannoy at Bertram Mills Circus 1935/36

Stand 90 – 1935 Radio Exhibition

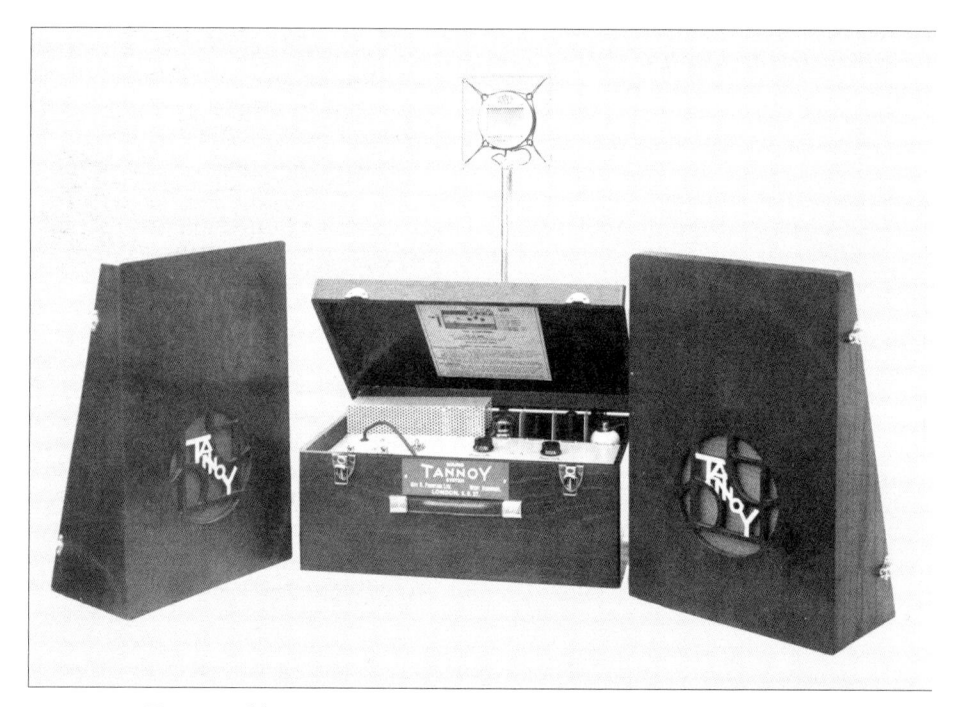

Transportable Amplifier with Microphone and two Loudspeakers c1932

400 Watts Tannoy Amplifier, one of the first to be Rack Mounted. Made at the Dalton Street Factory.

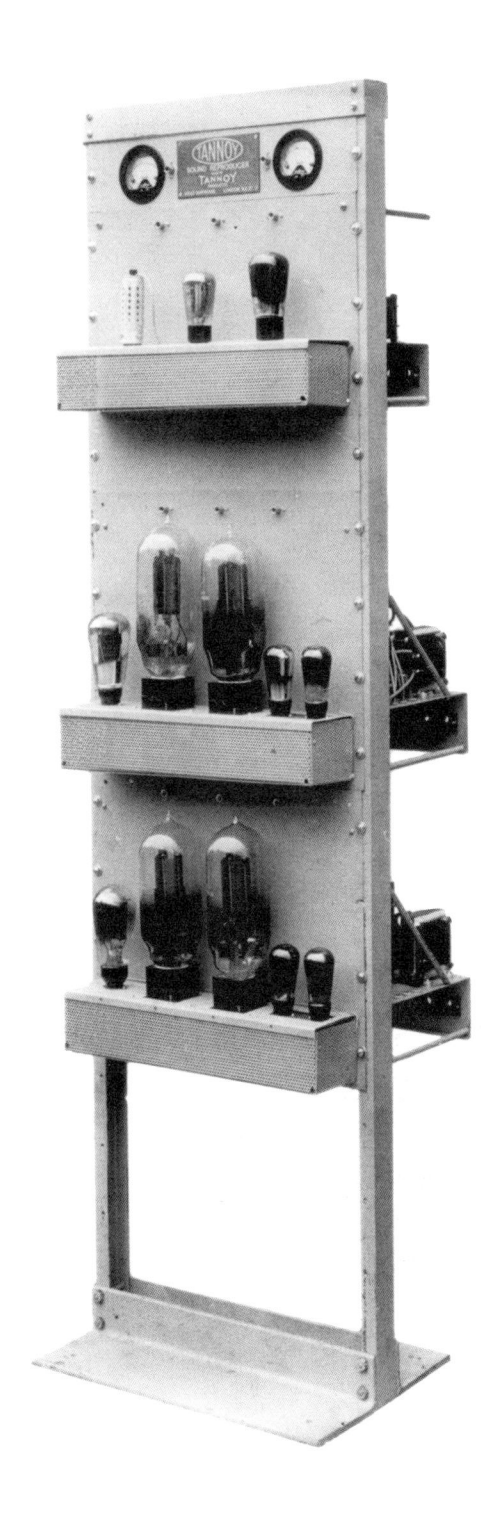

The first 'Daily Mirror 8' touring van 1932

'Daily Mirror 8' touring coach/van 1933

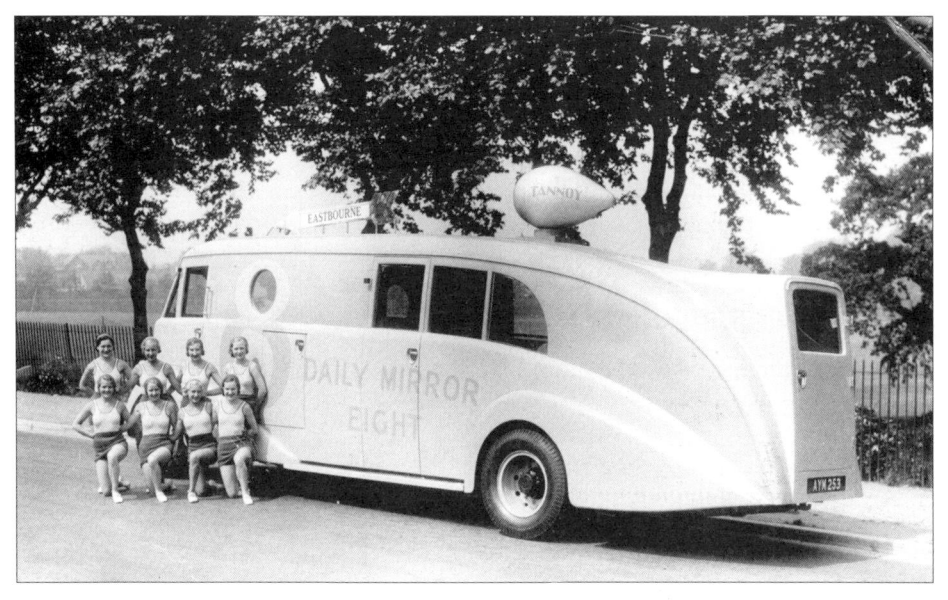

Above: 'Daily Mirror 8' touring coach 1934

Left: the tuning dial here is calibrated in metres but without station names, suggesting 1932-34 possibly for use in hospitals.

Right: here 'Droitwich' is printed on the tuning scale, indicating post 15th January 1934. Northern stations suggest it was intended for use in Northern England

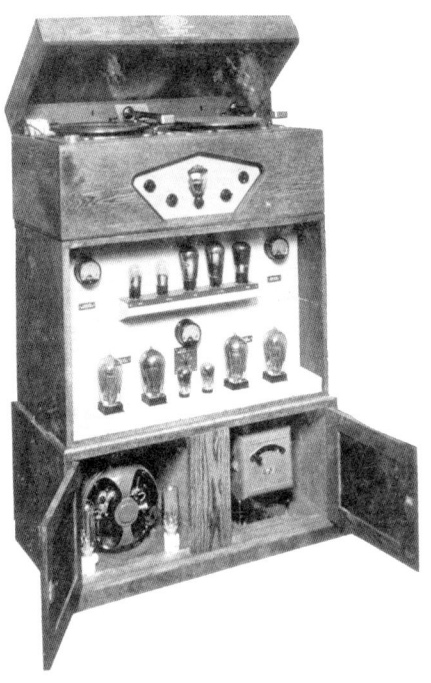

*Showman's Equipment.
Tuner Calibrated in degrees
indicates c1932*

*4 Waveband Radiogram
c 1935
The lockable doors and the
apparent absence of a loudspeaker suggests communal
use, probably in hospitals*

without consulting Guy, George went to see Leslie Odell of *British Relay* and asked him where they obtained their racks and, following Odell's lead he was able to buy the first two racks they needed for £3, 30/- each. Guy was typically furious for, according to Wheeler's account, he was getting a cut from *Camco*. It is more likely, however, that he had it in mind that the majority of the amplifiers which the factory was making needed to be portable or, at least transportable, and therefore built into cabinets.

Other railway companies in Great Britain followed the lead of *L.M.S.* and before long, a special range of rack-mounted, tropical equipment was ordered by the *Indian Railways*. The *Indian Railways* sets usually comprised two units with three 150 watts amplifiers in one and three *Westinghouse* rectifiers in the other, all of which had to be forced cooled.

Guy continued to fight against rack mounted amplifiers for some time and, apart from contracts such as the *L.M.S.* one, he continued to insist that much of the Tannoy equipment was built into cabinets, long after other manufacturers had adopted rack mounted amplifiers as standard. Even when the factory had changed over to making predominantly rack mounted equipment, Guy still made sure that at least some of the amplifiers were built into wooden cabinets. It must, of course, be admitted that by insisting on this, he was ensuring that his amplifiers were portable, and therefore adaptable. It must also be said that most of the Tannoy cabinets of the time were well designed and very pleasing to the eye and this probably appealed to him and to the artistic streak inherited from his father and grandfather. Nevertheless, his obstinate streak demanded that things were generally done his way, thus satisfying his almost uncontrollable ego.

The Tannoy range of radiograms was still attracting attention and, on 26th August, 1932 *Wireless World* reported on the Radio Show at Olympia that the Tannoy Standard radiogram was priced at 45 guineas and the Senior superhet radiogram at 60 guineas.

It was not long before extra space was needed for the coil winding operation and, in 1933, Guy acquired premises in Nettlefold Place, another dingy back street, behind shops near West Norwood station and it was here that Bill Haines set up the first separate winding shop. Once this had become established, the design of coils and transformers was placed in the hands of two design specialists, Norman Crowhurst and Philip Marks, both of whom later made major contributions to the progress of Tannoy, while a lady called Vi Metcalfe ran the winding shop. Vi Metcalfe later worked for John Logie Baird, winding coils at his workshop at Crystal Palace.

In August, 1933, Tannoy again exhibited at the Radiolympia Exhibition and publicity material shows that, among other items of equipment, the 'Standard' and 'Senior' models of the radiogram were shown with a range of amplifiers and loudspeakers, the latter incorporating the new 'Tannoy' logo on the fret. This logo had been designed by Alf Davey, who had been taken on as storekeeper when he left his previous job with a company making motorcycle sidecars. Although he eventually became Tannoy's Purchasing Manager it is very doubtful if he was ever adequately rewarded for his design which helped so much to bring Tannoy to the attention of the public. It was an excellent logo which served the company very well for many years. The TANNOY Trade Name, with the pointed ends was designed by a good friend of the family, Bill Truby, who was employed by *P.A. Reuter*. This was not discontinued until Tannoy was acquired by *Harman Industries* (the account of this is the subject of Chapter 15).

At that exhibition it was evident that Tannoy public address amplifiers were gaining attention for, on 25th August, 1933 *Wireless World* reported:

> Public address equipment formed the principal exhibits of this firm and many large amplifiers and horn type projection loudspeakers were shown. A heavy duty, moving-coil loudspeaker rated to handle 30 watts is also listed with various types of microphones.

The prices remained the same and the author's father replaced the two-valve wireless which he had bought from Guy in 1930 with a Tannoy 'Junior' radiogram. One wonders what sort of 'discussion' took place over the price paid for this!

Also in 1933, a readily transportable 100 watts public address system was available with the amplifier and twin turntables in one cabinet which featured a metal mesh front, behind which were mounted the valves and two meters which probably registered the output valve grid voltage and anode current. The metal mesh allowed the valves to enjoy a fairly free circulation of air for cooling.

By 1933 Tannoy was acknowledged to be the largest organisation in Great Britain specialising in the design and manufacture of public address equipment and early in that year the young Bill Haines visited the factory with his father as a customer where they saw Guy Fountain and a salesman, Mr. Wormy. Haines' father was a showman and an amplifier was later demonstrated to them on site by an operator, Peter Bray, during the Easter weekend. The sale was agreed for £120 and an amplifier, allegedly capable of 100 watts output, with twin turntables and four, 18" loudspeakers and a rotary converter was delivered. Haines recalled that the loudspeakers were very efficient, being energised magnet loudspeakers with their 18" cones having chamois leather surrounds and fitted into wooden cabinet, 3 feet square, made by *Camco*. His next meeting with Guy Fountain was a few months later when the equipment failed on a Saturday evening. His father phoned both the factory and Guy's house on the Sunday morning but there was no reply so he asked Bill to take his car and go to 25 Lancaster Avenue to see if he could arrange a quick repair. A very annoyed Guy Fountain answered the door and, after some argument, he decided to get his car out of the garage, a maroon coloured American 'Essex Six' saloon, and go to do the repair himself. This was achieved quite quickly as it was only a loose connection on the input socket.

Bill Haines' next meeting with Guy was in the following July when he was interviewed for a job. He had just completed his 5 years apprenticeship with *His Master's Voice* at Hayes and in their *Columbia* factory in Wandsworth and, as he was one of about 20 on the course, he considered it important to find alternative employment as quickly as possible. He was ushered into Guy's office in the newly completed Canterbury Grove factory and, after a general preamble and some questions on Ohm's Law,[7] he handed Guy his indentures and his final report. Guy's response was, "Christ! - if you can do half that you will suit me." He then asked Haines how much he wanted and, as he was getting £4.10.0d. per week at H.M.V., he asked for £5. This caused some consternation as Guy told him that George Wheeler was only getting £5, so they settled on £4.15.0d. and a promise of a rise to £5 in three months if his work was satisfactory. With typical impatience Guy wanted him to start immediately, so he did, working for Tannoy during his holiday. He then returned to *E.M.I.* to hand in his resignation and, having worked out his notice, he came back to Tannoy.

Bill Haines' family showground was adjacent to the Southern Railway lines between Victoria and Clapham Junction and it is believed that this was in the area which was, until it was redeveloped in about 1999, occupied by a car breaker's yard, with access from Eversleigh Road. This may seem irrelevant but, as will be recounted later, Tannoy owes much of its fame to equipment which was supplied to fairgrounds.

Among Haines' first allotted tasks were the preparation of the company's stand for the Radiolympia Exhibition and the move into the new factory which was being built in Canterbury Grove and which was occupied in March 1934. Little expense had been spared in the building of this new Tannoy factory with the result that when the start of the move was due, not long after the Radiolympia exhibition, there was little money left to buy new equipment and even less to spend on furniture. At the end of the show all the products, displays and publicity material were loaded onto lorries to take back to the factory. This is hard, heavy work and all the staff and representatives of other manufacturers had similar chores to do, after which they would repair to the nearest licensed premises and enjoy some well earned drinks. However this was not to be for the Tannoy staff who, as soon as the lorry was packed with their display materials and products, were told by Guy to trawl the deserted stands and find whatever they could in the way of tables, chairs, desks and filing cabinets – anything that looked like office furniture, and load this also onto their lorry. It was in this manner that much of the furniture and equipment for the new factory was acquired!

A few weeks later, In March 1934, the new building was officially opened with much pomp and circumstance by Guy's friend Freddie March, Duke of Richmond and Gordon, but it is very unlikely that His Grace ever knew anything of the manner of the acquisition of the office furniture and the chairs in which he sat. Had he done so, how eager would he have been to accede to Guy's request to perform the opening ceremony?

Other contracts which were awarded to Tannoy at about this time were to provide sound equipment for the announcements and gramophone record playing at various ice and and roller skating rinks. Among these were the ice rinks at Streatham and Hammersmith and the roller skating rink at Brixton. There were several such roller rinks in and around London at the time and they were very noisy places so the Tannoy equipment had to be loud. Roller skates were not so well made as modern roller blades; they had hard steel wheels which made a great deal of noise on any surface, particularly on the wooden floors of the skating rinks. In addition to this, their owners did not devote too much time to maintenance with the result that the ball-bearings inside the tiny wheels, starved of oil, could usually be heard rattling around in their races. Numerous other contracts were secured in hotels such as the Branksome Tower and the Dunholme Manor Hotels in Bournemouth, at London's Cumberland Hotel and in the 'Ace of Spades' Roadhouses, the most famous of which, perhaps infamous, was at Hook, on the Kingston by-pass. Dirt tracks at the Crystal Palace and Wimbledon Stadium were equipped by Tannoy, as were the Enfield open air swimming pool, the Olympia Sports Stadium, the Whitehall Club in Shrewsbury and many offices such as those of the *Blue Star Shipping Line* and both the *Daily Mirror* and the *Daily Herald*. Within the next two years the Municipal swimming pools at Barking, Twickenham and Clacton Pier had been added to the list.

Such was the progress of the company that Canterbury Grove was soon outgrown so Bill Haines moved the machine shop back to Nettlefold Place where some sheds were built to accommodate the production of loudspeaker horns. He had considerable difficulty in persuading Guy to purchase any new, even secondhand, machinery and he recalled buying the company's first sheet metal bending machine. Before that, he often used to take sheet metal, already cut to size, to Old Street, Finsbury, where a sheet metal worker had his workshop and he would bend it on the pavement. On one occasion, Haines took a chassis for a Tannoy 100 watts amplifier there to be bent and, realising just how unsatisfactory this arrangement was, he bought the machine there and then, for £7-10-0d. He took the machine to pieces to get it into the back of the car and then, with great difficulty, had to persuade Guy to reimburse him for it. That machine continued in use for many years. He also bought a couple of lathes and later asked Guy for the money, with equal difficulty. Later, in 1939, it proved necessary to move the machine shop again, this time to the premises which became known as Waylett Place – of which more later.

By this time Guy's insidious ways were already in evidence and George Wheeler recalled some rather typical illustrations of the devious things that Guy did, among which was an act that took place soon after the move to Canterbury Grove. Guy and George had hatched the idea of combining the wiring for the factory's own public address system (an essential feature of Guy's factory) with the wiring for the overhead heating equipment. This was not much of a success but, like many of his ideas, it just *had* to have a great deal of attention paid to it and much valuable time spent on it. Guy was so convinced that this would revolutionise factory wiring installations and become a money spinner that he rushed to the Patent Office and took out a patent in his name, excluding George.

At the 1934 Radiolympia exhibition the company stand predominantly featured amplifiers but there were still radiograms on show, in quite prominent positions. The smallest amplifier shown was the two-valve amplifier, type AC25 which had an output of between 6 and 8 watts. The type M25 was also shown and this was of particular interest as it could be operated on either a 6 volts or a 12 volts car battery. This may have been the first truly portable amplifier and it was almost certainly another of George Wheeler's designs.

Tannoy had, by then, started producing rack mounted amplifiers for certain specific customers, particularly for the *London, Midland and Scottish Railway Company*. So for some years both rack mounted and cabinet mounted amplifiers were in production and there are photographs known to have been taken in 1934 of Tannoy amplifiers mounted in racks for a radio relay company, almost certainly this was *Rediffusion Ltd*.

Guy's very strong preference for his amplifiers to be built into cabinets was not entirely a personal matter. He had started the amplifier business with portable equipment and he continued to favour portable sets which were, of course, more easily carried about when built into cabinets.

In another *Radiolympia* report, on 24th August, 1934, *Wireless World* recorded:

> One of the smallest amplifiers is the AC25. This is of the 2-valve type with an output of 6-8 watts. It is priced at 26 guineas, including loudspeaker.
> The M25 portable model is of particular interest in that it can be operated from a 6 volts or

The TANNOY Story

12 volts battery. Three class B valves are used in parallel in the output stage to give an output of some 8 watts and a rotary converter is provided for the H.T. supply. A gramophone pick-up and turntable are provided together with a microphone and horn type loudspeaker and the equipment is listed at 38 guineas.

So, early in the 1930s, the name of Tannoy started to become associated with the growing amplifier industry. The production of wireless sets and battery eliminators, referred to in the publicity as 'Mains Units', was continued for some years and the company also started to develop new ideas associated with sound amplifiers, even to pioneer them, for Tannoy was among the first companies in Great Britain to combine electric gramophones with wireless sets to produce radiogramophones. This was quite a logical development of the wireless and amplifier business and in 1931 Tannoy stopped making simple wireless sets to concentrate their attention on amplifiers and radiograms; quite a bold step at the time. It was suggested by one of the company's long-standing employees, Stan Livingstone (of whom more in later chapters), that Guy's justification for producing luxury radiograms was to establish contact with rich clients who might be in a position to purchase or to authorise the purchase of other Tannoy products.

In addition to radiograms for domestic use, the Tannoy management was far-sighted enough to introduce a special model for use in schools, and hospitals. Although they may have been available earlier, the first of these of which there is an illustration is the 1935 model which had an output of 12 watts. This was very much more powerful than any domestic radiogram of the time and it was more than adequate for the assembly halls and classrooms of most schools and it was housed in a somewhat plainer, more utilitarian cabinet than the domestic radiogram. Nevertheless, it was a pleasing, modern design, in polished light or dark oak that was so fashionable at the time and it is evident that the *Camco* cabinet displayed the very high standard of workmanship associated with all Tannoy products. The illustration shows the lid open to reveal an early record changer which, judging from its three record supports which rotated to release one record at a time, was almost certainly made by *Garrard*. Below this compartment, double doors on the front are shown open, exposing the tuning dial and other controls with a meter above it and it is interesting to note that these doors were lockable. Although it is not possible to read its label the meter probably indicated, as was the case on some Tannoy amplifiers, the final stage grid volts which would have given an indication of the level of the output power. Other controls are the volume control, the on-off switch, the tone control and what appears to be the wavelength switch. Beneath this panel is the well proportioned loudspeaker grille with the Tannoy fret, the whole being a very elegant and well balanced design.

Although by this time the company was well advanced in the design and production of their radiograms, there were some shortcomings, however trivial they may now seem. In 1934, largely due to the efforts of Peter Eckersley, the wavelengths of European broadcasting stations were re-allocated to reduce the inter-transmitter interference which did much to spoil the listeners' enjoyment of radio programmes. These changes took place on 15th January, 1935, but the B.B.C's transmitters were only slightly affected; most of the frequency changes being imposed on the continental stations. Many manufacturers of radios offered replacement tuning dials, calibrated for the new frequencies but Tannoy radiograms were calibrated in numbered, 9 kilocycle bands and purchasers were provided with blue prints indicating which stations were operating in which of the numbered channels. Following the re-allocation of frequencies, Tannoy simply offered replacement blue prints.

It is believed that it was in 1935 that the company received an order to install radio equipment in the Royal Train which required a considerable amount of research, experiment and development – development which was to continue for some years. George Wheeler was in charge of the project and, with some assistance, he spent much of his time at Wolverton, near to where Milton Keynes was later developed and where he was, in theory, supervising the installation of the equipment on the Royal Train. The equipment was required to perform two functions; to provide good radio reception in the royal compartments and to provide communication between the coaches. The term 'supervising' was, in the event, something of a euphemism for he had to carry out most of the installation work himself, with the help of a couple of assistants. At various stages of the project George had to ask for test runs, for which purpose the Royal coaches were coupled onto the back of a train to Scotland, usually the Flying Scotsman.

The greatest problem with the Royal Train installation was interference. Electricity was provided in the carriages for lighting (and, of course, to power the Tannoy equipment) by 48 volts batteries which were kept charged by a dynamo mounted under the coach chassis and driven by a braided canvas belt from a pulley on a wheel axle. The arcing at the brushes of these dynamos produced serious interference which was very difficult to suppress and which varied with the speed of the train. The Tannoy equipment was powered via a d.c. to a.c. rotary converter and another problem which was important to solve was that of getting a good earth connection which was difficult because the train's axles were floating in oil baths which acted as an insulator. On one test run, having made various adjustments under the coach when the train had stopped at Preston and at Carnforth, they arrived at Carstairs. Here George needed to make some more alterations to their suppression equipment under the coach and he said to the driver, "Can you wait for about 5 minutes while we change some equipment?" He then went underneath the train to take the covers off their installation. As he was disconnecting some of the condensers, the train started to move backwards and forwards. George said that he had never moved so quickly before or since! They also had a problem in providing an adequate aerial to receive the rather poor radio signals from the numerous transmitters then used by the *B.B.C.* and, at one stage of their experimental work, they used a kite to suspend the aerial above the moving train! Nothing was recorded, however, about what happened to this when the train passed under bridges. On the final test run of the Royal Train Guy Fountain accompanied George and his team on the journey and, following his extensive work on the Royal Train, George enjoyed making the claim that he was the only commoner ever to have slept in the Queen's bed! Although the initial installation was soon completed, further developments were incorporated over the years and it was not until 1940 that the installation in the Royal train was finally completed.

In the latter part of the decade, the company started winning contracts for several installations which helped tremendously to bring the name of Tannoy into the public arena. In the mid 1930s, Tannoy equipment was installed in many London hotels, the Waldorf and the Savoy being among the first, and in places of entertainment such as dance halls although the most important of these, the Hammersmith Palais, in common with all the Mecca dance halls, was not equipped until after the second World War.

During 1936 the factory was extended by the addition of a first floor above the front part only of the existing building and the company's capital was increased to £10,500 when the *Crofthill Investment Trust* took up 17% of the ordinary shares and 44% of the preference shares.

Early Progress In Public Address

CHAPTER NOTES

1 This entry in the show catalogue may not be true for, as will be recounted later, it has been said that Tannoy did not start making their own loudspeakers until 1935. Those which were offered for sale in 1931 were almost certainly bought in, and almost as certainly they would have been overpainted 'Tannoy' in very bold letters. It is thought that Tannoy were, at that time, working on loudspeaker designs.

2 The author's father had purchased one of these sets from Guy in 1930 which is now in the author's collection. It is still in working order although it has, over the years, been subjected to various repairs, most recently by Gerald Wells at the Vintage Wireless Museum, with the inevitable, perhaps regrettable result that not all its components are of the original types. This must be accepted for the condensers were made of wax impregnated paper and as the wax dries out it is unlikely that any of the original types survive in a serviceable condition. However, the set still works and is still in use with a *Triotron* loudspeaker.

3 Although there are references to Tannoy loudspeakers in trade literature and in the company's records from about 1930 onwards, T.B. Livingstone, of whom more later, was quite adamant that no loudspeakers were made by Tannoy until about 1935. But bearing in mind the various accounts of Tannoy loudspeakers alleged to have been made in the early 1930s, and the fact that Livingstone did not join the company until late 1938, it is possible that Livingstone's statement may not have been accurate.

4 The Swan and Sugar loaf was a favourite watering hole of the author's father who, after a day's work in London, frequently walked from South Croydon station to the 'Swan' for a drink or two before catching the No. 235 bus home to No. 7, Crest Road.

5 There is a reference in the company records of a family friend, Phyllis Mary Odell, of Harrow Weald, taking up 549 shares, (25%), In 1933.

6 Ron Rackham is acknowledged as having been something of a genius. He was responsible for several of the company's most significant developments which will be covered in detail in later chapters.

7 This is interesting for the author remembers a conversation with Guy Fountain during a holiday at Guy's holiday home, Carlton Cottage, at Cliftonville, Kent. The author was just about to start a course in Electrical Engineering and Guy asked about his future intentions. The only technical questions he asked were, "What is Ohm's Law?" and, "How does this apply to alternating current?"

IF IT'S TANNOY IT'S SOUND

FOUNDER & GOVERNING DIRECTOR

Guy R. Fountain

TANNOY
PRODUCTS
LIMITED

Head Office and Showrooms:
WEST NORWOOD · LONDON · S·E·27
Telegrams & Telephones: GIPSY HILL 1131 (6 lines)

CHAPTER FOUR

SWINGS AND ROUNDABOUTS

The previous chapter has dealt with the company's progress through the 1930s but there was a particularly important development in progress at that time which added considerably to Tannoy's status and reputation for, in 1932, Guy made his first *coup de maître*.

It has been said that the progress of Tannoy through the 1930s was something of a circus, but this is, of course, the cynical view. The fact is, that in January 1932, Guy was permitted to provide public address equipment to the Bertram Mills Circus at Olympia and this was truly a breakthrough. However, there had been a little 'behind-the-scenes' activity typical of Guy Fountain, who was the archetypal entrepreneur, in order to achieve this deal. It is generally accepted that Guy, by then a good friend of Bertram Mills, paid Bertram £100 to allow him to show what Tannoy amplifiers could do and that there was no charge made for that year's equipment. In subsequent years the equipment was hired to Bertram Mills at commercial rates.

The Bertram Mills Circus was one of the largest and most famous in Europe staging an annual show in London's Olympia as an alternative attraction to pantomime and in 1932 Tannoy supplied sound equipment to the circus for the first time. Freddy Cooper was in charge of the installation and a 250 watts amplifier was used. This incorporated two large, DA 60 transmitter valves feeding G.E.C. loudspeakers which were boldly overpainted 'TANNOY'.[1]

In view of the importance to Tannoy of the Bertram Mills Circus contracts, it is worth recording some details of this work including some of the amusing anecdotes about these installations, resulting partly from the technical problems and partly from Guy's petulant manner.

The TANNOY Story

The amplifier which was used in the first installation had been used previously for the Radio Exhibition in Bristol, an event which had been beset with difficulties, and its use at Olympia also had its problems as the operator and the commentator had to sit in a confined space underneath the public seating which in later years became part of the stables for the equine events. Freddy Cooper, a Tannoy Engineer, enjoyed telling the story of the time when the output transformer failed in the middle of a show and he had to fish out the broken ends of the windings with a couple of knitting needles just to keep the set going until the end of the performance.[2]

The name, 'TANNOY', in very large letters, prominently displayed on the loudspeakers and anywhere else where Guy thought he could get away with it, brought the company's name to the attention of the large numbers of people who attended the Bertram Mills Circus and this guaranteed Guy the excellent publicity which he so wanted, and needed. This contract represented some of the best advertising achieved for the company for the equipment literally 'spoke for itself' and drew the attention of the audiences to the loudspeakers and to the trademark 'TANNOY'. As a result the company quickly became very firmly established and for some years, seldom looked back.

In spite of the early problems and occasional failures, the first season at Bertram Mills circus was generally successful. Bertram Mills was well pleased and, based on this success, Tannoy was again called upon to provide sound equipment for the following show in 1933. By this time the company had produced an amplifier specifically for showmen, the GA 250, a 250 watts amplifier which was designed around an output stage also comprising four DA 60 valves. This installation was even more successful than the first with the result that Tannoy equipment was used for many years at the Olympia, with a break only during the second world war. The Olympia report recorded the fact that at this show Type 'A', Voigt 30 watts moving coil loudspeakers were used as well as various types of Tannoy microphones.

The DA 60 output valves were transformer driven and the transformers, together with all Tannoy's early coupling transformers, output transformers, mains transformers and chokes, were, of course, made by *Keston Manufacturing Co.*, which has been mentioned in some detail in a previous chapter. It was largely as a result of the success of the early Bertram Mills contracts that Guy felt that it was necessary to move the factory into yet larger premises and construction of the purpose built factory mentioned in the previous chapter was started in Canterbury Grove, West Norwood.

Following their first successful experiences with Tannoy equipment at Olympia, Bertram Mills asked for an amplifier for his travelling circus and in late 1932 a portable 120 watts amplifier was installed for him in a van. It was a three-wheeled Raleigh van and the power supply consisted of four large 12 volts batteries, hanging in steel straps below the floor of the van, with a rotary converter bolted to the floor under the shelf on which the amplifier was mounted. Above the amplifier were two loudspeakers in wooden cabinets with frets made in the new 'Tannoy' logo and these could be removed from their shelf and placed outside the van. The van was liberally adorned with Tannoy publicity and, of course, featured, very prominently, the company slogan: TANNOY, THE 'SOUND' PEOPLE.

Following the success of this installation, further orders followed and one of the Raleigh vans which was photographed containing slightly later equipment bore a registration number which was issued in April 1933. In January 1932, a gramophone amplifier, similar to the large gramophone reproducer which was mentioned in the previous chapter was introduced in a more basic form and aimed specifically at the fairground operators, priced at 38 gns.

Derek Pipe who later became the company's Chief Engineer, recalled that in January 1934 energised loudspeakers were used at the Bertram Mills Circus which required a supply of 110 volts d.c. for the field coils and the engineers had to beg, borrow or steal all sorts of equipment including d.c. power packs and accumulators to provide this supply. Their problems were further complicated by the fact that, on this occasion, it had also been decided not to install the loudspeakers over the centre of the arena but to mount them in the corners of the auditorium, a long way from the amplifier. At that time 100 volts speech lines had not been thought of, the output from the amplifiers was all at low impedance, and a problem arose from the fact that one side of the voice coil and one side of the field coil were common so that the connections to the loudspeakers were made with three-pin plugs, with one pin being the common lead. Inevitably there were mistakes and, if a plug were forced, it could be inserted the wrong way around with the inevitable result that the voice coil took the 110 volts d.c. and was destroyed. The result was both disastrous and expensive for, not only did they then have to replace the voice coil and the cone, but the guilty party also had to contend with Guy Fountain's rage; new cones were 25 shillings each which would now, in 2003, equate to about £30.

Another amusing difficulty arose from the use of energised loudspeakers when the insulation of the field coil in one of the loudspeakers failed causing a short-circuit. The coil overheated and eventually caught fire. Fortunately the fire caused no damage but the firemen created something of a stir when they attempted to douse the burning loudspeaker, rather over zealously, with a foam fire extinguisher. Apparently a lady in the audience caught much of the foam and considerable damage was done to her dignity and to her expensive fur coat. The local Fire Officer got a bit worked up about this and reported the matter to the London County Council who then banned the use of energised loudspeakers in the Olympia.

In one of the early shows, Bertram Mills asked if it would be possible to amplify the speech of the clown acts in the arena. This is now just a routine matter of fitting all the players with radio-microphones and then amplifying the signals into strategically placed loudspeakers, but in those days, such sophistication was not possible. In the first attempts to do this a small amplifier and loudspeakers were built into one of the props but this did not produce sufficient volume to reach more than the first few rows of the audience, partly because space constraints limited the size of the amplifier and partly because, when the volume control was turned up, feedback produced the most awful howls and whistles. They then tried using a carbon microphone hidden in one of the props connected to the main amplifier by a long cable trailing across the arena and with horn loudspeakers fitted above the arena on angle iron frames, but the only loudspeakers which they could obtain at short notice had 3 ohms voice coils while all the other equipment had 15 ohms coils, so these loudspeakers had to have little matching transformers fitted in them. They were also wired in a series/parallel arrangement and, inevitably, the matching transformers were sometimes forgotten with the result that sound quality was terrible. So, the following year they fitted what were known as PM/PS horn loudspeakers on angle iron brackets over the arena. PM/PS meant 'Permanent Magnet Projection Speaker' and these consisted of an 8" diameter cone loudspeaker mounted on a rectangular horn with a rear enclosure which housed a 100 volts transformer.

They later used amplifiers which were destined for use by the relay companies in South Wales and mounted on stands in the arena, in full view of the audience. These had 40 volts distribution lines but somebody forgot about this and connected 15 ohms loudspeakers to them and they, too, sounded terrible, George Wheeler was furious and, once again, they had to fit matching transformers to all the loudspeakers in considerable haste. So, in spite of the general levels of success achieved with these installations for Bertram Mills' Circus, there were many difficulties and problems, some of which are now quite amusing to recall, but they were far from funny at the time.

Bertram Mills also asked them to install microphones in the band so that the music could be relayed more satisfactorily to all parts of the arena. For this purpose some experiments were done using early condenser microphones. It is believed that these had been designed and possibly made by Jack Houlgate, by then Chief Engineeer, who had joined Tannoy in about 1935 having served an apprenticeship with *Johnson & Phillips* and having also worked for Paul Voigt. Although the performance of these microphones was good, they are said to have been rather unreliable, but when they did work, they worked well and they picked up the music very much better than carbon microphones. But once again they had not arranged the loudspeakers centrally over the arena but in a somewhat haphazard manner around the auditorium where it happened to be easy or convenient to mount them; on the corner pillars and over the entrances, and their performance left much to be desired. So, although the equipment was, in fact, performing very well, the end result was sometimes more than a little disappointing. But Guy's insistence that the name of his company, 'TANNOY', should be seen in large, bold letters on every possible opportunity, afforded him the very best of advertising and the Bertram Mills contracts did nothing but enhance this publicity.

Guy was quite adamant, throughout the Bertram Mills contracts, that there would be no amplification equipment other than Tannoy's in use anywhere in the building during the shows. In addition to the main performance in the arena there were other side shows and a fun fair in the adjoining areas of the Olympia. Occasionally a showman would come in and start making his announcements using his own amplifier, at which, if he noticed it, Fountain would almost explode. He would storm up to Bertram Mills or any of his staff who happened to be in sight and shout, 'Switch that bloody thing off! We can't have anything here but Tannoy.' Then someone would have to rush back to the factory to collect another amplifier; any amplifier, to lend to the showman and satisfy Guy's insistence that every piece of sound equipment was supplied by Tannoy.

By 1937 rack type installations which were being made for the Argentinian Navy, using type RP 50 amplifiers, were used in the Bertram Mills contracts. Guy Fountain had argued for years in favour of building amplifiers in cabinets but eventually he was forced, rather later than other manufacturers, to accept the principle of rack type installations, but they had still not settled on mounting the loudspeakers centrally over the ring and again they were fixed on pillars around the hall. With these amplifiers, and with the new ribbon microphones, performance was much better than ever before although the operator had to take great care to achieve the required volume and clarity while still avoiding feedback. Further sophistication had by then been incorporated as the 100 volts loudspeaker line with a common loudspeaker impedance of 200 ohms had been adopted as standard practice for installations such as this, so the complicated systems using series parallel connections and dummy loads were no longer necessary.

In addition to amplifying the circus acts and the band, much of the music was provided from gramophone records and a great improvement in the sound quality from recorded music was made in the following year. Until 1938 the recorded music was all on commercially available 78 rpm, gramophone records and the sound quality from these left much to be desired because they were played over and over again and wear inevitably caused surface noise which was amplified with the music. So, in 1938, the music was recorded on film, as in the cinema, producing an improvement in quality, a total elimination of surface noise and, of course, no wear so that the same music could be played many times at successive shows.

This type of installation, using RP 50 amplifiers, was used at Olympia until the outbreak of the second world war. During the war there were, of course, no performances of the circus and, by the time the war was over, the company had made further progress although there was evidence of some lack of a truly professional approach to business. In the early post-war years Tannoy enjoyed the benefit of a Sales Manager and, in addition to manufacturing equipment which would 'speak for itself' and advertise the company, attempts were made to improve the appearance of the equipment. In the first post-war circus installation some of the war-time rack equipment consisting of 60 watts amplifiers was used, looking both neat and professional, and this was arranged in such a way that it was in full view of the public. There were three separate amplifiers, one for the circus music, one for the fun fair loudspeakers and one for the speech circuit in the circus big top and the operator sat at a smart console containing two turntables, a microphone and the pre-amplifiers. This was one of several consoles which were being built for Butlin's Holiday camps and it was diverted or 'borrowed' from the camp at Filey, Yorkshire. But the following year this was not available so a dummy console was built, of similar appearance, in the hope that it would be suitably impressive and would generate additional business. But of course, the people who visited the circus were not necessarily the people who might generate business by buying amplifiers, nevertheless, Guy insisted for, whatever else happened, the name of Tannoy was being brought before the public eye.

At the opening of the circus each year, Bertram Mills hosted a formal lunch, predominently for members of the press, local dignitaries and, occasionally, Royalty and in the immediate post-war years it was decided that the speeches which followed these lunches would be amplified. Guy Fountain insisted that every opportunity to show off his amplifiers should be seized with much alacrity and he made sure that these speeches would be the object of his attention. However, his enthusiasm backfired on him because the lunches were originally held in the National Hall at Olympia, which was little more than a concrete box with very poor acoustic properties and the Tannoy amplifiers did little or nothing to enhance the audibility of the speeches.

Terence Livingstone, predictably always known as 'Stan', who had joined the company as a salesman late in 1938 had, by 1939, made considerable progress within the company and was closely involved with the installation of the equipment for that year's lunch. He recalled that in that year, a number of loudspeakers were borrowed, once again from the stores of the South Wales relay company, and that these were mounted around the room and that they operated at reduced volume levels. This type of amplification, using many low output loudspeakers instead of a few very powerful ones, may well have been the first experiment along these lines and, in all probability, this led to what later became known as 'sound reinforcement'. Tannoy can therefore make a reasonable claim to have pioneered the important technique of sound reinforcement.

Initially however, this was not too successful and George Wheeler insisted that the following year it would be done entirely differently, with horn loudspeakers pointing down from above the luncheon tables, hidden by a false ceiling of butter muslin. The operators of the equipment, including Stan Livingstone, had to arrange suitable mountings for the loudspeakers and seats for themselves above the luncheon guests and they peered through the muslin to see what was happening below them. Due to reverberation from the concrete walls, the performance was little better than the previous year's attempt and during tests which were in progress just half an hour before the guests were due to sit down, George came rushing up to them shouting, "Bloody useless, we have got to take all those loudspeakers down." So, while the waiters were putting the finishing touches to the lunch tables, a new set of loudspeakers was hastily put up but the results were little better. It is believed that this was one of the reasons for moving this function in later years to the Olympia's Addison Rooms which had much better acoustics. It was not long before more experimental work was done with large numbers of low output loudspeakers replacing one or two very loud, high output units, and the principle of sound reinforcement was more firmly established.

There was another amusing incident soon after World War Two when Guy decided that the luncheon speeches would be recorded. Tannoy engineers were developing direct acetate disc recording machines and he was keen to show them off, so he arranged for two Tannoy disc recorders to be sent to the Olympia with Ron Rackham and Stan Livingstone to operate them. All the speeches were recorded, totalling about $2^{1}/_{2}$ hours at about three or four minutes on each 78 r.pm disc. They worked in a tiny room with little ventilation, recording speech after speech, until they had nearly 50 records at their side and were almost ankle-deep in the acetate swarf, all highly inflammable and liberally dusted with cigarette ash! The Fire Officer might have come close to having a fit yet the results of their labours was a huge pile of records which, so far as is known, were never played.

In the early post-war years the loudspeakers which were used for the circus shows were those which had been developed for the Greyhound Racing Association and which were first installed at the New Cross Stadium. They were large horn loaded loudspeakers which were fixed, somewhat precariously, over the circus bandstand and the last-minute job was always that of getting the angles at which they pointed exactly right. The sheer effort of doing this; lifting and adjusting the heavy loudspeakers with numerous ropes, was exhausting and the reproduction of music was none too good so, within a year or so, moving-coil microphones and line-source loudspeakers were used instead. These consisted of 6, 15" dual concentric loudspeakers in each cabinet, suspended on either side of the bandstand and, if these were carefully adjusted, they could give very acceptable reinforcement of the music across the whole arena. (The development of the Dual Concentric loudspeaker will be recounted in Chapter 12). At this time the music was provided by a 16 piece band, about half of whom were said to have been Welsh Guardsmen and Scottish Guardsmen 'moonlighting' to augment the circus band; and their incomes! Norman Robottom recalled that in addition to the difficulty of hoisting these line-source loudspeakers into position, they also found that in the optimum position they blocked the view of some of the most expensive seats in the auditorium. Numerous adjustments had to be made to the positions of these heavy loudspeakers and, of course, union rules dictated that only 'riggers' were allowed to handle them and this led to further complications.

The speech was amplified using large horn loudspeakers which were none too elegant so they were soon replaced by wooden enclosures, each containing three 15" and one 12" dual concentric loudspeakers, suspended facing downwards with 'Tannoy' in bold 'Dayglo' signwriting. This was typical of Guy, he always insisted that as much publicity as possible was visible and the invention of 'Dayglo' paint played right into his hands, but more typical was the illuminated 'Tannoy' sign over the bandstand. He insisted that this had to be wired to an independent circuit so that if any act required the arena to be in darkness, when the lights were switched off, the 'Tannoy' sign was not affected by the blackout switch, and so remained ON at all times. When the speech loudspeakers were replaced a year or two later by the much smaller 'Victory' bowl loudspeakers, he insisted that they were fitted with 'Tannoy' pennants hanging below them. This caused some argument because they tended to obscure the aerial acts from some seats, but the audience could see the name 'Tannoy' and that was all that mattered to Guy.

Norman Robottom also recalled a time when he was engaged in

conversation with Cyril Mills[3] at the ring entrance, just before the circus opened, when Cyril suddenly pushed Norman against the wall. Norman wondered what was going on until he saw a huge bear rushing past him which might have knocked him down. He also recalled that many children, when visiting the circus, would deliberately get themselves lost so that they could have their names called out over the Tannoy.

Another incident recalled by Robottom was occasioned by the times when a special show would be arranged on a Sunday afternoon for television, usually abbreviated so that only the best acts were shown. It was not long after these that audiences started to fall off quite dramatically, leaving many rows of empty seats because, of course, so many people took the view that they could see all the best acts on television so why bother to go to the real thing. Guy Fountain soon took advantage of this situation by negotiating deals for large blocks of seats at much reduced prices and then giving these away to numerous friends and acquaintances to whom he felt he should dispense his own form of largesse.

But, to return to pre-war days, a natural progression from these circus shows was the sale of Tannoy amplifiers to smaller showmen, particularly the travelling funfairs which were often to be seen in towns and villages all over the country. Following the various contracts for the supply of sound equipment for the Bertram Mills circus, other circuses and fairground operators soon followed this lead and the company received many orders for amplifiers. The equipment, designed specifically for showmen, operating on 110 volts d.c., was introduced in 1938 and it was a neat and compact set in two cabinets. 110 volts d.c. was used in fairgrounds because this was the voltage generated by the dynamos mounted above the boilers of the steam traction engines which towed the stalls and rides from one town to another and, on arrival at their venue, generated all the electricity which was required by the fair. The amplifier and turntable, without autochanger, were in one cabinet which had an on-off switch, a volume control and a switch to select either microphone or gramophone. The second cabinet, in a smart, contemporary design, contained the loudspeaker. It did not feature the Tannoy fret although a large, black plate with 'TANNOY' engraved on it was fitted below the loudspeaker opening, with the letters boldly picked out in white. This was almost too big for the cabinet, throwing the design out of balance, but the all important point was that it was big enough and obvious enough to ensure that the name, 'Tannoy', was brought to the attention of the public. Tannoy's reputation was established on the quality of the equipment they were able to supply but, more importantly, on the basis of the excellent service they were prepared to give. The association between Tannoy and Bertram Mills continued for many years and culminated

The TANNOY Story

in the appointment of a director of Bertram Mills, Ronald Pickering, to the Tannoy Board in 1960.

The quality of after sales service to Tannoy customers, particularly showmen, and the ease with which service engineers could be contacted, was always of considerable importance to the company. Showmen worked mainly at weekends and always during bank holidays, so the company always maintained a small staff of service engineers at the factory to deal with any emergencies which might arise – anywhere in the country. As an example of their service, George Wheeler recalled the occasion when a fairground operator telephoned from Chipping Sodbury to report that his amplifier was not working; that the fair was due to open at 6 p.m. and that they could not manage without it. George rang around the factory and found nobody available to go to Chipping Sodbury to attend to the equipment so, after throwing some tools and spares into the back of his car, he drove from Norwood to Chipping Sodbury, well over 100 miles and a journey of about 3 hours or more in those days, and did the repair himself. On another occasion, George recounted that he had taken a big 500 watts amplifier to a function at the department store, *Bon Marche*, in Brixton where the transformer started smoking. He took the amplifier back to the factory and removed the transformer and managed to get three girls to come to the factory at night and work on it until 2 a.m. to repair it. He then took the girls to their homes and delivered the repaired amplifier back to Brixton.

Not even Guy himself was immune to meeting emergencies and he once drove his Essex 'Super Six' car, loaded with equipment, to Caernarfon, in North Wales, arriving there late at night in very heavy rain. He carried a GA 120 amplifier on the back seat, four large loudspeakers, (two on the front seat and two on top of the amplifier), and sixteen sections of Voigt horns, stacked inside each other, concertina fashion and strapped over the top of the car from the rear bumper to the top of the windscreen. The showmen were so enthusiastic at Guy's arrival that, much to his annoyance, they insisted on unloading the equipment and setting it up there and then. They were equally enthusiastic about the excellent performance of the amplifier.

Another example of Tannoy's after sales service was recorded in an unknown employee's notebook in which he wrote, 'When I was a young lad of seventeen I was summoned to the Chairman's office one day and he asked me to go home and put on my best suit and return to the factory by 2 p.m. At 2 o'clock I was taken in a Ford 'V8' shooting brake to Goodwood, travelling at 85 m.p.h. on the Guildford by-pass which was quite a thrill. On arrival I was ushered into the Duke of Richmond and Gordon's library to service his radiogram. On completing this task, I was asked by the butler if I would like some tea. I then started to follow him to the door but he requested me to stay in the library. He duly returned with the tea, laid out on a large silver tray, complete with silver tea service. It was quite an experience in those days to sit in the ducal chair and take tea in the manner of the gentry'.

To return to the subject of fairground equipment there were, much to Guy's chagrin, other makers of amplifiers whose equipment was better suited to fairground work. The most notable of these was Magnaphone, founded and owned by Mr. Robert Carter-Pedlar who, after serving in the army during the Great War, went on to university where he studied electrical engineering, mechanical engineering and forestry. He then founded the Magnaphone Company to provide P.A. systems specifically for fairgrounds and his was the first company to make a powerful enough amplifier for the purpose which would operate on a 110 volts d.c. supply without any intermediate equipment such as a rotary convertor. To make an amplifier powerful enough to meet the requirements of the showmen and work on 110 volts, Carter-Pedlar did away with the conventional coupling between one valve and another and coupled the anode of one valve directly to the grid of the next. He then had to apply an enormously high bias to the grid of the succeeding valve. This enabled a huge amount of power to be fed into a class 'B' output stage, but it worked. By this means he was able to build an 80 watts amplifier which operated quite successfully on 110 volts d.c., something which had not been achieved before, not even by Tannoy.

He also designed a loudspeaker cabinet specifically for fairgrounds which was more efficient acoustically than most and which was both smaller and stronger; very great advantages in equipment which had to be moved around so much. The loudspeaker was mounted on a baffle which was deeply recessed in the cabinet, about half-way between the front of the case and the back, and this had two great advantages in that it had a very long path between the two sides of the cone, considerably enhancing the bass performance and the loudspeaker usually remained undamaged if it was dropped either on its front or on its back; a frequent occurrence. With the advantages which his equipment offered over the competition, Carter-Pedlar was making tremendous inroads into the fairground business at a time when Tannoy was trying to do the same with conventional loudspeakers and the GUB 30 amplifiers which, although they were good amplifiers, were conventional and had to be supplied with power through expensive rotary converters. Rotary converters were also inefficient although this was not too important as there was plenty of spare power from the dynamos on the steam traction engines which powered the fairground entertainments and their hundreds of coloured lights. Carter-Pedlar was not immune from difficulties, however, for it was customary to install his ampli-

The TANNOY Story

fiers, generally 60 watts amplifiers, in the fairground pay-booth and there were occasional failures of his amplifiers due to coats being left on top of them.

With his superior showman's equipment Carter-Pedlar gradually developed a near monopoly of the fairground amplifier business and this was a considerable irritation to Guy who believed he had an established right to all of this business. But Carter-Pedlar had a problem in that he could not produce enough amplifiers in his rather small factory to meet the demand of the many fairgrounds; he was in a classic situation of over trading. He also had some difficulty in collecting payment from showmen because they were constantly on the move; they were not deliberately dishonest but quite often they just could not be found. For this reason he found himself in financial trouble and in 1938 Guy Fountain bought the business, the trade name that went with it and his successful designs for amplifiers and loudspeakers. Thus it was that Guy Fountain managed to gain the stranglehold which Carter-Pedlar had been securing on the fairground business. Guy also took Robert Carter-Pedlar into Tannoy together with his deputy, Tommy Newman. This was the good news; the bad news was that the fairground business came to a standstill a year later when the second world war broke out.

After Tannoy's acquisition of Carter-Pedlar's company, and as showmen's equipment was principally a Hire Department responsibility, Norman Robottom was often involved in supplying, or repairing, or replacing their equipment. He said that when visiting a travelling showground he would be under strict instruction not even to get the equipment out of the van until he had been paid for it, and this often resulted in him being paid large sums of money, sometimes amounting to several hundreds of pounds, in shillings and sixpences which he had to take into his van and lock the doors while he counted the money. Only then would he take the equipment out of the van and set it up.

Immediately after the end of the war the fairgrounds hurried to get back into business but it was not very long before the embryonic environmental lobby began to take shape and started giving fairgrounds a few problems. The basis of their complaint was that there was too much noise from these fairs and that the noise was usually somewhat discordant. Each stallholder in a typical fairground had an amplifier through which he played the music which he liked or considered appropriate for his type of show and through which he could shout his own "Roll up, Roll up", announcements. The cacophony generated by all these amplifiers blaring out different music, usually at maximum volume, was quite unacceptable and the complaints became more and more frequent. So Tannoy devised the 'A & B' amplifier system in which a central, 'A' amplifier, played the same music on all the sideshows with provision for each stall to have its own microphone and 'B' amplifier which, when its microphone was switched on, isolated the stall's loudspeakers from the main music amplifier and allowed the stallholder to make his announcements. This was still very loud of course, but it was much less annoying as all the stalls and rides played the same music and, in any case, the stallholder did not have to use such a high volume to make his announcements heard. This also eliminated the need, or more properly the desire, for stallholders to compete with each other by running their amplifiers at full volume to try to drown the sounds of their neighbours. This development by Tannoy had been available in 1939 but it was shelved for the duration of the war and re-introduced in 1946 with more sophisticated technology and better results. Tannoy's development of fairground amplifiers, developed largely from the Magnaphone designs of Robert Carter-Pedlar, was so successful that for the following five years or more the company had a near monopoly of fairground equipment. However, they were not always able to supply loudspeakers in sufficient quantites to meet the demand and many of these had to be bought in from *Rola* and *Celestion*.

Another development resulting from the company's success with showmen took place when it was realised that many Tannoy customers did not wish to commit large sums of their limited capital in expensive sound equipment and so they arranged to hire it. This led to the formation by Tannoy of Sound Rentals Ltd., who supplied Tannoy amplifiers on an annual rental contract, replacing them with more modern equipment as necessary on an exchange basis.

With the acquisition of Magnaphone, Tannoy inherited a man called Hyams who had been responsible for the financial side of Magnaphone and he was set to work under Tannoy's accountant, Abrahams. Stan Livingstone had personal memories of these two and recalls that when he joined Tannoy he was offered a salary of £1 per week but after about 8 weeks he had not been paid. He asked both Abrahams and Hyams in turn but both denied any knowledge of his position in the company, even when he produced his clock card. Abrahams told him to, "Go and see Hyams", and Hyams said, "Talk to Abrahams". Eventually he went to see George Wheeler who, after establishing the facts, ordered them to, "Give him a tenner now and pay him properly from now on". Abrahams admitted that he was just keeping things going as long as he could without parting with any money but the reason for this behaviour was never properly established.

The **TANNOY** Story

CHAPTER NOTES

1   The minutes of a meeting held in the company's offices over 25 years later, on 26th January, 1957, record that *Voigt* loudspeakers had been used on this contract and although *Voigt* were very strong in their design department at that time and made fine loudspeakers, possibly the best, it is now believed that what was said at that meeting was incorrect. It is almost certain that G.E.C. loudspeakers were used because, as George Wheeler recalled the event, only G.E.C. could supply them in the numbers needed in the time available.

2   This is the story as related to the author but one is left to wonder how knitting needles were obtained during a circus performance at Olympia and this casts some doubt upon the accuracy of this account. Nevertheless, it is accepted that a very makeshift repair was carried out to keep the amplifier working for the show.

3   Cyril and Bernard were the two sons of Bertram Mills. Cyril used to search the world for new circus acts while Bernard was in charge of all the animals and the presentation.

Tannoy Public Address Van with roof mounted 200 watt omni directional loudspeaker system, circa 1950

CHAPTER FIVE

THE DEVELOPMENT OF TANNOY IN THE LATE 1930s

There were, of course, several other developments which took place during the 1930s at the same time as the circus and showground contracts and one of these, probably in 1934, was as the result of an order to supply public address equipment for the Navy Week at Devonport. A furniture van was hired from a local removals contractor and this was just about large enough to take the necessary equipment and two men to Devonport where the men worked day and night for two days to set it all up, a task which would now take about a week. One of the Navy's problematical requests was for a microphone to be fitted inside the submarine with its lead connected to the amplifier so that when, during an exercise, they simulated the sinking of the submarine, the sounds of the exploding depth charges, as they might be heard inside the submarine, could be relayed to the spectators as realistically as possible. Tannoy asked for a small hole to be drilled in the pressure hull of the submarine and this was used to take the microphone cable through it with just an ordinary rubber grommet to seal it! Surprisingly it all worked quite well and, miraculously, the submarine did not sink.

The following year the Navy Week was moved to Chatham and again Tannoy supplied the public address systems. This time it was also necessary to install amplifiers and, in some cases radios, in many of the vessels including H.M.S. *Ajax*, H.M.S. *Leander*, H.M.S. *Birmingham* and H.M.S. *Malaya*. In addition to these, the main amplification system covered the whole of the dockyard area. These Navy Week shows continued until 1939 but, following the last show, some of the amplifiers and radios were inadvertently left on board the ships and, in one case, when the ship's communications receiver was knocked out by enemy action during the second World War, the Tannoy all-wave radio which had been overlooked was still functioning. Some time after the Battle of the

The TANNOY Story

River Plate, Captain Pennefather wrote to the company to tell them that it was only by this means that the crew of the famous H.M.S. *Ajax* heard from the *B.B.C. Empire Service*, when the ship was still off the South American Coast, a news bulletin of the result of the battle of the River Plate.[1]

In 1935 the company moved forward quite quickly with the opening of a branch office in Manchester, in Whitworth Street, with 'Mickey' Quick as its manager, and with the first appointment of another director, Keith Hill, who was also a director of *F.W. Lucas* of Brixton Hill, a company which supplied numerous components for the wireless and motor industries and equipped the third of the Daily Mirror Eight coaches described in chapter three. This was probably also the company which supplied vehicles to Tannoy and carried out maintenance on them before Guy established Tannoy Motor Company many years later, after the second World War. Keith Hill lived near Crystal Palace and was one of the '*Higgs and Hill*' family and he and his wife were close friends of Guy and Elsie. In the early days of the Manchester office there was a junior service engineer whose name is not known for certain but it is believed to have been Gourier. Many years later he became head of *B.B.C. Television Engineering* in which capacity he delivered lectures to children and this was said to have been a great honour. Not long after the establishment of the Manchester office, a branch office was opened in Bristol where Guy had his suspicions about the assistant manager who, he thought, was carrying on an extra marital affair. Nobody believed Guy at the time, thinking that he was just being suspicious as usual, but it eventually transpired that he was quite right.

Also in 1935 the company received an order for an intercommunication system for the Argentine Navy, a one-off in which Tannoy was a sub-contractor to the *Telephone Manufacturing Company*. Pat Healey was the General Manager of T.M.C. and he was very friendly with George Wheeler so he asked George if Tannoy would like to supply the amplification equipment. The Argentine Navy required systems which would perform the function of public address communications to be heard in all personnel movement areas on board ships as well as an aural communication system between ships. They specified that voice communications must be clearly audible over a distance of five miles, a requirement which might prove difficult to achieve today. The reason for this was that radio communications were deemed to be insecure and were subject to interference, so Tannoy devised a modified public address system using loudspeakers in metal enclosures. This order, although it was a one-off in this form, was the first of many contracts which were to be executed by Tannoy for the armed forces and it required the development of a special loudspeaker.

The Development Of Tannoy In The Late 1930s

The five miles requirement made it necessary to construct a loudspeaker which was powerful enough to handle 500 watts and this was designed by Jack Houlgate, the company's Chief Engineer, assisted by George Wheeler. The *Western Electric* '555' loudspeaker which was, as Stan Livingstone put it, the first 'classically' designed reverse throat pressure driver, had an aluminium strip voice coil, concentric rings machined out of the centre pole to load the diaphragm and every feature which goes to make an excellent loudspeaker. Jack Houlgate made a giant model of this with a 4" diameter voice coil of copper wire instead of aluminium to achieve the best mid-band efficiency. He found that he could make the aluminium diaphragm quite successfully but he could not make a suspension that would work satisfactorily, so he put an 'O' ring about half way along the voice coil and this allowed enough axial movement. However, it suffered the disadvantage that the magnetic gap was necessarily rather wide so he overcame this by saturating the magnet assembly. The result of all this was that the impedance remained very constant over the frequency range and a unit which was nominally 8 ohms at 400 Hz was still 8 ohms at 4 kHz. Thus it would absorb plenty of power over the speech frequency range and it would compensate to some extent for the lack of real working magnetic flux resulting from the large magnetic gap. The end result was a loudspeaker capable of handling 500 watts of speech and clearly audible over the specified distance.

The frame for Houlgate's giant loudspeaker was cast in three sections by a foundry at Tooting Bec Common and these components were then machined in the Tannoy factory, bolted together and painted white.

While working on this loudspeaker in the late 1930s, they built an amplifier for test purposes with an output of 500 watts with two enormous DA 250 output valves which glowed bright red and for which *Keston* had made a special transformer. This amplifier was situated in the development laboratory and connected to oscillators with keys to select different frequencies and noise levels. One day Guy came into the laboratory and commented that it was not very loud, whereupon George keyed a 40 db output while Guy was standing beside the loudspeaker. Guy was not amused!

Also in 1935 the company introduced a very neat 20 watts portable public address system for use on mains or battery in two cabinets. One cabinet contained the amplifier with a hinged lid which opened to reveal the controls and a large caged resistance which was presumably used to reduce the mains voltage for the valve heaters, indicating that it was probably suitable for both a.c. and d.c. mains, so the lid had to be kept open while the amplifier was in use. The second cabinet was in two parts which were held together in transit by buckle clips, each part containing a loudspeaker. At the same time, Tannoy

The TANNOY Story

introduced a very well built amplifier, in a wooden cabinet as Guy insisted, which produced 250 watts of sound energy for less than 1% of total harmonic distortion. If this was correct, and there seems no reason todoubt this claim, it was a remarkable achievement for it was nearly another ten years before *H.J. Leak & Co.* were able to claim that their high fidelity amplifier, the Leak 'Point One', the output of which was nowhere near 250 watts had, for the first time, achieved less than 0.1% total harmonic distortion.

On 20th March, 1936; in a review of commercial P.A. equipment in the *Wireless World*, many companies are featured, including *Ardente, B.S.R., (British Sound Reproducers), B.T-H., (British Thompson-Houston), Ferranti, G.E.C., Grampian Reproducers, Marconiphone, Philips Industrial, Reslo Sound Equipment, Sound Sales Ltd., Truvoice and Trix Electrical Co.* In all, more than twenty companies making sound amplifying equipment were featured and seven companies making loudspeakers specifically for P. A. work; *Rola, Celestion, Epoch, Goodmans, Magnavox, Voigt* and *R.&A. Sound*. In the article, the Tannoy equipment is described:

> The Firm of Tannoy Products manufactures a range of amplifiers giving outputs from 10 watts to 1 kW. The G.U.B. 10 amplifier works off a.c., d.c. or a car accumulator,[2] the output being 10 watts, the overall gain 70 db and the frequency characteristic is flat within 2 db over the range of 100 Hz to 5,000 Hz. The price, complete, is 34 gns. (The input is to a 600 ohms grid transformer, feeding a triode, resistance-capacity coupled to a phase splitting transformer which drives two small power triodes in push-pull. These valves provide the power for driving two, class B triodes which feed the loudspeaker load via an output transformer. All Push-pull transformers are designed to give a balanced output with equal phase shift on each half whilst adequate de-coupling in plate and grid circuits ensures stability and good frequency characteristics. For mains operation, a multiple plug connects all valve filaments in series via a voltage regulating barretter. The H.T.
> supply is from two, half-wave valves. The G.U.B. 10 is the ideal all-round amplifier, quality and reliability of the high standard associated with Tannoy.

This amplifier appears to be the main feature of early 1936 advertising. Another amplifier described was the GM 12 A, 12 watt:

> A 600 ohms input to a grid transformer fitted with a special shield to avoid hum, is connected to a W 30 screened-grid valve, resistance-capacity coupled to an HL 4 valve, resistance coupled to a phase splitting transformer, which drives two PX 25 valves in push-pull. The output transformer is arranged to feed one or two 15 ohms loudspeakers. The overall gain is 92 dB with output of 12 watts undistorted.

The article continues, interestingly:

> This firm specialises in the rack system and also manufactures loudspeakers of the horn and box baffle types, the former including a flat horn which limits ground and sky losses.

The Development Of Tannoy In The Late 1930s

Also on 20th March, 1936, E.C. Thompson discussed several outstanding examples of the use of public address systems but Tannoy gets a comparatively small mention. He wrote in *Wireless World*:

> 'When the electric gramophone pickup was introduced the amplification of gramophone music was a natural sequel. Probably half the P.A. work carried out today is concerned with the diffusion of recorded music at exhibitions, football matches, air displays and on fairgrounds. Sound equipment can be found on fairgrounds all over the country, unfortunately not all showmen possess an ear for music and some of them do not think that their amplifiers are earning their keep unless they are running full-out all the time. The Tannoy engineers who have to some extent specialised on fairground P.A. have had some amusing experiences. Not once, but many times, they have found a filed down nail in place of a gramophone needle in a showman's equipment. Some showmen consider the life of a gramophone record to be at an end only when the grooves have disappeared. On one occasion a showman's amplifier was sent back [to Tannoy] for repair, the complaint being that when the set was switched on, instead of music, a nasty smell was amplified. When the amplifier was put on test the complaint was fully justified; the smell was indescribable, and the test staff made for the door as one man. Eventually, one braver than the rest or with a less acute olfactory sense returned to find a dead rat cooking across the mains transformer'.

On 8th May, 1936, in the 25th anniversary issue of the *Wireless World*, Tannoy advertised another amplifier, the MU 5., although there was no detail in the advertisement of its performance. The MU 5 was a variant of the M 5 which was the basic amplifier; the MU 5 included a microphone and loudspeaker and the GMU 5 had, in addition, a gramophone turntable.

The great strides taken by makers of public address amplifiers is illustrated by an article which was published in the *Wireless World* on 22nd. May, 1936, entitled 'The Story of Public Address'. It comments:

> When one considers the excellence of the sound amplifying systems in use at the present time, it is hardly credible that it is only 14 years ago that the *Western Electric Company*, now *Standard Telephone and Cable Company*, the pioneers of public address systems, conducted their first outstanding demonstration at the Radio Exhibition at the Horticultural Hall. The success which attended this occasion was so unmistakable that it was not long before enquiries were being received from all parts of the country. By 1924 P.A. systems were definitely known and the company [*Western Electric*] was honoured with the then colossal task of equipping the Empire Exhibition with microphones and loudspeakers to be used in the opening ceremony by his late Majesty King George V.
>
> His Majesty expressed great interest in the system installed and visualised the vast possibilities open for it throughout the country. The first job of any magnitude, however, was the Rodeo at Wembley, a happening still fresh in the minds of us all. His Majesty again appeared before the microphone in 1928 at the opening of *Lloyds*' New Building and by that time P.A. systems were no longer looked on as an innovation, but actually expected by all orators addressing a large number of people.
>
> From this time events moved apace and the uses to which P.A. systems have been put are not without interest. It is not only at vast gatherings that these systems are used although their application to crowds is more easily understood. Small systems are now constantly in use for small dances and garden parties.

The TANNOY Story

By 1937 Tannoy public address equipment had developed to the point where a very compact general purpose system was built, in which the amplifier and turntable were in one quite small cabinet, with a detachable lid which contained the loudspeaker. However, photographs show that this amplifier was supplied with a rather cumbersome microphone although it is not certain whether this was a carbon microphone or a moving coil microphone which Tannoy started making in 1937.

It was at about this time that attempts were made to convince the B.B.C. that the amplifiers they were then using left much to be desired and Tannoy made a special amplifier to demonstrate to the B.B.C. It was Sir Adrian Boult who eventually persuaded the Corporation not to buy the Tannoy amplifiers, because he, and the other panellists, liked what they already had – largely because they were used to it. The fact that the Tannoy amplifier was better was disregarded.

Although the company was concerned almost entirely with sound equipment, there were occasional diversions, even as early as the mid 1930s. In about 1937 or 1938, Guy Fountain became involved with a Polish lady, whose name was said by Stan Livingstone to have been Madam Krapoweickei, who had carried out some experiments in a Polish hospital on the therapeutic effects of heat in the healing process of various parts of the body, particularly damaged limbs. She had learned that body tissue is susceptible to some extent to low levels of heat, particularly heat which is generated within the body without external burning. This heat had been produced by placing the part under treatment within a cable loop and passing low frequency radio waves through the coil. Guy got the company involved with this lady and made a few signal generators for her which were, of course, a primitive predecessor to microwave heating. These were installed in two or three hospitals where she was engaged as a Consultant. This is a good example of the availability within the company of facilities and resources which could be applied to entirely different projects or developments in spite of the fact that Tannoy was primarily concerned with audio frequencies and technologies. It might also have been argued that many of the company personnel may not have fully understood the application of frequencies above 10 kHz.

From this work Guy developed an interest in a company which made radio frequency generators and radio moulding processes. Radio frequency heating was shown at the 1947 Radiolympia exhibition but it has not been possible to establish which company made them.

The various developments, both technical and commercial, referred to in this chapter can be summed up, in the words of Winston Churchill, as 'The end of the beginning' of the Tannoy company. However, it seems appropriate to add

The Development Of Tannoy In The Late 1930s

at this point the story of Tannoy's work in the development of loudspeakers, initially to handle high output and concluding with thesuccessful introduction in the immediate post-war years of the Tannoy dual concentric loudspeaker. The facts, as related by Stan Livingstone, are as follows:

> Until about 1935, Tannoy did not make loudspeakers; they were all bought in. Pressure drivers were bought in from Reslo and cone drivers from Rola. The development of Tannoy loudspeakers can be divided into four segments:-
> 1. The CD4 cone loudspeakers, (a pre-war development).
> 2. The SD5 pressure units to replace Reslo, (a pre-war development).
> 3. High power loudspeakers for the Argentine Navy, (a one-off, also pre-war).
> 4. Higher power pressure units, 20 watts and 100 watts, which were used in various warning systems including Trinity House, (Predominantly a post-war development).
> 5. Wide range loudspeakers which were a combination of the cone loudspeaker and the reverse throat pressure unit, known as the dual-concentric loudspeaker. (a post-war development).

Reslo was run by a gentleman called Leonard Murkham with whom a serious dispute arose when Tannoy made some response curve measuring equipment for him which, he claimed, did not work, and refused to pay. Guy Fountain therefore decided that he would no longer buy from *Reslo* and from this decision the Tannoy SD 5 loudspeaker was developed. This had a spun aluminium diaphragm and an aluminium voice coil with twisted joints and it was a very good pressure unit; distinctly better than *Reslo*'s and, of course, its development was entirely the work of Jack Houlgate.

But loudspeaker designs and, of course, microphone designs were not the only important achievements of the company. Essential parts of any amplifiers in the 1930s were its transformers and these had to be particularly well designed and well made for them to perform their tasks with the minimum of distortion. Condensers of all types were the products of large companies such as *Plessey* and *T.C.C.* and resistors were obtained mainly from *Erie*. Both of these components had reached a high standard of reliability, stability and accuracy, but public address amplifiers were very dependent on good transformers. 600 ohms balanced input transformers, intervalve 'push-pull' driver transformers and output transformers for 100 volts loudspeaker lines all demanded low losses, very low distortion, low hum and low noise. These characteristics depended very much on how well-designed and how well-made these various transformers were. In this technique there was nobody better than Norman Crowhurst who joined Tannoy in 1935 and who was always known as 'Willy' Crowhurst. In 1937 he produced a series of design charts which anyone in the company could use. Not only were his designs particularly good in their audio performance, they were also easy to make and there was no problem in getting the turns on. He pioneered the use of cellulose acetate film as the inter-winding insulation which was better than the conventional 'kraft' paper by a factor of 3. This also reduced stray capacity and self inductance and made Tannoy amplifiers very stable. Tannoy were thus able to operate up to 20, 60watts amplifiers in parallel, with both inputs and outputs paralleled, and this was one of the principal reasons for Tannoy reliability. 60 watts amplifiers could be group connected to produce any required power and if one amplifier failed, the change in overall performance was negligible. The 60 watts amplifier was very reliable, the maximum anode voltage being 470 volts while most other manufacturers used transmitter valves for such high powers operating at up to 2,000 volts.

The Tannoy group system was very economical and they ran from 1938 to 1947 using only one basic amplifier, the 60 watts amplifier, and this also gave the company very real economies of scale. The success of this group system depended entirely upon exceptionally good input and output transformers, and 'Willy' Crowhurst provided the company with exactly what was needed.

Willy Crowhurst was a member of the Jehovah's Witnesses and he disappeared into the limbo of conscientious objectors from 1939 to 1945, he then returned to Tannoy and stayed until 1952. In 1953, Crowhurst emigrated to America where he was deeply involved in early cinema stereo systems and the 'Pespecta Sound' systems, which were used by *Paramount* and *M.G.M.*, were all his work. These systems required very accurate filter circuits to extract trigger signals from the film photo-audio track which were used to control the spaced out groups of loudspeakers to simulate movement of sound sources around the auditorium. Tannoy personnel really were a clever lot!

Another significant addition to the Tannoy personnel, if only temporary, took place in 1936 when E.A. (Bill) Preedy joined the company. His employment came to an early end after just three weeks following a difference of opinion with George Wheeler over wages. He had come to Tannoy with a promise from George that his wages would be reviewed after a week. Three weeks passed with no action other than extended promises so he left to take up a position with *Decca/Brunswick* and, after working there for a while, he went on to the *International Broadcasting Company*, following Norman Angier and others from *Decca*. (Preedy later returned to Tannoy).

Preedy's only recollection of his brief time with Tannoy in 1936 is that of accompanying a Service Engineer by the name of Ron Foster to the Blackfriars 'Ring', in the days of all-in wrestling, to replace the carbon granules in a hand held microphone which had been used by the referee to break up a contest. This was almost a weekly occurence.

In view of the acknowledged achievements of the company during the 1930s it is perhaps a little surprising that no mention has been found in the technical

The Development Of Tannoy In The Late 1930s

press of the time that Tannoy amplifiers were used extensively during the Coronation of King George VI in 1937. However, it was quite widely publicised that Tannoy equipment was used at some time in the late 1930s in the Royal Albert Hall for productions such as Hiawatha and Faust.

Not many records of the company's social events survive but in 1937, on Wednesday, 3rd March, there was what was referred to as 'The Annual Dinner and Dance', which was held in the Hollywood Restaurant, Princes, Piccadilly. At this event the toasts were as follows:

The Firm.
    Proposed by His Grace the Duke of Richmond and Gordon.
    Response by Guy R. Fountain.

The Staff.
    Proposed by Keith Hill.
    Response by S. Solomon and J. Houlgate.

The Visitors.
    Proposed by George C. Wheeler.
    Response by W.F. Taylor.

In 1938 Guy made an attempt to produce television sets although they were not entirely of Tannoy manufacture. He was said to have been a very good entrepreneur in that he would look around other manufacturers' equipment and combine the best features of several of them into a Tannoy product which, so far as the customer was concerned, was very much better than those made by the individual makers. His 1938 television incorporated a *Plessey* chassis and parts from other makers but, typically, he insisted on two points; the first being that it was contained in a much more elegant cabinet than any other manufacturer's and the second being that the audio circuitry was very much better than the original with big output, big loudspeakers and sound which was as near perfect as was then possible. The viewer could watch and listen to a television in the maker's original form and it looked and sounded like any ordinary set, but with the superior *Camco* cabinets and with the much better quality audio circuits which Tannoy designed and made, the Tannoy versions always looked and sounded very much better. This was achieved only at a high price but, if a customer were looking for something really special, and very elegant, Guy was very good at providing it; genuine, superior quality equipment. Incidentally, one always got the impression that he was able to sell these grand pieces of equipment to people who could well afford them and who wanted something special but whose personal contact might also have been useful to him. There is no record of how many of these television sets were made but it is thought that there were very few of them.

The TANNOY Story

While Bill Preedy was working at the *International Broadcasting Company* in 1939 he was involved with an outside broadcasting unit using American Presto acetate recording equipment. He contacted Tannoy during a lull in outside broadcast reporting, with the object of securing an outdoor job for the Summer. His luck was in and Preedy rejoined Tannoy as a Representative in the summer of 1939.

In June 1939 he was sent on a 'Daily Mirror Eight' tour, accompanied by Norman Robottom, an announcer provided by the *Daily Mirror* and, as Preedy recounted it, eight lovely girls. At Southend, Guy Fountain visited them and the tour Manager advised them all to count the physical fitness team after he had left! The coach had the names of the individual members of the Eight painted on its sides and it was surmounted by a large loudspeaker in a streamlined enclosure on its roof, so positioned that the public could be forgiven for thinking that it was a Tannoy spectacular instead of a *Daily Mirror* publicity event. Preedy regarded this tour as a heavenly experience, though technically difficult because, as has been mentioned in Chapter 3, so much sand managed to get into the rotary converter which supplied power for the amplifier in the coach. They went on to Newquay and it was while the show was there in late August that Bill Preedy was called away. On that fateful day, 24th August, 1939, the Tannoy staff were assisting the photographer in transmitting the photos to the *Daily Mirror* for publication next day and, on completion, they were asked if their announcer was around since he had been called to the Territorials and Preedy to the R.A.F.V.R.

After appropriate farewells and dinner, Preedy took his leave from the *Mirror* team and was soon posted to R.A.F. North Weald, which was one of the 11 Group Fighter Stations which were later the main targets of German raids on airfields during the Battle of Britain. At the height of the German offensive against these R.A.F. fighter bases, R.A.F. North Weald was very badly battered and in one raid the Operations Room received a direct hit and the Tannoy system was damaged. When urgent requests for assistance were made to Tannoy by the Commanding Officer, Group Captain Frew, Guy told him that one of his engineers was, as Guy inappropriately put it, 'luxuriating at North Weald'. It was a long, hot summer. The C.O. sought out Bill Preedy and explained that he could not order Preedy to assist with the restoration of the Tannoy system as he was then mustered as 'Aircrew Under Training' and had been waiting for training to start, having been on the Reserve List since he joined the R.A.F. Volunteer Reserve at Kenley in 1938, but that his help would be much appreciated. This help was willingly given and, headed by the Station Signals Officer, Preedy carried out a few minor repairs to the 3 R 60 amplifier, replaced the broken valves and had the system back in operation the same day, powered by an

The Development Of Tannoy In The Late 1930s

emergency generator which the Air Ministry Works Department had thoughtfully kept in reserve on the base. In this installation the Tannoy system not only provided a full public address service but, following this attack, the rack in which the Tannoy amplifiers were mounted gave considerable help in propping up a roof support beam in the Plotting Room which fell on it! Incidentally, as the war progressed other services were finding additional uses for the Tannoy 3 R 60 basic system but the number of installations increased significantly when the U.S. Army Air Force arrived.

The following December, Preedy was released from the R.A.F.V.R. and rejoined Tannoy where he was assigned to the installation of basic systems, the 3 R 60 which developed 480 watts employing multi source powering and extendible 60 watts power amplifiers. At about the same time, Ron Rackham was in the Territorial Army and, fortunately, he was still in the U.K.. He, too, was duly released back to Tannoy. George Compigne, who was involved with Tannoy outside service, was also a Territorial but was in Crete at that time. He was captured there and was a Prisoner of War for the next five years, returning to his old job with Tannoy at the end of hostilities. However, he did great work in Germany while working as forced labour in a railway repair yard, putting sand in the axle boxes of German trains, an excellent bit of war work by a Tannoy employee.

On a more personal note, about Guy that is, he bought his motor cruiser *Naiad* in 1938, named after a female water nymph, a Deity who presides over rivers and springs, from the Chelsea Yacht Club. It had two Chrysler engines and on one fateful occasion it was moored offshore at Birchington when bad weather had been forecast. Guy ignored the forecast and he also ignored the advice which he was given to move it to the safety of Margate Harbour. As a result of this, the following morning it was found to have been badly damaged in the storm. Apparently its mooring chain was known to have been in poor condition and contained a section of rope which wore through at the cleat and parted. The boat was washed onto a stone breakwater which pierced its side and, when it was found in the morning, it was discovered that it had been looted. By the time his son, Michael, got to it people were stripping all sorts of equipment from it. All the bedding was stolen and many fittings were unscrewed and taken. Guy arrived there late in the afternoon and it is said that he got in touch with the insurance company and convinced the Loss Adjuster that he had been on the telephone to them on the previous Friday to insure it. It was eventually repaired and sold.

The **TANNOY** Story

CHAPTER NOTES

1 It was not until late 1943 that the Empire Service was re-named the Overseas Service, subsequently, in 1965, becoming the World Service.

2 The use of the word 'accumulator' in the context of cars is interesting, the term ceased to be used at about this time.

Guy Fountain showing Countess of March coil winding in New Canterbury Grove Factory, 1934

CHAPTER SIX

TANNOY'S INVOLVEMENT WITH THE R.A.F.

The introduction to the R.A.F. was quite an extraordinary affair. In 1934, a comprehensive public address system was installed for the start of the first England to Australia Air Race, the MacRobertson Race, which was organised as part of the centenary celebrations for Melbourne.[1] The race started from R.A.F. Mildenhall at dawn on 20th October, and this was the first occasion when high impedance loudspeaker lines were used, operating at 40 volts, with a transformer in each of the dozens of horn loudspeakers mounted on poles around the aerodrome. It is said that the public address system kept the 60,000 spectators particularly well informed. There were, of course, many Royal Air Force and Air Ministry personnel present and it is fair to assume that they, too, were suitably impressed by the performance of the equipment. It has been particularly difficult to establish which company provided the public address system for this event as there are conflicting accounts in the documents which have been consulted, one account claiming that it was the *Telephone Manufacturing Company*. As recently as February 2002 it has been established from company archives that it was Tannoy.

The following year, 1935, was the Silver Jubilee year of King George V and as a part of the celebrations there was a Royal Air Force Review which was held jointly at R.A.F .Duxford and R.A.F. Mildenhall. The company submitted a tender to supply, install and operate the public address equipment for the review at these two bases which were a little over twenty miles apart. Tannoy won the contract but it was one of the first major events which Guy missed because he had made arrangements to take a holiday and, while it was being installed, he and Elsie were enjoying a cruise on the *Arandora Star* which had also been fitted with Tannoy equipment, leaving George and the staff to deal with the requirements of the show. George Wheeler recounted that in later years it became more apparent that when an important function or a large display required Tannoy amplifiers, Guy would be seen fussing around the factory for weeks before the event, like a hen with her chicks, getting in everybody's way and making unnecessary alterations just to be seen to be doing something, no matter how trivial. However, come the day, he would usually conveniently disappear and it was always assumed that this was to leave others to 'carry the can' if anything went wrong. George said that on many occasions such as this Guy ducked responsibility and George had to see things through.

This contract necessitated making 160 loudspeakers to cope with a total output of 1,600 watts from four amplifiers and this alone posed significant problems as the company encountered considerable difficulty in raising an overdraft to cover the cost of this work. A Tannoy amplifier producing about 400 watts output was installed at Mildenhall connected to a G.P.O. tie line to Duxford. It was by then a standard Tannoy practice to use an impedance of 600 ohms for long tie lines and this output was fed into the G.P.O. line to Duxford. The signal received on the tie line was then fed into the slave amplifiers at Duxford. The event, and the Tannoy installation, were both resounding successes and this was by far the greatest audio power that had been used on any public address installation in the country.

After the Review the Station Signals Officer, a Wing Commander, congratulated George on the quality of the equipment and on its excellent performance and said that he had been instructed to convey a similar message from their Majesties King George V and Queen Mary who had asked him to commend all those who had been responsible for the installation in the Royal enclosure. George Wheeler thanked the Wing Commander and, using the telephone beside the the P.A. equipment, he sent a telegram to Guy on the cruise ship which was then in harbour at Hambourg. The telegram said something like, "Operation successful, congratulations all round". Guy sent a telegram back by return to say "Well done". The Wing Commander also said, "When we come to do the R.A.F. Review at Hendon, the job will go to Tannoy."

Later, in the course of discussions with Group Captain Sizer,[2] George asked about R.A.F. Hendon in north London where, in those days, the principal R.A.F. display was staged annually. The first R.A.F. Tournament, as it was then called, was held on 3rd July, 1920. It was later re-named the R.A.F. Pageant, then the R.A.F. Review, and it took place at Hendon on the first Saturday of June each year until 1938. The reply from the Air Ministry was that it would not be possible to arrange for Tannoy to supply the public address equipment as the *Marconi Company* had been awarded the contract. "But", he said, "I'll see to it that you get in". However it was not until two years later, in 1937, that Tannoy received an offer to tender and the same Group Captain asked George to meet him at R.A.F. Hendon to discuss the details of their requirements for the coming Hendon Air Show. George went there on a particularly hot summer day and he and Group Captain Sizer walked around the R.A.F. base all morning discussing the requirements and eventually the Group Captain took him to the Officers' Mess for lunch.

George very seldom drank alcoholic drinks, he very occasionally had a tot of whisky for medicinal purposes but never at other times; even at his own wedding reception he drank only ginger beer. "What are you going to drink, Wheeler?", asked the Group Captain when they reached the bar. George thought that he could not ask for an orange drink, so he settled on a shandy, and much enjoyed it.

In designing the amplifiers for the R.A.F. Pageant it was found necessary to investigate and measure with some accuracy the sound levels produced by the amplifiers and loudspeakers that were to be used. So they set about designing and making an instrument to measure sound levels. This was done in conjunction with the *National Physical Laboratory* at Teddington. George Wheeler contacted Dr. Constable at the *National Physical Laboratory* who had been a student at the Woolwich Polytechnic with George and, with Dr. Davis, he had done some work with a simple, basic noise level meter for checking traffic noise. George told them that he felt sure that Tannoy could improve on this and he also put the suggestion to Norman Crowhurst, one of Tannoy's great technicians. Crowhurst designed various pieces of equipment including a switching arrangement, using a rotary switch, which altered the characteristic of the meter so that it closely matched the response of the human ear, known as 'A weighting', this is standard on modern noisemeters.

At that time, Tannoy had an extremely good Chief Engineer in Jack Houlgate, arguably the best electro-acoustic engineer in Europe during the first half of the 20th century and he devised a method of testing the characteristics of microphones. He placed a crystal microphone in front of a loudspeaker with its output fed into a control circuit which regulated the signal level to the loudspeaker so that the output of the loudspeaker remained constant. When a test microphone was placed beside the control microphone it was possible to measure the response of the microphone under test in relation to the sound which was being fed into it. When George Wheeler and Jack Houlgate took this to the *National Physical Laboratories* they were literally astonished; nothing like it had been attempted before. From then on, Tannoy could record the characteristics of microphones and, occasionally when this was considered necessary, they would send a microphone to the *N.P.L.* who would carry out a check on its performance at one frequency, usually 1,000Hz, so that if the Tannoy laboratory equipment were, say, 1 Db or so out at this level, they could easily check back and adjust their equipment.

Following this, and a lot more development work, the National Physical Laboratory produced a specification for a noise level meter based on a combination of their own experiments and Tannoy's work and, in late 1936, the Ministry of Transport issued a contract to construct 10 noisemeters, although it was not until many years later that traffic noise levels were officially subject to legislation. This work took many months to complete but eventually it was done and a very successful instrument was put into production. It was the first, and for many years the only accepted noise measuring meter. In ackowledgement of the contribution of the *National Physical Laboratory*, the instrument was called the *Tannoy/N.P.L.* Noisemeter but there is no doubt at all that Tannoy, under the guidance of Jack Houlgate, made the most important contribution to its development. Many other applications were found for the noisemeter and there is an illustration in subsequent Tannoy literature of six, *Tannoy/N.P.L.* Noisemeters in use by the *London Passenger Transport Board* for noise investigation.

At the Hendon Display, Tannoy achieved another 'first' for this was the first time that public address equipment was used air-to-ground during an aerobatic display. The installation was rather complicated because they had to fit a little microphone into the pilot's helmet and microphones small enough were not then readily available. A transmitter, which was not very good, was installed in the aircraft and the pilot's voice was picked up by the R.A.F.'s own receiver in the Air Traffic Control tower and fed into the Tannoy amplifier. The system worked and the pilot was able to enhance the entertainment value to the public by giving an interesting commentary on all the manoeuvres he was carrying out during a very impressive display of aerobatics. Another exciting feature of this Hendon Air Show was a formation fly-past by Gloster Gladiator (the type later used very bravely and to great effect in the defence of Malta) fighter aircraft with their wing tips tied together with bunting. Tannoy also supplied the sound equipment for the following year's Review, also at Hendon, but with the threat of imminent war, the 1939 review was cancelled.

Later that year George and some of the technical staff put the idea to the Air Ministry that they could carry out both entertainment and operational control of airfields with P.A. equipment, the technical staff had even prepared the necessary circuit diagrams but it was not until a year or more later that George met James Sutherland who was engaged to his sister and who worked at the Air Ministry. They met at George's parents' home and, in the course of conversation James asked George how he was getting on with P.A. equipment for the R.A.F. He replied that they were only working on ideas as they had not received an invitation to tender.

Tannoy's Involvement With The R.A.F.

Following that reminder, George telephoned the Air Ministry the next day and asked to speak to the officer responsible for issuing the contracts for P.A. systems and told him that he had no doubt that the contract would be based on the proposals which they, Tannoy, had submitted but that they had not yet received any tender documents. The officer told George that Tannoy were going to do the work but that he did not want to get involved in any project through Guy Fountain because Guy always wanted to do things his way and this did not necessarily suit the requirements of the Air Ministry. It was then discovered that in error, invitations to tender had been sent out to several companies but not to Tannoy, the reason being, as the Air Ministry spokesman said to George, "You can't do installation." George replied, "Don't tell me my job, I know what I'm doing." Eventually the Air Ministry Signals Officer sent Tannoy an invitation to tender and George told Guy. George and the Technical Department worked out a price and submitted it to the Air Ministry but they heard nothing for some time.

In August 1939 George received a telephone call from Group Captain Sizer asking him to go to Fighter Command H.Q. at Bentley Priory, Stanmore. George went as requested and again met Group Captain Sizer who said, "I want you to meet Air Vice Marshall Dowding." After a few preliminaries Air Vice Marshall Sir Hugh Dowding, Commander-in-Chief of Fighter Command, asked George, "What is your position? What authority have you?"

George replied, "I'm the Technical Director and General Manager. It is my responsibility to ensure that what needs to be done, is done."

"I want you to install a P.A. system at R.A.F. Biggin Hill." said Dowding. "How quickly can it be done?"

George replied that they could submit a tender which would give a firm completion date to which Dowding replied, "Never mind about a tender, how quickly can it be done?"

When George told him that it would take about three weeks, Dowding replied, "I'll tell you what I want, I want it completed in 48 hours." To which George replied, "Well, I suppose we'll have to do it then." Dowding then said, "I'll give you the names of 19 other fighter stations, I want them done in three weeks from today."

These were, of course, the fighter stations of No. 11 Group which became the principal targets of the Luftwaffe during the 'Battle of Britain' and the airfields from which the fighter squadrons which won that very critical battle operated.

It is interesting to note that the R.A.F. Station at Biggin Hill was established on 13th February, 1917 when the Wireless Testing Park was moved there from Joyce Green, Dartford. Some experimental work had also been

The TANNOY Story

carried out for the R.F.C. at Brooklands and for the R.N.A.S. at Cranwell but these were eventually merged at Biggin Hill. The purpose of this establishment was to carry out research and trials of telegraphy and, more importantly, telephony in military aircraft. Towards the end of 1917 the unit was accorded the more distinguished title, the Wireless Experimental Establishment. Possibly their most notable achievement was the development of direction finding and, in October, 1918, a Handley Page 0/400, equipped with a direction finding loop was flown to Paris and back entirely on wireless bearings. This development was the work of one of the wireless officers on the strength of the Wireless Experimental Establishment, one Captain P.P. Eckersley, previously mentioned in Chapter 1, who later became Chief Engineer of the *B.B.C.*

After accepting the challenge from Air Vice Marshall Dowding, Wheeler, on returning to the factory, telephoned F.H. Wheeler Ltd., electrical contractors, and spoke to Frank Wheeler's right-hand man, Mr. Lippett. "Whatever you are doing just now, drop it," he said, "get every man you can and call them off their present jobs, get all the necessary cable, poles and whatever equipment you need and get to Biggin Hill, you have to install a complete P.A. system there in 48 hours and another 19 installations in 21 days." George was able to do this because he had used F.H. Wheeler to install a system at a hospital near Redhill and by this time he knew Lippett quite well. So they literally flooded Biggin Hill with cables, poles etc. and did the job. Tannoy supplied, and *F.H. Wheeler* installed, the P.A. systems to those 20 R.A.F. bases in 21 days. *F.H. Wheeler Ltd.* was founded by Frank Wheeler, not to be confused with Tannoy's George Wheeler. Frank and Phyllis Wheeler later became close friends of Guy and Elsie Fountain. His company was eventually absorbed by Crown House as part of *Crown House Engineering Ltd.*

After some time, Frank Wheeler spoke to George and thanked him for what he had done which had, of course, put *F.H. Wheeler Ltd.* 'on the map'. These contracts were a great opportunity for the company and their successful completion gave them excellent publicity. Frank asked George, "Is there anything I can do for you?" George replied that he did not think that there was. Frank then said, "I've got a house in Cliftonville, near Margate, would you like me to give it to you?" But George thought that if Guy ever got to hear about it he would 'go through the roof', so he had to decline this kind offer.

A point was often made about Tannoy that the company was vertically integrated and made everything, but this was not always quite the case. They were unable to make some of the required equipment for these installations in suffucient numbers so, although they were able to build all the necessary 60 watts amplifiers, some drive units and microphones had to be bought from *Reslo*,

Tannoy's Involvement With The R.A.F.

some loudspeakers from *Goodmans* and *Rola* and, with one or two disastrous exceptions, the radio chassis were bought from *Plessey*.

Following this work, Tannoy public address equipment was installed in airfields, gunsites, tanks and submarines as well as in other shipping. In 1943 the 700th airfield installation was completed and thus it was that 'Tannoy' became synonymous with reliable communications. This was also, of course, the time from which the word 'Tannoy' became the generic term for public address equipment and began to be used in everyday conversation. The Air Ministry contracts came to Tannoy at a very fast rate and, to finance these contracts, they applied to *Barclays Bank* for additional loans and these were agreed without query.

It was at the time of the start of these Air Ministry contracts that Terence 'Stan' Livingstone joined the company. He was to have considerable influence over the the company in the ensuing years. He joined Tannoy in 1939 and stayed for 45 years, leaving in 1984 because he did not wish to be re-located to Glasgow.

One of the key issues for the company was the trade name, 'Tannoy'. When contracts were awarded for the R.A.F. airfields, the Ministry of Defence stipulated that the manufacturer's name must not appear on any of the equipment. However Guy, being the natural salesman that he was, wanted the name of Tannoy to appear on as much of the equipment as possible and in the largest, boldest way in which it could be done. He argued that the company's name was 'Guy R. Fountain Limited' and that 'Tannoy' was only the trade mark and, according to an unidentified newspaper report from the late 1970s, he told the Ministry, "If the name isn't on, you'll get no deliveries" So, having won this argument, the name 'Tannoy' appeared on every piece of equipment, as boldly and as obviously as he thought he could get away with it, particularly on all the loudspeakers, with the result that the name, once again, 'spoke for itself'. It was largely due to this that 'Tannoy' became the household word that it now is throughout the United Kingdom and much of the world and, to this day, public address systems and call systems, regardless of make, are often referred to as 'the Tannoy'.

On one occasion, never to be forgotten by George Wheeler, Frank Wheeler and Guy Fountain allegedly went on a tour of R.A.F. bases which were equipped with Tannoy public address systems. On such occasions they used to carry the relevant files so that if they happened to be stopped by the police, as travellers frequently were in wartime, they could substantiate their claim to be visiting R.A.F. bases. This time they were known to be going to Newcastle and staying at a particular hotel there. While they were away, George needed to talk to Guy so he telephoned the hotel and asked them to page Mr. Guy

The TANNOY Story

Fountain. The reply eventually came back that there was no Mr. Fountain staying there. George was puzzled. He was even more puzzled when, about ten minutes later, the telephone in his office rang and when he answered it he heard, "Hello, George, Guy here, what do you want?" The big question was, how were Guy and Frank able to register at an hotel during wartime under false names? In those days, hotels were legally required to check names and addresses of their guests from their identity cards but Guy and Frank were staying at the hotel under assumed names with a couple of girls!

Following the war, Tannoy again became involved with the Royal Air Force in an entirely different manner, that of designing and installing amplifiers in aircraft for propaganda work which became known as 'Sky shouting'. Initial tests were carried out near Bristol using two 100 watts loudspeakers mounted on a helicopter, facing vertically downwards. These experiments were none too successful but when two more loudspeakers were added, and when they were tilted forward from the vertical to reduce the effect of the turbulent downwash from the rotor, the system worked.

The following narrative was derived in part from 'The Valetta', by Bill Overton, and is believed to be a true account of the facts:

> 'By 1951 the Communist Terrorists in Malaya had killed 1,275 members of the security forces, and 1,828 civilians, including the High Commissioner, Sir Henry Gurney. Anti-Communist Terrorist operations were rapidly increased on the appointment in 1952 of Sir Gerald Templar. He made many immediate innovations in the anti terrorist warfare tactics and one of the first facts which he realised was that psychological warfare might turn the tide of the campaign. He very soon introduced propaganda, spread by means of the local radio and the press and he instructed the R.A.F. to intensify leaflet dropping. This did not always get to the target and he decided to introduce 'sky-shouting'. He instituted experiments using a *Dakota* aircraft which he borrowed from the U.S.A.F. and the experiments were sufficiently successful to persuade him to order three *Vickers Valettas* to be equipped with sky-shouting equipment. The first two, VL 277 and WD 160 were equipped at R.A.F. St. Athan in December 1952 and trials were carried out in the U.K. with VL 277 while WD 160 was sent to the Far East where it joined a transport squadron, No. 48 Squadron, at R.A.F. Changi in February, 1953. The equipment was made and installed by Tannoy and consisted of amplifiers feeding into four modified loudspeakers, each capable of handling an output of 500 watts, slung under the fuselage of the Valetta and angled to the port side. The system was powered by an *Enfield* 'Cub' 5.6 KVA diesel generator. Just behind the flight deck an acoustically insulated booth was installed with a reel-to-reel tape deck on which pre-recorded propaganda messages could be played, operated by a volunteer crewman recruited from the wireless trade groundstaff and, as he was also responsible for maintaining the generator, he was given a small extra allowance referred to as 'Crew pay'. He also had a microphone so that, when necessary, live broadcasts could also be made. The two voice *Valettas* went into service in March 1953 but their flying performance, (which was not particularly good in the high temperatures experienced over Malaya and Singapore), was (further) hampered by the drag of the line of huge loudspeakers under the fuselage.'

Tannoy's Involvement With The R.A.F.

The first sky-shouting sorties were made at 1,500 ft. above the ground but, when mountainous areas had to be targeted, in dense jungle, it was necessary to reduce the height to 800 ft. The Valetta was found to be none too successful over the Malaya jungle because it was necesary to carry out these flights at a slow speed, not much above the stalling speed of the aircraft, in order to achieve the maximum possible time over the target area for the messages to be clearly understood. Manoeuvrability was much impaired at this low speed which necessitated flying with flaps down and with high engine r.pm to compensate for the weight of the amplifiers and the diesel generator, and for the drag of the loudspeakers. This problem was exacerbated by the fact that many of these sorties had to be flown at or near mid-day when the air temperature was at its highest and turbulence was at its worst, and handling the Valetta in such conditions was quite dangerous. Also, at these high power settings, the noise of the Bristol Hercules engines was so loud that it tended to drown the messages in spite of the 2,000 watts power output and, when the microphone was being used, it picked up the sound of the engines and amplified it with the messages.

There were also occasional failures of the Tannoy equipment which caused problems and burned-out speech coils in the loudspeakers were frequent occurences. One of the operators noticed, however, that these failures occured predominently when the Hakka dialect of Chinese was being used. This dialect has many staccato, explosive sounds which were just too much for the loudspeaker coils and the equipment had to be modified, in addition to reducing the use of these particular words, before more satisfactory results were obtained.

Sky shouting Valettas were used from Feb. 1953 to Feb. 1954 and were withdrawn following the crash of Valetta WD 160 on the 4,000 ft. Mount Ophir. This illustrated the unsuitability of the Valettas for sky shouting and they were not used again for this purpose. This role was later taken on by the specialised Voice Flight, formed from 267 Squadron, and equipped with three Dakotas and two Austers. Sky-shouting was later employed during the Mau Mau Campaign in Kenya and in the Eoka Campaign in Cyprus using Percival Pembroke Aircraft.

Michael Fountain recalled that during the trials of the sky shouting equipment they had fitted four 500 watts amplifiers, connected to four 500 watts loudspeakers which were mounted under the fuselage of a Valetta at the R.A.F. base at St. Athan, Near Cardiff. Michael was under the aircraft listening to determine the level of background hum. He does not know exactly what happened but an impulse signal suddenly came through which came close to making him physically sick. Some years later, in 1956, Tannoy produced a lightweight, transistorised amplifer for air-to-ground work which weighed only ½lb per watt output, then a record.

There had, incidentally, been an earlier example of sky shouting techniques when, following the Great War, the Ottoman Empire was carved up and Britain gained control of much of the Middle East, all of it somewhat volatile. In an account of the Royal Air Force activities, several squadrons were engaged in suppressing numerous revolts in the region and it is recorded that at least one Vickers Victoria aircraft of No. 70 Squadron, which was based at Hinaidi, was fitted with an amplifier and loudspeakers in the campaign in Mesopotamia against Sheikh Ahmad of Barzan in 1932. Its purpose was to warn the civilian population of the villages of planned air attacks as an alternative to the leaflet drops which had previously been used; the warnings were given two days ahead of air raids to give them time to clear the area and distance themselves from the Sheikh's men. No surviving account of the effectiveness or otherwise of the technique has been found but it is on record that the amplifier and loudspeakers were supplied to the Royal Air Force by Tannoy. It is also known that in 1935 the R.A.F.'s sky shouting equipment was brought up to date and the class 'A' amplifiers were replaced with Tannoy class 'B' amplifiers fitted into Vickers Valentia aircraft.[3]

During the second World War the Royal Air Force also bought a small number of Tannoy Power Microphones but this detail will be covered in the next chapter.

Tannoy's Involvement With The R.A.F.

CHAPTER NOTES

1   The prizes were furnished by Sir William MacRobertson and three *de Havilland Comet* aircraft were entered, one of which was flown by Mr. & Mrs J. A. Mollison, (Jim Mollison and Amy Johnson). However, they were forced to retire with engine trouble at Karachi after flying there in the record time of 22 hr. 13 min.

2   Said by George Wheeler to have been the Chief Signals Officer of the Royal Air Force at that time. However, it has not yet been possible to confirm or confound this fact.

3   There is much evidence to support the belief that Tannoy supplied the amplifier for this work although an account in *Wireless World* of 22nd. May, 1936, which offers considerably less detail about these operations, credits this to *Standard Telephones and Cables Ltd.*, stating also that the aircraft concerned was a *Vickers Valentia* and that it was equipped in August, 1935.

Tannoy installation on an RAF airfield

No crystal set user should be without
THE NEW NON-VALVE MAGNETIC MICROPHONE BAR AMPLIFIER

Patent No. 248581/25.

Will work a LOUD SPEAKER direct from CRYSTAL SETS up to 6 miles or more from main Broadcasting Station; or make WEAK CRYSTAL or VALVE Reception LOUD and CLEAR in headphones under any conditions. Enables even VERY DEAF persons to hear FROM CRYSTAL SETS. Every Amplifier guaranteed.

Operates perfectly on one or two small dry cells.

No other accessories required.

NO VALVES, ACCUMULATORS OR H.T. BATTERIES.
NO DISTORTION.   NO FRAGILE PARTS.

NOTHING TO GET OUT OF ORDER.   A CHILD CAN ADJUST IT.

Price 34/- post free.   2 Dry Cells (lasting 3 months), 4/-.

Write to-day for illustrated literature, free.

May be obtained from any good Dealer, or from
Sole Manufacturers and Patentees:

NEW WILSON ELECTRICAL MANUFACTURING CO., LTD.,
18, Fitzroy St., Euston Rd., London, W.1.   Phone: Museum 8974.

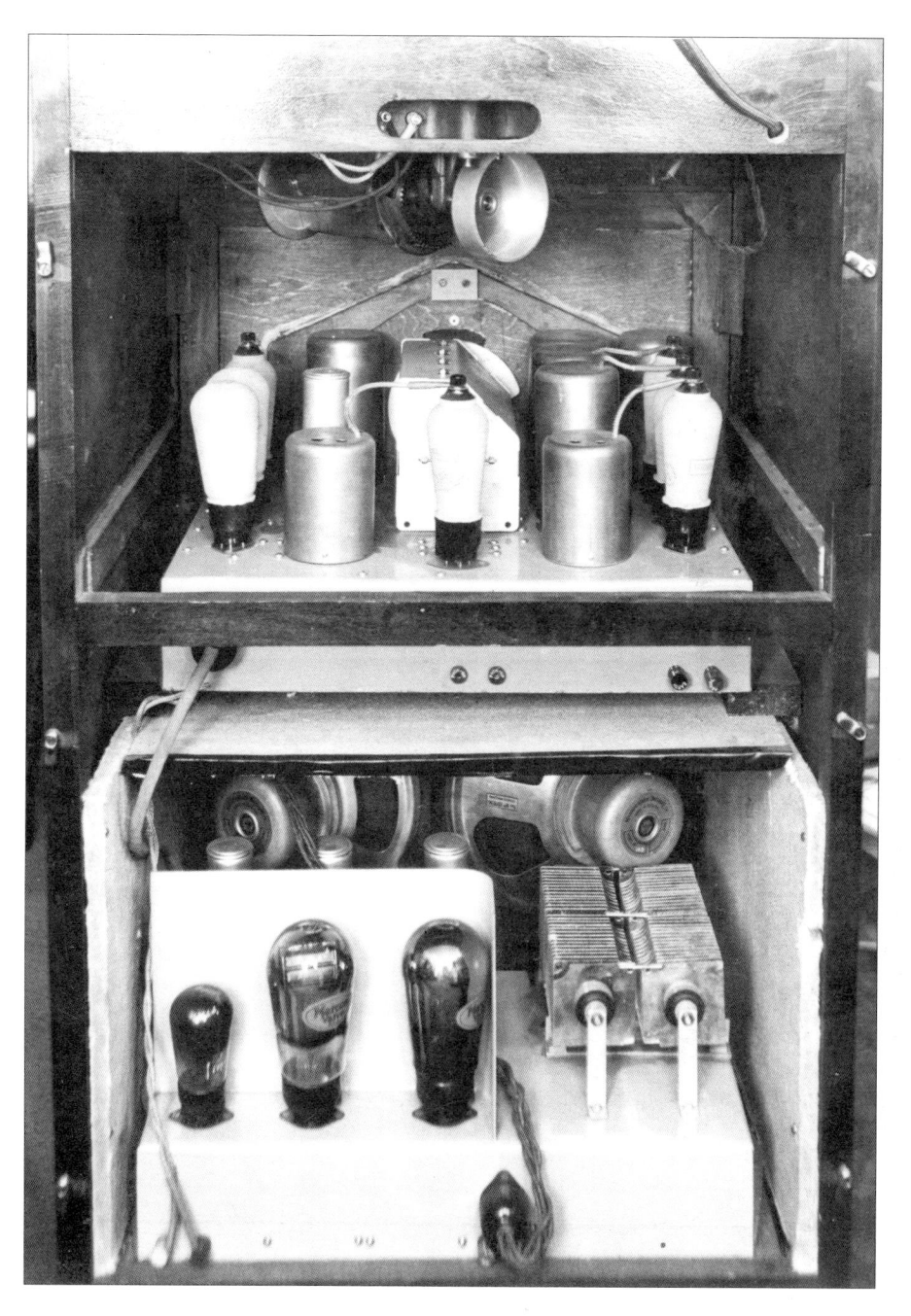

Interior View of a Tannoy Radiogram – probably a Tannoy Senior Model

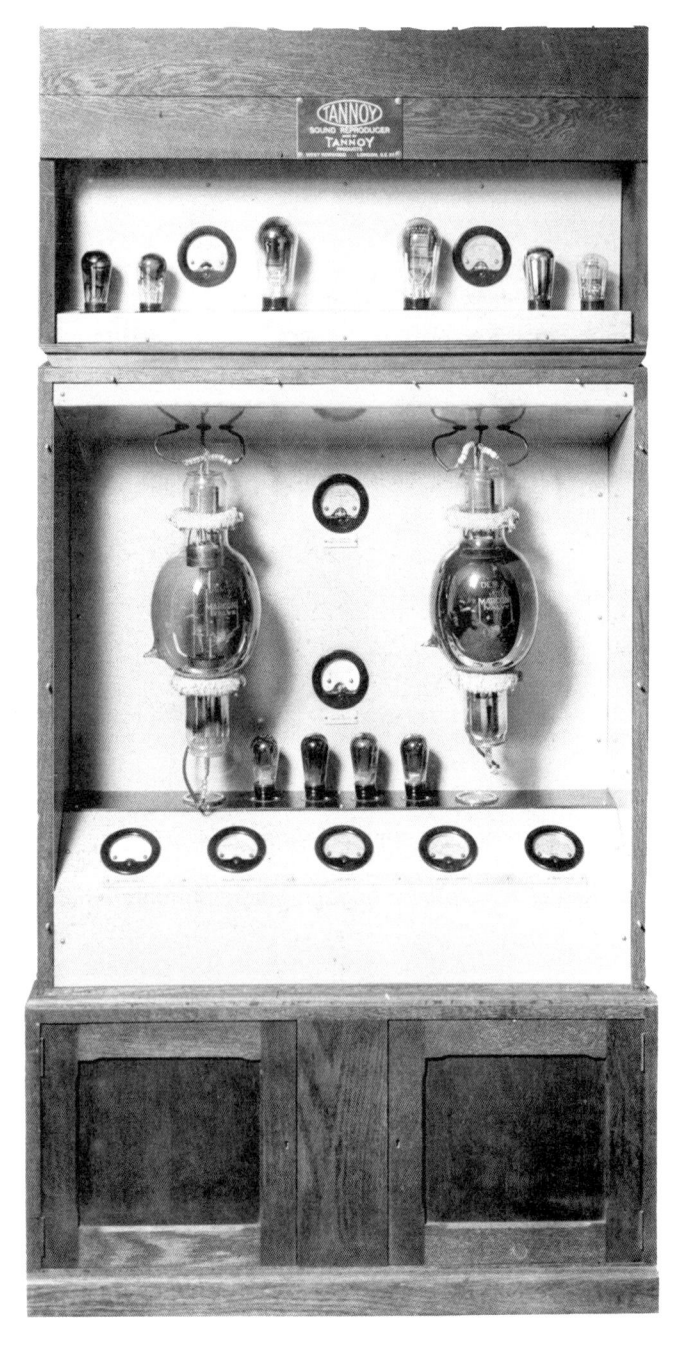

The line voltmeter here suggests post-introduction of 100 volt loudspeaker lines. Output valve type indicates pre-1937 when Norman 'Willy' Crowhurst made it possible to parallel up to 20 x 60 watts amplifiers.

Radio and gramophone amplifier for Naval installations 1935

*Above: The CD4 (15") Loudspeaker c.1935
Believed to be the first Tannoy-designed and made cone loudspeaker which remained in
production for many years*

*Left: SD5 pressure
Loudspeaker Driver
(also c 1935) was used
in all Tannoy Horn
Loudspeakers for many
years. Combined with
the CD4 (above) this
formed the basis of
Ronnie Rackham's development
work which
eventually created the
Dual Concentric
Loudspeaker*

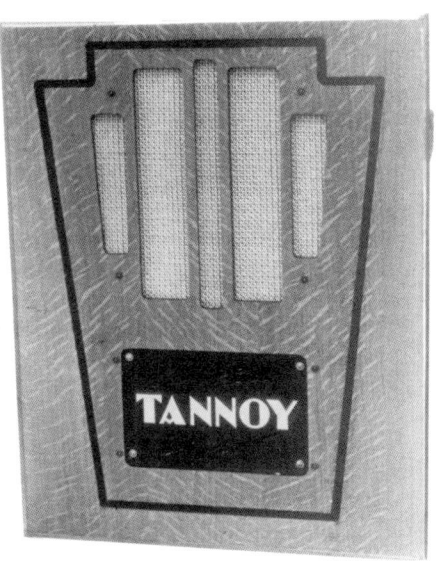

Above: 110v Equipment developed mainly for fairground use, 1938.

Below: Also 1938, Little & Large 110w and 5w P.A. Speakers

Power Microphone and the 'Collapsible Calamity' c1937

A late version of the portable P.A. system shown opposite. This 'Collapsible Calamity' features the rubber mouthpiece modification described in Chapter 7.

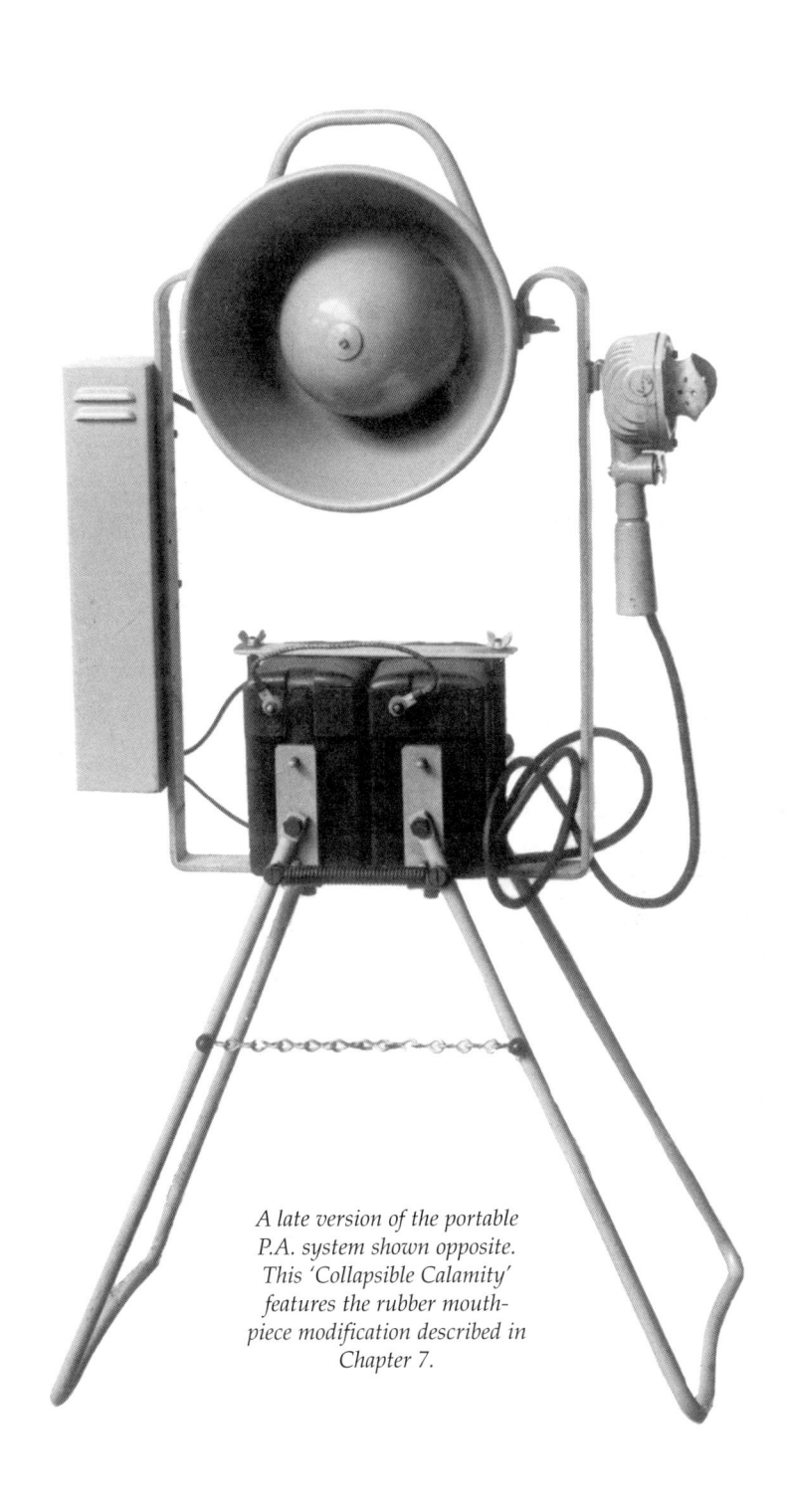

The Tannoy Public Address Installation at the 1937 RAF Review at Hendon. Although difficult to see on the photograph the trademark 'Tannoy' is boldly painted inside the loudspeaker horns.

Michael H Fountain, 2003

Michael Fountain at the controls of the sound reinforcement scheme for the Ottawa Legislative Assembly before shipment to Canada. The Tannoy Radiogram can be seen behind Guy Fountain.

George Wheeler (the first General Manager and 'midwife' at the birth of Tannoy) in his early days.

Left:
Ronald H Rackham –
undoubtably the genius behind
much of Tannoy's creative and
development work. The Dual
Concentric Loudspeaker which
has remained substantially
unchanged for more than 50 years
was entirely his brain-child.

Right:
T.B. 'Stan' Livingstone
who contributed so much to
this book.

The control panel in the House of Lords' Chamber with 'Stan' Livingstone in position.

Left: Dennis Terrett

*Right:
Claude Yates.
Committed the foul deed with the
potato up Mr Twentyman's
exhaust pipe.*

Above: Bill Preedy, the second General Manager at his desk. A photograph of the QE2 behind him.

Below: Philip Marks on a bicycle equipped with the valveless 'Power Microphone P.A. System 1940

Above: Four x 500 watts loudspeakers mounted on a DC 3 'Dakota' photographed on a 'Sky Shouting' sortie over Malaya.

Below: A Shorts 'Stirling Bomber' of No 15 Squadron displayed on a London bomb site to raise funds for the 'Wings for Victory' campaign c 1941.

CHAPTER SEVEN

THE TANNOY POWER MICROPHONE

About ten years after George Wheeler joined the company and triggered its move from wireless sets and battery eliminators to amplifiers and public address equipment, another newcomer to Tannoy brought a novel idea which, in its turn, started the company's progress along an equally fortuitous and profitable line of development. Early in 1937 Alfred Courtenay-Snell joined the company from *Clifford and Snell* of Sutton and brought with him the basis of the power microphone.

Even after the invention of the triode valve and the development of the valve amplifier, there was still a need for a sound amplifier which did not need valves; valves were fragile and required both high and low voltage supplies.

In the early days of the electronics industry, long before transistors and even before there were valve amplifiers, the only known way to amplify sound by electrical means was to drive a microphone mechanically, instead of vocally, with what was essentially an earphone and which could drive it much harder. During the Great War, *S.G. Brown & Company* had made what they called the *'Microphone Bar Amplifier'* which was different from any previous type of microphone in that it was a push-pull device. Instead of the diaphragm compressing the carbon granules on its down stroke allowing them to relax as it moved back, it actually drove the granules alternately in each direction, thereby increasing its effective power. Another advantage of the push-pull configuration was that the distortion was low and the current carrying capacity high and this increased the power output even more. In addition to this, it was driven mechanically by means of a little rod which connected it to the diaphragm of an earphone, which was, in turn, driven by another microphone or, in another popular application, by a crystal set. This device was used by the army during the Great War. After the war they were sold in large numbers in Government surplus stores to amplify the output of crystal sets and were still being made in 1927 by *New Wilson Electrical Manufacturing* of London W1 for the same purpose and marketed from 1926 by *Empire Electric Co.* of London NW1. They produced a reasonably well amplified signal though the quality was poor.[1]

In the early 1920s, *S.G. Brown* were advertising their '*Crystavox*' loudspeaker, a development of the Microphone Bar amplifier in which the amplifier and a horn loudspeaker were made as a single unit. This, incidentally, was sold at £6 and, in an advertisement, the accompanying *S.G. Brown* crystal set is priced, in tiny figures, at £2.

In about 1933 Alfred Courtenay-Snell thought that it would be an improvement if this could be driven vocally but to make it work it was necessary to do two things. Firstly; it had to be made to pass even more current, which he achieved quite simply by mounting eight of them on one chassis, and secondly – the really clever thing for which he must be credited – he made a properly designed mouthpiece which matched the acoustic impedance of the mouth to the effective stiffness of the diaphragm. The operator had to speak a specific distance from the diaphragm and to achieve this the microphone had a perforated metal mouthpiece which the user held over his mouth. It was not very hygienic, of course, but the user automatically held it at the optimum distance from his mouth. Thus, when he spoke into it there was a very much bigger movement of the diaphragm than had ever previously been achieved, greater than would have been the case without this ingenious acoustic matching device. The idea for this had come from *His Master's Voice* who had done a lot of experimental work on the impedance matching of diaphragms and horns in the development of their acoustic gramophones and recording machines with the result that their later gramophones had very big horns and, for the first time, actually reproduced the bass notes which were recorded on the records.

Courtenay-Snell was a partner in *Clifford and Snell Ltd.* a company based in Sutton, in an old chapel, nearly opposite where the Odeon theatre was later built and they made a piece of equipment called the 'Loudaphone'. This was installed on all *London Transport* underground trains and which could, until comparatively recently, occasionally be seen on the very old trains of the Northern Line. There is also one on display in a mock-up of a 1930s London Transport Underground train at the Transport Museum at Covent Garden. This consisted of a high current microphone with which the Guard could talk to the Driver at the other end of the train and hear his reply. But *Clifford and Snell* was then a very old-fashioned firm, with very old men running it and, although he was a partner in the company, Courtenay-Snell realised that he would have great difficulty in persuading these old gentlemen to back the development of his idea for a power microphone.

So, in 1936 he approached Tannoy and saw Bill Haines. Courtenay-Snell came to Tannoy with two rather tempting offers; firstly, he had the basic idea for a power microphone which worked, crudely perhaps, but it showed great promise; and secondly, he had access to some money from the *Banque Belge pour l'Etranger*. This was very tempting to Haines because seldom does a company get an approach from anyone with both a good idea and the money to develop it, occasionally they come with one or the other, usually neither. So Courtenay-Snell joined Tannoy in 1937 with the ability to raise some money and with the basis of the power microphone. In the event, the *Banque Belge* invested £6,500.

Jack Houlgate looked at the power microphone and immediately saw its potential and ways of improving it both electrically and acoustically. It was, of course, a very inefficient device. In crude terms it took 5 amps from a 12 volts battery which is 60 watts and, on a good day, if the operator spoke loudly enough, it would produce 3 watts of sound. But, of course, 3 watts into an efficient horn loudspeaker makes quite a lot of noise and if it is on or near a vehicle or a boat, obtaining 5 amps at 12 volts is no problem for it is readily available from the battery.

Now Courtenay-Snell was extremely good at mechanical design, particularly the mechanical design of castings. He could design the most complicated castings and he would always get the draw right so that the casting would come out of the mould without damaging either the casting or the tool. The company was therefore able to make a very attractive looking power microphone, based on Courtenay-Snell's idea but incorporating Houlgate's improvements, which would work for a reasonable length of time from 12 volts from a couple of motorcycle batteries. The power microphone was essentially an eight cell, push-pull microphone which was connected to a centre-tapped transformer. Initially the battery was connected in series with a large resistor to limit the amount of current through the microphone because it generated quite a lot of heat and it was necessary to prevent it from actually catching fire or burning the operator's lips. However, this was not too successful, so the resistor was replaced with a 12 volts, 60 watts bulb which used to wink in unison with the speech which was quite fascinating; high technology! The transformer and its attendant equipment was assembled in a box to fit into a motor car.

But Houlgate soon re-designed the microphone, using a solid block of aluminium, ¼" thick, with holes punched through it to form the eight cells. This enabled them to make the microphone a more compact and therefore a more practical, useable instrument. The holes in the aluminium block had to be perfectly smooth so they designed a tool which honed the bores as it punched them through the aluminium. The holes were filled with carbon granules and fitted with tiny disc-shaped pistons which were 20 thou thick and soldered to a 40 thou diameter brass rod. These were made by a drawing pin manufacturer and they were then sent to *Johnson Matthey*, the famous precious metals company in Hatton Garden, to be rhodium plated. These tiny piston rods were then soldered to an annular ring on a copper diaphragm which had been spun into the required shape by hand, using an ordinary lead pencil – a very soft one; grade 'F' – and the whole was then laquered to prevent corrosion. The blocks were sulphur anodised to insulate the surface and this was done by *Mercers of Sydenham*, although later the anodising was done electrically by Tannoy. The unit was then fitted into a cast aluminium case with an on/off push-button on the handle and with 18 fins on the back to dissipate the heat generated by the high current passing through the carbon granules. Development of this microphone continued for a while under Houlgate and Courtenay-Snell and an early version known, incorrectly, as the 'Valveless Amplifier', was fitted to a police car and a bicycle and shown at the 1937 Radiolympia Exhibition. Its efficiency was never good, although this was not important, and even the final production model delivered only about 8 watts of power while consuming about 5 or 6 times that amount of energy from the battery, but it served its purpose and served it well.

An alternative version was mounted on a complicated framework which could be unfolded and stood on the ground. However, such was the design of the frame, with spring loaded legs, that unless the operator was very careful he could not open or close it without mutilating himself on the sharp metal edges, so it was nicknamed the 'Collapsible Calamity'. Nevertheless it was quite popular because it was the only means of driving a loudspeaker which did not involve either valves or a rotary converter so it was an enormous step forward – and it worked. The prototype of the 'Collapsible Calamity' was presented by Bill Haines to Cranbrook School but it is not known whether it is still there.

The 'Collapsible Calamities' went into production in 1938 and they were originally all made by Bill Haines, with Vi Metcalfe in charge of winding the transformers. In 1938 about 800 were made for organisations such as the Civil Defence Corps, the Auxilliary Fire Service and for the Police. They were intended for crowd control during air raids but it is doubtful if they ever served this purpose.

As with George Wheeler's first amplifier, Guy Fountain, always the archetypal entrepreneur, recognised in the power microphone something which would give him the opportunity to experiment and, at the same time, give him some considerable amusement. So he had one fitted onto his car, which was a

The Tannoy Power Microphone

grey S.S. saloon. Guy also quite surely enjoyed the power which he could exercise over all and sundry by the injudicious use of the power microphone on his car, probably even using it to shout abuse at other road users. The author remembers an occasion, in 1937, when Guy and Elsie, with their children Jeanne, Michael and David, visited the author's parents, Douglas and Kathleen Alderton, at No. 7, Crest Road, in South Croydon, for Sunday lunch. As they approached down Ballards Way, near its junction with Ballards Farm Road, Guy's voice was heard resounding around the neighbourhood, probably for half a mile or so, shouting, "Come on Aldy, get those bloody gates open!"

Fountain often fell out with his fellow directors, including Courtenay-Snell, who had been appointed to a directorship in 1938. Snell left one Thursday morning soon after completing the design work on the Power Microphone with Jack Houlgate and went to work for *Standard Electric Ltd*. This was probably as late as 1939, not long after Stan Livingstone joined the company. Stan was always friendly with Snell and Snell had always been very civil to Stan and, on Stan's admission, he had learned a lot from Snell, so he liked him. Snell had been out that morning and, on his return, he came to Stan and said, "You won't be seeing me any more, Stan." When Livingstone asked why he replied, "Well, you know how it is." He leaned towards him and tapped him on the shoulder and said, "You want to watch that man Fountain, you watch him, my boy." Snell and Guy parted on very bad terms, in very typical circumstances, following a big shouting match.

When Courtenay-Snell had been with *Clifford and Snell* he had done a great deal of work for the Admiralty and he had acquired a large quantity of green, Admiralty linoleum. This was found to be ideal for the tops of Tannoy's benches! He was never asked exactly how he came by it.

Following Courtenay-Snell's departure, a huge amount of work was done to improve and perfect the power microphone and this was done by Jack Houlgate with help from Tony Anselm in making the necessary tooling (Tony Anselm's contribution is mentioned in more detail later in this chapter). In all applications of the Power Microphone, both civilian and military, it was used in connection with a reflex, horn-loaded pressure driver in the interests of electro-acoustic efficiency. This development work was not accomplished without considerable expense and, in 1940, the *Banque Belge* invested a further £9,500 in the company.

THE POWER MICROPHONE IN THE ARMY.
When the power microphone was launched upon the market, in 1938, it was in a cast metal body with cooling fins on the back, rigidly bolted to a cast metal mouthpiece which produced the acoustic matching. Courtenay-Snell had a

contact in the Ministry of Supply called Kelf-Cohen and he approached Kelf-Cohen with the power microphone. Courtenay-Snell told him that he had a microphone which would drive loudspeakers directly and could also drive the modulator in a transmitter without the need for a pre-amplifier, and it could therefore simplify mobile communications. The first proposed application was for use in tanks because the radio set in a tank performed two functions; not only did it talk to other tanks and its command headquarters but it also incorporated an intercommunication system which enabled the tank Commander, who was looking out of the top, to talk to the gun layer who could see absolutely nothing and to the driver who could see little more. For this reason, if the radio failed because the tank went over a big bump or, worse still, if it were hit by a shell, it became blind, deaf and dumb; a very unfortunate set of circumstances.

So a trial was arranged in which a Tannoy power microphone, in addition to functioning as an internal communication system, was also fed into the tank's radio. The idea was that instead of the radio driving earphones which were not really loud enough, the microphone drove little 800 Hz re-entrant coaxial loudspeakers fixed in convenient positions in the tank, i.e., one beside the driver's ear and one beside the gun layer's position, so they would be able to hear the tank commander under any circumstances. Above all, it did not matter so much if the radio set failed for the tank commander could still talk to the crew. Alternatively, the loudspeakers could be switched out of the circuit and replaced by headphones. Of course, the power microphone could also be used with the radio, assuming that it was still working, to communicate with other tanks and with their field headquarters. There was a switch on the control unit by which the loudspeakers could be connected either to the Commander's microphone or to the tank's R/T system. So every member of the tank crew was always in communication with the Commander and the Commander was always in communication with other tanks in the unit.

Livingstone carried out these trials and the first time they went over a bump they found a very obvious shortcoming; Livingstone was holding the microphone with the mouthpiece pressed against his lips and very nearly dislodged all his front teeth; there was blood everywhere. Also, by the time they had carried out the demonstration it was almost red hot, but all of this did not alter the fact that it had proved that the thing did work and would do the job.

The Ministry of Supply ordered them to redesign the microphone yet again and this was done very quickly by Courtenay-Snell and Houlgate. Now if anything like this were tried today with all the committee decisions and management input, with the Accountants inevitably also having their say, it would be amazing if it were achieved in under two years, but Courtenay-Snell and

The Tannoy Power Microphone

Houlgate managed it in considerably less than that, getting it into production again in about 2½ months. They made the microphone mechanism into a separate insert instead of being integral with the cast case, and this could be assembled and tested as an insert. They designed a new cast case which would accommodate the insert in such a way that the case would still function as a heat sink and, under considerable and understandable pressure from Livingstone, they replaced the cast metal mouthpiece with a moulded rubber one. This hasty re-design proved entirely satisfactory and the resulting power microphone remained in much the same form for some 40 or 50 years; surviving in produc-tion until long after the second World War.

The Ministry were so impressed with all this that they decided that they would like the power microphone to be totally independent of the switching of the radio set but, as Stan put it, the radio seemed to have been designed by people who had only ridden horses and were none too familiar with tanks, so Tannoy made a selector switch in a very strong metal box with a key which could be switched to 'Crew' if the commander wanted to communicate with the crew, to 'Radio' if he wanted to transmit, or to both simultaneously. This was something which had not previously been possible and was immediately recognised as a great advantage. But, as has been emphasised earlier, Courtenay-Snell was a brilliant man and right from the beginning he realised that this equipment was necessarily in a vulnerable place and that soldiers would step on the key switch and break it as they entered or left the tank, so he had a very strong piece of metal channelling fitted to the side of the box to protect the switch. The complete equipment gained the official title of 'Tank Emergency Crew Control No. 1', and it was not long before every tank in the British Army had this equipment installed. This was the first military application of the Power Microphone.

From this there sprang a whole range of military equipment. In addition to the 'Tank Emergency Crew Control No. 1', the main item was the artillery crew control equipment which was devised to control a battery of guns. Until this was introduced, artillery control was largely achieved by visual signals or by a one-way radio system but the Tannoy equipment was a wired system using a power microphone which was connected, via switching, to either four or eight coaxial loudspeakers, one sited adjacent to each gun. These loudspeakers incorporated a 'talk' button on the top of the box so that they could also be used as microphones, feeding directly into very sensitive, sound powered headphones which the gun commander wore to pick up the low voltage signal from the gunner's loudspeaker. There was, of course, no amplification in the reverse direction but, if the gun commander gave the order, 'FIRE', the gun crews could all hear the command and fire as instructed but if, for example, a gun failed to fire, the gun team could press the 'talk' button on the loudspeaker box and shout into the loudspeaker, telling the commander that the gun was jammed or whatever and, for the first time, the commander knew what was going on. The control unit was in a strong wooden box and required a 24 volts supply. The loudspeakers were buckled together in pairs so that the complete system was in three strong wooden boxes with webbing bandoliers so that they could be fairly easily carried, however, they were quite heavy. The loudspeakers could be operated at a distance of about a mile from the commander and this was adequate for the usual 4 gun arrangement. This was later extended to eight guns for which 2 units could be coupled together. This reduced the loudspeaker power but it was still adequate in most situations.

Another great advantage was security because it was completely separate from the radio whereas before the introduction of this equipment, using radio, as soon as the commander gave the order 'FIRE', anyone with a receiver, including the enemy, would know that the shells were coming and would take appropriate action. In this form the power microphone was given the official title of 'Telephone, Loudspeaking, No.2.' This, too, was still in production after W.W.2 and Edmund Newton remembers assembling them soon after he joined Tannoy in 1961. There was another compelling reason for adopting the power microphone for there was a shortage of valves in the early years of the war. Valve manufacturers were unable to keep up production to the levels demanded by military radio equipment and the shortage of valves was felt as early as September, 1939. This became acute in May 1941 and the shortage lasted until about April, 1943.

In the course of the research for this chapter, a letter was received on 28th October, 1992, from Mr. R.C. Gilbert of Cowes, Isle of Wight :

> "I noticed a request in *Practical Wireless* for information on Tannoy equipment. It was used widely by the Royal Artillery for communication with the guns. My experience was as an Electrician, Signals, attached to the 166th Newfoundland Field Regiment, Royal Artillery. Each field regiment had 24, 25lb guns, made up of 3 batteries of 8 guns, each battery consisting of 2 troops of 4 guns. Each troop had a set of Tannoy equipment consisting of the amplifier, (this was, of course, the control unit and transformer), heavy duty microphone and 4 loudspeakers. The latter were in heavy wooden boxes which clipped together in pairs to form a unit about 16" by 16" by 16". It was extremely durable equipment, the main defects being compression of the moving coil in the loudspeakers and the failure of the microphone cord. It was a very essential piece of equipment for, as you can imagine, communication between the command post and the guns during action was difficult."

The Tannoy Power Microphone

The 'Tank Emergency Crew Control No.1' and the 'Telephone, Loudspeaking, No.2' became quite popular with the troops, not only because they were so reliable, but because they found other uses for them. It was not long before they found that, quite frequently, due to the high current and high temperature, the carbon granules tended to fuse together, not firmly, but just enough to impair slightly the microphone's performance. So they adopted the habit of knocking the microphone against the side of the tank, or any other convenient hard surface, to loosen the granules; a simple remedy which worked well and which led to the secondary use of the microphone as a mallet for driving tent pegs! During the early research for this book Chris Bisaillion, of Ontario, supplied detailed drawings of the microphone and headgear assemblies of the 'Tank Emergency Crew Control No.1' and suggested that it might also be used as 'a club' if overrun by the enemy (see overleaf). Of the surviving examples, two of which were in the author's radio collection, not too many have much of their grey paint left. It was also found that when used operationally in cold weather, the microphone was seldom switched off because it performed so well as a hand warmer![2]

Later in the war, during the preparations for the Normandy landings, the Army wanted to carry out some very secret tests using the Power Microphone. The trials took place at Donnington but the security level was very high and Tannoy had to get Cabinet approval for George Wheeler and Jack Houlgate to go there. On arrival they were met by an Army Captain and were taken into the camp, passing through two very tight security checks, and when they eventually arrived inside they were shown what was referred to as a brainchild of Churchill's; a top secret item of equipment. There were three tanks coupled together and equipped with heavy digging equipment, the idea being to take these to France and dig a continuous trench all the way to Berlin. It sounded laughable but it must be borne in mind that the men who were to follow behind would be very well protected but, achieving a speed of only about half a mile per day, it would have taken a very long time indeed to reach Berlin. Tannoy came into the scheme because it was suggested that the control between the tanks should be effected by means of the Power Microphone and it was decided to put on a demonstration and they started two of the tanks but, unfortunately, the third tank had engine trouble and would not start.

So the demonstration was called off and it was arranged for Wheeler and Houlgate to return to London by train. On arrival at the station they found that there was no train for some time so the Captain suggested that they went into a nearby pub for a drink to pass the time. While they were talking, one or two local residents came in and addressed the Captain, "Hello, Joe, I hear you've got trouble with one of the machines up there." So much for security!

NO. 1 CDN.

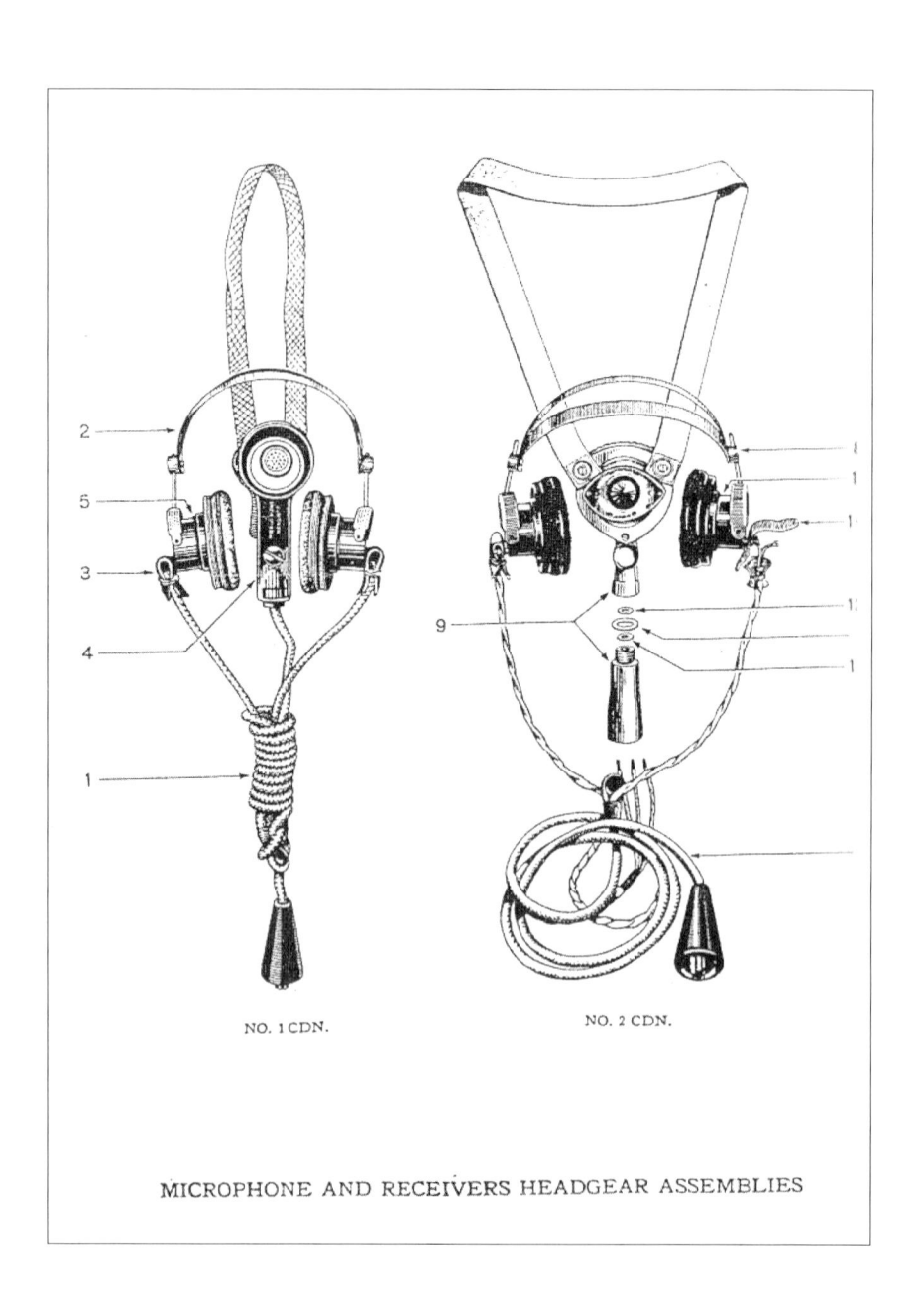

NO. 2 CDN.

MICROPHONE AND RECEIVERS HEADGEAR ASSEMBLIES

The Tannoy Power Microphone

However, such was the secrecy about the project that the purpose of a trench to Berlin is still unclear.

There is one more important application to which the power microphone was put, not directly connected with the Army, but loosely connected and quite significant. Immediately after the invasion of France on D-Day, 6th June, 1944, it was necessary to get weapons, ammunition, food supplies and fuel to the troops as quickly as possible, hence the huge floating concrete sections which were towed across the channel to build the 'Mulberry' harbours. Petrol was a difficult one as it would have been virtually impossible to ship sufficient fuel across the channel in cans to keep the vehicles running with the result that the invasion would have come to a halt a few miles inland; and it would have failed. This was foreseen and so Pluto was laid. P.L.U.T.O. was, 'Pipeline under the Ocean' and it consisted of huge flexible pipes which were laid across the English Channel through which vast quantities of petrol were pumped for many weeks. P.L.U.T.O. was the underwater section of a most ambitious pipeline which was laid from the refineries on Merseyside and which eventually reached Emmerich, on the Rhine just south of the Dutch border and about 50 miles south east of Arnhem. The under water section of this pipe was made in the *Siemens Brothers* cable factory at Charlton in a continuous process, the pipe being manufactured in the factory and run out onto very large cable drums, some 20 ft. in diameter, on barges floating on the Thames. After the invasion these were towed behind tugs and laid across the English Channel to provide the essential fuel supplies for the invasion forces. Because its production was noisy, instructions to the operatives in parts of the factory had to be conveyed by means of loudspeakers, and Tannoy Power Microphone installations, similar to the 'Telephone, Loudspeaking, No. 2', were chosen for this purpose.

Incidentally, on D-Day minus one, Engineers Ken Gregory and Bill Preedy were working on an installation in East Anglia and they were having dinner at a Thetford hotel when they received a telephone call from a supply tanker driver. He told them that *F.H. Wheeler*'s wiremen were incarcerated at the nearby East Wretham U.S.A.A.F. station, and that he had only just managed to escape the attention of the American Security Guards. They assumed, quite wrongly, that the U.S.A.A.F. security there was getting over enthusiastic so, after collecting Harry Astell, the *F.H. Wheeler* Area Manager, they drove to the base. About half a mile down the road they were stopped by armed guards and told that if they proceeded they would be detained. After brushing them off, they were taken under guard to the C.O. who, without giving any reason said, in effect, "I'm sorry, gentlemen, but you are now my guests". They were each allocated an Officer, to whom they might just as well have been handcuffed, and they were obliged to stay with their particular escorts, moving only when they did

The TANNOY Story

and sleeping only when they did. Next morning, after breakfasting in the Mess, they were told that they could leave. The mystery was cleared up when they got into their car. They switched on the radio to learn that it was D-Day and the secret was that all aircraft had been painted with the D-Day bands to give immediate identification and they had not been allowed to see these. Car radios had been banned throughout the war but they were allowed again by about March, 1944. This account confirms the overwhelming need for domestic radios in wartime.

THE POWER MICROPHONE IN THE ROYAL NAVY.
Some experimental work was carried out by the Royal Navy in which the power microphone was used to convey orders from the bridges of ships to movement areas and action stations but little information has been found of this work. Perhaps more important, and certainly more widespread, was the installation of power microphones in submarines and this is very interesting because submarines are divided into several watertight compartments and, at the time under consideration, communication between compartments was very difficult even with the bulkhead doors open. The crews had to rely on klaxons using coded signals and if something happened for which there was no code they had a problem. Now submarines suffer enormous shock problems from depth charges. When a submarine comes under attack from depth charges, the explosions do not always damage the pressure hull but everything inside that can break, does break and the first things that fail are the lights because the shock breaks the lamp filaments, particularly if they are switched on and hot (scenes of this happening occur in many films about submarine warfare). A conventional valve amplifier in use for communications between compartments would have been almost as vulnerable; the shock waves would have broken the valve heaters and the amplifier would be silent and there they would be, in the dark, with nothing but a klaxon and about half-a-dozen codes such as, 'Action stations', 'Dive'; 'Fire', 'Surface', 'Stand down', etc., but if something out of the ordinary happened for which there was no code, they were lost. It must be said at this point that valve heaters were, in fact, a little less susceptible to shock than lamp filaments because they were rigidly encased within the cathode which was in the form of a tiny nickel tube, coated with various metals, predominently barium. The delicate heater filament was thus given some support by the cathode but there was, nevertheless, some risk of failure due to the shock of explosions and it was desirable to eliminate this risk if possible. Following the success of the 'Telephone, Loudspeaking, No.2', Tannoy was approached to see if a similar installation could be made which would work in submarines and Jack Houlgate immediately thought back to *S.G. Brown*'s Microbar

The Tannoy Power Microphone

amplifier.

Houlgate constructed a special device similar to the workings of a moving coil loudspeaker but with two magnetic gaps, one at each end of the magnet assembly. Everybody thought that it was only possible to have one gap in a magnet assembly but Houlgate disagreed and decided on a gap at each end; and it worked, proving the others quite wrong. He then wound two voice coils on formers, one coil positioned in each magnetic gap, and had the coils driven electrically by a power microphone.[3] He then connected the coil formers mechanically to two more power microphones and by this means they were driven very hard; much harder than they could ever be driven vocally and, with 24 volts, which was readily available on board submarines, and taking nearly 10 amps, it was possible to get nearly 10 watts of sound out of each microphone, and 20 watts into lots of little loudspeakers – in the confines of a submarine this was very loud indeed. There were normally eight loudspeakers installed in various compartments of the submarine and, when all the lights had gone out and when nothing else electronic was left working, the submarine's captain had good, loud and reliable communication with all the important locations in his ship. This was a genuine valveless amplifier - and it worked. The system also incorporated a reply back facility in which, like the 'Telephone, Loudspeaking No.2', the loudspeakers worked as microphones and these energised the captain's headphones. It was even possible to connect a tuner to the system and recognisable music would come from the loudspeakers. This equipment, which was given the title, 'The Tannoy Broadcasting Alarm System', was introduced into the submarine fleet from early 1942 and it was not long before every submarine in the Royal Navy was equipped. The development of the Power Microphone for submarine use, as described above, was the ONLY piece of Tannoy equipment which can correctly be called a 'Valveless Amplifier'. All other uses of the Power Microphone, pre-war, wartime and post-war, used single Power Microphones with reflex loudspeakers of various designs.

Designer Philip Marks developed the submarine equipment one stage further and reasoned that if they could feed a warning signal into the circuit they could do away with the klaxon. So he thought of the idea of using a 24 volts vibrator, the output of which is a square wave, and feeding this signal into the microphone transformer. This was an excellent idea but he had overlooked the fact that the vibrators were not suitable for working into a highly inductive load such as a transformer, so after the vibrator had been in use for a short time it failed due to arcing across the contacts which soon welded them together. The fellow who came to sort this out was Dick Merrick, who ran the *Ferrograph Company* and had also worked for *Wright and Weare Ltd.*, and he devised a tuned feedback circuit to limit the arcing effect of the inductance. From then on, it was

The TANNOY Story

a complete success and the Tannoy system virtually replaced the klaxon.
This assembly was originally fitted into a large rubber mounted cast box but it was difficult to make and very expensive. Eventually Livingstone suggested to George Wheeler that they could reduce costs by doing away with Courtenay-Snell's cast box and by making the whole unit in a big pressed steel box with a channel around the outside to stiffen it and form a water-tight seal. Houlgate agreed, so Bill Haines made one and it was taken to the Admiralty who had doubts about its ability to withstand depth charge shocks. So it was then taken to the Admiralty Research Establishment at Bath where they had what was referred to as a depth charge simulator. This consisted of a 3" thick steel plate, 20 ft. square weighing nearly 22 tons, mounted on a huge spring, all of this in an enormous building. To simulate a depth charge, they bolted the equipment to be tested to the plate and then struck the plate, six times on each side and six times on each edge with a very large, heavy weight and they reckoned that this was approximately equivalent to the shock of a depth charge. It was a very crude test but the Admiralty could think of nothing better at the time. The Tannoy valveless amplifier passed the test and became a very successful piece of submarine equipment.

THE POWER MICROPHONE IN THE ROYAL AIR FORCE.

On 7th October, 2000, the author found a power microphone amongst a display of aircraft radio equipment at the Newark Air Museum and discussed this with Michael Fountain. It was concluded that this must be a mistake for it was believed that this was never used by the R.A.F. However, on a visit to Stan Livingstone three days later in St. Christopher's Hospice in Sydenham, just nine days before he died, Stan perked up and said, "Oh yes it was!" and with his eyes sparkling with enthusiasm, he told the full story.

During Bomber Command's great offensive strikes against Nazi Germany many aircraft were returning to England, severely damaged, to find that their bases were covered by blankets of thick fog. Diversion airfields were indicated to crews at their pre-flight briefings but these, too, were often fog bound. The result of this was that many crews died, and their aircraft were destroyed in needless landing accidents. Churchill issued an order to the effect that this situation MUST be rectified. The result was the invention of F.I.D.O., Fog Intensive Dispersal Operation. The system consisted of very large petrol burners in which vaporized petrol, burning on the same principle as the conventional blow-lamp or 'Primus' stove, produced intense heat with the minimum of smoke and lifted the fog from the runway. These burners were situated in vaporizer pits alongside the runway with, at a safe distance from them, control

The Tannoy Power Microphone

pits each with two operatives to open and close the petrol valves as instructed from the Air Traffic Control tower. These men received their instructions by means of the A.L.S. 23, 'Apparatus, Loudspeaking, No.23', which consisted of loudspeakers fed by power microphones; very similar to the 'Telephone, Loudspeaking No.2'. F.I.D.O. would disperse fog over the runway to a height of about 300 ft., making a safe landing possible, but at a price! F.I.D.O. consumed 250,000 gallons of petrol per hour at a cost, in those days, of £44,000. Needless to say, F.I.D.O. was installed at only 11 Master Diversion Airfields but a great number of Bomber Command aircrews were saved. Only one of these installations, at R.A.F. Manston, with a runway some 250 yards wide and about two miles in length remained in use into the 1950s. There was only one emergency post-war when an Avro Anson flying in low cloud and with an unserviceable radio was able to land safely.

Tannoy grew big during the war but it did so, as so many companies did, almost exclusively on military contract work. Tannoy was lucky in that what it was making was unique and could not be obtained elsewhere, in fact the power microphone was considered so important that a second factory had to be established to ensure security of production. The Ministry of Supply was quick to recognise that a bomb on the West Norwood site would have caused a major problem and rightly demanded that a second factory should be set up to make them. This was established near Dorking, Surrey.

By this time, Guy had become very friendly with Frank Wheeler, whose company, *F.H. Wheeler*, had carried out the installation of the Tannoy equipment in the R.A.F. Fighter Command airfields and, during the Battle of Britain, Guy's family stayed with Frank and Phyllis Wheeler at Sutton Place, about a mile to the west of Abinger. They later moved to a rented house called Cumnor, at Wonham Way, Gomshall and the author remembers staying there for some weeks. During this time, Michael and David went to school at Cranleigh.

At about the same time Tannoy evacuated its Accounts Department to the safety of a big country house called Minnickfold, near Beare Green and when the power microphone production was moved away from Norwood it, too, was moved to Minnickfold. Minnickfold is a very elegant 'black-and-white', Tudor style house which was built during the 1890s as a hunting lodge for the Admiral of the Fleet. The gardens were designed by Gertrude Jekyll and had a very long greenhouse which has since been demolished although evidence of the foundations of the piers could still, when visited by the author in 1997, be seen. The Power Microphone production line was installed in that greenhouse.

The TANNOY Story

There was a man in the company called Tony Anselm, formerly Anthoni Anselmi, who had responded to an advertisement for a Toolmaker under the impression that he would be making simple tools, even garden tools, but he was so adaptable that he very soon became an expert engineering toolmaker in his own right. He latched onto production processes very quickly indeed and, when it came to process design, he was probably ahead of his time and it was he who established the power microphone production in the greenhouse at Minnickfold. This was later transferred to Dorking where Anselm installed Tannoy's first moving assembly line, which he had designed, in a stable block in a side street to the south of the High Street. It was on the first floor of a building with a rope operated lift which enabled goods and equipment to be lifted into the workshop. The author has spent much time wandering around Dorking trying to identify this building and one which seemed to fit the description was located. However, a subsequent search with Michael Fountain has revealed that the building has been demolished and new offices have replaced it. The building was at No. 3, Dene Street.

On occasions during the war, Guy arranged for company dances to be held in the elegant surroundings of Minnickfold where, as has been recorded, the accounts department and the Power Microphone assembly were evacuated from West Norwood. Michael, then about 13 or 14 years of age, was allowed to play the gramophone records, through a Tannoy amplifier of course, which provided the music for these dances. That is, until he left one of his father's favourite records on top of the amplifier! Guy was absolutely furious and he really made Michael suffer. There had been a similar incident some years earlier: Guy had a record which he particularly liked to use in demonstrations when he really wanted to impress a potential customer. On this occasion, he found that he had left it at home at Lancaster Avenue so he sent an office boy to fetch it for him. As the lad arrived back at the factory he lost his balance and fell off his bicycle, cracking the record. Guy was absolutely furious and flew into a typical, uncontrollable rage, and smashed the cracked record over the lad's head.

There was another amusing incident in relation to Minnickfold when Norman Robottom was detailed to take a van to Minnickfold to collect some equipment for the factory. At the time he was quite fond of one of the company employees, Margaret Higgins, and he suggested to her that it was such a pity that she could not come with him. She went to her immediate superior and said that she was not feeling well and could she go home? So she and Norman set off for Minnickfold. On the way back, they decided to stop for a while at a well-known beauty spot, Ranmore Common, which overlooks Dorking. They bought a couple of bottles of cordial, parked the van beside the

The Tannoy Power Microphone

road and sat behind the hedge enjoying their drinks and each others' company and the view of Dorking when, quite suddenly, there was a rustling sound behind them and, to their astonishment, and acute embarrassment, Guy Fountain appeared. By an incredible, thousands-to-one chance, he'd happened to drive along the same road at that time and, believing that one of his vans had broken down, had stopped to investigate and found Norman with a young lady employee who was supposedly off sick!

Now Guy was extremely reluctant to let other companies know anything of the secrets of the power microphone, his power microphone. He wanted it all to himself and he certainly did not want any other company to get in on the act. However, under pressure, he did eventually have to allow this because the Ministry would not have the whole of the production vested in one company, even if it were split between two sites, and Guy was forced to accept the fact that another company would have to enjoy a share of this very lucrative action.

At the time Guy was friendly with Allen Clark, then Managing Director of *Plessey* who, in addition to making huge quantities of all sorts of electronic equipment for the services, also made the diaphragms for some of Tannoy's loudspeakers, particularly the SD 5. At the same time, Livingstone was on friendly terms with a man called Webb who was Chief of Testing and subsequently became a director of *Plessey*. Webb was always very complimentary about the power microphone but not about Tannoy's factory site and he once said, "If *Plessey* had to make things in a place like this, I would leave." However reluctantly, Guy was obliged to allow *Plessey* to take on some of the production of power microphones and, of course, to divulge the secrets of its design to them. *Plessey* made very large numbers of Power Microphones but, as usual, Guy insisted that even these had the name 'Tannoy' cast into their cases.

In those days Tannoy were delivering power microphones on a continuous basis and there was always another contract in the pipeline. So Jack Hudson, who was the Financial Director and Company Secretary, could more or less ring up the Ministry of Supply and tell Kelf-Cohen if there was a bit of a panic on cashflow and the next payment of, say, £10,000 would appear by the next post. This did not require sophisticated bookkeeping because everybody knew that Tannoy were delivering, everybody knew that there was another order coming along, everybody knew that they could pay their suppliers and, because they were all fixed price contracts (Guy would *never* go for costed contracts) even the Ministry did not mind.

The power microphone was in production throughout the war and, although orders slowed down very dramatically at the end of hostilities, there remained some demand for them. They were soon seen by military cadets from the Iraq, Iran, Egypt, and other Middle Eastern countries who came to Sandhurst for

The TANNOY Story

their officer training, some of whom visited the Tannoy factory and saw the production. They recognised a need for these in their own, expanding services and many export orders followed with the result that, during the Iran/Iraq war, the 'Telephone, Loudspeaking, No. 2' was still being supplied to several Middle Eastern countries.

There was, of course, some fuss about sending equipment to Iraq during the war but there was really no problem because it was regarded as defensive equipment rather than as offensive equipment. It was essential always to have a licence but if a company had a licence prior to an arms embargo it seems that they did not have to apply for another.

At one time Tannoy did experience a few problems, notably with payment for goods supplied, particularly in about 1958 when, following a *coup d'etat*, King Feisal and his family were assassinated and the military took over.

Tannoy had to deal through an agent, he was called Musa Ali and there came a time when Musa Ali fell well behind with payments so Tannoy wrote to him and sent him many telegrams, all of which were ignored. Eventually the company received a letter from Musa Ali's brother who was some way from Baghdad, to say, 'I hide here, I send money but not for a little while or I get shoot'. Guy Fountain had considerable doubts about all this and was reluctant to let them have credit but eventually the money was received and the company continued to supply power microphones.

To simplify somewhat the history of the course of the Iran/Iraq war, the Iraqis occasionally advanced but never very far and, as soon as the Iranians opened fire the Iraquis retreated and they lost everything. However, they had plenty of money because the Gulf States were pouring money into Iraq to try to keep the fundamentalists under control. Iraq, in those days, seemed to be the hero of the Middle East and in the late 1970s and early 1980s Tannoy was turning out power microphone equipment at a tremendous rate, often taking orders for 1,000 or 2,000 sets. It was Livingstone's responsibility to go to the Iraq Embassy to collect the money and he used to be 'received', with mint tea and all due ceremony and all this stood Tannoy in very good stead.

The Egyptian army was also equipped with power microphones and this was absolutely ideal for the company because every time they fought the Israelis they lost much of their equipment, but Egypt also had lots of money at the time so they just bought more microphones.

In February, 1958, when Egypt got together with Syria and formed the 'United Arab Republic', later to be joined by Yemen, power microphones were in great demand and Livingstone took Denis Blackmore, then the Company Secretary, to the U.A.R. Embassy. Relationships between the United Kingdom and various middle eastern countries were good, but they had to be handled

The TANNOY Story

with great tact and some delicacy and, in those days, contracts had to be interpreted by Swiss law if there was any suggestion of a dispute. On one occasion the Egyptians wanted to buy 2,000 power microphone sets and Livingstone and Blackmore visited the U.A.R. Embassy to negotiate the deal. The Embassy was guarded by armed policemen because it was believed that the Israelis were likely to attack the building and throw a few bombs in, so Livingstone took Blackmore in through the rather elaborate defences. Livingstone knew his contact there quite well who said, "Well, would you like a cheque for half of them now?" But Tannoy had not then signed the contract, let alone supplied any microphones so Blackmore said quietly, "This seems alright, Stan", so they accepted the payment there and then and eventually did a lot of business on informal lines such as this.

Edmund Newton, who joined Tannoy in the late 1950s, recalled an amusing episode during the later production of the 'Telephone, loudspeaking No. 2'. A query arose concerning the instruction plate which was screwed to the lid of the control unit and which read, "REMOVE THE UD", which the troops could not, of course, understand. It transpired that the young lady who was tasked with preparing these instruction plates had mis-read a rather carelessly written word, 'LID' in which the 'L' had been written too close to the 'I'. It is thought that 1,000 or more sets were issued with this mistake.

Some years later another very successful product for military applications was introduced, without the power microphone – the ALS 24 equipment. This was a 24 watts, integrated amplifier with a horn loaded loud hailer which was built into a very solid casting for mounting in vehicles and with a separate input mixer. Once again, Ronnie Rackham did the mechanical design work and Dennis Terrett was responsible for the electronics.

CHAPTER NOTES

1   The most recent reference to the microphone bar amplifier found by the author is an advertisement in the *Radio Times* of 23rd September, 1927 by the *New Wilson Manufacturing Company Limited* in which it is advertised at 34/-.

2   During a visit to the Army Signals Museum at Blandford Forum in 1999 it was found that the museum did not possess a Tannoy power microphone so the author's collection was reduced to one.

3   This was the very first series gap magnet assembly to be made and it later became the basis of the very successful Tannoy dual concentric loudspeaker.

A.F.S. Fireman using valveless loud hailer at show

CHAPTER EIGHT

1939–1945

Before the war there had been minimal money problems because Guy had acquired in rapid succession the financial support of Keith Hill, who had become a director in 1935, and Alfred Courtenay-Snell, the latter bringing with him backing from the *Bank of Belgium*.

Courtenay-Snell came with the nucleus of the power microphone and with some backing for this project. He was a nice man but slightly strange and he sometimes seemed to give the impression of being the 'Power behind the throne'. He told Guy that he could raise money with *Banque Belge*, who then invested in the company. Later, when Jack Hudson joined as the Accountant he, too, invested some money in the business.

The result of these acquisitions of personnel with their welcome financial contributions was that by the latter part of the 1930s the company was stable; it seemed that it was always possible to find the next person to invest in it. Like a lot of small companies it had tended to be run on a 'hand to mouth' basis but the support of Keith Hill and Alfred Courtenay-Snell made a major contribution to the company's stability and, but for their contributions, it would not have been in the sound financial position which it was in 1939 when the second World War broke out. Based upon this secure footing, the company's business progressed rapidly.

Not everything that Tannoy tried was successful. At about the time of the outbreak of the war the first electronic air raid warning system was under development; the development seemed to go on for ages. This consisted of a signal generator and amplifier in which the sound of the air raid warning was generated by a beat-frequency oscillator with a second, very low frequency oscillator to produce the rising and falling note of the 'Alert' signal. It even included a simulation of the sound of the gas warning rattle which was produced by a square-wave oscillator but, unfortunately, only six were ever

The TANNOY Story

sold. This was not at that time a wise investment of resources but later, in the 1950s, it was developed further to make equipment such as fog signals and chemical disaster warnings of which more later. Then, in 1940 they experimented with other means of handling very high power outputs and bought an old Great War searchlight, converting it into a very high power loudspeaker with about fifty SD 5 units, all with short horns attached. Each horn progressed from about 1" diameter to about 3" with a total length of about 2'. This was taken to Ranmore Common, overlooking Dorking from the North Downs, and demonstrated to representatives from the army. It worked very well indeed although its intended purpose was not recorded; neither was its effect upon the good people of Dorking.

Following the installation of Tannoy public address systems at the R.A.F. Fighter bases which stood alone in the defence of the United Kingdom during the Battle of Britain, the value of public address had been very quickly appreciated by the Air Ministry who ordered similar systems for many more of their airfields and, as has been recorded in chapter 6, by 1943, 700 complete public address systems had been designed and installed and were being maintained by the company at R.A.F. airfields throughout the country. The Royal Navy had a steady requirement for power microphones and associated equipment on board warships of all sizes and they were soon being installed in submarines, the Army needed huge numbers of 'Tank Emergency Crew Control, No.1' and 'Telephone, Loudspeaking No.2' sets, particularly the latter. These requirements resulted in the production of about 750,000 power microphones for the armed services.

The wartime use of Tannoy equipment was not confined to the armed services, for sound equipment played essential roles in civilian life. The 'Collapsible Calamity' has already been mentioned although very few of these were, in fact, used by the authorities for which they were intended. However, a little appreciated fact is that literally thousands of public address amplifiers were installed in factories throughout the British Isles and although there were other companies supplying similar systems, Tannoy secured at least their fair share of this business, perhaps more than a fair share. The *B.B.C.* 'Forces Programme' provided almost continuous light music for the entertainment of any troops within its reception area and its availability was taken up by thousands of factories, most of them producing munitions and essential war equipment, and broadcast throughout the production areas over their public address systems. The *B.B.C.* programme, 'Music While You Work', sometimes referred to – tongue-in-cheek – as 'Music While You Shirk', was a firm favourite which was broadcast twice daily from 23rd. June, 1940 and more than 8,000 factories, with more than 4 million workers, relayed the daily programme over their public address systems and, among the Tannoy employees, these factory installations were known as 'Music-While-You-Work' systems. As an indication of the importance of these programmes, one factory manager reported that there was a 20% fall in output when their public address system was out of action for a week. Another favourite was 'Workers' Playtime', hosted by Wilfred Pickles and with Violet Carson, who later played the part of Ena Sharples in the early Coronation Street programmes, at the piano. This was broadcast daily at lunchtime from factory canteens. However, Tannoy's involvement with factory public address schemes was not entirely a wartime phenomenon, many Tannoy systems had been installed in factories before the war, notably in clothing factories.

These Tannoy installations also offered emergency speech broadcasting cover to many industries in which workers could be stood down and sent to the shelters during air raids, thus minimising the danger to operatives. In some cases a single building with a suitable high point, notably the *Gillette* factory on London's Great West Road, was used to carry out surveillance of the surrounding buildings from whence warnings could be immediately passed to nearby production plants, if they had the good fortune also to be equipped with Tannoy public address, by means of tie lines. Such was the workers' faith in these systems that on one occasion when the power failed in a factory due to a V1 attack, the workers stayed in their air-raid shelters refusing to return to work, 'Until the Tannoy told them to'. During the V1 attacks the Tannoy emergency public address systems were an essential form of personnel safety. These emergency public address systems continue to the present day and are known as Voice Alarm Systems, for life safety support. (There is now a British Standard, BS 5839: Part 8, governing these systems which was written by a small team which included a former Tannoy employee, Dennis Terrett).

Many of the factories which were equipped with Tannoy public address systems were in the North of England or in Scotland, particularly in the west of these regions, so the company opened an office in Glasgow which was managed by a gentleman called Solly Gold.

Very soon after the start of the war all the workers, and the managers, were told by Guy to acquire bicycles and he also bought one because he reckoned that the factory was within cycling distance of Lancaster Avenue. He used his for about a week and then gave it up and it is not too difficult to imagine how the others felt. However, in due course, those who were regarded as needing the use of a car in view of the essential nature of most of Tannoy's equipment received petrol rations. In most cases these rations were quite substantial.

In 1942 there was the famous 'Wings for Victory' Campaign which was intended to encourage the civilian population of the country to give money

The TANNOY Story

towards the cost of building the huge number of bomber aircraft which were so badly needed to sustain the essential work of Bomber Command. A feature of this campaign was the placing of a *Short Stirling* bomber on a London bomb site and, of course, public address equipment was also required there. This was, of course, supplied by Tannoy.

During the second world war Tannoy gained control over a company called *Bex Electric Ltd*. The original company had been called *Lester Clarke Garages* and operated in Park View Road, Bexleyheath and, at the time of writing, 2002, the garage is still there, now an Alfa Romeo dealer. Livingstone once said that he considered Lester Clarke to be one of the most miserable men that he had ever met, though he admitted that Clarke was no fool. The motor trade was, of course, almost defunct during the war but in about 1942 there were two people working there re-winding starter motors and car dynamos. In about 1943 Frank Wheeler had joined up with Clarke and together with a man called Twentyman they had set up Bex Electric in Lester Clarke's garage premises. It has been said that Clarke contributed little to this arrangement but among his contacts was an employee of the local *London Transport* trolleybus workshops with whom he negotiated a lucrative contract to re-wind trolleybus motors which occasionally failed. Instead of replacing them with new motors, it became necessary to rewind them and Clarke had secured a contract to do this work, but he very soon ran into the problem of insufficient business.

When it became a part of Wheeler's company, *Bex Electric* started to grow, but not too quickly and Frank Wheeler soon came to the conclusion that it was not the fortune-maker that he had hoped it would be. However, they had managed to win a contract to make small electric motors for aircraft cameras, about 500 per month, which was quite useful, but no great deal. Guy Fountain, by then a quite well-established friend of Frank Wheeler whose company was, of course, doing a tremendous amount of installation work for Tannoy on the R.A.F. airfield contracts, was interested in this business and he had one really enormous advantage which stood him in very good stead; Tannoy had full approval for A.I.D., inspection and release (Air Inspection Department). Two men in Tannoy were authorised to approve goods and sign the release notes; Livingstone and a man called MacIntosh and, on the brown copy of the release note, the company would be paid. This was a very potent arrangement and it was decided that with the clearance authority which would result from being a wholly owned subsidiary of Tannoy, the process of clearance and approval of these motors, plus some pump motors for aircraft hydraulic systems, would be somewhat simplified. So Wheeler agreed to the acquisition of *Bex Electric* by Tannoy, following which there was a Board meeting. Bill Haines, unexpectedly, was asked to attend and he went to Bexleyheath with Guy

Fountain and, equally unexpectedly, he was elected to the Bex Electric Board as Production Director. Haines was allocated one share in the company but he never received anything for it when Bex was liquidated.[1]

So Livingstone was sent to *Bex Electric* to inject the A.I.D. approval into the company and another Tannoy engineer, Claude Yates, who was a great friend of Bill Haines, was put there as the factory Manager. Claude Yates had been taken on by Haines in 1939 without much experience – having previously worked for his family firm of Estate Agents – and he had been put on drilling holes in amplifier chassis. Claude used to do a lot of motorcycle scrambling on 750cc bikes and he took part in similar events in Austin Sevens – the '750 Club', a motor club almost exclusively for Austin Seven cars, still competes each year at Hawkhurst for a cup which was donated by him. After a few weeks of drilling he approached Haines and asked, "Mr. Haines, do you think I could sub-let some of these holes?"– a question which caused some amusement. Haines' response was to put him in charge of the drilling machines, later the presses, until he became a sort of general factotum, rising steadily until he became the Factory Manager at *Bex Electric*. Livingstone made the point that Claude Yates was an extremely nice person but he was not naturally good at running things (Stan recalled that, not unnaturally, he usually had his eye on the prettiest girls in the factory).

When Livingstone and Yates were sent to *Bex Electric*, Guy made it clear to them that Twentyman was not well liked by him and there was a loose understanding that his life was to be made difficult in the hope that he would leave. In the event, he was soon given his notice and dismissed, probably by Guy, but not before they had enjoyed a bit of fun at his expense. A week or two before he left, Norman Robottom, Claude Yates and a couple of others were discussing the matter outside the workshop one evening and, as Claude Yates put it, 'I drew the short straw'. Claude was commissioned to find a suitable sized potato and push it up the exhaust pipe of Twentyman's car, this being a favourite prank of many schoolboys at the time. The result was that either the car would not start or, if it did, the chunk of potato would be shot from the exhaust pipe with a very loud bang as the pent-up exhaust gases were released. The next morning the four of them were lined up against a wall, opposite the desk in Twentyman's office. He kept them there for more than half an hour in a vain attempt to extract a confession to the foul deed, but none of them ever let him know who had done the dirty work with the potato.

Bex Electric soon secured a lot more contracts with the Ministry of Aircraft Production to make various electric motors for aircraft and this was very successful business, making 2,000 motors per week at one time which was quite

The TANNOY Story

an achievement for what had been just a little garage in Bexleyheath.
George Wheeler, always had an eye to the main chance and he focussed his eye on *Bex Electric*. George's relationship with Guy was deteriorating so he had the bright idea of installing his father as General Manager at *Bex Electric*. George Wheeler's father had been a Government inspector at Woolwich Arsenal during the Great War and he was very knowledgeable about the manufacture of many things to do with armaments. He was also a very good mechanical engineer and he virtually ran the business, notwithstanding the fact that Yates was still there, although Yates eventually returned to Tannoy as Bill Haines' assistant. So Livingstone looked after the A.I.D. inspection with George Wheeler's father in overall control. The inspection was not entirely the responsibility of Stan Livingstone for a Ministry Inspector would make frequent visits to the workshop to check that correct procedures were being applied. Now in the manufacture of motors it was, of course, necessary to grind the ends of the shafts so that the bearings would fit accurately and Livingstone recalled that 'Old man Wheeler' could pick up a motor shaft and look at it and say, "You'll never get the bearing on that, Stan," and he was right; and it would only have been 2 thou oversize!

A big problem which they experienced was that the motor bearings were a push fit on the shaft and if the shaft was right all was well. The bearings were also a push fit into the housing in the motor casing and these motor casings were zinc-aluminium die castings. However, in the early stages of production nobody had thought too deeply about the performance of die-castings at 20,000 feet and, of course, they used to contract and expand over the very wide range of temperatures experienced in aircraft at such altitudes and two things used to happen. Firstly, the motor casings would contract enough to impede the function of the bearing, and secondly, when they returned to ground level and they were sent for testing, the motor casings would expand again in the nice, warm workshop and the bearings would fall out! This led to the development of high stability, aluminium alloy die-castings with a very low coefficient of expansion which the small electric motor industry now depends on. It became possible, for example, to make a carburettor with tiny holes for its needle jets which would remain the same size at 20,000 ft and well below freezing point as they were when the engine was running at its normal temperature on the ground.

At that time there was an enormous push to build more aircraft and, to make aircraft production simpler and to diversify production, pre-fabricated wiring looms had been introduced in which large looms of cables and junction boxes were made which could be fitted into the aircraft quite easily and plugged together and, if everything had been done right, it all worked. Now

Mr. TANNOY ON ACTIVE SERVICE!

June 6th, 1944—the supreme test!—thousands of TANNOY LOUD SPEAKERS went into action! With our land, naval and air forces, Tannoy Sound Systems were actively engaged in transmitting orders and instructions of vital importance.

As on D-Day, so on all the D-Days Plus—TANNOY SOUND SYSTEMS continue to give vital support to our victorious forces.

Where reliability and efficiency mean so much, the name is "TANNOY."

TANNOY
THE SOUND PEOPLE
GUY R. FOUNTAIN LTD.

"TANNOY"
is the registered trade mark of equipment manufactured by
GUY R. FOUNTAIN LTD.
Canterbury Grove, S.E.27
and Branches.
Phone : GIPsy Hill 1131

the cable looms could be made easily enough but not the junction boxes so Clarke secured for *Bex Electric* a contract not only to make the boxes but also to fabricate the wiring looms and they made vast numbers of these for aircraft such as the Avro Lancaster and the Short Stirling. This added substantially to the existing business of manufacturing 2,000 electric motors but it was entirely dependent on defence contracts.

Having secured control of *Bex Electric* Guy Fountain utilised the compnany for a short time after the war (until *Bex Electric* ceased trading) in the manufacture of rotary converters for Tannoy battery amplifiers and, using his contacts among travelling showmen, in the manufacture of electric motors for dodgem cars. Another company with which Guy became closely associated with was the *Static Condenser Company* of Wokingham.

In about 1943 a young lady called Joan joined Tannoy, having worked on the perfume counter at *Boots* in Oxford Street. She had been drafted into war work, as so many girls were, and was originally sent to the *Mullard* factory at Mitcham. However, this was difficult for her due to the long journey to and from work and she requested a transfer – she was moved to Tannoy.

Joan was probably the first person to make voice coils without formers and this came about because Tannoy were then making good quality moving coil microphones and Jack Houlgate felt that these would be even better if the weight of the moving parts could be reduced by eliminating the former for the coil. He set Joan to winding single layer coils with no former held together by "Durofix and Good Luck" and stuck onto a cellulose acetate diaphragm (also with Durofix). Joan was very, very patient and she had the necessary dexterity to make these tiny, delicate coils – a job to which she was well suited. They and the moving coil microphone to which they were fitted were a great success but, perhaps equally importantly, she later became Mrs. Livingstone.

Another wartime project which did not achieve a great amount of fame because it was, like so much wartime manufacturing, surrounded in secrecy, came as the result of an enquiry from the Royal Navy. One day during the war the company Receptionist telephoned George Wheeler to say that a Naval Officer had arrived and was asking to see someone in authority. When he was brought to George Wheeler's office he said, "We have a problem but this is all *Strictly Confidential*. The Germans are laying acoustic mines in the English Channel, near Portsmouth, which are triggered by the sound of ships' propellers. Can you make us a very powerful amplifier with a loudspeaker which we can fit under water to trigger these mines from a safe distance?" George replied that he did not really know whether they could or not, "But", he said, "why not try hitting the hull with a bloody great

The TANNOY Story

hammer?" After some discussion of the problem the Officer said that he was then going to the Admiralty and he would arrange for them to issue a contract to Tannoy to develop an underwater loudspeaker to trigger acoustic mines. Within hours, Tannoy received a visit from a number of Naval Security Officers because the Officer who had visited them previously had travelled from Portsmouth and had walked into the factory and discussed acoustic mines without reference to the Admiralty at a time when the Navy needed to keep their knowledge of the existence of these mines entirely secret. They vetted the whole factory, with a fine-tooth comb. However, they issued a small contract and Jack Houlgate, with George Wheeler, devised a filter circuit which operated from 2Hz to 200Hz and that seemed to help them although the results of their work was never communicated to them. Bearing in mind the secrecy which surrounded this project it is hardly surprising that no more than this is known about it even today.

Tannoy grew big during the war but it did so as so many companies did, almost exclusively on defence contract work; work which the company would not have been in a position to accept without the stability which its pre-war backers had brought. This stability enabled the company to channel substantial resources into the production of the power microphone and carry out the costly public address installations in the Battle of Britain airfields literally at a moment's notice. An indication of the inevitable growth of the company on the backs of these war-time contracts is illustrated by the fact that in 1939 the company had about 35 or 40 employees, a figure which grew to over 500 by 1944.

As has been recorded earlier, *Carrington Manufacturing* made the cabinets for Tannoy before the war. They made particularly fine, elegant cabinets for radiograms which sold well and, of course, the aesthetically pleasing cabinets for the special radiograms which were made for hospitals and schools must not be overlooked. When the R.A.F. public address systems and similar wartime contracts made demands on Tannoy for such large numbers of loudspeakers, *Camco* tried to make the required cabinets, most of which were grey boxes with the Tannoy fret. They also tried to make the very rugged boxes for the 'Telephone, loudspeaking No. 2' but these were hardly their style, nor had they ever been set up for mass production, having neither the necessary facilities nor the capacity. It was quality in which they excelled, not quantity.

However, Guy knew a man called Freddy Edwards who had made cabinets for the *Defiant* radios and radiograms for the *Co-operative* movement. *Defiant* came about as the result of the Radio Manufacturers' Association's interpretation of the *Co-op*'s dividend as discounting and, as the R.M.A. would not countenance discounting by its members, no radio manufacturer who was a member of the R.M.A. was permitted to supply their radios to the *Co-op*. But some manufacturers, including *Plessey*, decided to provide the radios for the *Co-op* by introducing a new range with a new name, specifically for the Co-operative movement and, as an act of defiance to the R.M.A., they called these sets 'Defiant' and F.W. *Edwards & Co.* were contracted to make the cabinets for them.

Now Freddy Edwards and his brother were able to cope with mass production and took over from *Camco* as Tannoy's loudspeaker cabinet maker, making some 400 or 500 R.A.F. loudspeaker cabinets for public address systems each month, plus the cabinets for the 'Telephone Loudspeaking No. 2' sets, in lots of 5,000. Initially Edwards used to make the cabinets and send them to Tannoy for the loudspeakers to be fitted but later it was found to be easier to send the loudspeakers to Clerkenwell and get Freddy Edwards and a couple of girls to fit them into the cabinets. Livingstone and McIntosh used to go to Clerkenwell each week and do all the testing and inspecting there, put the A.I.D. stamp on everything so everybody got paid, and despatch the loudspeakers straight to their destinations. Incidentally, although they were never actually corrupted by this somewhat doubtful procedure, Freddy Edwards, through means best known to himself, kept MacIntosh and Livingstone well supplied with butter throughout the war (butter was rationed to 2 oz. per person per week).

During the war there was a fair amount of behind-the-scenes activity and, for example, authorities devoted huge resources of both time and money to eliminate black market trading. Nobody ever knew exactly what was going on within Tannoy, and it was certainly nothing approaching black market trading in severity, but it is thought that Guy had something of a fiddle going with Freddy Edwards because Edwards used to visit Tannoy every Friday and he and Guy used to disappear into the toilet, it was believed to hand over cash. Eventually the whole works came to know about it, not least because Freddy Edwards, rather indiscreetly, talked about it. George Wheeler confirmed that there was an awful lot of fiddling going on with suppliers etc. and this was common to many industries at the time.

Now Edwards had a man working for him called Timms but he left because, he claimed, Freddy Edwards was such an impossible man to work for. Timms said that he was often inebriated and even when he was sober he was pretty difficult. Strangely enough Freddy's brother was quite charming and it was often joked that there must have been, somewhere, a charming milkman. Freddy had the reputation of being uncouth and it was said that he was sometimes so drunk that he was virtually incapable of running his business properly. So Timms left and started his own cabinet works called *Lockwood & Co.* and he managed to

The TANNOY Story

cream off some of the Tannoy loudspeaker cabinet work from Edwards. In fact Tannoy business represented too large a share of his production and for this he eventually suffered when, some years later, Tannoy went into temporary Receivership.

Just before the end of the war, in late 1944, the shares owned by the *Banque Belge pour l'Etranger* were transferred to Guy Fountain who then owned all but one of the company's shares.

CHAPTER NOTES

1   The pump motors referred to were almost certainly feathering pump motors for feathering the propeller of a failed engine.

"OVER THE TANNOY!"

The vast number of TANNOY SOUND SYSTEMS used by the Fighting Services bear eloquent testimony to the quality of this famous sound equipment.

By virtue of their indefatigable war service, their proved reliability and efficiency, TANNOY SOUND SYSTEMS are destined to play a large part in the reconstruction to come.

TANNOY, the SOUND Service, means:—

- (1) Choice of an extensive range of equipment;
- (2) Advisory Service on acoustic problems;
- (3) After-Sales Service second-to-none.
- (4) Rental Schemes and Hire-Maintenance to suit all.

"TANNOY" is the registered trade mark of equipment manufactured by
GUY R. FOUNTAIN, LTD.
West Norwood, S.E.27, and Branches.
Phone: Gipsy Hill 1131

TANNOY
"THE SOUND PEOPLE"
GUY R. FOUNTAIN, LTD.

THE LARGEST ORGANISATION IN GREAT BRITAIN SPECIALISING SOLELY IN SOUND EQUIPMENT

CHAPTER NINE

THE RABBIT WARREN

From a reasonably tidy, ordered start when the purpose built factory was opened in 1934, Guy embarked on a series of necessary expansions in which, in addition to extending the factory both vertically and horizontally, he acquired various other properties in and around Canterbury Grove until the production area became fragmented and somewhat disorganised. Inevitably, this became known as 'The Rabbit Warren'. Guy had several opportunities to redevelop the various sites and he often talked about it but he never actually took the plunge; it seems that he enjoyed his little rabbit warren of buildings, gradually acquiring properties over the years, some of which were purchased by the company, some by the family and some leased.

Lansdowne Hill is a turning west off Norwood Road, very near to the point at which Norwood Road ends and becomes Knight's Hill. About 50 yards up Lansdowne Hill there is a fork junction at which Canterbury Grove branches off to the left. Canterbury Grove is divided by a railway line which crosses it rather less than 100 yards up the hill and only a footbridge joins the road to its remaining half-mile or so. The original 1933 factory was a single storey building on the south side of Canterbury Grove but this was extended upwards in 1935-36 with the addition of a first floor on the front part only. There were four little cottages beyond the factory, between it and the railway, and these were bought by Guy Fountain but it was not until 1940-41 that two of these cottages were demolished and the factory was extended horizontally with a front which matched the original factory.

Before much of this took place, during the mid 1930s, it became necessary to expand the business and several nearby properties were acquired when they became available. Just after Norwood Road runs south into Knight's Hill, opposite St. Luke's Church, is a small back street called Nettlefold Place, a rectangular crescent, if this is not too much of a contradiction, with two entrances from Knight's Hill. In the early 1930s some workshops were purchased on the south side of the southern access to make a winding shop for coils and transformers following the break with the *Keston Manufacturing Company*. In later years this was converted into a new machine shop, a spray shop and a metal store and the machine shop was equipped with belt driven machines powered by an overhead shaft. These premises, which looked like a rather tatty old car repair workshop, were hidden behind corrugated iron gates and the spray shop was a ramshackle, lean-to shed which was so small that when it was necessary to paint racks, which were only 64" high, they had to wait for good weather so they could be sprayed outside. This cannot have been a very satisfactory arrangement for, to complicate matters, the finished goods from these workshops had to be carried from there, along Norwood Road and up Canterbury Grove to the factory for assembly.

On the west side of Norwood Road, to the north of its junction with Lansdowne Hill, No. 348, on the corner of Waylett Place[1], was one of three shops together with Nos. 350 and 352, which were leased by Tannoy. These had been built by a Bert Truscott, whose family Fountain had known for some years, who had intended using the first floor as a sweet factory and the ground floor as a supermarket but, due to the war, he never achieved this. Tannoy leased these premises from Truscott in June or July, 1939 at a rent of £400 p.a. and moved into the first floor in August, preferring not to take the ground floor as it had no natural light It is said that Truscott never forgave Bill Haines for this deal because he was persuaded to grant Tannoy a ten year lease. Within a month or so, war was declared and the machinery was moved from Nettlefold Place into these premises which, although they were not actually in Waylett Place, were always referrred to within the company as 'Waylett Place'. When the machines were being installed Bill Haines was on holiday in Great Yarmouth, having left full instructions regarding the installation including the specification for the main driving belt which was to be 6" wide. While he was away he received a phone call from Guy moaning about the expense of a 6" belt and arguing that they should make do with a 4" belt instead. Having done all the calculations, including the heavy load of the spinning lathe for forming loudspeaker horns, which was operated by a man called Bert Major, he was

The TANNOY Story

sure a 6" belt was needed, but Guy insisted on buying a 4" belt. In the event, the 4" belt would not drive all the machinery so Haines had to replace it with a 6" belt when he came back from his holiday.

Soon after Tannoy moved into 'Waylett Place', (No. 348 to 352 Norwood Road), Lambeth Borough Council took over the front part of the ground floor, partitioned it into cubicles, and used it as an air raid shelter. At about the same time when, as Livingstone so aptly put it, the Norwegian Government 'saw the writing in the snow', the back of the ground floor of Nos. 348 to 352 was taken over and allocated to the Royal Norwegian Navy as a supply depot. However, during an air raid one night, an incendiary bomb came through the roof of Waylett Place, finishing on the ground floor, convincing the Council that these premises were not ideally suitable for use as a shelter, so they vacated them. Tannoy returned to the front part of these premises although the Norwegian Navy Suppliers continued to operate their supply depot throughout the war from the back part.

A few yards up Lansdowne Hill there is a very narrow right of way to the right (the north) called Sydenham Place, which gives access to the backs of the Norwood Road properties and just beyond this there is another opening which led to a long row of garages. These garages were owned by a Mr. Cox and had originally been built in the 19th century as stables for the horse-drawn trams. Tannoy rented these garages but eventually acquired them from 'Old man Cox', as he was known and thereafter this area was referred to as 'Cox's Yard'. This was used during the war as an extension to the factory and it included the spray shop, moved from Nettlefold Place, and stores.

In March, 1944, in what is believed to have been the last raid on London by piloted aircraft before the V1 attacks began, some explosive incendiary bombs fell on the area, including Cox's Yard which was completely destroyed by fire and one of Tannoy's more devoted employees, Tom Thumbwood, a paint sprayer, was in the premises at the time. The story is that he saw the bomb come into the building and went to extinguish it with a sand bag but, as he did so, it exploded. Miraculously, his injuries were only slight. However, as Tannoy's work was deemed to be of national importance, authority was quickly granted for Cox's Yard to be reconstructed as a purpose built machine shop and for Waylett Place to be repaired. When this work was finished there was a celebration party in the front offices, predictably called 'The Phoenix Party', on 24th March, 1945 at which, it was said, some 'home truths' came out; 'home truths' about Guy Fountain and the opinions of his staff about him.

In the fork of the junction of Canterbury Grove and Lansdowne Hill, almost opposite the main factory, there was a very old triangular house which accommodated a café which, in the years before Tannoy had its own canteen, was run by Mrs. Russell and Mrs. Albert and this serviced the personnel with sandwiches, snacks, teas and coffees. When this building was vacated Tannoy took it over and used it for storage but this became rather exciting because for some reason it was filled from the top downwards. Being a very old, creaky building, originally a house of three or four storeys, by the time the top two floors were full, the building was found to be unsafe, with bulging walls, so it had to be shored up. Tannoy kept this for some time and when it was eventually vacated it was popularly supposed that it did not have to be demolished, it just fell down. The site was never redeveloped and is now, in 2002, used by street traders as storage space.

Alongside Nos. 348 to 352 Norwood Road was one end of the little crescent[2] which is, in fact, Waylett Place and Guy bought a row of cottages along the back of this crescent. Their fronts faced the backs of the Norwood Road shops and their rear elevations adjoined the 'Cox's Yard' premises. He renovated them very basically and let them, but they were eventually condemned and demolished and the land became a car park which still, in 2002, remains.

Between the northern entrance to Nettlefold Place and Canterbury Grove, and behind the main factory, is another little back street called Bloom Grove. From an unimpressive start, Bloom Grove divides into two short roads forming a fork with large, semi-detached Victorian houses on each side and with a triangular area of grass between; the further boundary being the railway line. The company acquired two of these houses, it is believed they were the second pair on the right hand side, Nos. 16 and 18, which had tiny gardens backing onto the rear of the main factory. Tannoy was quite good at knocking holes in walls and they knocked one in the back of the factory creating an access to these two houses in Bloom Grove, with a covered way through one of the little gardens. The ground floor was made into a canteen where some really excellent fare was provided by Miss Edie Davis and the upper floors became the accounts department where the accountant, Jack Hudson reigned and Stan Livingstone recalled that he was often referred to as, 'The terrible Mr. Hudson who is not counting the money!' The accounts department was virtually sealed off from the rest of the company and it was said that one needed a passport to go there. He was a very large man, quite likeable but rather roguish and, in common with his employer, he was said to be quite well acquainted with the gin bottle. Hudson later became a director and the company secretary.

When, soon after the war, the company acquired more vehicles it was decided to employ a motor mechanic by the name of Marshall and create a garage. This was done by adapting a small building which was in Canterbury Grove, near to the electricity sub-station and adjoining the eastern side of the main fac-

The TANNOY Story

tory. The purpose of this was to achieve a worthwhile economy by maintaining all the company vehicles and it was also decided to create the 'Tannoy Motor Company' although this was only on a letter heading, to obtain trade discounts on vehicle parts. The fact that a mechanic was employed by Tannoy also made it much easier for Guy to do some of his little fiddles; especially if they entailed work being done on his car or, for that matter, on any of his many diversions such as his experiments with a jet-powered boat or his 'Chris-Craft' speedboat.

Just after the war when the Norwegian Navy vacated the ground floor of Nos. 348 to 352, Norwood Road, Tannoy acquired other shops in Norwood Road, No. 356 and the upper floor of No. 358. No. 356 was owned by United Dairies but it was let to Barkers for restoring old furniture. Tannoy leased this from Barkers but, in 1953, Michael Fountain bought the freehold from United Dairies, a condition of the purchase being that it should not be used as a dairy. At the time of writing, January, 2002, Michael still owns this freehold and this condition still stands. Tannoy Marine was located in No. 356 with a cabinet workshop behind it and with the laboratory above. Then Tannoy took the the upper floor of the adjacent dry cleaner's shop, *Achille Serre*, knocked a hole through the party wall and extended the laboratory in there.

Tannoy still occupied these buildings, including the re-built Cox's Yard, when, in 1947, the company went into receivership. Almost the first action of Norman Wild, the Receiver, of whom more is recorded in Chapter Eleven, was to vacate the main Canterbury Grove factory and let the premises to *Cossor Radar*. Cox's Yard was let to a Mr. Victor Cianferani who established his company, *Marcantonio Ice Cream* there, using it as his factory and using the corner shop, No 348 Norwood Road, as one of his retail outlets. Later, Tannoy was able to re-use this corner shop as a Hi-fi showroom and reception area but there was a condition in the lease which required the front to present the appearance of a shop so Tannoy had to have a curtained display window with photographs. From the reception area there were stairs to the first floor where there were offices in the front and the machine shop, assembly area and the test department behind. On the second floor, under a mansard roof, was the drawing office, the allocations office and the purchasing office.

Norman Wild then reduced the company to its 'core business', that is to say, public address equipment, and he abandoned the many little side lines which had been allowed to evolve. The cabinet department became necessary because Norman Wild was moving Tannoy into the growing high fidelity market for which they required good cabinets. This was supervised by a Mr. Cullis but there was also a wonderful man called Frank Venables, who is said to have always had a 'dewdrop' on the end of his nose and to have smelled of wintergreen, but he was an excellent cabinet maker as well as being an accomplished violinist. Frank Venables who had been with the company for a long time had, over the years, made up many of the experimental designs, particularly those of loudspeaker cabinets.

When the company started making progress under the Receiver more machinery had to be acquired so that by about 1955 the machine shops occupied the whole of the ground floor of the Nos 348 to 352 Norwood Road.

Tannoy had bought the houses in Bloom Grove with the intention of developing the whole site but Guy was quite content to leave things as they were. He was not over ambitious; not a waster with money and if the business provided him with the kind of luxuries he wanted he did not seem to care whether the company became any bigger or not; he was always reluctant to take any major step unless it seemed to him that its success was an absolute certainty. In later years there was much talk of the possibility of the redevelopment of adjoining freeholds which they had acquired; grand plans were prepared and talked of in grand ways but Guy never had the courage to go through with them and he let the matter drag on and on until the company was no longer in a strong enough financial position to proceed with them and Tannoy continued to be a rabbit warren of adjoining properties with all the attendant inefficiencies. Had Guy felt secure enough to proceed with these developments, the resulting expansion would have resulted in a much larger international company but it seemed that he did not feel that he could adequately handle such a situation: he seemed to enjoy having total power over a moderately sized company rather than having slightly less power over something which might outgrow him and overtake him.

A house in nearby Rosendale Road, West Dulwich, was also acquired and used for additional stores due to a shortage of storage space in the main factory. Numerous items were kept there and it was always necessary to wait for a van to collect all the items which had been requisitioned for the day or, if anything was urgent, someone had to make a brisk walk to collect what was needed. On one occasion, Dennis Terrett was sent there to collect a small prototype loudspeaker cabinet that Frank Venables had made in the small cabinet workshop which had been established there. The sight that greeted Dennis was of Frank, knee deep in wood shavings, putting the finishing touches to a mahogany toilet seat for Guy Fountain!

Because it did not grow, it ran into problems because a business such as Tannoy has to expand; there has to be room for people in the company to progress further up the ladder, which there was not, and so they kept crossing swords with Guy and probably stayed with him only because they had had their confidence in their own abilities destroyed by him. Ronnie Rackham was a typical example of this in spite of the fact that he was acknowledged to be a brilliant engineer in the field of electro-acoustics and the country's second most competant engineer in this field after Jack Houlgate, from whom he learned the greater part of his knowledge.

Grandiose plans were drawn up to re-develop Canterbury Grove in anticipation of greater sales and higher levels of production and, by the 1960s, Tannoy had certainly become the leading audio company in the U.K. and was very well regarded world wide. If at that time there had been sensible expansion, and an adequate career structure offering scope for advancement, the company could have attracted young engineers who would have stayed and who would have carried the technology forward. Tannoy would then have become a major company or part of a major group if, of course, the Fountain family had wanted to sell their interests in the company, albeit at their price. Among those who decided to leave the company soon after the war was Jack Houlgate and this was probably the greatest loss of all to Tannoy. He joined the *B.B.C. Engineering Research Department* where he carried out further research into sound recording and reproduction and worked on the *B.B.C.* fine-groove recording system which was an interim between the standard 78 r.p.m. groove and the microgroove which became the standard for long playing records. He is believed to have been teased by personnel at the *B.B.C.* regarding his background in Tannoy who referred to Tannoy equipment as 'All high and no Fi', or 'High output, low Fidelity'. These taunts, of course, were spitefully inaccurate for Houlgate had helped Tannoy lead the field in high fidelity sound reproduction equipment (see Chapter 14).

There came a point, soon after the war, when a South African Company, *Proctor*, wanted to manufacture Tannoy equipment under licence because of the severe restrictions on what could be imported into the country but Guy thought that they would not maintain the standards and quality which, he felt, only Tannoy could provide. He lost this, and several other opportunities, of allowing overseas manufacture under licence because he felt that the situation could get out of hand, out of his control, and he would lose the advantage. He was over cautious in this respect and this prevented a great deal of potential coming to fruition. This attitude and these actions frustrated many people in the company with great ability and the weaker ones succombed to his power and remained with him; others who had the courage to leave did so, and fared well.

In the early 1950s, *Cossor Radar* moved out of the Canterbury Grove factory and Tannoy moved back in. In these premises there were the cabinet workshops, supervised by Fred Cullis, and a large hire department with much of its work devoted to sound reinforcement schemes and multi-lingual interpretation equipment. The site was visited by the author on several

The Rabbit Warren

occasions, particularly in October, 2000. By this time the original factory, although still in use, had all its windows boarded up and its front wall liberally adorned with the most appalling graffiti; it was a very sorry sight. However, the line on which the building was extended towards the railway line is still clearly visible from which it would seem that not too much attention was paid to bonding. There is also a slight difference in level between the original factory and the matching extension towards the railway with a resulting step in the roof levels. To the east of the factory where the electricity sub-station had been, tolerably presentable workshops and offices have been built and these were in use by a building company. The triangular site where the cafe and later the rather unsafe stores were situated was a fenced yard which was used for storage and unpacking by the Norwood Road street traders. Nos 348, 350 and 352, Norwood Road, 'Waylett Place' were occupied by *Iceland* with a snooker club above. In Waylett Place itself the site of Guy's old cottages which were often referred to by company personnel as 'Vermin Villas', was still in use as a car park.

Sydenham Place has a narrow entrance from Lansdowne Hill and gives access to the backs of the shops in Norwood Road. It is a very untidy place and one building is occupied by a trader, Tom Draddy, who deals in secondhand books. He is a keen local historian and has taken an interest in the history of the site and learned that it was, in the 17th century, a farmhouse. No building could possibly look less like a farmhouse than the present buildings, nor could its land look less like a farm. Nettlefold Place still contains only commercial premises and Tannoy's old workshops still look very tatty and are in use for car repairs. The pair of houses in Bloom Grove, once the accounts department and the canteen, have reverted to dwellings although, predictably, now divided into several flats and looking much the worse for wear.

The Thurlow Arms, the pub in Norwood Road opposite Lansdowne Hill where the first purpose made Tannoy amplifier was installed in 1929, has enjoyed a rather chequered history. It was named after Edward, Lord Thurlow, 1730 - 1806, at one time Lord Chancellor of England. When visited by the author in the mid 1990s it was a very dirty, very shabby and very run-down public house but there were plans to refurbish it. This was done but since then, to the shame of the local authority for permitting this, it has been re-named twice, the second time being in November, 1999, since when it has been 'Jack Stamps'.

Incidentally, further north along Norwood Road and on its eastern side, was an open piece of land with a very old house, Serbia House, where Sir Hiram Maxim once lived and it was there that he designed a fairground ride with very large airships or zeppelins going round which was used at the Crystal Palace.

The TANNOY Story

The house was used to accommodate Serbian refugees during the Great War, hence its name. He also tested his Maxim machine gun on a bit of spare land there. This house fell into disrepair but to the left of it was an old building like a two-storey garage and at one time the Tannoy hire department was located there, run by Jim Whiting with Jefferies as his assistant. This building was always referred to as 'The Tram Depot' although it was not, in fact, on the site of the tram depot; that was next to it. The tram depot became a furniture depository and is believed to be still in use as such. It must also be remembered that the accounts department and the manufacture of power microphones was moved to the safety of Minnickfold during the war and that the power microphone plant was later established in Dorking.

From the above, it should be abundantly clear that Tannoy, under Guy Fountain's leadership, developed into a badly fragmented, somewhat disorganised conglomeration of little workshops and offices and it is little wonder that *Plessey*'s Chief of Testing, Webb, made his comment to Stan Livingstone which is recounted in Chapter 7, that he would leave *Plessey* if he had to work in similar conditions. By the same token, it is surprising, very surprising, that Tannoy progressed so well and became such a market leader in the field of sound engineering – but it did.

CHAPTER NOTES

1   Originally called Thomas Place and it was here that John Weller started making his *Weller* cars, later to become *AC Cars*.

2   Another 'rectangular' crescent.

BUCKINGHAM PALACE

15th May, 1945.

Guy R. Fountain, Esq.,
Governing Director,
Messrs. Tannoy Products,
    Canterbury Grove,
    West Norwood, S.E. 27.

Dear Sir,

        The King desires me to convey His appreciation to you and the members of your staff for so kindly making the arrangements for the musical programmes which were relayed to the loud-speakers outside Buckingham Palace during the Victory celebrations.

        These programmes, as you know, were a great success and I would be grateful if you would kindly express His Majesty's thanks to all concerned.

        Yours faithfully,

P. Legh

        Master of the Household.

CHAPTER TEN

THE END OF THE BEGINNING

Like so many companies which enjoyed a near monopoly of essential war equipment, Tannoy prospered and grew during the war years but, of course, when hostilities ceased there was less need for this equipment and demand fell to a trickle in comparison with that of previous years. This was when the almost inevitable difficulties started, difficulties which were exacerbated by the fact that Tannoy had acquired a number of small companies such as *Bex Electric* and, as Guy was such a bad delegator, these acquisitions stretched his managerial capabilities to the point when he could no longer properly control his companies.

It was not only the demand for Tannoy equipment that ceased, even more importantly, there was a rapid decline in the payments. There was a brief period of grace when companies were supposed to sort themselves out but when Tannoy had worked out all the figures, they found that they owed money to their suppliers and that there was nothing left in the kitty to cover these debts. This was simply the result of very poor financial control and it left Tannoy in a precarious position. Then, for much the same reason, *Bex Electric* folded, but Clarke had maintained his interest in the property and when Tannoy moved out in about 1946, he started to get his first, very small allocations of new cars and he returned to the motor trade. Fifty five years later there was still a car sales business on the site.

So the first evidence of the end of the beginning for the Tannoy Company

The End Of The Beginning

became apparent quite soon after the war. This came as something of a surprise to some, probably even to Guy, who thought, perhaps dreamed, that everything in the garden was lovely following their undoubted success during the busy days of the war. However, the company was soon in trouble, largely because, in addition to the lack of formal control over finances, Guy was dictating company policy without reference to George Wheeler or to anyone else and the Purchasing Manager had been writing orders for equipment, at Guy's insistence, when there was no reserve of money to pay the suppliers. Another major problem arose as the result of a misjudgement with the two amplifiers on which they had set great store; two portable battery powered amplifiers, the AB.24/AC/60, (a 24 volts amplifier with 60 watts output) and the AB.12/AC/25, (a 12 volts amplifier giving 25 watts output). Neither of these generated any worthwhile sales.

Another major problem which arose immediately after the war was the inevitable shortage of materials and Livingstone recalls that the company was often unable to manufacture much of their basic equipment because of this. At these times, they had many workers literally idle but Guy preferred to keep them on, giving them all sorts of things to do and not caring too much if they occupied their time in knitting and crossword puzzles as long as they were there because, when materials became available, sometimes at short notice, their skills would be needed.

One commodity which was in very short supply after the war was paper and, in common with most industries, the company had great difficulty in producing brochures. The production of Tannoy's literature was operated rather informally, on a day-to-day basis by a man called Tom Cowling who prepared both the drawings and the text. He also drew the cartoons for the wartime and early post war advertisements. On one occasion he reached the stage at which he had prepared a brochure but it could not be printed because he could not find a local printing company with enough paper. Livingstone, very foolishly he subsequently admitted, saying that he would never have considered doing it in later years, contacted a friend who had a position of some standing in local politics and a big printing works. Livingstone asked his father to visit this company on behalf of Tannoy and he learned from them that they had just printed some instruction books for another company and had quite a large stock of surplus paper, so they were persuaded to print the catalogues. However, this was very near the time that Tannoy finally went into receivership and, in the event, the print company were never paid.

But in spite of the warning signals there was a great deal of euphoria among the company's executives who had enjoyed the sweet smell of success and, of course, they had been so immersed in the day-to-day problems of keeping pace

The TANNOY Story

with the war-time demand for Tannoy products that they had little time to worry about what might lie around the corner. Of course, they thought, there would be a demand in peacetime for public address equipment; showmen would get back on the road; more railway stations would need Tannoy systems; circuses would start again and new applications for Tannoy products would arise. However, the euphoria was somewhat enhanced, and looming problems were temporarily overshadowed, by an immediate requirement for a substantial amount of public address equipment for the Victory celebrations which were planned in many venues around the country, particularly, of course, in London. The first of these took place in front of Buckingham Palace and in The Mall in May, 1945, immediately after the declaration of Victory in Europe, 'V.E. Day'. Tannoy was the obvious choice to supply, install and operate all the necessary amplifiers, microphones and loudspeakers which were used for the announcements to the public and to relay music for entertainment throughout the celebrations: they did it, and they did it well. Michael Fountain, then in the army in Glasgow, joined in with that city's V.E. Daycelebrations and among many acts of joy and bravado which were enacted, he managed to get four men onto his Panther 250 cc. motorcycle, riding rather dangerously around George Square.

Following this parade Guy Fountain received a letter from the Master of the Household of Buckingham Palace, dated 15th May, expressing the appreciation of His Majesty King George VI to all those in the company who had worked so hard to contribute to the success of the event. This was the first time that public address amplifiers were used at Buckingham Palace and similar equipment was used in August to mark Victory over Japan, 'V.J. Day'. Soon after this Tannoy was awarded a contract to install public address and simultaneous interpretation equipment at the United Nations Headquarters in Paris.

But the greatest parade was the big Victory Parade through London which took place the following year, on 8th June, 1946, in which many thousands of the armed services took part together with representatives of the Civil Defence units, the Home Guard, the Air Raid Wardens, the Fire and Ambulance Services, the Women's Voluntary Service and the many reserved occupations such as the Women's Land Army, munitions workers, miners, doctors and nurses who had all played their vital parts in contributing to the eventual victories over Germany and Japan. Organising the parade through the streets of London was a huge operation and this, together with the need to inform and control the many thousands of spectators who flocked to London to watch the parade, required much planning and, inevitably, a great deal of public address equipment. The Victory parade was, of course, a great success and the Tannoy equipment which was used to such effect along the routes which included the

Strand, Trafalgar Square, Whitehall, Parliament Square, Birdcage Walk and the Mall, made a major contribution to this success. Michael Fountain, who had joined the company during the previous month, was stationed at the Palace of Westminster and he operated the equipment for that area which was situated inside the Victoria Tower.

Although there was a considerable drop in demand for the company's products, all was not lost for the relaxation of wartime restrictions and the immense feeling of relief which was felt throughout the country, led to a desire to participate in all sorts of entertainment which had been abandoned, or severely curtailed during hostilities. Dance halls re-opened, horse racing and dog racing flourished, sports events gained momentum and cinemas and theatres were crowded; many of these requiring amplifying equipment. Tannoy supplied many dance halls with good quality amplifiers and they equipped greyhound stadia, race tracks and speedway tracks with public address systems. Bertram Mills was back in business and another friend of Guy's, Billy Butlin, was expanding his famous holiday camps in which Tannoy had started installing public address equipment just before the war. These required high quality systems which Tannoy designed and installed, casting the net wider to encompass *Pontins* and *Warners* Holiday Camps as well. The systems which had been provided for the Victory Parade were subsequently adapted and used at a number of *Greyhound Racing Association* stadia to provide good quality music at a time when, as Livingstone so aptly put it, 'People sat and listened in an orderly manner between events instead of killing each other.'

Among the dance halls were the Hammersmith Palais, owned by Claude Langdon and with Lou Praeger's Band in residence, and the *Mecca Group*, which was founded by a Polish immigrant, Carl Hyman, with Alan Fairley. Guy met these gentlemen and contracted to hire Tannoy equipment to the Hammersmith Palais and to *Mecca* dance halls such as the Lyceum, the Café de Paris and the Streatham Locarno.

By this time Michael was working with Tannoy. He had left Dulwich College and volunteered for service in the Army as, by doing so, he would qualify for a University Short Course and he went on the last of these courses at Glasgow University. Having volunteered, he was enlisted at the age of 18, on 2nd April, 1945, and went to Glasgow on 9th April where he was attached to the Royal Artillery and did a six months University course which covered subjects such as engineering, surveying, etc. After this short university course, he then had to do his basic training of about 8 weeks, attached to the King's Royal Rifles at Bushfield Camp, near Winchester. From there he was posted to Bakewell, near Matlock, Derbyshire to await an O.C.T.U. course and it was

The TANNOY Story

while he was there, shortly before Christmas 1945, that he contracted pneumonia. He managed to get home for Christmas leave although he became more seriously ill while at home and his illness soon progressed to pleurisy with the result that he was admitted to the Middlesex Hospital, London. His condition deteriorated still further and he developed empyema which necessitated surgery to drain a lung. Medicine was not, of course, as advanced as it is now and he had to stay in the Middlesex Hospital for three months, being allowed out briefly to attend his sister Jeanne's wedding which had been delayed until March so that he stood a better chance of attending. He was then invalided out of the Army, being judged unfit for further training, and his father gave him the choice of going on to University or of joining Tannoy, he chose Tannoy and joined in May, 1946, just in time to play his part in Tannoy's contribution to the Victory Parade. Against considerable opposition from Guy, Jeanne married Squadron Leader Alan Campbell Shirreff, an R.A.F. fighter pilot who was, at about that time, the Captain of the R.A.F. cricket team. Michael's brother David also encountered fierce opposition from Guy when he chose to make the Evangelical Church his career. Guy was wrong on both scores for Jeanne's marriage and David's career were equally successful. Later in 1946 there was another very notable achievement for the company when the word 'Tannoy' first appeared in an English dictionary.

When Michael was taken into the business Guy insisted, quite rightly, that he should start at or near the bottom, so he started as a laboratory assistant, helping Jack Houlgate and Ronnie Rackham in the 'Pink Room'. This was part of the development laboratory and it was so named because it had been built as an experimental acoustic laboratory and lined throughout with perforated, sound-absorbing tiles which had been painted pink. Its central item of equipment was a crystal sound cell microphone which was used for calibrating other microphones, loudspeakers, pick-ups and other pieces of equipment. Under Houlgate, Michael was employed in making any small items of special equipment which were required by the factory or by the test laboratory and, of course, keeping the place clean and tidy, so he gained a great deal of valuable experience with a broom. He later worked his way through most departments of the factory, including the machine shop where he learned to set up a lathe, then gained further experience as a Salesman and as a Field Engineer, travelling around the country doing repairs and installations of Tannoy equipment. Among the installations on which he worked were several of the *Butlin's* Holiday Camps which gave him the opportunity to meet many of the 'Redcoat Girls'. He had also been involved with the installation at the greyhound stadium at New Cross where, in addition to dog racing, motorcycle speedway races also took place and, with his keen interest in motorcycling, he secured a spare time job there in April, 1948, and for two years he was the speedway announcer on the Tannoy public address system. There had been an earlier application of Tannoy equipment in similar circumstances for it had been installed in pre war days at the Crystal Palace dirt track races. Michael was paid £3 per week in cash for this which considerably enhanced the £6-10-0d. per week which he was paid by Tannoy although, in addition to his salary he was also paid 1½d per mile for any travelling he had to do for the company in his car.[1]

Following his initial training under Rackham in the Pink Room, Michael commented that Ronnie Rackham was one of the nicest people that anyone could hope to meet; he was kind, gentle, unassuming yet brilliant. He was a great innovator, with incredible creative ability but he was never given the credit which he should have been given. He had joined the company as a young man in its early days and he had developed great design ability being a very skilled draughtsman. His design skills extended to cabinet work and he designed the G.R.F. loudspeaker enclosure. Eventually, shortly before his retirement, he designed another excellent loudspeaker cabinet which was named the 'R.H.R.' after him at the insistence of David Bissett-Powell, who had joined the company in about 1966 and, by the time of Rackham's retirement, had risen to the ranks of the senior management. There will be more of David Bissett-Powell in later chapters.

Although the story rightly, and chronologically belongs some way in the future, it seems proper to record now the incidents surrounding Ronnie Rackham's retirement. David Bissett-Powell, having insisted that Rackham's achievements for the company be perpetuated in the name of one of its best loudspeaker enclosures, wanted to send Ronnie and his wife, Mollie, around the world as a retirement present, but there was no money in the budget to pay for this. So he asked Ronnie to design a loudspeaker enclosure, with no constraints, which would be Ronnie's ideal cabinet. When this was completed, David worked out the costings and approached all the distributors in the Far East and told them what it should cost them, but he then told them that he was going to charge them an extra £100 on their first orders and that the surcharge would be used to pay for Rackham's travel around the world. He also told them that they could enjoy his services for a day while he was with them. Rackham's trip took 3½ weeks and it was when he returned that it was learned that his health was failing.

Following the Victory Parade, the next really big requirement for outdoor public address equipment was the first post-war Henley Royal Regatta to which, as Engineer Bill Preedy put it, unless one was wearing a funny schoolboy cap and a blazer or, in the case of the ladies, one's skirt reached at least the regulation four inches below the knee, one was not allowed in, par-

The TANNOY Story

ticularly to the V.I.P. enclosure or to the riverside marquee. This event happily coincided with Tannoy's ability to produce rather better quality music than that which had been possible for the victory celebrations on V.E. day and V.J. day.

When it was first suggested that there should be a public address system in the steward's enclosure the organising committee were absolutely horrified; such an idea was almost anathema to them, they could not possibly contemplate such vulgarity. However, the proposal was eventually accepted, reluctantly by some, and a system was supplied by Tannoy's hire department. It was decided to install four loudspeaker bowls known as 'Victory Bowls', on a tree so that anyone wishing to listen to the commentary had to get quite close to the tree to hear it. In later years, when the Regatta Stewards became more accustomed to public address systems, they decided that either they would have a proper installation, or they would have nothing, so they opted for a complete installation with loudspeakers in all the stands. As an indication of the level of acceptance which public address eventually gained at Henley, a very well known *B.B.C.* announcer, John Snagge, was employed to present the commentaries when he was not actually giving his commentaries to the *B.B.C.* audience.

At some of these events they had commentators in boats at three points on the river, not on the river bank, and in those days there were no such things as radio microphones so these had to be connected to the bankside amplifiers by cables. Of course, these had to be watertight, including any joints so, a week or so before the regatta, the Tannoy engineers had to start preparing the equipment on site, armed with a primus stove and quantities of pitch, so that they could make watertight joints with pitch set in old tins. The Tannoy engineer in charge of the installation was Dave White and he rather enjoyed himself because he could not be bothered to book hotel accommodation and set up his little camp, with his tent, behind the Steward's enclosure. The microphone cables, which carried additional conductors for the operators' headphones, were laid along the river bank or just underneath it and were anything up to a mile in length. This introduced an awkward problem which came close to getting the Tannoy engineers into serious trouble. Many visitors to the event came in their own little boats and they occasionally caught their boat hooks on the cable, with distastrous results; everything on that link would be lost. On one occasion, on the last day of the regatta when there were thousands of people watching, Norman Robottom and others were on board the official Steward's launch, with flag flying, creeping along the bank looking for a fault which had developed in the cable while all the gorgeous young ladies were sitting on the bank with their shapely legs dangling in the water. There arose shouts of disgust at Norman and at the other Tannoy engineers, "You dirty bastards, we'll send for the police." Norman said to them, "We're looking for a break in our cable."

"Yes," came the reply, "we know all about that." And so the abuse continued. Norman said later that this was almost too much for them; it was not as if they did not have enough trouble without all that aggravation.

Norman told of another amusing incident when Raymond Glendenning was doing the commentary for the *B.B.C.* Racing had finished for the day and Raymond Glendenning was waiting to file his evening report to the *B.B.C.* He was standing just below Norman who, with a colleague, was listening to a radio for the tennis results from Wimbledon, which was on at the same time. On their radio they heard, 'We are interrupting the programme to go over to the Henley Royal Regatta for a report on the day's racing'. Norman looked down and saw Raymond Glendenning deep in conversation while the radio was broadcasting nothing but silence. So they whispered to one another, "Shall we tell him? Shall we tell him he's supposed to be on the air?" In the event they decided to keep quiet. Eventually a *B.B.C.* engineer came rushing over to Glendenning and told him that he was supposed to be giving his summary of the day's racing but, by the time he had composed himself and started his talk, his time was up and all that was heard on the radio was an announcer in London saying,'. . . and that is all from Henley'. Raymond Glendenning was quickly faded out.

In addition to the professional commentaries by *B.B.C.* personalities, many commentaries over the public address systems were given by University students, particularly when their own colleges were competing, and they were told what to say and what not to say. For example, they were told not to refer to the 'R.A.F. Four' but to the 'Royal Air Force Four'. One classic mistake which did get through, however, occurred during a race between Lady Margaret College and Jesus College when the announcer's voice came over the Tannoy system, loud and clear, saying, 'Lady Margaret is making a lot of water over Jesus.' Considerable attention had to be devoted to this commentary in subsequent years to avoid the risk of inexperienced commentators making similar gaffes.

Since the Regatta was very much a prestige event it was considered that the CD 4 loudspeaker in the so-called 'Victory Bowl' enclosure should be improved. The CD 4 was an extremely good 15" loudspeaker, designed, of course, by Ron Rackham, but it was not really a high fidelity loudspeaker. The 'Victory Bowl' was a two piece casting which made the CD 4 unit reasonably weatherproof but it was still a big cone unit which produced a good sound. Ron Rackham's idea was to bore out the pole piece of the CD 4 and mount the SD 5 high frequency pressure driver onto the back. He added an elementary cross-over unit to protect the SD 5 from being subjected to high power, low fre-

The TANNOY Story

quency signals, which may have caused it to destroy itself. This was mounted between two of the castings initially intended for the 'Victory Bowl' but with an 8" spacer to enable it to be used outside without there being too much of a weather problem.

Although a little crude in terms of a wide range loudspeaker, these performed quite well but Ron Rackham had seen a very elementary patent specification taken out by *Western Electric* and assigned to the *British Thompson-Houston Company* of the U.K. This showed, not very clearly defined, a pressure driver behind a cone unit with the centre pole of the cone unit bored out to form the beginning of the horn. The horn was then continued with the 15" exponential contour of the cone unit. So Rackham designed a reverse throat pressure driver to mount on the back of the cone loudspeaker. He originally intended cutting out concentric rings in the centre pole of the cone unit but this was both very difficult to achieve and expensive to manufacture so, instead, he decided on a multiplicity of holes to connect the pressure unit to the centre pole of the cone driver which, in turn, was bored out exponentially to form the beginning of the horn, the continuation of the horn being the exponential cone of the CD 4 (The CD 4 was already a curvilinear type because it was calculated that this produced fewer sub-harmonics than a conventional conical cone and in any case, it produced an altogether nicer sound). Whilst it was not a particularly accurate exponential curve it provided sufficient loading down to about 1 kHz which was reckoned to be the cross-over frequency. In the event, Tannoy could provide some really good quality music and very clearly audible announcements which made a useful contribution the enjoyment and the success of the regatta. The loudspeakers were, of course, made so that the name 'TANNOY' was very prominently seen as part of the cast casing.

Norman Robottom spent most of his years with Tannoy working in the Hire Department and he told the story of Tannoy's first involvement with 'cloak-and-dagger' work; possibly the only such involvement. One day he was told to take a microphone and amplifier and various other items of equipment to London to a block of flats in Baker Street. On asking what the job was, the answer was, "You'll be told when you get there." Arriving at the address, a man let Norman and his assistant in and explained to Norman that his work took him away from home quite frequently and that his wife was sure that he was up to no good while he was away; that, in modern parlance, he was 'playing away'. He, in turn, wanted to know what his wife did during his absences. Michael Fountain was also involved in this job and helped to install a very sensitive microphone, type 420, in the bedroom, under the pelmet, with a cable to the amplifier and a tape recorder in the room above. The outcome of this is not, of course, on record.

However, while the successes of such installations as the Henley Royal Regatta were being acted out, Tannoy was facing considerable problems of finance, administration and control. This has been touched on earlier in this chapter but the fact is that their wartime contracts with the Ministry of Supply had not required any sophisticated book-keeping and this led to two things:
a. There was no financial control structure, and
b. They would get involved in things for which there was no financial provision.

Stan Livingstone likened this method of working to that of a shopkeeper who believes he is doing well provided that the till is full. He would open the till, take out the money and have a good lunch although, strictly speaking, it was not his own money.

When the war-time contracts faded away in 1945, there was still a comfortable amount of cash 'in the till' and Guy believed that this would keep the company going while new products and ideas were developed. But many of the new ideas were Guy's own ideas and, while it must be admitted that some of them were of immense interest, it did not necessarily follow that the company was capable of developing them until they could be turned into commercial successes. So, all too often, money was taken from the 'till' and spent on endless development work; on ideas which would never sell, and this was, of course, a major problem.

It is quite possible, however, that another circumstance had made asignificant contribution to the shortage of money within the company because, during the war, companies had to accept the imposition of anadditional tax, Excess Profits Tax. In the case of Tannoy, for example, the company had made a profit of £3,000 in 1939 and in 1940 this had risen to some £70,000 so that the extra £67,000 was defined as Excess Profit and this was taxed. It has been said that Guy offset this initial demand by buying a secondhand Bentley for himself, a move which did not go down at all well in some quarters.

As an example of Guy's attitude to their problems, he asked George Wheeler to chair a committee to co-ordinate ideas for the development, production and marketing of various projects. The committee prepared a report on their proposals, which concluded that most of the projects then under consideration or under development should not be pursued. They submitted their findings on a Friday afternoon. On the following Monday Guy summoned George to his office and asked, "What the bloody hell are you playing at, giving me rubbish like this?" So George told him that they had spent a great deal of time considering the matters and that their report detailed their policy proposals, including their recommendations to abandon many projects which they considered would not become commercial successes, to which Guy replied, "I've

The TANNOY Story

built up the name of Tannoy and we ARE going ahead." So George asked where the money was going to come from, to which Guy replied, "Money is nothing whatever to do with you, you just get on with your job." George replied, "We have done our job, we must cut back on these projects." Now this took place at a time when most components were still in short supply and many were obtainable only against a licence, so he asked Guy, "What is the point of making large amplifiers and loudspeakers if we cannot obtain the record player decks to feed them?" But Guy just would not listen and most of his pet projects had to be continued.

George Wheeler recalled further difficulties which were experienced by the company during the post war years for, in the winter of 1947 which was one of the coldest winters on record, power was in very short supply and a form of electricity rationing was introduced in which power could be used on only three days each week. Occasionally, when Tannoy broke the rules, somebody would alert the appropriate authority and a man would turn up and complain that the company had soldering irons working and he told the Managers that they must switch them off. So George's father was sent down to R.A.F. Kenley and he collected an R.A.F. 3 kW generator which was soon installed in the yard just inside the factory gates to keep the factory going. The generator had a metal canopy and should have been fuelled by pressure hose into the fuel tank which was just below the canopy. However, fuel could only be obtained in large drums, so a hole was cut in the canopy so that the petrol could, with great difficulty, be poured in from above.

There were several unsuccessful projects on which much time and money were spent and one of these was the silent speech microphone, the development programme for which went on for a very long time. The original microphone had a close fitting mouthpiece so that the sound of the operator's voice was contained within the mouthpiece with no audible emission of sound; hence its name. The design work and the development of the prototype went on seemingly for ever but not one was ever sold because it never worked, but its costly development was, to all intents and purposes, funded 'out of the till'.[2] There had been a similar unproductive development during the late 1930s in the first electronic air raid warning system.

Another unsuccessful early post-war product was an ac/dc amplifier. This made quite a significant contribution to the company's downfall because they had not done their homework thoroughly and had not remembered that many places which were still supplied by d.c. mains were, in fact, supplied at 110 volts. This particularly applied to showmen's entertainments, most of which were still supplied with 110 volts d.c. from dynamos mounted on their steam traction engines. Tannoy had designed their universal amplifiers to operate on a d.c. supply of 220 volts and, when they were plugged in to many supplies, the little pilot light on the panel glowed, and so did the valves, but no sound came out. This proved to be a costly mistake.

Another development project which was a personal hobby-horse of Guy's was a very large and very luxurious radiogram which was combined with what was, in those days, a large-screen television set, monochrome of course, which was destined to secure Tannoy a commanding position in the domestic equipment market. It was built to a particularly elegant design, in a beautiful corner cabinet veneered with burr walnut of the finest quality and it was aimed firmly at the luxury market. Nothing but the best was good enough for it and Guy insisted that only the finest of equipment would be incorporated. This was, of course, just before the introduction of long-playing, vinyl gramophone records and, to ensure the enjoyment of recorded music for any satisfactory length of time, it was necessary to incorporate an automatic record changer. These had been available for ten years or more and were made by several companies, notably *Garrard* of Swindon who, debatably, made the best. But Guy wanted to be certain that only the finest and most reliable record-changer would be used in this prestige set which anticipated the music centres of the 1980s and which was virtually a complete home entertainment system, so he wasted a great deal of time searching for something better. He tried the *Rocola* changer from Staines, a complicated piece of machinery which turned the records over to play both sides, after which it returned them to a slot to the side of the cabinet. However, it was not very reliable because, after playing both sides, it was said to be a 50-50 chance whether the record hit the slot in the cabinet and it had a tendency to throw records around the room; not at all desirable with the shellac records of the time which were very brittle. Guy also tried record changers by *B.S.R.* and *Collaro* but he invariably settled on *Garrard*, because *Garrard* were usually at the forefront of the technology.

After the prototype set had been built, and tested endlessly in the laboratory, it was realised that they really had achieved a truly excellent, luxurious piece of equipment which looked elegant and, more importantly, sounded superb. Guy was particularly proud of it and, as happened quite often with his favoured products, he decided to show it off in his own home. There was, however, one minor problem for it was discovered, too late, that it would not come out of the room; it was too big to pass through the door! Obviously, if it could not be moved out of the laboratory door, it would not go through the average sitting room door either, and the project, which had consumed huge sums of money from the 'till', was dropped. Tannoy never again went into production with television sets and made only two prototypes.

There was another luxury radiogram built into a similar, walnut veneered

The TANNOY Story

corner cabinet. It was not inelegant, just a little 'over-the-top' to use the modern idiom. In the lower part of the cabinet were the radio and amplifier chassis and two record storage drawers, above these were two drop-down doors, the lower one concealing the controls and the upper one giving access to the record changer. Above these was a rather large, and none too handsome rectangular loudspeaker grille. It was none too handsome because this, too, had originally been intended to incorporate a television set but this idea was dropped and the aperture for the television screen was used for the loudspeaker, hence its very plain appearance. Only one of these was built and it is believed that this was eventually converted into a cocktail cabinet for use either at Tudor Lodge or at Carlton Cottage, Cliftonville, Guy's two residences.

These projects, on which a great deal of time and money were expended, contributed to the first downfall of the company but the situation which led to the appointment of a Receiver was largely brought about by overstocking and by the lack of control over money, particularly the latter, and exacerbated by these money consuming projects.

Yet another typical case of an item of equipment which did not sell was Tannoy's venture into direct disc recording, using acetate discs. During the early 1940s, when the *B.B.C.* was pioneering the techniques of on-the-spot broadcasts from war correspondents at the various battle fronts, they were unable to record such commentaries because there was no suitable, portable recording equipment available. The only recording machines the *B.B.C.* had were very large studio recorders which were extremely heavy and they were certainly not portable; barely even transportable. Now the Germans were ahead because they had wire recorders and the *Armor Corporation* in America had also started making wire recorders. It is believed that Armor were really food manufacturers but the story is that they had been talked into making wire recorders because they had a metal working department for making cans and this was deemed to be suitable for much of the metal work involved in the manufacture of wire recorders.

Guy Fountain had a friend, a man called Reginald Simon, of *Simon Sound Ltd.* Reg Simon had lost one arm and one eye and, to prove that it made no difference he always drove the biggest motor car he could afford. Soon after the war he had an Austin Princess and Livingstone said that a ride with Reg Simon was very much a 'white knuckle' ride because of his restricted vision and the difficulty he had in coping with the very heavy steering, notwithstanding the fact that he had a knob attached to the steering wheel. But in the early days of the war, Simon was a very good friend of Cecil Watts who was well known for his design work on disc recorders and who had devised a fairly reliable acetate recording disc (he later made accessories such as the 'Dust bug' which is men-

151

The End Of The Beginning

tioned in the *Wireless World* report on the Tannoy 'Senior' radiogram). Watts had worked out how an even thickness of acetate could be deposited on an aluminium disc but, as he worked from his home, he had no production facilities. However, Reg Simon had the facilities and was able to make the small disc recorders which Watts had designed for the B.B.C. He had designed both the cutter and the tracking mechanism, a parallel tracking mechanism which even included a crude, but reasonably effective scrolling mecha-nism to operate the automatic stop on the play-back machine. This scrolling mechanism had to be worked by hand and overdrove the tracking mechanism, but the operator had to be very quick to lift the cutter off the disc to avoid it cutting through the acetate and damaging its stylus on the aluminium.

Reg Simon went to the B.B.C. and told them that he had a man who could offer them a portable disc recorder and the B.B.C. jumped at the idea. This was a tremendous success although correspondents had to be physically strong to carry them as they weighed about 70 lbs. It was transportable rather than portable but many of them were lugged around the battlefields and the correspondents' commentaries were broadcast on B.B.C. news programmes within a day or two. These recorders were very successful and Simon did quite well out of them and it is said that he was able to give Watts quite a handsome consultancy fee.

There was a great exhibition at Olympia in 1946 at which a lot of German equipment was shown, when all their patents were open and when it was permissible to copy them without a licence, this being part of the war reparations. *Boosey and Hawkes*, the well known musical instrument company, started to make the German wire recorder while E.M.I. made the tape machines. But for various reasons both mechanical and electrical, the early tape recorders had problems with speed stability; they were quite satisfactory for recording speech but nothing else. At the same time the film industry was getting very interested in post recording; i.e. recording the dialogue in a sound studio after filming on location. They realised that taking the microphone out into the middle of a swamp, for instance, while the actress cried, "Help", was not very practical, it was much easier to get her to say "Help" later in the studio, and this produced much better results. So Reg Simon built a small disc recorder for the film industry based on the Watts machine but, in the event, this was not very successful because the circuit design left much to be desired. It was essentially a slightly improved version of the wartime recorder but it had only one input and no monitor loudspeaker. Its frequency response was not much better than that of the original war correspondents' machines and it was not deemed good enough for recording film sound tracks. With the introduction of wire recorders and, later, tape recorders, the need for

The TANNOY Story

Cecil Watts' disc recorder quickly disappeared.

But Guy had taken an interest in direct disc recording and Tannoy was approached by *British Acoustic Films*, then part of *Gaumont*, at Shepherd's Bush. Shepherds Bush was also the home of *Bush Radios*, hence the name. *British Acoustic Films* asked Tannoy to design and produce a complete disc recording system for them using Reg Simon's recording deck, designed by Watts, but with improved electronics. Now at this time Tannoy had just developed a new range of amplifiers, the 'Traders', one of which had an output of 20 watts. These amplifiers were the result of a rather loose trading association with *E.K. Cole & Company*, 'EKCO', under which Tannoy amplifiers were supposed to be sold by EKCO dealers; a scheme which was not successful. They had 3 inputs, a tone control and a master control similar to the input mixers which later became standard equipment on amplifiers. Their 20 watts output was sufficient power to drive the recording cutter and with a little correction it produced quite a good response. So Tannoy built one recorder in a wood cabinet, rather like an old-fashioned wooden refrigerator, on castor wheels, with rounded corners. It was painted grey and incorporated the 20 watts 'Trader' amplifier and a monitor loudspeaker in the bottom. This was fine, it sounded quite good and *British Acoustic Films* ran a few tests although it is said that their tests could, and should have been somewhat more thorough. Nevertheless, they ordered 6 of these recorders. By this time Reg Simon had realised that electronics was not really his strong point but still felt that he could make what he called a 'Super professional recorder' with a 16" turntable. This was effectively a bigger and better Watts recorder; better engineered, and Tannoy bought one of these. Unfortunately it was never paid for because it was delivered just before the Receiver was called in.

So Tannoy made the 6 disc recording machines for British Acoustic Films. Guy Fountain was, at that time, very interested in *Sound Systems Ltd.* of Dublin, who had influence because they were part of a big group and they were courting the *Irish Broadcasting system*. The Irish Broadcasting system were looking into studio recorders and in 1947, shortly after Stan and Joan Livingstone were married, Guy suggested that Stan should take one of the disc recording machines to Ireland and demonstrate it to the *Irish Broadcasting* authority.

So the machine was shipped over to Ireland and Livingstone enjoyed his first flight in an aeroplane. On arrival he went to the Sound System's H.Q. where he thought that he had better check the recorder to make sure it worked properly. He said something into the microphone and played it back and it sounded quite good but, as he was not familiar with the sound of his own voice, he was unsure of its performance so he put the microphone in front of an ordinary radiogram, played a record and recorded the music. When he went back to the beginning of the record and played both at the same time it became obvious that there was a problem; there was a difference of about half a tone. However, he managed to get through the demonstration because Sound Systems had a lot of spare amplifiers and amongst them they found a 60 watts mains transformer. He used the primary of the mains transformer as an auto-transformer to boost the on-load voltage to 240 volts and with this, the motor just about kept going at the right speed, but it became rather hot. This episode brought the whole project rather rapidly to an end because *British Acoustic Films* soon discovered what he had done and quickly lost interest.

After the old *'Lancaster Motor Company'* was bought by *Dagenham Motors* and so named, Guy had later re-registered the old name for himself, probably to spite John Portwine. He once thought of using the name for his transport department but, in the event, he just kept the name and called the transport division, 'Tannoy Motor Company', and he was able to obtain trade terms on all parts purchased. Previously, panel beating repairs had been done by *Lucas of Brixton Hill* but some time later an excellent panel beater, who rejoiced in the name of Wally l'Enfant, was lured into joining the Tannoy machine shop for specialist work.

There was an odd-job man at about this time called Sam Bray who was no stranger to the bottle. He worked for Tannoy from 1939 until 1942 and, after serving his time in the Army, he returned in 1946 and stayed for thirty-one years although he was frequently dismissed. He carried out numerous functions but when he was caretaker he used to lock the factory at night then, with an adequate concentration of alcohol in his system, he would fall asleep under a bench. Occasionally Guy would return to the factory at night to check things for himself and, when he found Bray in a stupor, he would sack him there and then, but somehow Bray always managed to bounce back after a few days.

It was not only technical problems which contributed to the company's difficulties for Guy had also created personal problems which had their effect upon the company. Very soon after the war, he decided to establish a presence in Ireland and 'Tannoy Ireland' was formed. Guy made several visits to Dublin and in the course of these visits he became acquainted with Maureen, a waitress who had previously been married to an American serviceman. Guy took a shine to Maureen and their relationship developed until she virtually became his mistress and moved to England where Guy secured accommodation for her near to the Crystal Palace at Sydenham.

Guy felt an obligation to support Maureen, whose maiden name is believed to have been McDonald, and he looked for a business remote from Tannoy to suit this purpose by registering it in her name and, in about 1948, he was approached by two brothers, the McGinty brothers, who worked in a former

The TANNOY Story

butcher's shop in Brighton making plaster and cement garden ornaments. It is believed that they managed to convince Guy that they could make plaster loudspeaker cabinets so he bought the McGinty brothers' company, probably for very little. They developed a range of plaster loudspeaker cabinets which were quite pleasing to the ear and many of them were installed in *Butlin's* holiday camps, but although they were in production for a year or two, they were not very successful as the corners were vulnerable and tended to chip and break and it was also found that it was difficult to fix components into them, so much so that they had to fix mounting rings in them to support the loudspeakers. Installation contractors particularly disliked them because it was usually necessary to fix a terminal box inside the cabinet and there was no satisfactory way of doing this. Another drawback was their weight but this high mass made them sound very good. This company became *Sound Plastings Ltd.* Stan Livingstone also said that there was a later arrangement in which Maureen received a pension of £10,000 p.a. for 5 years which allegedy came from the sale of *Tannoy Marine* although it is not certain whether this is fact or fiction.

At the time of Guy's attempts to break into the television market a Mr Bushnell was the manager of the service department and he had the necessary skills to service the television chassis. He had previously been in charge of the Chemistry department at the Norwood Technical College where exposure to various chemicals, exacerbated by years of heavy smoking, had given him a very severe lung condition which resulted in almost continuous coughing. After the failure of the television venture, Bushnell was detailed to do any repair work required on Guy's own television set and those of his friends whom he wished to favour. He used to rejoice in telling the story of the occasion when he was told to go to Maureen's home to repair her television, a job which took him a great deal longer than any previous repair work he had done because he found the set suspended from the ceiling in her bedroom!

The imposition of purchase tax eventually brought another big problem to this little company when regulations came into force. The company had been able to sell these garden ornaments because so many people were busy rebuilding their houses and turning their 'Dig for Victory' cabbage patches back into gardens. This was creating a large demand for garden ornaments and, by an oversight, they initially escaped the purchase tax net.

Now Jack Oldfield, formerly with Col. Colley, of whom more later, was made Sales Manager of this little company and he had a contact in *Carter's Seeds* who gave him many names and addresses of seed distributors so he did not have to spend much time in researching potential customers for the garden equipment and ornaments. This made his job very easy and when he contacted these distributors and negotiated deals with them, business boomed. But in

1948 purchase tax was extended to cover virtually everything, not just luxury items, and the garden ornament business quickly collapsed, adding to Guy's problems.

While all these events were being enacted, both within the company and those relating to Guy's nefarious personal affairs, Guy was enjoying the many luxuries which his lifestyle demanded. The holiday house which he acquired from Frank Wheeler, Carlton Cottage, in Princes Drive, Cliftonville, was often 'Open House' for friends and relatives and the author remembers several holidays there with 'Uncle' Guy and 'Auntie' Elsie and with Jeanne, Michael, David and various school friends of David's, particularly Derek Quitman, in the years following the war. During these holidays nobody, other than Guy, ever paid for anything. The house had a particularly comfortable sitting room, with french windows opening onto a deep veranda and a pretty front garden. Over the road there was a wide area of garden, well maintained by the local council, with tennis courts. In the sitting room there was a large, elegant, walnut cocktail cabinet, resplendent with interior mirrors and with brilliant lighting which came on as the drop-down door opened, automatically lifting the lid at the same time, at which Guy enjoyed dispensing alcoholic hospitality with characteristic generosity. This cocktail cabinet was, of course, adapted at great expense to the company from a television cabinet. But more importantly for teenagers such as Michael, David, Derek and Julian, there was, in the adjoining dining room, a very fine radiogram at which the young members of the party enjoyed playing their favourite records by artists such as Tommy Dorsey, Harry James, Bing Crosby and others.

A memory which is very vivid indeed is that of sharing one of the large bedrooms with David and Derek and seeing Guy come in to say 'Good night', with a few carefully chosen words in spite of the fact that he had quite probably 'had-a-few', accompanied by loud sucking noises and a great deal of excavation work with the silver toothpick which he always carried in his waistcoat pocket, and concluding with a very generous and loving parental kiss for David. Douglas and Kathleen Alderton had seldom been given to displays of affection within the family, neither in public nor even within the privacy of the home, and these moments of closeness between Guy and David came as something of a surprise, especially when, but an hour or two earlier Guy had, in all probability, displayed an outburst of his violent temper aimed at David or one of his siblings.

From Carlton Cottage he would often take his guests out, on one occasion to the *Rediffusion* relay station at nearby St. Peters where Tannoy equipment was installed and, on the return journey, he demonstrated the noise, and the power, of his Bentley with its exhaust silencer cut-out which was operated by a lever

The TANNOY Story

situated between the front seats. This was probably illegal even then, but the additional power and awful noise was great fun.

One evening it was decided that the party would go to the cinema in Margate. However, it was not that simple for, instead of just going along like ordinary citizens, Guy insisted on telephoning the cinema manager beforehand, making it abundantly clear who he was and letting it be known that he expected some ten or twelve seats in the front row of the Dress Circle to be reserved for him. On arrival, about ten minutes late, it was found that the start of the programme had been delayed for the party and it was only when all were comfortably seated that the music was faded, the lights dimmed, and the programme commenced. Guy just loved that, and expected it!

As has already been recorded at the commencement of Chapter 2, Guy had a tendency to try anything new, particularly new electrical equipment and gadgets and, very shortly after the war, probably in 1946, he had an electric lawnmower – something almost unheard of then. It may have been an early commercial electric mower but, by the same token, he may well have thought of the idea himself and had a conventional engine-driven model fitted with an electric motor. He also made a point of buying the latest ideas in portable radios and, at a time when 'portable' really meant 'transportable' and when battery radios usually had to have at least 90 volts h.t. and $1^{1}/_{2}$ volts l.t., he bought a couple of miniature portable radios from America, measuring about 7" by 4" by 2" with very small, miniature valves which worked quite well on 45 volts from a tiny battery. This is yet another of the author's clear memories of Guy Fountain for he took great pleasure in showing these off to the various visitors at Carlton Cottage during an Easter Holiday in Cliftonville in 1946.

Stan Livingstone recalled an amusing event when, on the occasion of a Radio Industries Club lunch at the Connaught Rooms in 1948 or 1949, Guy somehow committed himself to returning to the factory as a passenger in Livingstone's car, probably, it was said, because of a blazing row with whoever had taken him there. Stan's relationship with Guy was by then very volatile and Stan agreed to the lift with some reluctance. Stan then had a Ford '8' which he had inherited from Bill Haines, and Bill Haines was also travelling with them, sitting in the back seat. Stan recounted that it was 'quite an exciting' car with its single transverse front spring which lacked some stability and he thought to himself, 'this is where I win'. "Well," Livingstone told the author, "I didn't drive dangerously but my driving was 'rather exciting'. Guy just sat there, white knuckled, and we soon arrived at the Elephant and Castle where the big one-way system was then under construction. There were many possibilities of which I took advantage and Guy remarked, 'Next time I think I'll go

The End Of The Beginning

by bus.' Whereupon Bill, who had not said a word since they started and who was not noted for his spontaneous humour said, 'You bloody nigh just did '!" There was another occasion when Guy wanted to tour a number of Tannoy installations, including those in Leeds and Manchester, as well as the offices of the *Daily Express*. Bill Preedy was driving and, when Guy shouted, "Pull over, pull over!" Preedy did as he was told whereupon Guy got out and adjusted both the wing mirrors so that he could see behind, never minding about Bill Preedy's vision.

The Radio Industries Club had its own public address equipment for use at lunches, meetings and similar functions and this featured a gold plated Tannoy microphone mounted on a stand modelled on a television transmitter aerial mast. It was widely thought, perhaps assumed, that it had been donated by Guy Fountain but this was not the case. Guy had, in fact, charged them for it.

As a further illustration of Guy's capricious ways, two former employees of the company, Ernie Marsden and Dennis Terrett, told the author the story of the occasion in 1935 when Guy Fountain, while prowling around the factory as he often did, came across a young lad standing near the goods inwards area with his hands in his pockets, apparently doing nothing. On being challenged by Guy the lad quite happily admitted that he was doing nothing so Guy asked him what his weekly wage was. Guy then took out his wallet, handed the appropriate sum over to him and shouted, "you're sacked!" He then went back to his office feeling very pleased with himself, blissfully unaware of the fact that the boy was employed by a delivery company called *Carter Patterson*.

The lack of financial control in the company has already been discussed and this cannot be stressed too much, but there were other matters in which more formal control could, and should have been exercised. Apart from Tannoy Marine, which catered for Guy's 'Nautical Novelties' and which became very successful in its own right, the various functions of the companies were carried on side-by-side without any clear divisions of responsibility; it was a sort of conglomerate mess which was typical of the way in which Guy liked to run his business. But through the 1930s and during the war years the different manufacturing tasks gradually became more important as separate entities and should have been more clearly defined. Tannoy Marine has been mentioned and the Hire Department also became a part of the Tannoy Products Ltd., but there was no clear distinction between the manufacture of Tannoy equipment such as amplifiers, loudspeakers and microphones, and what had, by then, become known as Systems Engineering; the production of large, specialised sound schemes and process control systems. The need for formal divisions soon became more apparent but the lack of such control, together with lax

The TANNOY Story

financial arrangements, contributed to the difficulties in controlling the companies. Not even the costing of Tannoy's contracts was done on a formal basis; calculations were based on a 'rule-of-thumb' which was : 2 x material costs plus $4^{1}/_{2}$ times labour.

So, by the late 1940s the company had run into a considerable cash-flow problem and a contributory factor in this was the fact that they had anticipated large volume sales of public address equipment and had spent substantial sums of money building up stocks, including Trader amplifiers; but the sales did not materialise. As has already been seen, Tannoy was forever embarking on new projects and the company even attempted to break into the television market which was a bad move. These problems were often generated by Guy's personal feelings about whether he thought ideas submitted to him would be worthwhile for the company. His reaction to proposed developments depended not only on how the proposal was put to him but also on who had presented it and, in essence, he had to assess whether it would be seen as being one of his ideas. He was also a Director of the *Static Condenser Company* at Wokingham from whom Tannoy used to buy condensers. They, too, had financial problems and Guy thought that it would be a good idea to pull them into the group and help them with finance, which he did. This move gave Tannoy a large part of the production of paper and foil condensers but it exacerbated the company's money problems.

The poor control over the company's finances was largely the result of a lackadaisical attitude which had been allowed to develop while the military contracts were occupying the attention of the management. During the war there had been fixed-price running-contracts for airfield installations and for the various items of equipment which incorporated the power microphone. With these running-contracts the Ministry of Supply could be approached for money at almost any time and they would always pay, either against what had already been delivered or, occasionally, against future commitments. After the war, Tannoy was still involved with the R.A.F. airfield contracts which were still being supplied, albeit at a much slower pace, but these, too, had their financial problems. Tannoy had been awarding wiring contracts to companies doing the installations on the airfields, predominently *F.H. Wheeler*, and there came a time when *F.H. Wheeler* had no money to buy the necessary cable and Tannoy had none left in the 'till' to pay *F.H. Wheeler*. Frank Wheeler naturally became uneasy when the cable manufacturers who had been supplying him also wanted their money so it was he who, perhaps reluctantly, was partly responsible in 1947 for highlighting the situation which put Tannoy under the threat of Receivership but, as his company was also in difficulty this was quite understandable. Added to this, Guy had not treated Frank Wheeler entirely fairly and their relationship was, by this time, strained.

One day, Frank Wheeler telephoned George Wheeler who had, by then, been appointed to the board and said, "Could I see you, privately and confidentially?" When they met, Frank told George that he was very worried because Tannoy owed his company over £70,000 and, in spite of his best efforts, he could not get the money. George speculated as to whether Tannoy had been paid for the contracts in question, and Frank Wheeler replied that he'd learned Tannoy had been paid in full.

Next morning when George arrived at the factory he spoke to Denis Blackmore, the Company Secretary, and told him that Frank Wheeler had been asking for money and that he, George, was very concerned. The fact that George had introduced Frank Wheeler to Tannoy had led to a most successful association which lasted throughout the war, and it was some embarrassment to him to learn that there was such a large sum of money outstanding. Denis was equally embarrassed by this confrontation and, although he was well aware of the situation, he did not know whether he ought to discuss it.

George went immediately to Guy and started by reminding him that it had been he who had introduced *F.H. Wheeler* to Tannoy. Guy asked what this conversation was leading up to and George said that Frank Wheeler had told him that Tannoy owed his company over £70,000. Guy responded to the effect that it was down to Air Ministry, as they were the ones who owed F.H. Wheeler. George then said that this was not what he had been told; he understood that the Air Ministry had paid Tannoy. Guy then became rude and said that finance had nothing to do with George.

The result was that Frank Wheeler set in motion the issue of a writ. Guy, realising the severity of the situation, pulled what Livingstone regarded as one of his master strokes; he went to *Barclays Bank* and took out a debenture. Within a few days, *F.H. Wheeler* issued a writ to recover the money owed to his company. Blackmore then went to *Barclays Bank* and told them what was happening with the result that, in order to guard their debenture, they put in the Receiver. The appointed Receiver was Norman Wild who came to the factory on a weekly basis and, according to Michael, he was a very charming and pleasant man who summed up Guy very quickly indeed. There was also an official Receiver, Ross Hindle, who came once a week on behalf of the other unsecured creditors. The company was in Receivership for the next three years.[4]

The TANNOY Story

CHAPTER NOTES

1   Occasional spectators at the dog racing events were the author's mother, Kathleen and her close friend, Elsie Fountain. They devised a system of betting in which they watched the dogs being paraded prior to each race and laid their money on any dog which did a 'woopsie' before the race, reckoning that, being that much lighter, it must win.

2   Some time later, in the late 1960s, Dennis Terrett was to design an improved version which consisted of the insert of a type 420 micro phone with a foam rubber mouthpiece and an internal coiled pressure release tube, which worked well and may have exonerated the original thoughts and attempts. The type 420 microphone was a particularly successful Tannoy design of moving coil microphone with an alumini um diaphragm and a chromium plated front bezel. It was very robust and therefore popular and they were used in many installations such as the holiday camps where it was named the Desk Unit Control, so it became known as the Duck. Not many of the improved silent speech microphones were sold and Dennis made each one, including shaping the rubber mouthpiece by hand. The rubber for these came from a large sack of pieces which Guy had obtained, together with some fire hose, in order to make fenders for his boats.

3   It was said that Carlton Cottage, which had once been offered to George Wheeler, was acquired from Frank Wheeler by Guy as a 'benefit in kind', possibly at a special price, perhaps even as a gift.

4   The company which went into Administration was Guy R. Fountain Ltd. but there was also Sound Rentals Ltd., a small company at that time, and Guy tried to transfer the assets of Guy R. Fountain Ltd. to Sound Rentals.

TANNOY

12-INCH 10-WATT CABINET LOUDSPEAKER
LS/10/CX

This Loudspeaker is intended to provide the highest quality reproduction of speech and music combined with adequate power handling capacity, it will find its main application in theatres, dance halls, etc., and indeed anywhere where performance and good styling are of the first importance. A Special 12" Unit fitted with a high flux density magnet system and having a curvilinear cone, together with the acoustically designed cabinet, results in a frequency response far superior to that normally associated with direct radiators. The Loudspeaker Cabinet is of the rear enclosed type, with the result that it may be mounted against walls or across corners without the quality of reproduction being in any way impaired.

Frequency Range ... ... 70–7,000 c.p.s.
Impedance ... ... 1,000 ohms (10 watts at 100 volt line)
Dimensions ... ... 9½" × 19" × 19"
Weight ... ... 29½ lbs.
Finish ... ... Natural Oak

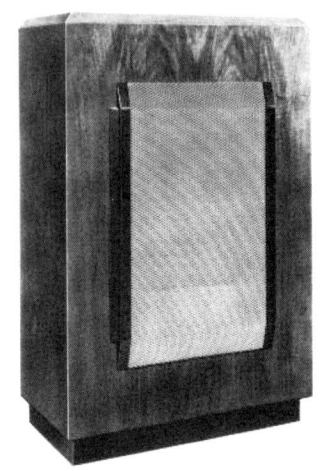

12-INCH DUAL CONCENTRIC BASS REFLEX LOUDSPEAKER

The introduction of this entirely new Loudspeaker System enables reproduction of a standard hitherto associated only with the Research Laboratory to become a reality on all Public Address installations.

The "Dual Concentric" principle of Loudspeaker construction was pioneered by TANNOY and enables a very wide frequency response, together with outstanding spacial distribution to be obtained from a Loudspeaker no larger than the conventional direct radiator.

Inter-modulation distortion and other faults inherent in even the best types of single Loudspeaker systems are completely eliminated. The fact that the level frequency response is obtained by making the system completely aperiodic enables very high overall gain to be obtained, particularly when this Loudspeaker is used in conjunction with Microphones having controlled directional characteristics.

Frequency Response ... 50–12,000 c.p.s. ± 3 dB
Impedance ... ... 1,000 ohms (10 watts at 100 volt line)
Dimensions ... ... Width 23"
                        Height 34"
                        Depth 12"
Weight ... ... 45 lbs.
Finish ... ... Oak, Walnut Veneer or Grey and Black

CHAPTER ELEVEN

ADMINISTRATION 1947–1950

When Norman Wild came in as Receiver he established much needed financial control systems and, having investigated the Rabbit Warren, he closed two factories which had been predominantly engaged in making equipment which would not sell; the original Canterbury Grove factory and the rebuilt Cox's Yard, and he streamlined the company to its 'core business'. The main factory building was let to *Cossor Radar* and Cox's yard, as recorded in Chapter Nine, became *Marcantonio*'s ice cream factory. The remaining creditors were secured, if this could be regarded as security, by a lot of stock which was stored in two big huts. This stock was somewhat mysterious to Wild and he wondered if it was any good and he asked Livingstone if it would sell. Much of it consisted of magnets and Livingstone replied, "Some of it is good, some of it is of quite high value." He also told Wild that he knew a company who would buy them and although they would not pay what they were worth they would pay cash, and that was *Electradix*. So Leslie Dixon came over from *Electradix* and said, "That lot's worth £500", and took them. How payment was arranged Stan Livingstone never knew.

When Wild took over the company there were still the three or four big direct acetate disc recording consoles made by Tannoy, two of which had been used to record the speeches at one of the Olympia lunches and one which had been used on the trials for the *Irish Broadcasting* system. One of them had also been used to the amusement of family and friends to enhance the Christmas festivities at Tudor Lodge and the author remembers a typical, vitriolic family row

Administration 1947–1950

which developed between Guy and Elsie when she discovered that a microphone had been secreted in the ground floor washroom to record some potentially embarrassing conversations. Elsie was absolutely furious, and rightly so.

Stan Livingstone became involved in the discussions about the disposal of these recording consoles because he alone knew what they were worth on the open market. Wild, of course, did not know and neither did Guy although he would not risk his reputation by admitting it. The disc recorders were probably then worth between £500 and £600 each.

But Wild was a rather ruthless man, he had to be, and soon after he arrived he asked George Wheeler, "What is your title?" George replied that he was Technical Director and General Manager. "Oh", said Wild. "How many people have you on the staff?" George was not sure and hesitated. Wild said, "Never mind exactly how man. Is it 400 or 500?" "Well," said George. "Call it 450." So Wild said, "I want you to get rid of 300 of them." "I can't do that." said George, to which Norman Wild replied, "Let's get this quite clear Mr. Wheeler, if you can't get rid of 300, you will be one of them."

In the following weeks, during the early stages of Norman Wild's receivership, Guy was totally unco-operative; he did everything to stall Wild's work. Wild was a very straight, honest man and if anyone were honest with him he would act fairly with them. Guy, on the other hand, never worked that way; he never went the straightforward way in his dealings with anyone, let alone Wild, and he reckoned that he had Wild in the palm of his hand. He was very wrong. One day there was a telephone call to George from the City office of *Barclay's Bank*. "Wheeler?" asked the caller. "Yes," said George. "Wild here, I want you to come and see me." So George made some excuse to Guy for a day off, telling him that he had to do something next morning and he went to the City to see Norman Wild. On arrival Wild said, "Look here, Wheeler, I'm fed up with all this. I'm getting nowhere; I'm getting no information, no help, nothing at all out of Fountain. I want to get rid of him." Wheeler said, "That's up to you." "Well, could you run the company?" "Yes," answered Wheeler, "I could run the company practically but I think that you would have all sorts of problems." "Well, think it over, I'll give you 48 hours. I'll get rid of Fountain and you can take it over and see what you can make of it."

The next day Guy called George into his office and said, "Well, how did you get on with Norman?" George said, "I don't know what you mean". "Well," said Guy, "you've been to see Wild." George replied, "Look, what I do in my time is my own business." "Oh, I know what he said, he offered you the opportunity to take the factory over. What are you going to do?" To which George replied, "I'm not prepared to discuss it in any way at all, I'm not saying any-

The TANNOY Story

thing." Wild had, of course, reported back to *Barclays Bank* to the effect that he had interviewed George Wheeler with a view to him assuming control of the company and to make something of it. But Guy evidently had a spy within *Barclays* who had tipped him off.

George Wheeler also recounted, "Guy did some diabolical things; he pulled some very doubtful tricks. He came to me one day and asked me to prepare a paper on public address equipment to be presented at the University of Belfast and I said, 'Yes, O.K.', naturally believing that I would also be responsible for presenting the paper. So I went right back into the history of sound, to the achievements of the Greeks and the Romans in the acoustic designs of their theatres. Houlgate wrote a detailed account of the design of microphones and loudspeakers and various others wrote sections of the paper, depending on their particular specialities. One covered installation and another wrote a section on the design of amplifiers. When we had prepared our papers we submitted them to Guy so that he could read them over the weekend. On the following Monday when we went to see him to collect our papers he was not in his office and when we asked his secretary when he would be coming in, she said that he was in Ireland. He presented the papers himself! With no formal technical background this took a lot of nerve, but he was not at all short of that."

When the company went into receivership it became fairly obvious that the cabinet business was going to be a bit of a problem but Norman Wild was no fool and, having agreed willingly to the continuation of the loudspeaker manufacturing business, he realised that it would be greatly to their advantage to be making their own cabinets. *Sound Plastings,* who were still making some loudspeaker cabinets, was not actually a part of Guy R. Fountain Ltd. so, just as long as Sound Plastings supplied cabinets at reasonable prices, all was well with that arrangement and they got paid. He also allowed Sound Rentals to continue in business because they operated in a similar manner.

Wild streamlined the company creating the opportunity to develop some very successful projects, in contrast to the unreliable mix of successes and failures which Guy had spearheaded, and it was during this time that two major developments took place, one being a 'Systems Engineering' achievement, the other being the perfection of what became the most important piece of equipment ever to come from Tannoy. The first of these was the development and perfection of sound reinforcement schemes and the installation of Tannoy equipment in the Palace of Westminster, the second was the famous Tannoy 'Dual Concentric' Loudspeaker.

THE PALACE OF WESTMINSTER.
Soon after the war, the House of Commons was rebuilt following its destruction

by enemy action in 1941 and, against stiff competition, a Tannoy sound reinforcement system was ordered and installed there in 1951. This system had been designed by Ron Rackham with the help of Philip Waples and, in 1948, when the Members of Parliament were still sitting in the Lord's Chamber following the destruction of the Commons, a test and demonstration set had been installed temporarily in a small section of the House of Lords so that it could be assessed and compared with schemes offered by *Philips* and *Ekco*. The problem of feed-back, particularly acute with a microphone operating at up to 15ft. from an orator, had to be beaten while, at the same time, satisfying the aesthetic standards laid down by the Ministry of Works. The root cause of instability in a closed auditorium was due, and still is, to standing waves which produce a condition of sympathetic resonance or feedback; the electro-acoustic engineer's curse. At the time there was very little guidance on the subject from academics but the B.B.C. were also looking at the problem because in auditoria where there was a need for interaction with an audience it was necessary to provide a public address facility without the plague of feed-back and its characteristic whistles and howls which would ruin a broadcast.

George Wheeler, with his customary pioneering attitude but without much expertise, decided to try out an electro-mechanical device which consisted of a transmitting loudspeaker rotating in a gimbal with slip ring contacts, rather in the manner of the *Leslie* loudspeaker which was employed at the time in electronic organs to provide tremolo and vibrato effects. The theory was that by constantly rotating the loudspeaker standing waves would not build up, but the experiments were doomed from the start. Once, just as a result seemed possible, the device suffered a bad attack of disintegration and the revolving loudspeaker flew apart. This ended part one of the story and more practicable methods of eliminating feedback in sound reinforcement schemes were investigated.

By this time the principle of sound reinforcement in which a large number of low power loudspeakers are used to provide clear, but quiet and unobtrusive sound to each seating place instead of a few very powerful loudspeakers, had been well established and this was the system proposed for use in the Palace of Westminster. By employing such a system there was very little risk of sound from these small loudspeakers impinging upon the adjacent microphones and therefore there was very little risk of feedback occurring. However, to reduce the risk even further, a circuit was incorporated into the amplifiers in which the loudspeakers nearest to the microphone in use were automatically muted, and the next surrounding loudspeakers were reduced to half power. However, there were a few complaints in the early days from members who said that their loudspeakers were working only intermittently.

The TANNOY Story

Some years later, in the mid 1960s, an additional circuit was incorporated into the system to complete the elimination of standing waves and this was the work of Dennis Terrett who supervised the installation work in the Palace. He had read about some experiments which had been carried out in America and he put the idea to Ron Rackham who told him to go ahead and devise a suitable circuit. He achieved this by improving on the American method and by designing a circuit which delayed the signal by 5 cycles. The extra gain measured was an average of 10 dB with a shift of -5 cycles so that the muting of the loudspeakers was no longer necessary so this facility was switched out when the frequency shifter was added in about 1965.

There has to be a large number of microphones hanging from the roof of the chamber to ensure that every member is in close proximity to at least one of them and, with so many microphones, the gain achieved was far too small if all of them were in circuit at the same time. So experiments were carried out with an automatic system called 'Speech Operated Disconnection of Microphones' in which the loudest signal fed to the amplifier, that of the microphone closest to the member then speaking, triggered a circuit which automatically cut out the other microphones. This inevitably became known, to the delight of technicians and members alike, as S.O.D.O.M. But this had its drawbacks as there was very rapid switching of microphones during heated debates and if, for example, a member made a controversial statement during a speech and a member on the other side of the house shouted, 'RUBBISH', the 'Rubbish' would come through loud and clear and the member actually delivering the speech would be silenced, a most unhappy and unsatisfactory state of affairs. So S.O.D.O.M. was soon replaced by a manual control system but, of course, no provision had been made to accommodate an operator. In the event, the control equipment was installed in what had been a small store room, little bigger than a broom cupboard which, conveniently, was in the south west corner of the house, opposite the Speaker and, after removing a small section of the fine oak panelling, it was fitted with a darkened glass window overlooking the chamber. When the author visited this in late 2000, it still resembled a cupboard, with barely sufficient room to work, but it is all that can be provided and, in any case, it is just sufficient and it has at least been made tolerably comfortable. The operator has, in front of him, a diagram of the chamber with each microphone represented by a button so that, knowing the intended order in which the members are likely to be called, he can select the microphone closest to the expected speaker by pressing the appropriate button. Of course, it is not always possible to know in advance who will be speaking at any given time so, in these circumstances, the operator can select a group of microphones as near as can be judged to the member who is speaking by pressing several buttons simultaneously and,

Administration 1947–1950

when he has established which microphone is actually the nearest, he can press the button for this one again, automatically switching out the adjacent, unwanted microphones. The button for the selected microphone is illuminated. For use only in extreme circumstances, the Speaker has the means to disable any microphone with an override switch.

Michael Fountain and Stan Livingstone were both involved in the early experiments in the old House of Lords and in the trial section of the chamber they employed pressure units below the backs of the seating driving long, acoustically damped tubes, the tops of which were about 1½" diameter and covered with a protective grille. These terminated at about ear level with one outlet for each seating position. They were all carefully balanced and with the wiring hidden under the cast iron grating sections of the floor which were covered by matting. These were not particularly successful although they did prove the viability of the principle of providing a small loudspeaker for each seating place. The final design for the new House of Commons Chamber incorporated specially designed loudspeakers and grilles let into the decorative woodwork above the leather backs of the seating, close to the members' ears. These, combined with the cardioid uni-directional microphones which were designed by Ron Rackham, completed this unique achievement and the design of these microphones was so good that their response to sound reaching them from behind was virtually nil. They were suspended on long wires from the ornate ceilings of the chambers and the installation was duly completed. Another Tannoy engineer who was closely associated with the design and installation of the original systems was Ernie Marsden who, with others, recounted the story of Guy sacking the delivery boy.

Later, when the House of Lords was refurbished, a similar Tannoy scheme was installed there too, although initially the loudspeakers were incorporated into the order paper rails which were fitted to the backs of the benches. They also incorporated sockets for the hand held earphones, like lorgnettes, which some seemed to prefer to the loudspeakers. The control panel in the Lords' Chamber was installed in the gallery, high above the floor of the chamber, and incorporated into an architectural feature.

Norman Robottom recalled the problems which they encountered at the start of the parliamentary year when members of the House of Commons were summoned to the upper Chamber to hear the Royal speech. The Tannoy microphones were considered to be an unacceptable incumbrance and had to be wound back into the roof out of sight and, of course, no Tannoy engineer was permitted to be present. The result was that members of both houses experienced some difficulty in hearing the Royal Speech.

In television programmes from the House of Commons, the loudspeakers

The TANNOY Story

can be seen as circular, bronze coloured grilles at intervals in the backs of the members' benches, just above the green leather seat backs.[1] In the Lords they are similar grilles, now deeply recessed into the red leather. Since the B.B.C. started live television transmissions from the Palace of Westminster there have been many criticisms levelled at Members of Parliament and at their Lordships who are often seen to be languishing upon the benches, apparently resting in comfort and, in some cases, sound asleep. Not so; they are, in fact, almost certainly listening quite intently to the course of the debate with their ears close to the Tannoy loudspeakers.

Beneath the Commons chamber, is an additional control room for use during 'secret' sessions. In this room the operator's control panel was so arranged that he could not hear the members taking part in the debate and his only means of determining who was actually speaking was by viewing the chamber through a periscope which gave him a reasonable view of the proceedings. This was a rather unsatisfactory arrangement which made the operator's work very difficult; but it satisfied the demand for secrecy in certain circumstances although it is believed to have been used only once, during the Suez crisis. On one occasion, while maintenance work was being carried out, one of the Tannoy engineers, who was a keen film collector, left a reel of acetate film on top of one of the equipment cabinets. Unaware of this, another engineer put his hot soldering iron on the film can with the result that a great deal of acrid smoke was generated. The Palace firemen were called to deal with it and the engineers were given a severe ticking off as it could so easily have exploded. So, what Guy Fawkes' men had failed to do, Guy Fountain's men nearly did! As Dennis Terrett said, "We, at least, got as far as lighting the fuse!"

In 1952 Winston Churchill, having returned to the Commons as Prime Minister, had started developing the hearing problems usually associated with age and he derived only minimum benefit from the sound reinforcement system at his seat. He rejected the use of a hearing aid for cosmetic reasons since they were, at the time, both crude and cumbersome. At this time a Mr. Victor Foot, a part-time inventor, had produced in his two-room factory at Wandsworth a hearing device which was cosmetically acceptable but technically inefficient. It comprised an electro-inductive diaphragm of about $3/4"$ in diameter mounted in the top of a dummy fountain pen which could be clipped to a breast pocket and activated by an extremely strong modulated field loop which could be positioned under the carpet. At Churchill's place it worked, but a heavy price was paid in the form of a scorched carpet over the energising coil which required more than 1 kW of power.

The Lords' Chamber is sacrosanct and the heavy hand of Victorianism abounds and causes problems when applying contemporary sound

Administration 1947–1950

reinforcement equipment. Somewhat surprisingly, one such situation is said to have occurred during the time when miniskirts were in fashion. The sound for the Peeress's gallery was produced by miniature loudspeakers fitted in the front of the gallery, at floor level. When the younger, contemporary Peeresses arrived to hear the debates during this era, wearing the fashion of the day, it is understood that there was much concern regarding the possible effect upon their Lordships' blood pressures. 'Modesty curtains' were duly fitted, presenting the electro-acoustic engineers with yet another almost impossible problem. In addition to this, the rear rows of seating do not have the convenience of red leather upholstery in which to secrete the miniature loudspeakers. These difficulties were finally solved by the installation of pressure units located under the seating, fitted to acoustically damped conductor tubes, terminating at a 1" hole in the linenfold panelling, at a convenient height in relation to the listeners' ears.

There was also a requirement for continuous recording for the Hansard writers and this was subject to a separate contract. At the time there was no suitable recording equipment available, neither in Europe nor in America, so Tannoy had to modify whatever equipment they could procure. They used a magnetic tape recorder which was situated in the Hansard Editor's office. The machine used was a cassette recorder using very large cassettes and with the tape running at $1^{7}/_{8}$ inches per second. There were two tape cassettes loaded, one in operation and one at stand-by. After about 20 minutes the stand-by tape became the duty tape, with a small overlap. The tape was then changed to be ready for the repeat sequence. For monitoring purposes the recorders were modified by the provision of additional heads to provide a 'read-after-write' facility to ensure that the recording was actually on tape and not, as is standard practice, of monitoring the signal at the recording head. Thus, when the Hansard writers employed this facility they were able to confirm a satisfactory recording, delayed by the transposed head distance which was approximately $1^{1}/_{2}$ seconds. Somewhat later, in the 1970s, these recording facilities were extended to the committee rooms with the recording equipment located in a two-storey Portakabin structure on the roof.

The original Tannoy systems naturally employed thermionic valves and by 1972 it was deemed necessary to upgrade the equipment and in 1973 and 1974 fifty additional Tannoy microphones were installed together with new solid state systems, using silicon transistors, which could operate on a 50 volts battery during power failures. These new Tannoy systems incorporated even more sophisticated electronics than the original schemes but nobody had devised a phase shifting circuit which could offer any improvements on Dennis Terrett's original design, so this was retained.

The TANNOY Story

Soon after these systems were commissioned, an electricians' strike was threatened. Bill Preedy and Dennis Terrett were involved, checking the emergency supplies to the Palace of Westminster with the Resident Engineer, Colonel Harris. Col. Harris pointed to a massive heavy duty switch which gave the Palace two alternative supplies, in the 'up' position it was labelled 'Victoria' and in the down position, 'Westminster', saying, "We are completely covered". However, a number of car batteries were rushed to the House and connected up and tested in an emergency mode. It worked, which was just as well for immediately before the House sat the power supplies from both Victoria and Westminster sources were cut at the main intake point. Resourceful members, who used torches in the Commons Chamber to read their order papers, were cautioned by the Speaker who said that these were classed as lanterns and were forbidden in the Chamber! The Speaker then went on to say that members should 'speak up' as the sound reinforcement system was not working but the Hansard report for that day goes on to report that in fact the sound system was working and, '. . . the Speaker corrected his previous statement'.

A measure of the standard of excellence which the Tannoy schemes achieved is well illustrated by the fact that when the *B.B.C.* started some experimental broadcasts of proceedings on 9th June, 1975, their engineers installed their own microphones, made by *A.K.G.*, and carried out exhaustive trials on them but it was found that the noise level was just 3 dB better than the Tannoy microphones which had been in use for 25 years or more. So, when regular broadcasts started on 3rd. April, 1978, the *B.B.C.* used the Tannoy microphones with the addition of two new ones at the Despatch Box. When television broadcasts started from the House of Lords on 23rd January, 1985 and from the House of Commons on 21st November, 1989, it was again found that the old Tannoy microphones could not be bettered so, once again, they were retained. These Tannoy microphones remained in use for both the sound reinforcement systems and the *B.B.C.* transmissions until 1992 when those in the Commons were replaced, followed in 1994 by those in the Lords when all the Tannoy equipment was finally decommissioned and replaced by new schemes which were designed by Southampton University. The Tannoy microphones and loudspeakers had been in service in the chambers for some 45 years! Incidentally, it has been said that the new microphones look like *A.K.G.* units, which were made by a *Harman* company and it was, of course, *Harman* who later took control of Tannoy. The response of the original system was level from 100Hz to 8kHz, +/- 2dB, including the microphones and loudspeakers, i.e. from mouth to ear, and this was achieved with minimal electronic correction.

Much emphasis has rightly been laid on the brilliant work carried out by Ron Rackham on the design of the installations in the Palace of Westminster, but

Administration 1947–1950

Dennis Terrett made the point that the work of Philip Waples must not be overlooked. Dennis worked as Philip Waples' assistant during the original installation in the Palace of Westminster and also on the system in Ottawa and he said that Philip Waples was an exceptionally able electronics design engineer and Bill Preedy described him as a 'Five-star Genius.' When Waples left Tannoy there was a very big hole in the design ability of the company.

One day, just before the commissioning of one of the Tannoy systems in the Palace of Westminster, Guy turned up there in his Rolls Royce and was absolutely furious when the Palace Police would not let him drive into the Palace yard. He would not, of course, consider parking his car elsewhere and walking in; he demanded to be allowed to park his car in the Palace yard. Tannoy's man there at the time was Victor Bachelor who, by nature of his duties in the House was allowed to park his car in the yard so Guy was absolutely livid when this privilege was not automatically extended to him. "Don't you know who I am?" he roared, "I'm Guy Fountain, Governing Director of Tannoy and my company is installing the sound equipment here." The policeman said the he did not really care who he was. He was not allowed to bring his car inside. Eventually Guy saw Vic Bachelor and asked him why he had not been allowed in with his car but neither Vic's reply nor the final outcome is on record. On another occasion when Guy was visiting the engineers and much enjoying walking through the 'corridors of power', he insisted on going through a doorway clearly signed, 'MEMBERS ONLY', ignoring the doorkeepers. It so happened that the Sergeant at Arms saw him and called out, "Stop Stranger," at the same time starting to draw his sword from its sheath. At that Guy stopped in his tracks and followed the Tannoy engineer to safer ground.

It was widely thought that Ron Rackham should have been put forward for an Honour in recognition of his important achievements with Tannoy through the war years and particularly for his work in perfecting the systems for the Palace of Westminster, but it is believed that Guy, being intensely jealous and unable to let a subordinate overshadow him, blocked this saying, "If anyone is to receive an honour, it should be me." Bill Preedy recalled it as another 'Look at me' or 'Do you know who I am?' situation with Guy Fountain who, it seems, decided that he should pay a visit to the Queen. Eventually, and with great difficulty, a meeting was arranged with the Master of the Household. The first problem arose when, as was customary, they entered the Palace via the Ambassadors' Entrance and not through the main courtyard. The next problem was that, on entering the ballroom the Master of the Household was not there. In order to amuse Guy during the delay Bill Preedy took the opportunity of showing him the Knighting Stool so he could rehearse for the much anticipated accolade. When Bill Preedy noticed that the Master of the Household was

The TANNOY Story

approaching from the picture gallery Guy retreated into the depths of the ballroom, apparently in a state of panic, pretending to examine one of the Tannoy dual concentric loudspeakers.

The success of the schemes in the Palace of Westminster led to similar installations being ordered for several other legislative assembly buildings including the House of the People in New Delhi, (1950), the House of Commons in Ottawa, (1952), Legislative Assemblies in Regina, Manitoba and Edmonton, all in Canada, the Legislative Assembly in Cochin, in south-west India and the International Monetary Conference in Istanbul, (1955). Instantaneous translation systems were another requirement in many debating chambers. Tannoy helped with the design and installation of a six language simultaneous interpretation scheme in the Palais de Chaillot, Paris, for the 1951 session of the United Nations Organisation and a similar system was soon ordered from Tannoy for their permanent buildings in New York and Geneva. A Tannoy debating and interpretation system was also installed in Church House, Westminster and, in addition to sound reinforcement and interpretation, the Tannoy systems, known as the '8000' system, incorporated vote counting facilities and were claimed, probably quite correctly, to be the most advanced systems of their kind. Tannoy sound reinforcement schemes were also provided in the Queen Elizabeth Hall and in the New National Theatre in Romania.

The challenge of competing for projects such as these was that each installation was expensive and tied up considerable financial resources for a comparatively small company. The tenders for the Bangladesh Assembly in Dacca and for the International Monetary Conference in Istanbul make this clear. The complete system for Dacca was priced at £633,000 including £445,000 for closed circuit television, £113,000 for sound reinforcement, £34,000 for an electronic voting system and up to £32,000 for simultaneous interpretation. The installation in Istanbul amounted to £249,000 for interpretation equipment, £35,000 for a recording system and £27,000 for closed circuit television.

Stan Livingstone was responsible for the installation of the Tannoy equipment in the Romanian Theatre and on one occasion, when he was returning from a progress meeting, his aircraft had a stopover in Moscow and Stanley took the opportunity to visit the radio studios there which used Tannoy monitor loudspeakers exclusively. While arranging his onward flight home his passport was taken from him and he was escorted to the upper floor of the terminal building which proved to be a detention area. No reason was given to him for his detention, that is to say not in English, and no communication was allowed throughout his three days detention during which he had to take his meals in the restaurant, accompanied by an outsize female guard of the Russian Security Department. When his passport was returned, still no reason was given for his detention and he resumed his journey home to a very worried Joan and to an equally worried Tannoy staff. The reason was eventually discovered. Harold Wilson, then the Prime Minister, had insisted on the return to Moscow of a number of Russian Embassy staff who were deemed to be undesirable and this had triggered a tit-for-tat game at which the Russians were very apt. This was a very worrying experience for those such as Stan who had been chosen to be the pawns in this diplomatic game of chess.

Starting in 1955 and continuing for some thirty years, Tannoy developed and installed audio frequency loop simultaneous interpretations systems for a large number of multi-national government and commercial conferences but perhaps the most active time for installations such as these was 1959 when sound reinforcement and/or interpretation schemes were provided for the Saskatchewan Legislative Assembly, the Senate Chamber in Ottawa, the Fiji Legislative Assembly, S.H.A.P.E. Headquarters in Paris and the N.A.T.O. Talks in Mayfair, London. Many notable amplification and sound reinforcements installations were carried out by Tannoy at about this time including:

County Hall, the GLC Chamber.
Mecca Dance Halls.
Pontin's Holiday Camps.
The Connaught Rooms.
Kingsway Hall.
Bentalls Department Store.
Bulmers Cider.
The Royal Exeter Hotel.

The Baltic Exchange.
Butlin's Holiday Camps.
Warner's Holiday Camps.
Petters Engines, Slough.
Streatham Ice Rink.
The Pascall Sweet Factory, Mitcham.
Darwins of Sheffield.
Lots Road Power Station.

In addition to these, Tannoy public address systems were installed in the many stadia owned and run by the *Greyhound Racing Association*, notably the White City stadium at Shepherds Bush, West London.

The subsequent replacement systems in the Palace of Westminster and many of the important Tannoy systems which followed from them were supplied in later years. For example, following the installation of solid state systems in the Palace of Westminster in 1973 and 1974, further development of this equipment took place and, in 1977, installations were commissioned for the Governments of Malta and Syria. It also seems appropriate to record at this point some of the earlier experiences of Norman Robottom, although they rightly belong to an earlier time.

Norman Robottom remembers one of the difficulties which they encountered with the early simultaneous translation systems which was caused by the

The TANNOY Story

soundproof booths in which the interpreters sat. Not only were they very heavy and therefore difficult to transport to the building where they were to be used but the walls of the booths were made of a timber based material which had been processed with formaldehyde and, when the booths became warm, the operators started coughing during their work, to the consternation of their clients.

On the occasion of the meetings of the War Debts Commission, which was convened in 1950 at Lancaster House, Norman Robottom was working on the installation of the interpretation equipment when he was approached by two rather fierce looking men who announced to him that they were from M.I.6. They asked him about the equipment he was installing and said, "How secure is this system? Can anything be heard via this equipment in any other area of the building?" When Norman tried to assure them that all was quite well; that it was simply low power amplification equipment which would not transmit anywhere, they asked him how long it would be before he had finished. He told them that he would be done in about 30 minutes and they said that they would be back. When Norman had completed his work, they set a metronome in front of one of the microphones and then used some form of probe to find out if there was a signal anywhere which could be regarded as a security risk. They even probed among the live cables in the electricity distribution board, thankfully without killing themselves. They were soon satisfied when their probe picked up nothing but a B.B.C. programme although they were able to hear the metronome when they attached the probe to the outside door knobs of the room but, as there would be two rather large Marines on duty there at all times, they went away happy.

Norman Robottom was then made responsible for operating the equipment during the conference and this entailed selecting the correct microphone for whoever was speaking. This should have been easy as the delegates were, of course, supposed to address their remarks through the Chairman, thus giving Norman time to see who was going to speak and to select the correct microphone. However, they seldom observed the correct procedures and there was often a delay between a delegate starting to talk and the interpreters getting his words. The very highly paid interpreters would then knock furiously on the windows of their booths and gesticulate madly at Norman who was doing the best that he could and was, of course, paid only a tiny fraction of the salaries which they enjoyed.

On one occasion, on a very warm day, Norman went to the 'gents' during a break in the conference and found himself standing next to Anthony Eden who said, "Hello" to him. Norman replied, "Hello, Sir", to which Eden replied, "It's far too hot to be cooped up in here on such a lovely day as this, I'll try to wrap it up quickly." Soon after the meeting re-convened, Eden announced, "I call this meeting to order, does anyone wish to make a statement?" Then, almost immediately he said, "This meeting is adjourned until 9 o'clock tomorrow morning." He banged down his gavel, looked at Norman, gave him a broad smile and winked.

On another day, a Monday, when the conference was not due to re-convene until the Wednesday, the factory received a phone call for Norman at 3 o'clock from the Palace of Westminster to tell him to get into his van and get to Lancaster House quickly as they were waiting to start. Norman drove Tannoy's little Morris Eight van like a lunatic, breaking the speed limit, and drew up outside Lancaster House. When he leaped out of the rather tatty little van the security police yelled at him, "Stop, Stop! You can't leave that thing here." Norman quickly told them who he was and that the conference was waiting for him and, changing their attitude, they ushered him up the stairs and opened the door for him. When he arrived in the conference room he saw that all the delegates were waiting for him so that they could start work.

Norman was also involved in a number of seances but it was not long before he had to ask Jim Whiting, who was in charge of the Hire Department, to take him off this assignment, most of which took place in the Kingsway Hall, London. He said that there were some really strange things going on which he just did not understand. He had to install sound equipment to amplify the proceedings and on the stage there was a seat, rather like a big box, just big enough for someone to sit in, which was covered with black velvet and this was where the medium was going to sit. Norman asked where the microphones were required and he was told that they wanted three microphones and that they should be a few feet in front of this box, at varying heights. Norman thought that there would be a few technical problems with this arrangement and he asked if they could be placed a little closer but he was told, "That will be alright." He was quite concerned about this, believing that the microphones were much too far from the seat but he was repeatedly told, "That will be alright," almost as if they were telling him to mind his own business and just get on with what he was being paid to do.

When he had finished setting up the equipment, he took a break and went out for a cup of tea and, on returning to the hall he found it well filled, so he sat down at the mixing panel which he had installed to control the three microphones. The medium, a woman, then sat in the box and Norman heard some very unreal voices coming from the microphones which he was monitoring, not just a woman's voice, but various voices including male voices and one of a child. He could tell which microphone the child's voice was coming through and, at one point, it sounded as if the voice was speaking very closely into the

The TANNOY Story

microphone, a matter of just a few inches, yet Norman could see that it was four or five feet away from the box. He felt quite uneasy about this and he was sure that something rather wierd was happening. Now when a voice is too close to a ribbon microphone, it tends to emphasise the low frequency elements of the sound and Norman kept turning down the gain control of this microphone to compensate for this, yet there was nobody near enough to the microphone to cause the problem.

On another occasion, Norman thinks that this was also at the Kingsway Hall, the Medium had apparently established contact with a newspaper boy from many years earlier, late in the 19th century and, of course, long before the development of electronics and sound amplification. The young lad's cockney voice was apparently coming from the medium who was sitting in the box. Towards the end of this contact the voice said, "I bet that bloke from Tannoy's wonderin' wot's goin' on!" Norman could never work out whether this was genuine, however wierd, or a set-up, and he found this experience so disturbing that he had to ask to be taken off the job.

Now, returning, quite properly, to the events during the years of Receivership, there was another amusing incident which Norman Robottom recounted which illustrates the quality and the reliability of Tannoy equipment of the time in a rather surprising manner. He was asked to take a portable amplifier to Dover during the channel swimming season, the idea being that it would be used in the little support boat which would be rowed across the channel with a young girl who was attempting the swim, so that words of encouragement could be called to her by her supporters in the boat. At the quayside they had to lower the amplifier, the battery and all the other equipment down into the little boat on the end of a rope. Unknown to any of them, the rope had been stored close to a battery which had been tipped over, allowing some sulphuric acid to come into contact with it. The rope, weakened by the acid, broke as they were lowering the amplifier into the boat and the inevitable result was that the boat capsized, tipping all the Tannoy equipment into the sea. However, the water was quite shallow there and the boatman managed to hook everything out of the sea, covered with seaweed and sand and apparently useless. They could not possibly obtain replacements in time for the start of the swim so Norman borrowed a hose and washed the silt out of the amplifier and the microphone and opened all the cases to lay the chassis out to dry in the sun. Later that afternoon, when everything looked more or less dry, he tried it and, miraculously, it all worked, even the microphone, so they were able to go ahead with the swim as planned.

The Royal Aircraft Establishment's bi-annual air shows at Farnborough were a great money spinner for Tannoy and these contracts ran for several years. For these events towers of 100 watts column loudspeakers were powered by 1 kilowatts amplifiers and this arrangement was so effective that it was possible to hear the announcements quite clearly over the noise of the aircraft performing their displays. The level of background noise from the aircraft was not the only problem which Tannoy engineers had to overcome, for the spectators, numbering many thousands of people, watched the displays from vantage points along much of the length of the runway, set back at a reasonably safe distance of course, and there was always a considerable distance between the front rows and those spectators right at the back of the viewing area. Because they were spread along the the runway, there was a major problem with sound delay such that if loudspeakers mounted along the length of the spectators' arena had been connected to the same amplifier, the time lag would have meant that spectators at any given point would hear the announcements two or three times, maybe more, depending on how much volume the loudspeakers produced and how far the spectators were from those loudspeakers which they could hear. This would have been completely confusing and announcements would have been unintelligible. So the Tannoy engineers devised an elaborate delay mechanism for the various amplifiers by means of a magnetic disc recorder with several play-back heads arranged at different points around the magnetic disc so that each amplifier's signal was delayed by exactly the right interval to ensure that the output of its loudspeaker was accurately synchronised with the sound from the adjacent loudspeakers, all along the line. This required some ingenious equipment and much experimentation to ensure that the time delay on each amplifier was accurate, but they did it – and it worked. In later years the magnetic disc recorders were replaced by magnetic tape recorders using a continuous loop of recording tape and with multiple re-play heads.

Guy Fountain occasionally visited the air shows and the Hire Department crews were forewarned of his visits. The first instruction from the 'Guv'nor' was to remove sufficient of the portable security fencing, provided for the safety of the public, to surround his Rolls Royce, giving it the prestige of a prime exhibit. Bill Preedy recalled the last show at which he was present, when, having dealt with the requirements of the bi-annual Rolls Royce show-off, he was then commanded to acquire a large ladder and place it against the side of a mobile radar station. Guy then had a chair placed on the roof as an appropriate viewing point commensurate with his station. It was not long before a member of the R.A.F. Police was despatched to have the offending object removed, presumably because it was believed to have caused a malfunction of the radar equipment. There followed a heated argument punctuated by frequent repetitions of the question, "Do you know who I am?" after which he was removed from his vantage point. On sub-sequent days the Tannoy crews were

The TANNOY Story

instructed to keep the offending policeman under surveillance, for which purpose they were equipped with high power binoculars, and any miscreant action was to be reported to Guy immediately.

The foregoing accounts illustrate the success of so-called 'Systems Engineering' projects during the period of Receivership. In the next chapter the success of the famous Dual-Concentric Loudspeaker is recorded.

CHAPTER NOTES

1   George Wheeler had discussed the requirements of the scheme with the Architect, Sir Giles Gilbert Scott, who told him that they would be constrained by the aesthetic requirements and that many things that Tannoy would like to do would not be acceptable; hence the tiny loudspeakers built into the backs of the benches with grilles which were designed by Sir Giles.

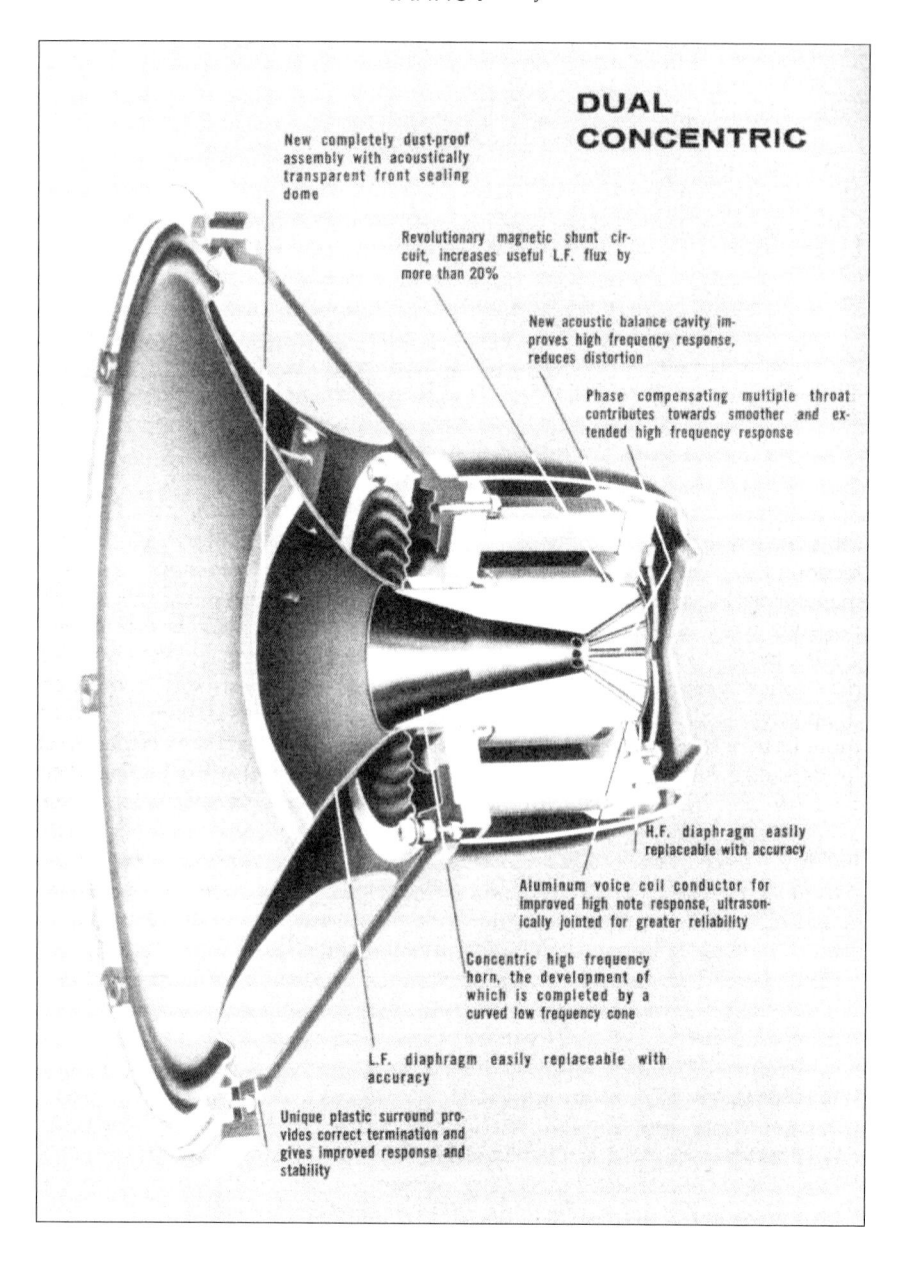

The **TANNOY** Story

DUAL CONCENTRIC

New completely dust-proof assembly with acoustically transparent front sealing dome

Revolutionary magnetic shunt circuit, increases useful L.F. flux by more than 20%

New acoustic balance cavity improves high frequency response, reduces distortion

Phase compensating multiple throat contributes towards smoother and extended high frequency response

H.F. diaphragm easily replaceable with accuracy

Aluminum voice coil conductor for improved high note response, ultrasonically jointed for greater reliability

Concentric high frequency horn, the development of which is completed by a curved low frequency cone

L.F. diaphragm easily replaceable with accuracy

Unique plastic surround provides correct termination and gives improved response and stability

CHAPTER TWELVE

THE DUAL CONCENTRIC LOUDSPEAKER

The most important achievement during the period of administration, the most important of all Tannoy achievements, was the development and perfection of the Tannoy Dual Concentric Loudspeaker. The company's development work on loudspeakers can be divided fairly equally between pre-war and post-war work and the progress in pre-war developments has been recorded earlier, in Chapter 5. Following the war the most notable achievement was the dual concentric loudspeaker although, to be fair, this progressed from some of the pre-war loudspeaker work for, since 1935, this had been the subject of much thought by Jack Houlgate, following his successful design of the very powerful loudspeaker for the Argentine Navy. He wanted to design a loudspeaker which would be a considerable improvement on anything which had been available hitherto and which would be truly worthy of the accolade, 'High Fidelity'. He had given a great deal of thought to the matter for some years, particularly during those boring hours during the war when he was obliged to spend his time on rooftops at night, firewatching. He had also designed and made a moving-coil gramophone pick-up for George Wheeler at this time.

The idea of a reverse throat pressure driver with the cone being the continuation of the horn was registered by *Western Electric* in America in 1936 and this was assigned to the *British Thomson-Houston* company in Britain but they did not use it. The *Western Electric* '555' was the first reverse throat loudspeaker and it was developed for the cinema industry. In the early days of the talking pictures a 10 watts amplifier was quite an achievement and this needed very efficient loudspeakers so horn loudspeakers had to be used, usually situated behind the screen which had tiny perforations to allow the sound through. These horn loudspeakers often did not sound too good for their quality left much to be desired, but they could be heard in large auditoria. All manufacturers who made horn loudspeakers at that time made them in a conventional manner and, so far as is known, the *Western Electric* '555' was the first reverse throat loudspeaker to be made commercially.

In the process of developing the principle of the power microphone for use on board submarines Houlgate had, as has already been recorded, confounded all the 'experts' by proving quite conclusively that a magnetic circuit could have two gaps; and work. His designs worked extremely well. After Jack Houlgate's departure to the B.B.C. his equally brilliant understudy, Ronnie Rackham, combined and refined these ideas and, after working on them for some years, he eventually perfected the Dual Concentric loudspeaker. Only a few days before he died Stan Livingstone stated to the author, quite categorically, "Ron Rackham was entirely responsible for this achievement. The detail design of the dual concentric loudspeaker, its development, its manufacturing specification, its excellent performance and its superb quality were entirely the achievements of Ron Rackham."

As part of his experimental work for the Henley Royal Regatta Rackham had made an experimental 15" dual concentric loudspeaker using the magnets of two CD 4 loudspeakers, stacked one behind the other to provide the working flux and this had the additional advantage of providing the length required for the initial horn loading of the high frequency unit. He made the high frequency unit with a duralumin diaphragm which was mounted on a very light, soft iron plate based on the SD5 loudspeaker which was the first pressure unit made by Tannoy. The SD 5 was used as the driver for all Tannoy horn loudspeakers. He then fixed this modified SD 5 loudspeaker onto the back of the CD 4 magnets which he drilled out exponentially so that the sound from the SD 5 came out through these magnets, the exponential form being continued by the cone of the CD 4 loudspeaker. He provided a cross-over at about 1,100 Hz and this was the basis of the Dual Concentric loudspeaker. He made two versions, one with a high impedance cross-over for use on 100 volts circuits which was soon discontinued; and a 15 ohms unit.

To develop the idea further, he reverted to Houlgate's successful magnetic circuit with two gaps and made a magnet assembly with the rear gap surrounding the voice coil of the pressure unit and with the front gap taking the voice coil of the cone unit to make one neat, viable assembly which, after a great deal of development work, he perfected in the Dual Concentric loudspeaker. The 2" diameter voice coil of the low frequency unit was wound with copper wire and was situated in the front gap of the magnet assembly while the smaller voice coil of the high frequency section was wound with aluminium wire. To equalise the sensitivity between the two drive units an exclusive magnetic

The TANNOY Story

shunt was used to decrease the flux in the high frequency gap. The high frequency voice coil was attached to the outer diameter of the dished, duralumin diaphragm to keep the mass down to a minimum and to extend the high frequency response. On the concave side of this diaphragm, and very close to it, was a machined, phase-correcting multiple throat which ensured that the sound radiation from all areas of the diaphragm arrived at the beginning of the exponential horn in phase. At the termination of the horn, which was machined out of the centre pole of the magnetic system, the horn expansion was continued by the curved low frequency diaphragm. In the ideal case a low frequency diaphragm should move as a piston whereas in practice, with a simple diaphragm, the cone flexes so that parts are moving forwards whilst others are moving backwards, or are stationary. This causes partial or complete cancellation and a peaky response. To alleviate this the Tannoy research team developed what they named the 'Girdacoustic' system in which a number of triangular cross-section ribs were attached to the rear of the diaphragm to add strength and rigidity.[1]

It was a really excellent piece of equipment and a very long way ahead of all its competitors and when he had perfected it, it was shown at the 1947 Radio Show, but nobody in the company quite knew what to do with it. It had a very level response and would handle a great deal of power but its great disadvantage was that it was so good that it showed up all the faults in contemporary recordings and radio transmission techniques.

The first effort at selling it was to offer it as a standard sound source to research laboratories. One was sold to *A.K.G.* in Vienna and one to the *Turner Microphone Company* in America, but what really started it along its road to success was that, following an article in *Wireless World*, the General Post Office Research Laboratories at Dollis Hill, in North London, bought one. They did some tests on it and promptly bought six more as standard sound sources for testing microphones and other equipment, after which Tannoy could state in their publicity material that they were suppliers of official sound sources to the G.P.O. Some 25 years later the G.P.O. returned these loudspeakers to Tannoy for testing and it was found that they were still performing perfectly, nothing had changed, so Tannoy sent them back with a note of thanks. Yet 1947 was a bad year for Tannoy as the company started to founder, but Norman Wild, the Receiver, was impressed with the fact that six loudspeakers had been sold to Dollis Hill so he asked if this equipment was saleable to anybody else. Very conveniently, just down the road in Kennington, was the *Decca* factory and *Decca* had just introduced their hugely successful 'Full Frequency Range Recording' system for producing gramophone records. With the introduction of *Decca*'s 'f.f.r.r.' – as it was known – the reproduction of music from gramophone records was dramatically improved and, for some considerable time, *Decca* were a very long way ahead of all their competitors. To complement their 'f.f.r.r.' records, Decca needed a reproducing system which would bring out the best in these new records so they introduced a very fine new gramophone, the Decola, which had three loudspeakers in the lower part of the cabinet. Although multiple loudspeakers were not then unknown in good quality instruments, notably the *McMichael* 'Twin Supervox', RV8 of 1933 and their 'Model 135' of 1935, they were not a regular feature as this was some time before the introduction of commercial stereophonic recording but, suffice it to say, the Decola was a truly excellent instrument. It was also a particularly elegant piece of furniture being housed in a very well designed cabinet veneered with burr walnut. However, although it was originally equipped with very good loudspeakers, the Tannoy Dual Concentric loudspeakers were very much better. There was a very good reason for *Decca* making their Decola as a gramophone and not as a radiogram for, at that time, purchase tax was applied to all radios but not to gramophone record reproducers. However, they fitted the Decola with a convenient slot into which a purpose made radio tuner could easily be fitted so that buyers had to pay this tax only on the radio chassis.

At about this time Stan Livingstone was transferred from a rather loose association with the Tannoy Laboratory to something which was called, 'Trade Sales', the idea being to try to find out what Tannoy could make in quantity and sell in bulk. Stan did not then have a car but there were buses and he went to *Decca*, less than four miles away, carrying a very heavy and rather cumbersome 15" dual concentric loudspeaker. He saw a gentleman called Norman Mordaunt who was under the impression that Stan was looking for a job because he knew that Tannoy was in trouble but, as he had lugged a heavy 15" dual concentric loudspeaker into his office he was not inclined to throw him out. Together with a man called Thompson – who ran *Thompson, Diamond, Butcher*, a wholesale radio and record distributor which was partly owned by *Decca* – Mordaunt looked over the loudspeaker and, after hearing it, they decided to keep it. After a week Stan telephoned them and they told him that they thought that it was fantastic, "We're going to make a luxury model of the Decola which we'll call the *Knightsbridge* but we expect to put only about 20 of them into production. Unfortunately only a 12" *Goodmans* loudspeaker will fit into the cabinet of our current Decola. Can you do anything?" Stan asked them to give him a couple of weeks and he would see what could be done.

Livingstone told Rackham that he thought they stood a chance of doing business with *Decca* if they could make a 12" model, so Rackham started to make one. He found an old, broken *Goodmans* 12" loudspeaker which provided the frame and used the magnets for the SD 4 which were quite

The TANNOY Story

suitable, but he had a problem finding a suitable cone. Stan took the problem to Norman Wild and explained that to make a cone would involve expensive tooling which he would not want to undertake. Wild asked who else made loudspeaker cones and Stan told him that he thought that all sorts of people such as *Goodmans* and *Celestion* had cone forming machinery. "Ah," said Wild, "*Celestion* are in the same position as Tannoy and a friend of mine is the Receiver." If he gave the man a call would Stan like to go over and maybe find some suitable cones? So Livingstone was sent by bus to *Celestion* at Thames Ditton and went to the stores where he found a great mountain of exponentially curved, 12" cones with 2" diameter voice coils – exactly the right cones. This was, indeed, manna from heaven! The storekeeper said he'd been instructed to let him have some. How many did he want? Stan said that six would do, so he gave him ten.

'To cut a short story long', as Livingstone later recounted, he took the cones back to Rackham and, with a lot of assistance from Bill Haines in making the machined poles etc., Rackham produced a 12" dual concentric loudspeaker in about 10 days. Stan took this to *Decca* who were then putting three *Goodmans* 12" loudspeakers into their Decola. They replaced the centre one with the Tannoy 12" dual concentric unit and the result was nothing less than a revelation. They then asked if Tannoy could make the accompanying two bass loudspeakers as well. This really presented no problem as they could get the frames; they had the magnets and they could get the cones. So Stan said, "Yes", and Mordaunt asked him for a quote.

Livingstone rushed back to the factory and saw Bill Haines who did some quick sums and Stan personally typed the quotation, very badly as he was no great typist and electric typewriters were unheard of, and posted it to *Decca*. He gave them a week to think it over, then phoned them and was asked to go and see them again. When he arrived at the *Decca* factory he was told that they had made up a Decola using the Tannoy loudspeakers and they wanted to change immediately. Stan then told them that the Receiver would, of course, want an order and he was told that they had already made out the order, they would like 1,000 dual concentrics and 2,000 bass units. Norman Mordaunt very gently picked Stan up from the floor and settled him in a chair, asking if he would like to take the order back with him to show he'd been doing something useful in these last few days. The order led to the sustained production of the 12" dual concentric loudspeaker and, for three or four years, they continued buying the cones from *Celestion*.

At that time, on so-called 'Trade Sales', Stan was entitled to a commission of 1%, Guy Fountain being under the illusion that he would never sell anything. But this time he had come back with a firm order for 1,000 dual concentrics, just the bare loudspeakers, without cross-over units or anything else, which sold at about £17 each and 2,000 bass loudspeakers at about £9-10/- each; approximately £36,000 worth of good business which, on just two comparatively small items, was almost unheard of. This, of course, brought a gleam into Norman Wild's eye but a big, worried frown on Guy Fountain's face who said, "Well of course, Stan, you realise this isn't really a Trade Sales deal, this is a head office sale." Whereupon Wild looked Fountain straight in the face and said, "Guy, we're talking about *my* ******* *money*, not *your* ******* *money*!" He then sent Stan straight down to *Barclays Bank* at Tulse Hill to open his first account on the basis that they couldn't pay him in cash because the envelopes were not big enough!

During these negotiations for the sale of the dual concentric loudspeaker to *Decca*, Tannoy received a letter from *British Thompson-Houston*'s solicitors with a copy of the registered design virtually saying, 'What about it?' Livingstone, on the point of securing the order from *Decca* for use in the Decola gramophone, could see the order going down the drain so he asked Norman Wild for his advice. Norman said, "Don't worry about that my boy, forget it completely. You just get on the bus and go down to Kennington and see Decca." Nothing more was ever heard about it. How Norman Wild managed to appease *B T-H*. and secure for Tannoy the right to make these loudspeakers was not recorded but he must have done some very clever talking. However, there is no argument that the *Western Electric* patent specification is quite clear; the specification is for a pressure driver of some type radiating through a horn, the commencement of which is a part of the magnet assembly and the continuation of which is the cone of a direct radiator. It is thought that the differences in the detail design on which Norman Wild succsssfully negotiated the appeasement of *B.T-H*. and their solicitors was probably based on Ron Rackham's development of Jack Houlgate's very original idea that a magnetic circuit containing two gaps would work satisfactorily, replacing the two separate magnetic assemblies as specified by *Western Electric*. It has also been suggested that his argument may have been further strengthened by detail differences in the profile of the cone as it is not entirely clear whether the *Western Electric* patent specified that the cone should be of exponential form.

Another company, an American company called *Altec Lansing*, wanted to make them but were not as brave as Norman Wild nor as ingenious as Ron Rackham and they used two magnets, one behind the other and, in the middle of the cone they put a little multi-cell horn. This was also sufficiently different from the *Western Electric* design to be acceptable, but it never came near to matching the success of the Tannoy loudspeaker.

It was not long before the news of this loudspeaker filtered down to the

The TANNOY Story

Decca recording studios who were, with their 'f.f.r.r.' system, the prime recording studios in the World. They had developed the first commercial feedback cutter and with this, they were producing their f.f.r.r. records. These reproduced sound up to 14 kHz at a time when other studios regarded it as a real bonanza if they could achieve 8 kHz, and they had also developed a special pickup to play them. They ordered a number of dual concentric loudspeakers for use in their studios and the news of this spread everywhere. Dr. Dutton, of *E.M.I.* studios, visited Tannoy and by this time Ron Rackham had also designed the G.R.F. and Autograph horn loaded enclosures for the Dual Concentric loudspeaker, so Dr. Dutton bought a number of G.R.F. enclosures for their Abbey Road studios in 1951. They were soon sold also to *Philips*, to studios in Eastern Europe and almost everywhere and Tannoy very soon took over from *Altec Lansing* in the manufacture of high quality monitor loudspeakers.

George Wheeler claimed to have taken a major part in the development of the Dual Concentric loudspeaker and he once said that he had taken out the patent for it but, to counter this claim, Livingstone was quite adamant that it really had little in common with the Argentine Navy loudspeaker on which Wheeler had worked under Jack Houlgate apart from the fact that it had a reverse throat similar to the Western Electric 555.

Other successes followed the introduction of the dual concentric loudspeaker. When Tannoy had gone into receivership, the company had placed many substantial orders with Timms' company, *Lockwood & Co.*, for loudspeaker cabinets but, of course, when the Receiver took over, there was still a substantial outstanding debt which was not paid. Timms just about survived and Livingstone told him that if he could weather the storm, in two or three years he would get something. In the event he was paid as the others were, 5/- in the pound. However, Livingstone and Timms remained very good friends. Then, in the 1950s, Timms won the contract for making the *B.B.C.* monitor loudspeaker cabinet which had originally been designed to accommodate an Altec Lansing loudspeaker, but there were no dollars to buy these so Tannoy took advantage of the situation and the dual concentric unit was fitted instead. The situation then was that Timms' company, *Lockwood & Co.*, had the licence to provide the B.B.C. monitor loudspeaker cabinets, Tannoy could make 15" dual concentrics at the drop of a hat and together they built up a very, very big business.

These were also the heady days of the expansion of commercial television and *Marconi* was the prime, world-wide supplier of T.V. studios. Tannoy had successfully sold the idea of the *Lockwood* - Tannoy - *B.B.C.* monitor loudspeaker to *Marconi* so nearly every studio was equipped with these monitors and, through the good offices of Jack Houlgate who was by then working for the

The Dual Concentric Loudspeaker

B.B.C., the B.B.C. studios adopted Tannoy pick-up cartridges as well. This connection which Tannoy had established with the television studio business led to *Granada* approaching the company when they secured their early franchise. It is believed that Bernstein, a leading light in the Granada expansion, declined to go to *Marconi–H.M.V.* Their chief engineer came to Tannoy and, having heard for himself the excellent performance of the dual concentric loudspeaker, bought a large number of G.R.F. enclosures, about 60 of them. They may still be there.

Guy's project to develop a luxury radiogram, described in Chapter 10, was built while Ron Rackham was developing the Dual Concentric loudspeaker and it is believed that Guy's radiogram incorporated an early prototype of this.

Tannoy Products, meanwhile, was getting involved with various other developments, some of which were successful; some were not. One factor was that the growth in ordinary domestic tape-recorders was just beginning and there was a great opportunity for Tannoy to jump on the band wagon. This market had been stimulated to a large extent by a man called Colonel Colley, whose company, *Thermionic Products Ltd.*, made a tape recorder called the 'Soundmirror'.[2] The Soundmirror was an American conception and Colley had wanted to secure a licence from the *Brush Corporation* of America to build them in the U.K. so he spent his last £1,200 on a half page advertisement for the Soundmirror in a prime place in the *Sunday Express*, on page 3, under the Giles cartoon. He then went to America and said to Brush, "Look at this, you had better give me the licence." They looked at it and liked what they saw and somebody checked on the circulation which, in those days was second only to the *News of the World* and, thinking that he must be a real tycoon, they gave him the licence. He operated his business from a private house just behind a pub in the Lambeth Road and, by coincidence, the pub was of some interest to Livingstone because his maternal grandfather had once been the licensee.

The Soundmirror was designed as an item of furniture, like the popular table model radiograms of the time, and it was built into an elegant walnut veneered cabinet to stand upon a table. There were doors to each side of the loudspeaker grille; that on the left giving access to storage space for the microphone and the mains lead and that on the right concealing the controls. The recording tape, 'Butterfly' brand, was made by *Samuel Jones & Co.* of Camberwell and the premises occupied by their workshops later became a shopping precinct called the Butterfly Centre after *Samuel Jones'* trade mark. But it was this tape which led to the Soundmirror's downfall because it was a paper tape with the iron oxide deposited on it. Colley bought the iron oxide from Brush and he assumed, not unreasonably, that when it came to coating the paper tape *Samuel Jones & Co.* knew what they were doing. But they had never coated iron oxide

The TANNOY Story

before so that, after the tape had been run through the Soundmirror a few times, there was not very much of the coating left and a mass of iron oxide clogging the magnetic gap in the recording head, completing the magnetic circuit and making the head almost ineffective. This took some time to happen and was not immediately apparent.

Although this disaster with the tape was a major setback for the Soundmirror, Col. Colley had a man called Trevor Johnstone who did the selling for him. Now Johnstone was an excellent salesman and he managed to sell a large number of Soundmirrors which Colley's factory could not, initially, make quickly enough. When they eventually managed to make them, the tape failed. This was not the greatest of ventures but, by the time of this failure, Col. Colley had taken a lease on some very expensive premises in Jermyn Street (renamed from German Street during the Great War to overcome sensitivities), where he had the whole floor of a building, believed to be above a tailor's shop. Nothing comes cheaply in Jermyn Street and he had to find a way to pay the rent so he thought of the idea of making little models which soon became so fashionable; the ornamental drinking ducks which swivelled to dip their beaks in a glass of cold water. Their necks formed part of a thermometer with their large, bulbous bodies as the reservoir and, when the bulb reached room temperature the liquid rose up in the long neck, raising the delicately balanced centre of gravity so that the ducks tilted forward and dipped their beaks. When their beaks touched the water, the liquid in the stem was cooled, contracted, and the ducks swung upright again, only to repeat the process, seemingly for ever. They adorned many homes at the time and became a real money spinner for Col. Colley.[2]

The reader might well wonder where all this is leading to so, to return to the story, Guy Fountain was also very friendly with a big, fierce man, Leslie Odell, who ran relay stations in Wales and somehow Odell and a friend called Terry MacNamara gained control of the *Baird Television Company* which had been in trouble for quite a long time. The first thing he decided to do on taking control of Baird was to make the cheapest television possible and sell it in large numbers. It was cheap but potentially dangerous because it had a line output transformer on which the fly-back voltage was 6,000 volts and if it were touched while the set was switched on there was a very strong possibility that the person doing so might not live to tell the tale. Still, as long as the high voltage components were not touched and the set was switched off at the mains when not in use, they should be alright. Guy Fountain acquired some of these sets which he gave away to friends and to various other people whom he wished to favour. Gradually, though, Odell realised this was not a good piece of equipment to sell to the public because, as Stan Livingstone jokingly put it, he could not afford the coffins. However, he realised that tape recorders were fairly easy to make and not likely to be lethal and, when Colley's Chief Engineer at Thermionic Products joined him they went into production with tape recorders but they soon found that they had another problem because they were unable to make the microphones. So they rang Stan Livingstone and invited him to visit them and gave him a large order for moving coil microphones which Tannoy could make quite well and, in the event, Stan managed to sell them about 200-300 per week. Apart from the power microphones which were still in great demand, the microphones for these tape recorders became the biggest volume production item for Tannoy; and they were quite profitable. But the venture was somewhat underfunded and it was not long before Baird, too, was in difficulty.

All was not lost for Tannoy, however, because *Baird* was then merged with the old *Scophony Company* which had made very successful, large screen projection television sets which used a system known as the 'Jeffree Supersonic Light Control Cell' and all sorts of other weird devices which, it was said with some exaggeration, involved 'millions of volts'. As early as 1936 Scophony were producing large screen television sets and, in the late 1930s and using the same system, they had even projected television pictures onto a cinema screen. *Scophony-Baird* put a man called Friedlander in charge and he really built the tape recorder business up until they were making and selling 1,000 tape recorders each week and, of course, buying 1,000 microphones each week from Tannoy. Being a man with his eye very much to the main chance, Friedlander built the business up to its peak and, when he realised that people like *Grundig* and *Philips* would become really big in Britain, he started negotiations with *E.M.I.* The *E.M.I.* company had a near stranglehold on television at that time because they had the patents on the cathode ray tube for the receivers and on the iconoscope which was the heart of the camera and, with the huge sums of money they were making it was rumoured that they bought almost anything, including *Scophony-Baird*. It was also popularly supposed then that anything that *E.M.I.* bought soon went down the drain and, after climbing for a time, *E.M.I.-Scophony-Baird* also failed with the result that the microphone contract with Tannoy, by then amounting to some 5,000 per month, evaporated. Nevertheless it had run for a few years and had been a very profitable line for Tannoy while it lasted.

By 1950, largely under the guidance of the Receiver, Norman Wild, the company had become reasonably profitable inasmuch as he had whittled the company down to its core business and had established the necessary financial controls so that everybody knew where the money was, where it came from and where it would go and in the following year the creditors were all paid off, that is to say, they received all that they were going to get, 5/- in the pound, and the

The TANNOY Story

bank's official Receiver who had run the Creditors' Committee departed.

Just before the Receiver departed George Wheeler left the company. By this time George Wheeler and Guy Fountain were, quite understandably, on rather bad terms and George said that there were many times when important decisions were necessary and Guy would not take responsibility; he just ducked the issues. On these occasions the decisions were left to George who had to take responsibility for them, right or wrong, although Guy usually contrived to take the credit if the results were particularly favourable. George, as General Manager, occupied the next office to Guy and if Guy was in a good mood he would pass all the incoming mail straight out to him for action or for distribution but, if he was in one of his typical black moods, he would distribute it himself so that George was often unaware of what was going on.

One day when George had been in the factory, he returned to his office where he found a note marked 'G.C. Wheeler' propped up on his desk. He could tell straight away that it was from Guy so he opened it immediately. The author has been informed that the note was full of the most severe criticism, although the exact content of the note is not known. George stormed into Guy's office but he was not there, so he went back to his own office and spoke to his secretary who had been appointed by Guy, and demanded, "Where's Mr. Fountain?" "He's just left, he's going up to town." George tore out of the factory, jumped into his Jaguar and raced after him. Michael and several other members of the staff saw him leave and it became a company joke that George reversed down Canterbury Grove at such speed that they swore he changed gear!

He guessed which way Guy would go and caught up with him in Gallery Road, Dulwich, passed him and forced him into the pavement and confronted him saying, "What do you mean by this?" Guy replied, "Have you read it?" To which George replied, "Yes, what do you mean by it? I've been with you for 21 years, I sit in the next office to yours and you do not have the bloody courage to come and sack me, you have to send me a letter like this. You can't even face me with this. Well, you know what you can do with your bloody job and I'll tell the Receiver that when I see him. I'm giving you 30 days notice here and now." "Now look, George, hold your temper, don't do anything hasty." said Guy, and he tried his best to retrieve the situation.

In the following weeks Guy did all he could to persuade Wheeler to change his mind and stay. He spoke to George's wife; extolling all his virtues, he even tried to persuade Michael to speak to George and on the Sunday before the expiry of his notice George and his wife were invited to take drinks with Guy and Elsie at Tudor Lodge. During that visit George told him, "I'm sorry, I will not stay with you any longer; I've had enough." George received a fine, green suitcase as a parting present from Guy – after 21 years.

When asked why he resigned, George Wheeler said, "He undermined everything I did: he loved to talk about Michael running the business and he would quite happily go away for a month or more but then he would come back and rearrange everything. He would countermand many decisions which Michael and I had made and insult him in front of others just to show who was really the boss. He would also undermine all those, particularly Bill Haines and myself, who were backing Michael just to teach us a lesson for doing so. I could spend a weekend with him and he would be entirely amicable; he would be quite charming but, on the Monday, he would pick an argument which would result in the most terrible row. It was behaviour such as this which led me to submit my resignation." The letter which Guy had left on George's desk was not atypical for there was an element of cowardice in his personal life, but in business he had very great courage.

A remark which was often made by George Wheeler was, "I was Guy's business son, Michael was his family son, and if Guy had been been able to accept the fact that others could take over, he could have retired and Michael and I could have run the company and Tannoy, which Guy had created through his undoubted entrepreneurial skills, would have survived successfully." Michael, too, was experiencing considerable difficulty with his father and their relationship became very strained. Guy was beginning to spend more time away from the factory and during these absences Michael was allowed to run the company for considerable periods of time, making many necessary and difficult decisions but, on his return, Guy would countermand many of Michael's decisions just to show that he was still in control. In front of other people he would talk of Michael as 'My wonderful son, who is running the company for me', boosting Michael's confidence, only to destroy all that he did at a later date. However, Norman Robottom said that, in spite of the trauma of working under Guy Fountain, it was quite an unique company to work for. It was neither too small to perform – nor so big as to become impersonal: it was almost like working for a family. This comment was endorsed by Dennis Terrett who said, "One did not work for Tannoy, one became a part of it."

There are many comments on record about Guy's erratic behaviour and Michael said that his father was driven by the most terrible ego. "He could be very nice, very charming, very generous if it suited him but he frequently had to buy his friends. There were times when he could enjoy weekends with his friends and employees, being thoroughly pleasant and, perhaps, playing cards on a Sunday afternoon or evening and all would be well. But, if he was in a black mood on the following day he could be very unpleasant, even obscene, and it was quite impossible to judge his mood changes. I could never have a party at home because we never knew when or if he would appear, nor in what condition he would be. If he was not the worse for drink, and creating hell, he would be trying to get off with any girls who were present." This side of his character was also mentioned by George Wheeler who said, "I remember the time at Dalton Street when Elsie's youngest sister, Joyce, came to me and told me that she was having trouble with Guy but, of course, I could say very little except to tell her to push him away; that was all I could do."

It has already been recorded that Guy had great courage in his business ventures but he was also a coward in his personal affairs. In the course of an argument with Jim Whiting who ran the Hire Department, Whiting grabbed Guy by the neck and threatened him. Guy was absolutely terrified and screamed at Whiting not to hit him. On another occasion when the Receiver was called in, Guy would not come to the meeting but stayed at home.

As a further illustration of Guy's erratic behaviour, ranging from kindness and generosity to near violence, Bill Haines recalled that he had an agreement with Guy Fountain when he was married and Guy did the dirty on him then. Guy said, "I'll make your salary £7.10.0d. per week and after a time there will be another 10/- per week." But when Haines went to him to ask for the additional 10/-, Guy said, "That's at my discretion," and he did not get it. "On the other hand," said Haines, "he could be so kind, and often generous, and he could be a most likeable person. Sometimes his generosity came with a price to pay and sometimes it was at the expense of the company. On one occasion he invited me to spend a weekend at Carlton Cottage, in Cliftonville and, at the end of the weekend he said, 'Before you go home, take your car up the road and fill it up with petrol and put it on my account'." On another occasion Guy felt sorry for Philip Waples who, having married at a rather young age had two mouths to feed, and potentially more, and was evidently feeling the cold during a particularly severe winter and was unable to buy a new overcoat on his rather low income. Instead of considering a rise in his salary, Guy gave him a cast-off overcoat! What made this gesture all the more ridiculous was the considerable difference in their builds although Bill Preedy later thought that Guy had given Waples one of Michael's, Michael being much taller than his father.

Bill Preedy also received a similar gift of a suit. He was summoned to Guy's office one day and told to be sure that nobody would witness the event and Guy told him that his appearance did not match up to his aspirations for the more senior members of his staff. Guy then rummaged behind his chair and brought out what Preedy later described as looking like the proceeds from a car boot sale. The suit was in a large, pretentious check pattern and Preedy said that it would have been more suitable attire for a Bookie's Runner. Guy then said, "Get it altered to your size, I don't think much is involved, you're roughly my size." Preedy never wore it; he kept it in his wardrobe for many years as a daily reminder of 'what sort of mean old b****** he was working for' and as a reminder to 'count his fingers if he ever shook hands with him'. He also sought every means to make Guy pay for this insult. Eventually it was passed on to the Salvation Army. At this time Preedy was a Regional Sales Manager and he had negotiated a low salary and a relatively high rate of commission at a time when he anticipated the completion of a number of large projects that he had worked on for some time. Within a year this proved correct and his bank balance began to look rosy at which time Guy decided to make him an Executive Director – on a fixed salary and no commission.

Titular promotion was general practice at the time, backed up by a key to the Directors' toilet. Having reached these giddy heights as Director of System Sales, Engineering and Rental business, Preedy was called to Guy's office one Saturday morning to be confronted by a disconsolate Guy, full of self pity, to tell him about the fact that Jim Whiting, then the only company Director from the ranks, had committed the grave crime of grabbing him by the throat and ramming him into a corner of his office, no doubt in a fit of pique. Jim was, of course, fired from his management of Systems Hire but the reason for Guy disclosing this happening to Preedy was to tell him that he was to take over total control of Systems Operations which then included sales, engineering, rental, hire and maintenance although both he and Guy were too upset to discuss money.

One day Ron Rackham was painstakingly showing Norman Robottom how to centre the cone of a 12" dual concentric loudspeaker when he was spotted by Guy. Suddenly there was an angry shout, unmistakeably in Guy's voice, "Rackham, get on with your work!" Rackham, equally short tempered, went bright red with fury and threw the loudspeaker across the workshop, smashing it into dozens of little pieces.

One little story of Stan Livingstone's indicates that the Fountain system did not always work; at the exhibition of the Radio and Electrical Components Manufacturers' Federation at the Grosvenor House Hotel, Tannoy shared a three sided stand with Plessey – Tannoy occupying one side and *Plessey* the other two. *Plessey* hung a huge banner across the stand with the word, PLESSEY emblazoned on it in huge letters. When Fountain arrived there was an explosion. He sought out Mr. Clark, the M.D. of *Plessey* who was a big man with a big tummy. Guy was, of course, a little man, a very little man so, when he went to remonstrate with Clark the best thing he could do was to prod him in the stomach and say, "Move your ******* sign." Allen Clark replied, "It's my sign, that's where it is, and that's where it stays." Fountain went away, furious.

Livingstone was somewhat worried about what might happen if Guy

The TANNOY Story

Fountain came back so he, too, sought out Allen Clark and said, "Excuse me, Sir, do you think we could move that banner? I shall have terrible trouble with Mr. Fountain if he sees it effectively over his stand." Allen Clark gave Stan an avuncular smile and said, "Yes, it is a bit large, isn't it? I'll get my men to change it." That afternoon Fountain came back to deliver one last tirade to Allen Clark and looked up and said, "Who moved that sign?" so Livingstone said, "Well, it was Mr. Clark." "Why did Clark move it?" and Livingstone replied, "Because I asked him to." Guy left in silence and Stan enjoyed the pleasure of not being spoken to for a fortnight or more.

To return to more appropriate matters relating to Tannoy's recovery, the end result of all the successful developments under Norman Wild's leadership was that the company was, once again, firmly established technically and it was on a very sound financial footing. Guy desperately wanted to regain control of his company so he approached an old friend, Joe L. Fairbrother, for a loan. It is reported that Fairbrother lent Guy £50,000 and with this he was able to re-purchase the company for £45,000 and use the remainder for its immediate cash needs. Once again, Guy Fountain was at the helm of Tannoy, though perhaps not very securely.

CHAPTER NOTES

1 John Gilbert writing in 'Gramophone', September 1976.

2 At the time of writing, July 2002, there is an example of the Soundmirror at the Chalkpits Museum, Amberley, Sussex.

3 The author remembers this well from his association with Col. Colley's son, John, a fellow student at Faraday House Electrical Engineering College from 1947 to 1950.

The Dual Concentric Loudspeaker

CHAPTER THIRTEEN

GUY BACK AT THE HELM

The situation then, in 1951, was that Guy R. Fountain Ltd. was in liqidation and Joe Fairbrother's money enabled Guy, under the banner of Sound Rentals Ltd., to buy the assets of Guy R. Fountain Ltd. Guy changed the name from Sound Rentals to Tannoy Products Ltd. and this became the new trading company. He then bought another public address company, Selby Public Address, and re-named it Tannoy Rentals Ltd. which then went into the installation and rental of public address systems in a big way. In yet another move to protect the name, TANNOY, Guy registered a new company, Tannoy Ltd., to own and protect the TANNOY trade name, but also to carry out Research and Development, obtaining its funding by licencing the trade mark, TANNOY, to the other Tannoy companies including, in due course, Tannoy Marine, Tannoy America, Tannoy Canada and Tannoy Ireland. But Guy was also concerned about the risk of losing the name, 'Guy R. Fountain Ltd.' following the earlier liquidation of this company so he re-registered Guy R. Fountain Ltd. in about 1960. Tannoy Rentals were, of course, responsible for the installation and maintenance of all rented Tannoy systems such as holiday camps, dance halls, factories and the *Greyhound Racing Association's* stadia but not for the systems in the Palace of Westminster. The Static Condenser Company and Sound Plastings Ltd. were still associated companies.

The period of receivership under Norman Wild had done the company a lot of good because, as has been stated, it had pared the company down to its core business, established proper methods of financial control, and had ensured that money was no longer just thrown around without formally accounting for its use. Work was properly costed and the re-structuring of the company really saw it through quite successfully for some fifteen years until about 1967 when things started to go slightly awry again, not tragically awry, but there were difficulties. It was also at this time that Michael left the company. However, it was not until about 1971 and 1972 that matters started to go seriously wrong again. Meanwhile, for 15 or 16 years Tannoy prospered once again.

It was during this more successful era that many of the sound reinforcement schemes in the various government debating chambers around the world were installed, with levels of success which equalled or surpassed those of the schemes in the Palace of Westminster, among which was the public address and instantaneous interpretation system in the United Nations Headquarters in New York. These installations came under the general heading of Systems Engineering and it was during this time that Systems Engineering emerged, quite rightly, as a separate division and with great success, so much so that it represented the major part of the company's prosperity in the ensuing years. Not only was it responsible for many sound reinforcement and instantaneous translation systems, but it was also responsible for successes such as the public address system in the re-developed Euston Station.

Railway travellers were very well aware of Tannoy loudspeaking equipment on station platforms and in railway terminals which had started in 1932 at Blackpool but, when London's Euston Station was rebuilt in 1952, the huge main passenger concourse was completely covered by only two Tannoy Vertilinear loudspeaker units, one at each side of the arrivals and departures indicator panel, and these enabled perfectly clear announcements to be heard over the whole area of the concourse without the need to subject passengers to an unbearable level of sound. This project was designed by a rare, practically minded architect who was not afraid to take advice from the specialists who were called in to ensure that the fundamental requirements were at least given an airing. The visual aspect of siting the recently developed column loudspeaker systems was important. These loudspeakers, known as 'Vertilinear Loudspeakers', formed acoustic lenses which ensured an even distribution of sound over a wide angle horizontally and minimal levels of sound vertically above and below their centre lines. It was thus possible to spread the sound very clearly throughout the area of the huge concourse, with very little sound travelling downwards to be reflected off the floor or upwards to be echoed from the roof. To enhance this advantage still further the roof structure, which is the principal offender, was treated with a recently developed, sprayed-on sound absorbing substance which set into a rugged surface and which reduced the standing wave pattern which would otherwise have resulted in reverberation, while at floor level the people milling around the concourse offered a variable level of sound absorption. By siting the two vertilinear loudspeakers to the sides of the wide passenger information display board, maximum absorption by passengers combined with the controlled horizontal direction of sound propagation ensured that all announcements could be heard clearly over the whole area of the concourse.

Tannoy was also involved with the early expansion programmes at Gatwick Airport and one of the major problems there had been overcome by Tannoy design engineers using an Ambient Noise Adjustment circuit which became known as A.N.A. In many public address schemes variations in the announcers' voice levels were automatically compensated for by an Automatic Gain Control but, more importantly, the Ambient Noise Adjustment circuit compensated for the continually changing noise levels generated by the passengers, depending on how busy the airport was at any time. In the concourses of the first new buildings the *British Airports Authority* planned to install advertising cubes suspended from the ceiling. Tannoy suggested that these would be ideal loudspeaker sites, with a line source loudspeaker in each corner so B.A.A. called in Southampton University to verify the expected performance of these installations. Dennis Terrett recorded that these proposals were agreed at the next meeting without opposition and it was supposed that they did so because they realised that Tannoy really did know what they were talking about.

Dennis Terrett had joined the company in 1951 and his first task had been in the assembly shop, winding the speech coils for the SD 5 loudspeakers. These were wound by hand onto a mandrel to which a paper former was attached and the thin, double-cotton covered wire was then fed onto the former as the mandrel was turned, by hand. During this process the adhesive was painted on using a small artists' brush. The adhesive was solvent based and acetone was freely used in the operation and, as the day wore on, Dennis began to feel quite strange and tired. He put this down to boredom but some time later he realised that he was, at the time, becoming quite a glue sniffer. Fortunately he was given other jobs to do after a few weeks and these did not have the same effects, but today the Health and Safety officials would have a great deal to say, not only about the free use of acetone, but also about the fact that there were many open acetone bottles on the benches. With people smoking and using soldering irons the risk of fire was high.

As if that were not bad enough, one of the processes was that of plasticising the surrounds of loudspeaker cones using trychlorethylene, which is an anaesthetic. This, too, was in open bottles on the benches and it was brushed onto the cones where it readily evaporated around the operators who were invariably smoking. Another source of considerable risk was the de-greasing tank which was next to the spray shop and men were frequently to be seen leaning over the tank, lowering items to be de-greased into the hot trychlorethylene vapour and with cigarettes hanging from their lips. This vapour, when introduced to heat and to the various by-products of smouldering tobacco, produces phosgene, a poisonous gas which was widely used as a weapon during the Great War.

During the winter of that year it was so cold in the factory that Dennis Terrett frequently saw condensation freezing into ice on and around the benches and many of the workers kept their coats on at work and wore mittens to keep their hands warm. However, early in 1952 he was transferred to the laboratory to work for Ron Rackham as a laboratory assistant. It was not much warmer there first thing in the morning but, as the test equipment warmed up, things improved. His first day there was very nearly his last for the factory intercom phone buzzed and he picked it up and said, "Hello". Being his first day, he was blissfully unaware that the system buzzed with a continuous note except for calls from Guy Fountain when the buzz was intermittent, demanding immediate attention. The voice on the phone asked to speak to Mr. Rackham to which Dennis replied that he was not yet in. The voice then asked for Mr. Waples with the same result. Then, with a cough and a grunt, the phone went dead. When Ron Rackham came in he received an urgent message to contact Mr. Fountain who demanded to know to whom he had spoken earlier? Rackham explained that Dennis was new and did not recognise either Guy Fountain's call or his voice and that in future he would. Luckily for Dennis, the event was passed over. His crime had been that of not addressing Guy Fountain as 'Sir', a point on which he characteristically insisted, a possible alternative being 'Mr. Fountain' or, for the favoured few, 'Governor'.

In Dennis Terrett's early days in the laboratory, printed circuits were just coming into use and one of the frustrations to be endured in the design stages of any new piece of equipment was that all printed circuit designs had to be shown to Guy for his approval. This was to make sure that the tracks were not too close together and that they were not too narrow. What might he think if he saw today's technology which requires the use of a microscope to see the separation and width of the tracks? There was always a shortage of test equipment which meant that much valuable time was wasted in making equipment in-house and in repairing old equipment instead of buying new. There was a *Cossor* oscilloscope which was fitted with a metal visor because its tube was none too bright; this used to lose its earth connection and the consequent discharge would take one by surprise across the eyebrows when looking at the screen! There was a *Furzhill* oscilloscope which consumed mains transformers at an alarming rate, mostly due to the lack of space for an adequate core size and, when Dennis first joined the laboratory, there was just one *AVO* meter.

During the 1950s a large number of microphones were manufactured for use with gas-masks. A test rig was used to ensure that there were no leaks of gas through the microphones and, as there was a flow of air through part of the rig,

The TANNOY Story

a gas meter was leased from the local gas company to measure this flow. After three months the gas company sent a man to read the meter!

In 1953, Tannoy secured another contract of some importance when the company was again contracted to provide public address equipment in the streets of London, this time for the Coronation of Queen Elizabeth II. On this occasion Trafalgar Square was a big problem because, unlike the comparatively narrow area of a street where it was possible to guarantee how far each person would be from a loudspeaker, in the wide expanse of Trafalgar Square a spectator could be at very different distances from adjacent loudspeakers which would, of course, cause a big problem: he or she would hear everything twice; perhaps more than twice, and the customary arrangement of loudspeakers hanging from almost every lamp standard and any other structure of a suitable height, would have been quite useless.

Once again the response to this problem which fell from everyone's lips was, "Let's ask Ron." Ron Rackham came up with the solution; they would use a single sound source to cover the whole of Trafalgar Square! Rackham designed some very large bass-loading horns for the CD 4 unit, so-called 'W' horns, which loaded them down to about 50Hz. He then made some special, modified CD 4 loudspeakers with very high magnetic flux using very thick plates of magnets. He decided on aluminium wire voice coils and, with a suitable crossover network, he produced horn loaded loudspeakers with an efficiency of something like 50% which were quite capable of handling the required 200 watts. A group of these was mounted on a steel frame and hoisted onto the roof of Malaya House. The results really were an electro-acoustic triumph. It was possible, with this system alone, to hear the music being played in Westminster Abbey quite clearly over the whole of Trafalgar Square. On the day, with all the systems working, the crowds who were waiting some distance from Trafalgar Square, in Whitehall, also heard the full tones of the organ, including the deep bass notes, rumbling down Whitehall a few seconds after the rather emaciated noise coming from the other manufacturers' loudspeakers which had been mounted along the roadside. But in Trafalgar Square, the sound was truly magnificent.

Guy Fountain was always interested in the sea and ships, hence the title of this chapter, and the small craft marine division of the company, Tannoy Marine, was formed to develop marine equipment such as the gas detectors, named 'Sniffa' and 'Super Sniffa', automatic ventilators named the 'Ventair' and the 'Ventalite', an electronic anemometer, a wind direction indicator and the 'Hey-Loh' loud hailer. These were often referred to by employees at all levels, perhaps rather contemptuously, as 'Guy's Nautical Novelties', but some of them were quite successful and many small pleasure vessels still, in the new millennium, have examples of these Tannoy developments, particularly the ventilators. Tannoy's Senior Design Engineer responsible for the development of most of these devices was Ron Rackham but the ventilators were designed by Bill Haines and the gas detectors by Dennis Terrett who was also involved in devising a means of preventing water from passing through the ventilators.

The gas detectors were produced to detect the presence of butane gas in the bilges of boats and, being a heavier-than-air gas and used in boats for cooking, it represents a serious but invisible danger. The basic Sniffa worked by osmosis but the more widely used 'Super Sniffa' was a catalytic device in which four coils of very fine platinum wire, coated with palladium, were wound on asbestos-type string in the form of a double helix, like the coiled-coil filament of an ordinary light bulb, and connected to form a Wheatstone's Bridge. Two of these were then coated with a catalyst mixture in an oxide form dissolved in formaldehyde and a current was passed through the coils to reduce the catalyst to the base elements on the wire and string, thereby making those coils more reactive to the hydrocarbon gases to be detected. A very weak current was passed through this wire generating a small rise in temperature but the presence of any hydro-carbon gas caused its temperature to rise a little more, raising its electrical resistance. This change in resistance caused an imbalance in the bridge circuit which was measured to indicate the presence of the gas. A more sophisticated model of the Super Sniffa, called the 'Sniffette', was connected to a meter on the boat's instrument panel to give a continuous indication of the level of any butane in the bilge.

When Dennis Terrett was working on the design of these gas detectors, he had a full size cylinder of hydrogen gas to reduce the catalyst. As a measure of safety the cylinder was put on the flat roof adjacent to his window, with a tube through the window to his bench. There was still a major problem which was due to the spontaneous combustion which takes place when hydrogen is introduced to platinum; this being the principle of some gas lighters. After a few pops and bangs the rest of the laboratory staff thought that Terrett should be doing this work elsewhere, anywhere but in the laboratory and, as a result of their concern a shed was erected on the flat roof so that he and his assistant, Patrick Mason, could blow themselves up with impunity. Part of the development programme was to verify the sensitivity of the detectors and this was carried out in a steel box of about 20 litres capacity, with a transparent door hinged at the top. Measured amounts of hydrocarbon gases were introduced and the reaction was noted and after each test a spark was generated in the box until the gas and air mixture was ignited. This resulted in a fireball and a minor explosion forcing open the door which was held closed by a magnet. This sometimes took Terrett and Mason by surprise and they both endured singed hairs on their arms but, of course, the other laboratory staff were comparatively safe.

The Ventalite was a simple ventilator panel, made of clear plastic to allow light to pass through it, but the Ventair was slightly more sophisticated. There were two models of the Ventair, the more expensive of these being powered by a small electric motor. The Tannoy anemometer was usually mounted at the mast head and was connected to an instrument on the boat's panel to indicate the wind velocity, an optional extra being a circle of coloured lights which indicated the wind direction.

In the early days of the development of the Sniffa, an experimental Tannoy gas detector was installed on an immigrant ship to Australia to detect refrigerant leaks in the plant which chilled the refrigerated holds. This device was unexpectedly put to a real test during these trials when it detected a genuine refrigerant leak. At first, the system was assumed to be faulty but it was soon realised that the equipment had, in fact, detected a gas leak. The success of this incident led to many further orders for the device.

There was some justification for the contempt shown towards Guy's ideas for some of them were not at all successful and skilled workers and technicians were often obliged to devote many hours to research and development of ideas which were never likely to succeed. Among these must be listed Guy's attempts to build a water-jet propelled speedboat on which a great deal of company time was wasted. *Dowty Ltd.* had produced a jet propelled boat and Guy decided to out-do *Dowty*. He asked one of Tannoy's technicians, Alan Ingram, to construct a turbo system which was essentially a boat with its propeller in a tube, driven by a lawnmower engine. Guy had several other employees in the factory working on it and, when it had been built, he obtained the permission of the Dulwich Estate Governors to test it on the boating lake in Dulwich Park. He had the boat tethered to two large stakes via a couple of spring tension scales to measure the thrust while the engine was revved up by Paul Worters to its maximum power. Paul Worters was one of several skippers on Guy's luxury motor cruiser and, when he was not under orders to work on Guy's boat, he doubled up as a factory caretaker and as Guy's chauffeur. Guy spent hours on this boat but there was so much resistance to the flow of water through the jet pipe that it was never a success. Bill Haines was often furious at the amount of time wasted and at the number of occasions when various people were required in the factory and could not be found because they were otherwise engaged.

More successful was the 'Hey-loh' loud hailer which was another triumph for Ronnie Rackham and which was originally marketed by Tannoy Products. This was predominantly an item of marine equipment and responsibility for its sales was transferred to Tannoy Marine in time for the 1962 Boat Show where Tannoy Marine had an enormous stand. Incidentally, a Tannoy Hey-Loh was used in one of the James Bond films, *Live and Let Die*, and it can be seen clearly in a speedboat chase in which there is a huge conflagration caused by fuel on the water. This was eventually returned to the factory for repair and was found to have been badly scorched. There was also a large scale model of the *Canberra* at the show which had first been shown at the Brussels International Show. There were telephones beside the model and it was possible to dial one of twenty locations on the ship and hear detailed information about that part of the vessel, in one of three languages. The master tape had been produced by Tannoy and Michael Fountain had recorded the English version. There are further details of the Tannoy equipment on board the *Canberra* later in this chapter.

There was a small boating business a little way along Norwood High Street which was run by Eric Coleman. He was brought into the company by Guy to help run his marine craft interests. He found himself at Guy's 'beck-and-call' for much of his time, occasionally acting as Guy's chauffeur, running errands for the factory or for Guy's house, even driving into London just to collect theatre tickets. He also had to keep up with the business of his section to keep the sales coming in and he would often get a ticking off from Guy for the lack of success, but he could not reply by telling the truth; that Guy had been causing him to waste his time.

There was a time when Guy Fountain had a distributorship for Healey Boats and this was the first time that Stan Livingstone realised that Guy was not quite the businessman he was thought to be because he did not seem to understand the difference between an agency and a distributorship. Healey had made Guy a distributor to take boats into stock and sell them, but Guy expected to act as an agent, selling boats first then ordering them from Healey. Such misunderstandings became a problem with the overseas distributors of Tannoy equipment because Tannoy could control their stock, inspect their books, everything. But an agent can operate exactly as he pleases as long as, eventually, he wins orders and gets his commission; he is under no obligation to his principals at all; he can even accept the agency and do nothing about it while he is busy selling for the competition.

Another 'signal' success story for Systems Engineering, if the pun can be forgiven, was the development of electronic fog warning signals for lighthouses and lightships around the British Isles, based on the trials of electronic fog signals which were carried out for Trinity House at Dungeness Head in Kent. This was a complete breakaway from the traditional air pressure fog signals. The system consisted of a lensed array of sixty, 100 watts high pressure loudspeakers, designed by Ron Rackham, each working into a short horn which was horizontally exponential and vertically linear and which formed part of the concrete structure. The horizontal polar dispersion covered an angle of $270°$ and

The TANNOY Story

the effective range exceeded five miles. In the early Tannoy fog warning systems the signal was generated mechanically but this was not a great success, so an electronic signal generator was soon substituted, the signal being fed into a power amplifier giving a total output of 6kW and this was the system which replaced the conventional air pressure fog horn. There were two stacks of pressure units at Dungeness Head, the North stack being the permanent fog warning while the South stack was used for trials. This was a great success and many Tannoy fog warning signals were installed throughout the British Isles and on board Trinity House lightships, but the largest installation was in Canada, on the St. Lawrence River. The Tannoy fog signal systems, first adopted by Trinity House in 1953, survived for many years and the last of the Trinity House systems, at Dungeness Head, was not decommissioned until October, 2000.

The large concrete structures enclosing sixty loudspeaker drivers was fine on land based installations but this system could not be used on many off-shore lighthouses nor on lightships so, between 1965 and 1968, Ron Rackham set his mind to finding a solution to this problem. He found it by designing a single loudspeaker which was capable of handling 500 watts. During 1952 a 1,000 watts loudspeaker had been constructed, the magnet for which was so heavy that it took two men to lift it. Dennis Terrett recalled that to magnetise it a coil of wire was wound on the centre pole before assembly and this was connected to a large bank of electrolytic capacitors via a heavy duty, solenoid operated contactor. The capacitors were charged up to 250V and then the solenoid was energised, producing a magnet. The magnetic flux was measured and the operation was repeated several times until the increase in the strength of the magnetic flux stopped, at which point it was considered that saturation had been achieved. The project was later shelved due to problems experienced with the robustness of the diaphragm, but the 500 watts version was a great success. This had a 6" diameter voice coil which was coupled to a ring trough diaphragm with a strong, double suspension system, the unit being designed to work into a reflex horn. It was a narrow band loudspeaker which operated only from 500 Hz to 1,500 Hz but, with a modified voice coil it would reproduce intelligible speech. Its sensitivity was 142 dB @ 1 metre, for 1 watt, an all time record and an assembly of four of these was clearly audible over eight miles at sea. In 1960 he also developed a successful solar powered audible fog warning system. This was marketed through Tannoy Marine for use on lightships as well as on board small pleasure vessels; on any boat, that is, where power supplies are limited.

Another success story for Systems Engineering was the supply of flameproof public address loudspeakers and installations to the petro-chemical industries. Tannoy was for a long time the sole supplier of flameproof and intrinsically safe public address equipment to the whole of the U.K. petro-chemical industries and this success, like so many others, was entirely due to the genius of Ron Rackham. He designed a pressure loudspeaker in which the sound from the diaphragm passed through concentric circular slots in a thick steel plate. These were long enough, and narrow enough, to ensure that any sparks which might be generated by a failure of the voice coil would be quenched by the mass of the plate acting as a heat sink. With these loudspeakers, and following the development of North Sea oil exploration, many Tannoy flame-proof fog signals with a range of up to six miles were installed on oil rigs.

A later version of the flameproof loudspeaker, undoubtedly the best ever, incorporated what can only be described as an open cell metal sponge. This was once featured on the television programme, 'Tomorrow's World' and it is believed to have been an *I.C.I.* product called 'Retimet'. The day following the programme Ron Rackham checked it and applied for a patent for its use as a flame trap for flameproof loudspeakers. There was found to be very little interference with the acoustic path through the material; the frequency bandwidth being unaffected and with no colouration, and it proved to be a vast improvement on any other form of flame trap in use.

A very small part of this business was held by *Marconi*, but their installations were none too successful and they tried to sell their share of the business to Tannoy. *Marconi* actually came cap-in-hand to Tannoy and said that they had a few contracts which 'did not fit into their big scheme', so what about buying it? Such was the measure of Tannoy's success in this field. Another development which was on vaguely similar lines was the Tannoy 'Temperature Resistant' equipment which was made for steel mills and rented to them by Tannoy Rentals.

In 1959, Tannoy Systems Engineering developed a monopoly in induction loop communication systems for hazardous installations such as those which then existed in the production of coal and gas. Once the gas had been extracted the residue of hot coke was forced out of the retorts by a mechanical pusher, driving it out into waiting trucks to be quenched. The procedure was that the train driver manoeuvred the train so that an empty truck stopped at one end of a particular oven and the pusher operator located the pusher at the other end of the same oven. The oven's contents, almost white hot coke, was then pushed into the truck. Occasionally, due to poor communication between the operators, things would go wrong so that the coke, instead of going into the correct truck, could go almost anywhere including, perhaps, into the locomotive which, as Stan Livingstone put it, was very uncomfortable for the driver. So Tannoy devised a system in which the locomotive driver was able to communicate with the pusher operator to ensure that both pusher and train

The TANNOY Story

were aligned with the correct oven. This system was operated by an induction loop around the workshop and it worked extremely well although, in the interests of total safety, the men who drove the locomotives would not work unless the Tannoy induction loop system had been tested that morning and had been proven to be working; if not, the union would pull their men out. The only competition Tannoy had in these induction loop systems was from *British Thompson-Houston Ltd.*, but they gave up after about 3 contracts because two of their installations did not work and they were replaced by Tannoy systems.

Tannoy used to sell equipment such as this by demonstration, eliminating the need for advertising. They adopted a principle previously expounded by Norman Wild who used to say to Stan, "Whatever you do, me boy, charge for it." The principle was that they costed a demonstration very approximately and if, say, it worked out at £1,000 they would quote the customer £1,500, knowing that if the contract was awarded, the price of the equipment would be about £4,000 or more. So they used to tell customers such as *I.C.I.* or *Dorman Long* that a demonstration would cost £1,500 but if the customer bought the equipment, that amount would be deducted from the price. This safeguarded the buyers and works engineers because in all cases such as this, they would be responsible to their middle or top management, and they had to safeguard their positions. So, when their bosses asked if the equipment was really alright they did not just produce a piece of sales literature which said that it was alright, they would be able to say that they had it on site, they had seen it, heard it and touched it and they knew that it worked well and by this means Tannoy soon enjoyed a country-wide monopoly. This method of sales by demonstration was a great success for, on the rare occasions when a demonstration did not lead to a sale, Tannoy's costs were well covered by the demonstration fee. Large overseas contracts soon followed because many of these process plants were built by the principal construction companies such as *Bechtel* or *Kellogg International* who would do turnkey operations and they would build installations overseas just as they had in Great Britain. For Tannoy the business was almost automatic as Tannoy very soon found their name on the approved list of sub-contractors.

Following the successes of the installations in the Canadian Legislative Assembly buildings and of those in the United Nations building in New York, Tannoy Canada was established in 1960, under the management of Freddie Towler and his wife, Mary. After establishing Tannoy Canada the Towlers established Tannoy America, also in 1960. It was about this time that Ronald Pickering[1], an Accountant and a Director of *Bertram Mills Circus*, was appointed to the board of Tannoy, followed in 1962 by Stan Livingstone and it was not long before Michael Fountain became the Managing Director of the company. Michael then visited the Towlers and Freddie told him that he wanted to buy premises for Tannoy America on Long Island to replace the rented premises which they initially occupied. So Michael and Freddie bought the land and built premises for the company without telling Guy. Michael eventually told his father about this and Guy was furious but, of course, it was a very valuable asset.

THE Q.E.2
In the Autumn of 2000, in the first issue of the *Journal of the Institute of Sound and Communications Engineers*, Bill Preedy wrote an account of Tannoy's work on the design and installation of the Sound and Emergency Communications systems on board the QE2. The article was aptly entitled, "The 'Trials' of the QE2". Much of the following account is based upon his article.

Towards the end of the 1950s, the then *Royal Mail Shipping Line* ordered three passenger and refrigerated cargo vessels for their South American service. These ships, which were built by *Harland and Wolff* at Belfast, were among the first to be equipped with three phase a.c. power supplies and the availability of 240 volts, a.c. allowed a breakthrough in the design of marine public address installations which were referred to, in marine circles, as Sound Reproducing Equipment or S.R.E. systems. These liners, the *Amazon*, *Aragon* and *Arlanza*, were equipped with Tannoy passenger and crew broadcast systems, including integrated entertainment services, and the passenger cabin facilities included multi-channel entertainment and automatic override for emergency broadcasts.

During their construction, *Harland and Wolff* received a contract to build what was ambitiously described by its designers as 'The Ship of the Century' the *Canberra*, and Tannoy was again contracted to design and install the S.R.E. systems. The equipment was located close to the ship's radio room and the Radio Officers were responsible for its operation. One of the problems was heat dissipation since at that time, 1959, thermionic valves were still used and, due to the obvious need for immediate system access, the heaters had to remain 'on' at all times to eliminate the 'warm-up' delay. The result of this was that the confined space where the equipment was located had to be fitted with a forced ventilation system supplying refrigerated air to the equipment.

By the time Tannoy was contracted to design the S.R.E. systems for the QE2, transistors were in common use and these allowed a complete revision of the design of the audio systems which covered public address and entertainment facilities in public rooms, passenger cabins and crew accommodation, and public address at all crew stations and in machinery areas. This installation required some $4^{1}/_{2}$ kilowatts of Tannoy amplifying equipment to feed 1,800 loudspeakers with six programme channels in the cabins and staterooms. In addition, simultaneous translation equipment was provided in the 600 seat

The TANNOY Story

theatre.

All these systems included both local and general emergency override. In addition, lifeboat and raft stations were provided with audio intercommunication which was controlled from the bridge wings. The installation was designed to function from a 50 volts d.c. supply which, in the event of failure of the ship's power system, was provided by a standby system of nickel cadmium batteries. The loudspeaker lines were limited to 50 volts r.m.s. to comply with the Lloyds and Marine Safety Standards prevailing at the time instead of the customary 100 volts r.m.s. which was used on conventional land-based installations.

The S.R.E. systems had to be built to conform to stringent marine safety standards which were in force at the time and it was possible to reproduce by electronic means the ship's fire orders, boat drill instructions, and even the ship's bell. Not all sounds were reproduced by entirely electronic means for, in order to provide the necessary fog warnings which, by convention, consisted of a bell at the bow and a gong at the stern to indicate the 'lay' of the vessel, recordings made of the bell and the gong on board the R.M.S. *Queen Mary* were played over the appropriate circuits to two, 100 watts loudspeakers at each station.

The ship was constructed by *John Brown* at their Clydebank yard and she was taken on twenty-four hours technical acceptance trials in order to prove all the systems and services, including a timed 'measured mile' off Arran and turning trials at maximum speed and, at the end of the trials the builder's flag would be lowered and replaced by the owner's pennant. This was to have taken place on 29th November, 1968 and all was proceding to plan when, early in the afternoon the ship, which had been cruising at about 31 knots, lost all power and came gently to a halt at the mercy of wind and tide. No information was available to the passengers on board but they later learned from the B.B.C. news that water had accumulated in a high pressure steam feed producing a potential turbine explosion in one of the two propulsion units. A newly developed computer had sensed the danger and activated the shut down of all machinery at risk. It was later possible to limpback into the Clyde on the one unaffected turbine and anchor off Helensburgh for the night.

With such a prestigious liner it is usual to follow these trials with a shake down voyage to the South Atlantic to which senior executives of other shipping lines and VIPs associated with the construction of the vessel are invited to take part. Owing to the delay in completion and the many problems which had been encountered, the invited guests were mainly *Cunard* personnel and their families with a large contingent of technical heads of the many contributing companies, plus various VIPs concerned with the QE2 construction. By this time, those directly involved no doubt thought that a 'QE2 bug' was active, particularly when those invited guests who were due to fly to Scotland on the Sunday before Christmas 1968, were faced with an airline strike. A special train was chartered for the tortuous journey, starting from Southampton and calling at Olympia for London based guests and Preston to pick up *Cunard* staff from Liverpool, arriving at Gourock, Strathclyde, for embarkation by tender late that night, in rough weather. Elsie Fountain had died on 28th August, 1966 and, by this time, Guy and Maureen were married and were among the invited guests.

It was a very tedious journey for all concerned, with Guy becoming more and more intolerable by the hour and his temper did not improve when an academic looking individual chose to seat himself, with two carry cots, each containing a young child, very near to Guy and Maureen. When, some time later, Willy Hall, the Superintending Engineer of *Cunard*, came round to see how his personal guests were faring, the gruff response from Guy was to the effect that some sex maniac with two squawking kids should be dumped from the train. Willy asked who he was talking about and Guy pointed to the source of his disaffection. Willy said, "But that man is my senior Electrical Engineer." Guy was in no way put out and immediately replied, "Well, you should put him on night work!"

Christmas day on the shake-down voyage saw the ship in sunny climes and the festive programme included cabaret artistes and the various entertainments were enhanced by the Tannoy sound equipment and by the use of early radio microphones. However, one of the groups, who had previously performed on the old *Queen Elizabeth*, brought their own ac/dc equipment and, in near suicidal ignorance of the subtleties of the ship's power supplies, set up their amplifier with its microphone and stand on the new theatre stage, which was part of the aluminium superstructure of the ship. The technical reader has possibly guessed that the polarity of their amplifier was reversed. The resulting performance was, to say the least, original and, with extreme good luck, the leading performer did not lick the microphone as was his usual habit!

The return to the QE2's home port of Southampton was made without major problems and, following an on-board conference, the remedial work was carried out by *Thorneycroft*, as was subsequent maintenance. But many of the special fixtures and fittings for sound and lighting in cabins and bathrooms had 'disappeared' in Scotland, so great efforts had to be made to re-manufacture replacements in time for the re-scheduled maiden voyage to New York, on 2nd. May, 1969.

The test programme provided the opportunity to design systems and products across the range of contractors' specialisations and, so far as Tannoy was concerned, this brought on line the essential elements and techniques which formed the basis of the subsequent Emergency Communications Systems,

The TANNOY Story

which are specified wherever it is necessary to broadcast potentially life saving instructions and guidance.

The liner business was built up in parallel with other shipping business but passenger vessels offered the best potential since this was a relatively untapped market for effective personnel safety communications. In the case of the Q.E.2 this was integrated with the entertainment system which had six channel cabin entertainment with automatic restoration to speech communication in times of emergency with clear, intelligible speech and, if necessary, in more than one language.

Liner installations completed by Tannoy were:-

1958 - 1959 The Royal Mail fleet of *Arlanza, Aragon* and *Amazon*. Built by *Harland and Wolff* at Belfast.
1960   P. & O. *Canberra*, 'The Ship of the Century', also built by *Harland and Wolff*.
             (These ships were the last to be installed with thermionic valve equipment).
1968   Cunard. 'Q.E.2'. This ship was equipped with silicon transistor equipment using power amplifiers and basic modules developed specifically for this contract, but which subsequently became the standard equipment for all Tannoy Systems Engineering projects.

The builders of the 'Q.E.2' were initially *John Brown* at Clydeside although even when the ship was on her quite disastrous trials, financial pressures brought about a change to three companies.

During a decade the company also won contracts to equip three cable laying ships which required S.R.E. systems. These vessels also required process control systems. In addition, Tannoy equipment provided essential back-up to the cable laying and cable recovery operations.

Michael Fountain was M.D. at the time Guy had formed Tannoy Marine to suit his own egotistical demands. Guy insisted that when Tannoy won major contracts for installations in large ships, the business had to go through Tannoy Marine so that he could bleat that the turnover of Tannoy Products was not up to scratch. Michael once sent him a steaming report stating that Tannoy Marine was a small craft division and Guy had no right whatsoever to absorb into Tannoy Marine the profits of work such as the *Canberra* contract. But Guy insisted that anything with even a remote connection with any vessel must go through Tannoy Marine in order to boost the performance of his own holdings. After Michael left, those companies which were family owned such as Tannoy Limited, Tannoy Rentals and Tannoy Products, were constantly being diminished as Guy funnelled the profits into other companies, particularly

Tannoy Marine. Tannoy Marine also enjoyed the advantage that it made no financial contribution to the development of its products, although it enjoyed the benefits.

Two more significant achievements were made in 1958, one being the introduction of the Tannoy Variluctance, stereophonic gramophone pick-up cartridge. This was the first ever British designed and British made magnetic stereophonic cartridge and its performance was such that it was an immediate success and remained so for many years. The second success was that of the first sales of the Dual Concentric Loudspeakers to Japan; sales which have been maintained to that country at a very high level ever since.

In 1960, being a lover of the sea, Guy had purchased a fine, 47ft. diesel yacht, the *Albaquila*, which he used not only for his personal pleasure and aggrandizement but also for the development of marine equipment such as echo-sounders, gas detectors and ventilation systems. Soon after he bought this fine vessel he decided to take it to Henley for another Royal Regatta and he moored it by Henley bridge, on the opposite side of the river to the V.I.P. enclosure, where he hoped to be able to hone his sycophantic skills by offering open house to the rich and famous. Much of his thunder was stolen, however, when he found to his intense irritation that the famous comedian, Max Miller, 'The Cheeky Chappie', had moored his boat at the next mooring; Guy was not amused!

The control point for the Tannoy public address system was within the Regatta enclosure which was designated for the use of the most important spectators and once again, Norman Robottom was involved (he had also been the very competent operator on the 'Daily Mirror Eight' tours). Norman, for his own safety and for that of his fellow engineers, had brought a pair of powerful binoculars to keep Guy under surveillance. This idea worked quite well until one evening whilst making his usual check he found himself looking straight down a superior pair of binoculars, in Guy's hands! At the conclusion of the regatta, the privileged spectators who had their own luxury cruisers from which to view the races and on which they could dispense hospitality, used to slip their moorings and motor up stream, but this was not good enough for Guy. He insisted on going the other way, through the remainder of the competitors and showing off to the spectators on the banks, resplendent in his blazer and peaked cap.

During the following year, in 1961, Tannoy Rentals reached the peak of its holiday camp business with public address systems installed in no less than 155 holiday camps. Also at about that time, the company was making every effort to secure the contract to install sound systems for the *Central Electricity Generating Board* at Ferrybridge power station in Yorkshire. This project was to

The TANNOY Story

comprise public address in all areas and an all-important intercommunication system between the control desks, with an interlink between the two systems. As the contract also included installation of all necessary cables and equipment, it was worth a great deal of money.

To secure the contract it was necessary to mount a demonstration in another power station and Hams Hall power station, near Birmingham, was selected. Dennis Terrett was the engineer in charge of the project and he and Ron Rackham manufactured a special ribbon microphone with noise cancelling properties and an amplifier rack with sufficient power to meet the requirements of a large number of horn loudspeakers. The noise cancelling was achieved with typical Rackham genius. An ordinary ribbon microphone is bi-directional; that is to say, the ribbon responds to sound reaching it from the front and from the back but not to sound reaching it from either side, so the microphone's response to sound from the sides is minimal. Rackham made a ribbon microphone in a case with suitable damping behind it, making it omni-directional, and then arranged a lip guard which ensured the correct juxtaposition of the ribbon and the mouth of the speaker, thus ensuring maximum response to the voice with minimum interference from extraneous noises; and it worked. On the appointed day Rackham insisted on loading everything into his estate car and the severely depressed state of the suspension clearly demonstrated that this was quite a load! Bill Preedy was also going in his own car but Rackham was determined to take all the equipment in his car. There was another problem in evidence in that there was very little tread left on the front tyres of his car, a point which others had brought to his attention some time before this journey, but Ron replied that racing tyres were much the same and, in any case, with little or no tread on the tyres, there would be a greater area of rubber in contact with the road surface! Dennis Terrett was very apprehensive about travelling with him but Rackham insisted and somehow they arrived safely at Hams Hall.

Guy's mean streak was much in evidence during this demonstration for it was written into the conditions that all personnel on site had to wear protective headgear. So Guy, in order to save a few coppers, looked through the pages of *Exchange and Mart* and responded to an advertisement for hard hats. When these arrived it was found that they looked like old American firefighters' helmets, with a protective extension over the wearer's neck. Terrett said that he felt an absolute pratt wearing it and, on one occasion, when he was struggling to get into a very crowded lift on the site, a voice at the back said, "Come in mate, we won't laugh at you." Guy was so fond of looking for bargains for the company that *Exchange and Mart* became known among Tannoy personnel as the *Director's Gazette*.

The demonstration was a great success and the order was certain, however, with Rackham's car once again loaded for the return journey it started to rain a little. At this point Dennis expressed to Bill Preedy his concern about travelling back with Rackham in his heavily loaded car and with bald tyres, and argued that it made good sense to lighten the load in Ron's car by letting him travel back with Bill. As they approached Hendon on a dual carriageway Bill looked in his mirror and saw Ronnie's car performing a graceful pirouette along the road. Fortunately there were no other vehicles on the road as he made very good use of the full width, finally coming to rest with a badly buckled front wheel resting against the kerb. A very shaken Rackham sat in his car while Bill Preedy and Dennis Terrett changed the wheel for him to complete the journey to West Norwood. A set of new tyres was fitted the next day.

The hard hat episode can be followed by a further anecdote about Guy's mean streak for he was also very reluctant to consider any applications for increases in his employee's salaries. It became a tradition that *Wireless World* was circulated among the more senior members of the engineering staff who had a habit of looking in the 'Situations vacant' columns for better paid jobs and ringing round them with bold, coloured pencils before the magazine was sent to Guy's office for him to read it,

Returning to the subject of Guy's 'seafaring' activities, there are several tales of his erratic behaviour. Stan Livingstone recalled that he was once at the Morris Motors factory at Cowley, working in the roof on a Tannoy installation. This was before Elsie Fountain died and Denis Blackmore who was, by then, the company Secretary, telephoned him.

"Do you think that you and Joan could go up the river with the old man in his boat tomorrow night?"

"Well," said Livingstone, "it's not impossible." Denis said, "Well, you can get yourself twenty quid out of the petty cash." Stan thought perhaps he didn't mind after all, so he and Joan went along. To start with it was a perfect occasion; Guy could not have been nicer. But the situation changed somewhat as they made their way up river when Guy said to his wife, "Elsie, let's have a sandwich, shall we?" So Elsie produced some brown bread and some fruit and she opened a tin of corned beef. There was a little refrigerator on the boat, so the tin was very cold with the result that the beef slipped out of the tin quite easily and it fell on the deck. Guy went absolutely mad and shouted at Elsie in a disgusting and atrocious manner; he went on and on at her, much to the embarrassment of all present. When it was all over Joan Livingstone said to Elsie, quietly but quite clearly so that all could hear, "If Stanley ever spoke to me like that, just once, I'd hit him – and leave him." On another occasion Guy was on board with Maureen and others when Elsie was seen approaching. It is report-

The TANNOY Story

ed that Maureen perfected a hasty dis-embarkation into a dinghy on one side of the boat only seconds before Elsie boarded on the other!

The military side of Tannoy's business must not be neglected because this was being further developed during these years and, from 1953 to 1966 Tannoy was the sole supplier of transportable public address systems to H.M. Forces. Almost every item of audio equipment then in use by the Services, from little loud hailers to the massive 2 kW amplifiers used in sky shouting aircraft, came from Tannoy and were proprietory Tannoy designs. Of course, news of these achievements had spread throughout the world with the result that Tannoy supplied equipment to the armed forces of many other countries.

Whilst considering these Systems Engineering successes, the production and sales of items such as microphones, loudspeakers and small amplifiers must not be overlooked, particularly the Dual Concentric Loudspeaker. Stan Livingstone had been promoting the Dual Concentric Loudspeakers for use as studio monitors, with considerable emphasis on the Japanese market. He did this without reference to Guy who might have tried to prevent this but, as it happened, it was very successful and this developed into a very worthwhile volume of business which continues in the 21st century. Tannoy also made the first shielded ribbon microphone which was quite scientifically designed. It was an improved ribbon microphone with a disc behind it to maintain the high frequency response which tended to fall off. This was a marked improvement on the performance of conventional ribbon microphones and they were also, to a large extent, directional. Tannoy was also the first company to make and patent a loudspeaker with an acoustically damped surround to the cone. Originally this was done experimentally by fixing pieces of adhesive tape at regular intervals around the edge of the cone but the success of this experiment led to further development of the principle, known as 'doping' the surround, a principle which is now universal. So, between about 1948 and about 1960, Tannoy was a very innovative company at the forefront of audio developments.

Since the mid 1950s Tannoy had been moving into the domestic high fidelity market which required them to make very high quality cabinets and they still had Frank Venables, of 'dewdrop' and 'wintergreen' fame. From these modest beginnings with Venables, the company's cabinet work developed and became very big. Frank Venables seems to have been highly respected by Guy for his skills with wood and, in addition to his work in the cabinet shop, he was obliged to spend endless hours varnishing and french polishing Guy's boat. He also doubled as the Butler at 102, College Road, the house into which Guy and Maureen moved after Guy sold Tudor Lodge following Elsie's death. However, his Skippers did not survive long for he was for ever sacking and recruiting new Skippers for his boat, one of whom was Paul Worters who lasted longer than most. However, Guy was really only a fair weather sailor; he would never sail with *Albaquila* across the channel. If he wanted to cruise the continental north coast, he always went over by ferry and met the boat in France.

There are many anecdotes which illustrate the sort of man Guy Fountain was and the first chapters recount his early life and the factors which moulded him but, with the sweet smell of success in his nostrils he gradually became a rather different person. The author remembers him as a man of unexpected extremes; at one moment a kind, generous and friendly man but, almost at the next moment, a man in a frenzy of bad temper; very bad temper. The episode of the little boys, Michael and David, anxiously waiting for their father to tire of experimenting with their new train set in the basement of the house at Lancaster Avenue is drawn from personal experience and the author also remembers various happenings while on holiday with the Fountain family at Carlton Cottage, Cliftonville, in about 1946. 'Uncle Guy', as he was known to the author, would swing unpredictably from one extreme to another; from kindness which could hardly be equalled, to demonstrations of a temper which was violent to say the least of it; from a mean streak which would not allow him to spend a few coppers on a treat for his children to a level of generosity which could hardly be imagined.

Mention has also been made of Guy's somewhat nefarious nocturnal activities yet he undoubtedly applied dual standards. Calendars which featured scantily clad girls were never permitted in the factory and when one member of the drawing office staff left the company, Guy commented that he had 'Trouser trouble'. Once, on a visit to Eindhoven with Ronnie Rackham and Stan Livingstone, it was suggested that the three of them should go out for an evening but Guy declined, saying that he was tired and was going to have an early night. The following morning, when they settled their bills, it was noted that there was an item on Guy's account for the previous day entitled, 'Special room service'.

At the factory he frequently ordered members of his staff to carry out personal tasks for him, many of which were of no benefit to the company, but he was the Governor. Edmund Newton recounted two such events, the first of which took place in about 1970 when he was a junior draughtsman in the drawing office. Guy was negotiating the lease of two adjacent flats in Dolphin Square, the idea being that these would be combined to make one large flat for himself and Maureen. He instructed the Chief Draughtsman to send someone to Dolphin Square and the job fell to Newton, the most junior in the Drawing Office. He was to obtain the floor plans of the flats and trace these so that Guy could work out what furniture would fit, and where. Having traced the floor plans he was told to bring them back to the drawing office and mark all the

The TANNOY Story

rooms out in 1 ft. squares on the drawings so that Guy could move cut-out templates of the proposed furniture to various positions. However, the project fell through and, so far as is known, the lease of the flats was never taken by Guy. Eddie Newton said that he was also instructed to carry out a similar exercise in the garden at Guy's home, making a scale plan of the garden and again marking this out in 1ft squares so that Guy could prepare his detailed plans of what should be planted, and where. Not long after this, Newton was also instructed to do much the same on Guy's boat, *Albaquila* and he remembers that the boat was absolutely loaded with Guy's 'nautical novelties'. It seemed that almost every concievable electric or electronic gadget that was then available was on board. It did, of course, have a Tannoy 'Ventair' extractor fitted but it also had radar, an echo sounder, a Tannoy anemometer and wind direction indicator, a very advanced radio installation, a Tannoy 'Hey-Loh' loud hailer, (gold plated), an electric bilge pump, a Tannoy gas detector, and much more beside. Eddie Newton commented that the fact that it was so loaded with equipment may have been the reason why Guy refused to take it across the channel to France, always insisting that Paul Worters had to sail her across the channel to France where Guy and his guests would meet him.

He also frequently adopted the principle of 'Divide and Rule' and often enjoyed taking a member of his staff aside and interrogating him about others. Dennis Terrett said that on these occasions they were always on their guard and very careful how they answered any questions. It was quite common to be summoned to his house for this purpose and, on one occasion, Dennis was told to go there at 4 pm. On arrival he was offered a drink but he replied that it was rather too early for him, but Guy replied that he was about to have one so he accepted in order to avoid offending him. He said he would like a small scotch. This was dispensed as a very large scotch, in a tumbler, clearly intended to lubricate his vocal chords. Sure enough, there were questions about his colleagues to which Dennis contrived some very carefully constructed replies. When it was time to leave he was very concerned about the quantity of alcohol he had consumed and he drove home very carefully. Fortunately drinking and driving was nowhere near so forcefully proscribed then as it was in later years, otherwise it would have had to be a taxi journey.

Norman Robottom recalled the different reactions of members of the staff to summonses via the 'Tannoy' from Guy or from Michael when Michael was the Managing Director. They would be somewhat apprehensive about a call from Guy, wondering what they had done wrong or what they had said to upset him but, as Norman said, when Michael called they would walk into Michael's office and often be greeted with the question, "Have you heard the one about. . .?" Dennis Terrett added that the telephone operator was responsible for making the public address announcements which included calling staff to the telephone to take calls, both internal and external. One of the frequent calls was, 'Mr. Fountain please, toll call.' Everyone took this as a warning that Guy Fountain was on the prowl and made themselves look very busy but the true meaning of this announcement was also well known to all, it meant that Guy's cup of tea was waiting for him in his office.

CHAPTER NOTES

1   Ronald Pickering's father, Russell Pickering, was *Bertram Mills* company secretary. His company was *Clarke, Pickering and Partners*.

Guy R. Fountain

CHAPTER FOURTEEN

GUY STILL AT THE HELM

Possibly the most amusing illustration of Guy's unpredictability is the story of his invitation to John and Marion Gilbert to take a holiday with him in Monte Carlo. The tale is based on John Gilbert's account to the author.

At the 1956 Radio Industry Club Dinner, Guy was in conversation with John Gilbert who was a well known correspondent and a regular contributor to *Gramophone* and several other magazines associated with music. Guy commented on John's appearance, saying that he did not look at all well, to which John replied that he had recently been quite ill. Guy's immediate reaction, a typical act of spontaneous generosity, was to invite John and his wife, Marion, to take a holiday with him in Monte Carlo.

During the next few weeks the details were arranged between them and on the appointed day John and Marion went with their luggage to the Tannoy factory where Guy's Rolls-Royce was waiting, complete with its trailer and his rather luxurious 'Chris Craft' speedboat.

On leaving the factory, with Guy at the wheel, they drove towards Dulwich where John, not unnaturally, expected that they would collect Elsie from Tudor Lodge but, much to his surprise, they drove past Tudor lodge and over the hill to a house near to the Crystal Palace, where Guy left John and Marion in the car saying that he would not be long. He soon returned with someone whom John described as 'a rather large lady' who was introduced to them as Maureen, she stepped into the car, and off they went. John thought that Maureen must be Guy's secretary and that he still had business to conduct with her, perhaps on the way back to the factory and it was therefore even more surprising to them when Maureen remained with them as they drove out of London towards Dover and it was some time before it finally registered that Maureen was, in fact, coming with them on the holiday and that Elsie was not.

They arrived at Dover where the Customs officer asked to check all the details of both the car and the boat and it was only at this point that Guy realised to his horror that he had left all the documents relating to the boat in his office. With his temper mounting, he telephoned Stan Livingstone at the factory and issued instructions for the documents to be brought to Dover by motorcycle as quickly as possible but it was some three hours before they arrived; three hours in which Guy's frustration and anger boiled up into a typical show of 'Fountain' rage, causing some embarrassment to John and Marion, and also to Maureen.

When the papers arrived the party returned to the Customs shed whereupon the officer, whose suspicions seemed to have been aroused, decided to check the engine number of the speedboat, but Guy had packed much of his luggage in the boat, all of which had to be removed to allow the Customs officer to gain access to the engine to verify its number. At this time, petrol was still rationed in France and Guy wanted to take as much as possible with him for the boat and the car so, in addition to filling the tanks of both car and boat, there were several cans of petrol amongst the luggage in the boat and this also had to be unloaded. Guy had also had an ingenious pump fitted in the boat to feed petrol to the car from the boat's tank, the idea being that this would increase the distance he could travel through France without having to stop to buy expensive, rationed petrol and, not unnaturally, Guy's disposition was further aggravated by the thought that this system would be discovered and that this would lead to even more trouble with the Customs Officer.

While Guy was busy with the Customs officer, he passed his briefcase to John, asking him to look after it for him saying that it had all the maps for the journey in it so that they could plan their route while on the ferry and eventually, after a long delay which only served to increase Guy's frustration still more, the Customs officer was at last satisfied. John then helped Guy to re-pack all the luggage into the boat, and they boarded the ferry. Once they were well out to sea, Guy asked John for his briefcase and told him that it contained £1,000 in £1 notes. At that time there were currency restrictions in force and it was permissible to take only £50 out of the country in cash. It is not difficult to work out who would have been held responsible if the Customs Officer had decided to inspect the briefcase.

Their arrival at Calais and their passage through Customs and Immigration passed without further incident and they set out on their long drive through France and they eventually arrived in Switzerland. Guy had planned the journey to take them through Switzerland where petrol was more readily available and less expensive.

Eventually they arrived in the South of France and Guy pulled up at an hotel

The TANNOY Story

where he had much enjoyed his previous visits and where he knew that there was a crane to lift the boat off its trailer and into the water. While Guy supervised the unloading of the luggage, he asked John to go into the hotel and book two double rooms. This John did, and he was shown two very pleasant rooms and, when the hotel porter had taken their luggage up to their rooms, the receptionist asked for their passports. John and Marion handed over their passports and Guy gave him his own. The receptionist then asked Guy for his wife's passport and Maureen handed over hers which was not only in her own name but was, of course, an Irish passport. On seeing this the receptionist asked if they were married and when Guy said that they were not, the receptionist replied, "I'm sorry Sir, but you cannot stay here."

This caused further embarrassment in the party, and Guy was once again angry, pointing out that he had stayed there several times before and that he particularly wanted to stay there again where he could lift his speedboat into the sea, but it was all to no avail, the hotel manager was called and he, too, adamantly refused to allow an unmarried couple to stay. So, amid huge embarrassment, all the luggage had to be brought down from the rooms and, once again, packed into the boat and the car; a situation which Guy, of course, found very humiliating and which did nothing to calm his temper. Guy had not known that since he had last stayed at the hotel, it had been taken over and that the new owner insisted on observing the French law which then forbade unmarried couples staying together in hotels. So Guy decided that they would have to go on to Monte Carlo where he had a friend who could get petrol for him free of tax because the boat was classed there as a 'Sea going craft'.

John Gilbert recalled that the onward journey to Monte Carlo was nothing less than a nightmare. It was one of those occasions when Guy's temper became absolutely uncontrollable and the atmosphere in the Rolls-Royce was almost unbearable. John was sitting in the front passenger seat, next to Guy, where he had a very much better view of the busy road ahead than Guy and at one point they were forced to come to a standstill behind a long queue of stationery vehicles. Guy decided that he was not going to wait with the other motorists, he was going to jump the queue. John, who could see ahead, advised him not to do so as there was a bend about 100 yards ahead and he could not see around it, but Guy insisted that there would be nothing coming and pulled out to pass the queue.

As luck would have it, there was something coming, a large British coach loaded with tourists from a Midlands town came round the bend just as Guy pulled out to pass the queue and they came to an abrupt halt, nose to nose, the huge coach and the Rolls-Royce with its luxury speedboat on its trailer. The coach driver passed a few typically choice remarks which were hardly complimentary either to Guy's driving skills or to his manners and he insisted, quite rightly, that he was not going to give way and that Guy would have to reverse back to the tail of the queue, trailer or no trailer. Meanwhile, the traffic beside them had started to move slowly and Guy decided that he would get himself out of trouble, and salve some of his hurt pride, by slipping into the first gap which he saw in the line. Looking in his mirror, he saw a space which was big enough and moved into it, expecting that the car behind would give way to him. However, he realised two inescapable facts only just too late; one being that the gap was not as big as he had judged it to be, the other being that the second vehicle was definitely not going to give way to him as he expected, nor could it, for it was on the end of a long tow-rope, being towed by the car in front! The resulting chaos of car and tow-rope, Rolls-Royce and Chris-Craft, took about half an hour to to disentangle and eventually, after more heated discussion they were able to proceed on their way towards Monte Carlo. From then on the atmosphere in the car was quite unbearable, and they completed the unpleasant journey in stony silence. They were all heartily glad when at last, without further incident, they arrived in Monte Carlo.

On the following day, the friend whom Guy had mentioned earlier, arranged for him to obtain some tax free petrol and allowed him the use of a crane to lower the boat into the water but as John and Guy were doing this, dressed in shorts, John felt a tap on his shoulder. Turning round he found that it was Peter Collins, at that time a leading motor racing driver who, in the Italian Grand Prix at Monza and in spite of the fact that he was lying third and needed only to maintain this position to win the Championship, magnanimously pulled into the pits and handed over his Ferrari to the team's No. 1 driver, Juan Manuel Fangio, whose car had suffered a steering fault. Fangio chased after the two leaders but was not able to win the race; one of them, however, dropped out and Fangio came in second, giving him enough points to secure the Championship. Peter Collins, who was so sadly killed two years later during the German Grand Prix, had recently married and had set up home on his yacht in Monaco harbour. He asked John if he knew Sir James Scott Douglas, to which John replied that he knew him well, even referring to him as 'Jimmy'. Sir James Scott Douglas was also quite well known as a racing and trials driver.

"Well," said Collins, "that's his yacht next to that of Onassis but he's on my boat just now, come aboard and meet him."

Peter Collins then looked at Guy Fountain and asked John, "Who is he?"

John replied, "That's Guy Fountain, Governing Director of Tannoy." So Peter said, "Bring him along, and bring the ladies as well, come aboard as soon as you can."

John told Guy of this conversation and he was a little perplexed when Guy

The TANNOY Story

told him, "Fine, you go ahead with Marion, and Maureen and I will follow when we are ready."

So John and Marion went aboard and to their surprise, there was Sir James and his party, which included some rather beautiful young ladies, enjoying themselves on Collins' boat and it was not long before Sir James asked John what he was doing in Monte Carlo and when John told him he added that Peter had invited Guy aboard as well.

"Who is he?" asked Sir James.

"He's Guy Fountain, the M.D. of Tannoy." replied John.

"Wait till that bastard comes aboard, I'll tell him just what I think of him and his company!"

Eventually, some 20 minutes later, Guy and Maureen came aboard, Guy resplendent in white trousers, brown and white 'co-respondents' shoes, blue blazer with the badge of the Royal Thames Yacht Squadron and a peaked cap!

At that moment John was talking to Sir James and he said, "Well, Sir James, may I introduce my friend Guy Fountain?". To which the response was, "Who are you?"

"I'm Chairman and Governing Director of Tannoy." said Guy, using a term which he had invented and which greatly appealed to his inflated ego.

"That bloody organisation," replied Sir James. "You ought to be shot."

Obviously Guy was extremely upset by this outburst but in the course of the following conversation the reason for it became clear. Apparently, some three months earlier, Sir James had sent an order with a cheque for two loud hailers but there had been no response whatsoever and the loud hailers had never arrived. After some discussion during which Guy offered profuse apologies, he turned to John Gilbert, addressing him rather in the manner of a master addressing a servant and saying, "Go back to the hotel and fetch my loud hailer and I will make a present of it to your friend." Turning to Sir James, he said, "I'll telephone my son who will send another from the factory in a day or two."

John eventually felt he could leave the party for a few minutes and went to fetch Guy's loud hailer, a Tannoy 'Hey-Loh', to give it to Sir James. Typically for Guy Fountain, his own 'Hey-Loh' was gold plated, but nevertheless he gave it to Sir James.

Later, Guy telephoned Michael at the factory to instruct him to send another one by airfreight which arrived some two or three days later, John Gilbert was asked, perhaps instructed, to collect it from the airport at Nice and, a little while later, John and Marion took the Chris-Craft over to Monte Carlo harbour to visit Sir James and to deliver the second loud hailer. As they boarded the yacht, Sir James was roaring with laughter and asked if they had brought the loud hailer, to which John replied that he had, and that it was the same as the first except that it was not, of course, gold plated.

Sir James commented that it was absolutely marvellous and worked very well, "But", he added, "after you and Fountain had left the other day, I called my Chief Engineer and handed him the gold plated loud hailer and asked him to try it out, which he did, and it echoed all around Monaco harbour. I then explained the story of how I had obtained it to which my engineer replied, "Well Sir, that's very interesting, but the truth is that we ordered them from *Pye*, not from Tannoy."

Later in the holiday, Guy was often quite unpleasant unless he had his own way and after about a month John and Marion felt that they could take no more of Guy's behaviour and they decided to return home. John asked Guy if he could borrow the car to go to Nice to see if he could come to some arrangement with *British European Airways* as he had, by then, very little money left. However, Guy insisted on driving him there and accompanying him to the airline office. While he was waiting in the queue, John again felt a tap on the shoulder and another voice said, "Hello Johnny, what are you doing here?"

John looked around and saw a man, dressed in shorts and an open necked shirt but, having been surprised by him and away from his customary environment he could not work out who he was. Meanwhile, Guy was standing apart from them and did not hear the conversation. John looked at the elderly man and apologised for not recognising him.

"Of course you do, you and Dick Whiteley cost me five pounds when we played snooker at Mansfield." (It has not yet been possible to identify Dick Whiteley positively but it seems almost certain that he was connected with the *Whiteley Electrical and Radio Company*, manufacturers of sound reproducing equipment including microphones and loudspeakers, whose factory was at Victoria Road, Mansfield.)

Then John remembered him, and he also remembered the customary sober business suit instead of the shorts. He asked John what he was doing there and when he was told that they were trying to get back to England but had very little money left, his new found acquaintance told him that Dick Whiteley was coming to Cannes the following day on board the S.S. *Chusan* and he felt sure that Dick would be able to organise something for him. John and Marion then left, returning to the hotel with Guy driving, but the following day John asked him to take them to the station where they bade their farewells and boarded a train to Cannes.

John and Marion arrived in Cannes and were soon taken on board the *Chusan* where they explained their predicament to Dick Whiteley who, as expected, offered them a spare cabin which he had on the ship, and so it was that they returned from their turbulent holiday, enjoying travel at its luxurious best on board the *Chusan*. They did not see Guy again for about a month when he was, of course, perfectly sweet and charming once more.

Michael recalled that his father also used to invite people to stay with him in Majorca but, once there, they often had to toe the line and do much as they were told, just as John had to in Monte Carlo. Back in Norwood he would sometimes take friends, acquaintances and business associates to lunch at Tudor Lodge. After lunch with Elsie he would occasionally take his guests 'over the hill' to spend the afternoon with Maureen and expect them to be equally friendly with both Elsie and Maureen. Some were able to accept this but others found it embarrassing. When the family was staying at Cliftonville, he would often arrange for Maureen to stay in a nearby hotel so that he could go and visit her.

On 28th. August, 1966, Elsie Fountain died and, somewhat too soon afterwards Guy told the family that he was going to marry Maureen. Michael told him not to force her on the family with undue haste because they would not accept her. They felt so much bitterness about the unhappiness that her presence had brought to their mother Elsie that they were very reluctant to accept Maureen. However, Guy married Maureen about a year later at Camberwell Registry Office, after which there was a reception at the Savoy Hotel. Needless to record, not one member of the family attended.

However, to return to business, the company continued along its successful path through the 1950s and 1960s but, in about about 1969 Livingstone started to worry about the company's future development. This was when electronic technology started to change very quickly indeed and although Tannoy attracted some young technicians who would have been capable of taking the company forward into that technology, none of them stayed for very long because they regarded audio as a bit boring and old-fashioned and they all wanted to get into computer and digital technology and the more advanced forms of electronics. So, by about 1969, Tannoy was a company which was falling behind the advances in technology, not falling behind with acoustic technology, but falling behind with the electronic technology. In addition to this it was an ageing company for Guy's big boast at the time was that he had 35 people who had been with him for more than 25 years and many who had been aboard for 35 years or more. This was a very good thing to be proud of but it did not produce an expanding company and a company such as Tannoy has to expand and, in common with many others, Livingstone was concerned about who was going to be left to pay his pension. He later said that had he then known more about the pension scheme he would not have been worried for when he eventually retired he received a pension of £22 per week which at the time was very acceptable.

However, Tannoy was not entirely in the doldrums for, at about that time, the company's exports of very high fidelity monitor loudspeakers to Japan were then starting to develop and this became very big business which Livingstone and others had to negotiate. It still continues to this day, but the situation developed in which there were contracts which Tannoy was unable to fulfil because the company had not kept abreast of the developing technology. Tannoy was frequently invited to quote for equipment and Stan found that they could not make what was required simply because they had insufficient knowledge of the new technology which was needed with the result that, little by little, the company started to go downhill. There was also a tendency for panic to set in which created the setting for the philosophy; 'what you can quote for, you quote low', in order to secure some business, so they finished up in about 1972 just as they had some 25 years before with dwindling reserves of money, so the company eventually abandoned its consumer electronics systems which could not compete with those of companies such as *Thorn*, *Sobel* and Arnold Weinstock's *Radio and Allied Industries*.

Livingstone thought, probably quite rightly, that they should go into the studio console business because this was truly audio and it seemed to have a good future for development. It also looked like the way in which Tannoy should and could progress and, at the time, the company secured a very big contract with the Romanian authorities to put an audio console and all its associated sound equipment into their new opera house. Livingstone and Rackham saw the plans and invited a quotation from another, unnamed company and virtually doubled it using the argument that they must be able to make it for twice the price. They also argued that it would be Tannoy's prototype for which they would get paid. Their little scheme worked; Tannoy won the contract, gained the additional experience and were paid for it. The scheme was a great success for Tannoy and it was an equally great success for the Bucharest Opera House.

During this contract Livingstone received a further indication that things were going wrong when he found that suppliers were telephoning him to say that they had not been paid for the components they had provided. *Gabriel House* was the agent for the company which then made the loudspeaker cones and Tannoy had also sourced some rather good faders from Switzerland which were not freely available elsewhere. Both these organisations telephoned to say that they had not been paid for their goods, to which Livingstone replied, "I don't believe you." So he went to see Denis Blackmore who said, "Well, you know, they are a bit far down the list, Stan." But the final indication came on a somewhat lower scale of importance when it was found that they were not paying Jimmy Leach, the proprietor of the *Mixing Bowl* restaurant in West Norwood, who did the catering for the company's '21 Club' meetings. The '21 Club' was formed to celebrate those employees who had served the company for 21 years and their luncheons were held in the *Mixing Bowl*. There were three months between meetings and when Livingstone tried to arrange one of these lunches he found that Jimmy Leach had not been paid for the previous one. This was the Christmas meeting of 1973 and in January 1974 an amazing thing happened.

Company Secretary Denis Blackmore, called the Production Manager, a Mr. Barry, and Engineers Stanley Livingstone, Bill Preedy, Ron Rackham and Bill Haines to a meeting in the showroom where there were already three other gentlemen who had come from *Exchange Telegraph*. These gentlemen were introduced and it was announced that they were interested in buying the company! Livingstone said that they were all astonished but, unfortunately, Denis had not then learned a most important lesson: he made the mistake of introducing them to Guy Fountain with the result that they were quickly sent away. Within a few weeks a whole host of companies including G.E.C., *Philips, Pye* etc. came down with a view to buying the company and, in some cases, such as with *Pye*, they got on very well and came quite close to striking a deal. Bill Preedy was then the U.K. Sales Manager and he used to show people around the factory and make it look as if it was worth lots of money. With *Pye* in particular all seemed to be very well organised and they progressed as far as telling the Tannoy staff not to worry as they would have a good pension scheme etc. Then one afternoon, after Guy had had a 'happy' lunchtime, it was just impossible for them to avoid meeting him and he was introduced as 'Mr. Guy Fountain, Chairman and Governing Director'. But Guy's rude reaction to them was to say to their Accountant and their Sales Director, "Unless you've got a million pounds in your pockets, there's the ******* bus stop." And that was the end of Tannoy's association with *Pye*. Bill Preedy later commented that a principle of survival which he found to be essential was: 'Never expose a valued client to Guy Fountain until the ink on the contract is dry'.

Early in 1974, the dual concentric loudspeaker production had a major problem. *Kurt Muller*, a German company, were making the special cones required for the exponential matching of the H.F. and L.F. sound components of these loudspeakers. They had a factory in High Wycombe where these cones were manufactured and this was severely damaged in a fire which not only devoured their entire stock of Tannoy's cones but also destroyed the essential tooling. Spare tooling was not kept at their German plant as was expected so the production of dual concentric loudspeakers at West Norwood came to a standstill until the dedicated tooling could be replaced. The consequential loss policy provided £150,000 cover and Tannoy decided to maintain the assembly staff at the Canterbury Grove factory in the hope that a miracle would happen, but no such miracle came about and the £150,000 was squandered on the largest ever production of knitting in West Norwood. This occurred immediately before the arrival of *Harman International* on the Tannoy scene; at a time when there was a full order book for Systems Engineering, which required many dual concentric loudspeakers, and at a time when the sales of dual concentric loudspeakers could only go up.

During the lead up to Harman's entry into Tannoy history, it seemed as if an invisible 'For Sale' notice had brought a number of interested companies onto the scene, most with derisory offers. G.E.C. had in mind an offer of £50,000 but this, and other similarly derisory offers, were based on recognition of the fact that a high proportion of the staff were members of the '21 Club', with the inevitable high cost of redundancies. It was during a visit by two *G.E.C.* executives that a bomb warning was received by the telephone operator and the prescribed broadcast was made to clear the factory. Personnel were required to line up in Lansdowne Hill to be counted. Livingstone and Preedy, considering the importance of the potential purchasers, hastily bundled the *G.E.C.* executives into Preedy's car and drove them up to nearby Royal Circus where they had a good view of the factory and any possible explosion. The telephone operator, as instructed, telephoned Guy at home where he was dealing with correspondence with his secretary, then Roy Saunders. Guy, on hearing the bomb alert, hurriedly took off, still in his carpet slippers, saying to Roy, "I must be with my boys," rather in the manner of the Captain of a sinking ship. Upon arrival at Lansdowne Hill, where the assembled ranks were waiting, he hurried into the works and into his office and broadcast to the workers outside, "This is the Governor speaking, all come inside and have a cup of tea." On this occasion, Livingstone and Preedy did not clinch a deal for the company.

At this fraught time, between 1973 and the arrival of Harman, Livingstone and Preedy were placed in the position of salesmen of the company business, and had also to try to untangle many of the associated financial and stock problems. The last stock taking exercise really brought home to them an understanding of the age of the Tannoy company and, above all, of its stock of components. One could not help overhearing the comments of those who were sorting parts in the darker corners of the storage area, such as, "Do you remember when these were used on the first station installation at Birmingham?" and, "I wondered where these G.U.B.10 parts had got to." It became something of a 'memory lane' event. When the counting was finished, the valuation showed that a very high proportion of stock had not been needed for ten years or more. At a subsequent session with Denis Blackmore and Ron Pickering, Preedy and Livingstone could only then confirm that Tannoy was in serious trouble.

But just before the eventual sale of the company, there was another interesting technical development. In 1973 Preedy was summoned to the Public Services Agency offices at St. Christopher House in London to meet a senior

The TANNOY Story

Procurement Officer. His opening words were, "Can your company make bells talk? I have contacted all the major fire alarm companies without success." Fortunately, Tannoy had realised, some years earlier, that the common alarm bell was 'tongue-tied' and, as with the R.A.F. stations and the factories during the war, there was a necessity, in an emergency, to communicate specific instructions which could be conveyed only by means of the spoken word. This was also, of course, the *raison d'etre* for the Tannoy valveless amplifiers in submarines. The wartime systems, both military and civilian, had been designed with possible damage to the equipment in mind and they included suitable back-up facilities to ensure security of the systems at all times. Just before this meeting the terrorist outbreak by the I.R.A. had caught the authorities out and this explained the urgency of their enquiry. At the time, people associated bells with the ultimate means of communication in the event of fire and, on hearing fire bells, they usually carried out the appropriate fire drill, evacuated their buildings, and assembled at designated assembly points outside. The Ministry needed to act as a matter of great urgency following an incident in which the staff of a central London building had been warned by means of the fire bells to evacuate their building following a bomb alert and, obeying their customary instructions, they had moved into the roadway to be counted, but the bomb exploded in a car parked in the road resulting in many casualties and some deaths.

Time was of the essence and a proposal was made to utilise existing cabling, which was used for fire detection and bell systems, and to replace the bells with loudspeakers. Fortunately this occurred when the company was changing over from germanium 24 volts to silicon 50 volts designs and there was a range of amplifiers readily available which had been well tested on the QE2. Tannoy was therefore ready and willing to accept a contract to convert all Whitehall buildings, a contract valued at £1.2 million. Following this the company very soon received follow-on contracts for the Palace of Westminster, Buckingham Palace, the Law Courts and numerous other Government buildings and this work led very rapidly to the perfection of the Tannoy Vocalarm Integrated Security Communications Systems. These systems had the advantages of being able to simulate the traditional bell or siren alarms plus the ability to give precise instructions by means of the spoken word. Instructions could be given by an announcer using the microphone on the command unit or by means of pre-recorded messages on either tape or disc. More than one command unit could be connected to the equipment and, using the disc or tape inputs, music could also be relayed over the system with alarm or emergency speech override. The equipment also incorporated alarm actuating systems, triggered by break-glass actuators or by fire sensors. The equipment had another great advantage in that the loudspeakers could also function as microphones so that the security staff could switch distant loudspeakers to the input circuit of the amplifier enabling them to listen to suspicious noises or conversations and take appropriate action. They were thus able to monitor all areas within the building.

Soon after completion of the installation in the Palace of Westminster, during a visit of the Chief Engineer of *United Biscuits*, Bill Preedy received a telephone call from the 'Gentleman Usher of the Black Rod', better known, perhaps, for his annual attempts to vandalise the door of the Commons Chamber before the State Opening of Parliament. Admiral Sir Frank Twiss was then Black Rod and he asked if it was necessary for the Lords to share the same evacuation signal as the Commons? The signal in the House of Lords was changed to incorporate a higher tone! Throughout the rooms and corridors of the Palace of Westminster there were still in evidence, at the time of the author's visit (October, 2000) the signal and voice alarm loudspeakers and, although most of these had been painted in the course of redecoration, nearly all of them were the original loudspeakers, still in use and many of them still showing the unmistakable Tannoy logo.

It was no coincidence that Tannoy was well prepared to produce this equipment for, as has been said above, the wartime factory and military public address systems had incorporated some of the facilities required and, in any case, the company had been working on the designs for some time in anticipation of the demand which was brought about by the deteriorating security situation. Bill Preedy was the driving force behind this work and he was the main inspiration to the systems engineering team. He also advised the many authorities about what should be done to provide reliable communications to the occupants of their buildings in anticipation of such events. The authorities, however, had thought that there would be no bombs on London so, when the first bombs did explode, one being at the Old Bailey, there were many telephone calls to Preedy asking him to explain again what Tannoy could do.

In many more government buildings the fire bells were removed and loudspeakers were connected to the existing cables, with the necessary amplification and command equipment connected to the other end and additional loudspeaker positions were provided where it was found that the original fire alarm system had not kept up with alterations to the buildings. The time scale for this work was counted in a few weeks, not the months which would normally have been expected. Other client organisations took an interest and they received the same response, among these was the *B.B.C.* who explained to Dennis Terrett that it was their policy to obtain competitive quotations. Dennis then asked who they had in mind as Tannoy were the undoubted pioneers of this equipment which was unique to Tannoy. After some discussion they agreed to oper-

The TANNOY Story

ate a single tender contract with Tannoy, to their advantage, with the well tried and tested Tannoy systems in all their principal premises within the U.K.

At the time there was only the Code of Practice for fire alarms and this did not take into account this state-of-the-art, Tannoy equipment, so this had to be accommodated in the specifications and, eventually, a new Code of Practice, based on Dennis Terrett's recommendations, was adopted.

Another development, which was a Tannoy first, was a surveillance system. It has been mentioned that the loudspeakers could be used as microphones for provide monitoring facilites and, to clarify this, it was developed for use by security officers to listen for unusual sounds without leaving their posts. They could then alert the police who could surprise the intruders and, on at least one occasion, the criminals are known to have expressed their astonishment at being caught since there had been no alarm sounded to warn them. This had been developed from the introduction of talk-back facilities in industrial P.A. systems so that individuals in all areas of a factory installation could communicate with their bosses. There were very many other examples of the widespread abilities of Tannoy systems during these years covering installations as diverse as the hostile environments of heavy industry to the more tranquil rooms of museums. However, all of this was not enough to secure the company's survival without outside assistance, and Guy's erratic behaviour and the manner in which he treated most of his employees, particularly those in positions of some authority, were contributory factors to the company's eventual passage towards the almost inevitable take-over.

By this time the deterioration in Michael's relationship with his father had become particularly difficult for him to handle and this resulted in acute depression and many sleepless nights. Bill Haines stood up to Guy at least as much as anybody did and, in later years, Michael came to realise just how much Bill had stood up for him in his disputes with his father. Bill Haines spent many years in his later life with his former Secretary, Peggy and when he died, Michael wrote to Peggy and expressed to her his appreciation of the support he had been given by Bill. In her reply Peggy said that she had known of this and of the many battles which Bill Haines had fought for him.

Michael said of these times, "My difficulty was that as he was my father I could not bring myself to treat him in the way in which he treated me; I should have done so but I'm not made that way; I could not round on my father so I just had to put up with it until I decided to leave, by which time I had lost all my confidence and I had no idea what to do next. It was during this time that I felt the need to get away from my father as often as possible and I found excuses to supervise, however loosely, several important installations amongst which were the United Nations building in Geneva where we were installing the instantaneous multi-lingual interpretation system and a similar installation, also for the United Nations, in the Palais de Chaillot in Paris."

In the later years of Guy's control of the company he would go away to his holiday home in Majorca and he often talked of retiring there but he would never actually make the decision to go. Many of the senior management, including Michael, used to wish that he would go away and leave them to run the business but although his breaks in Majorca became longer and longer, he would always come back and, on his return, he always felt the need to show, in one way or another, that he was still in charge. This did much damage to Michael as Managing Director because it undermined his credibility and his authority and the continuance of this behaviour on Guy's part eventually forced Michael's resignation. He reached the point when he had had enough; he could take no more. Life was fine when Guy proudly showed him off as his son and the Managing Director but, away from the limelight Michael was not allowed either to fulfill that function or to progress with it. Worse still, he was often given the freedom to proceed with ideas which he felt were right for the company only to have to suffer the frustration of having them stopped subsequently by Guy. Michael finally resigned in July, 1967 but it was a terrible decision for him to have to make.

Michael later spoke of his father as, "A strange man with an uncontrollable ego which dragged me down until I could take no more". Others have said that Guy Fountain's main problem was insecurity in that he had started with nothing and he was haunted by this all his life: he felt that all around him were conspiring to ensure that he finished up with nothing. But nothing was further than the truth. After all, until the Governor is very rich, what chance does anybody else stand?

Michael submitted his resignation to Denis Blackmore and said that he had received no support from Guy and he also drew attention to the fact that he had received none from Blackmore. After Michael submitted his resignation a similar set of circumstances arose to those which had prevailed after George Wheeler resigned. Guy was all sweetness and light and he did everything to persuade Michael to change his mind. He offered to send Michael and his wife, Jenny, on a world cruise so that when they returned Michael would feel better and would go back to him. He never really believed that Michael would actually leave; it was always his strategy to take people to the brink but he never expected that they would actually say, "That's it, I've had enough." He always reckoned that he would be able to coerce them back one way or another, even by the use of bribery. What Guy did not realise was that if only he could have controlled his ego and delegated authority, he could have sat back in luxury and enjoyed a pleasant, comfortable retirement on the proceeds of the labours of others.

Michael later said, "My father never forgave me for leaving him and he then tried to turn my brother and sister against me so, by this attempt to manoeuvre them, Guy upset them as well. He really seemed to think that he owned the family but, in believing this, he had finally succeeded in turning his whole family against himself." When he left the company, Michael was persuaded by his father to retain his Directorship of the company although Michael did not allow this to last for very long; he finally severed all ties with the company on 24th November, 1970.

Much has been said in the foregoing chapters of Guy Fountain's petulant manner and his mood swings and a little has been recorded of his surprising generosity and of his kindness and of the occasional examples of his sympathy and understanding. At a meeting of the 21 Club which was held on 15th February, 1957 Guy's better nature and the lighter side of his character had emerged, illustrating his interest in the history of his company and his appreciation of humour, even when he was himself the butt of some of the jokes. There was some discussion at this meeting about preparing a document which was to be called 'The Big Book'. This was to have been compiled by members of the 21 Club to record the history of the company and to include as many amusing anecdotes as could be recalled by the members, including those about Guy which may not have been too complimentary about him. At the opening of that meeting Guy Fountain said, "Among the various functions this club performs, I would like to include social amenities, but I would like the predominating function to be the compilation of historical references, anecdotes, circumstances, equipment, designs, particularly the intriguing ones, not necessarily the outstanding ones, but the intriguing ones from an historical point of view. For instance, during the last meeting, George Compigne mentioned an occasion when some artist – I forget the artist's name – blew the voice coils out of the loudspeakers by dropping the mike. Each of these anecdotes, in the end, will resolve into quite an interesting chapter of 'The Big Book' when it is produced."

Among the amusing anecdotes which arose from this meeting was one which was recalled by Mr. Mears who said, "I remember the time when you (Guy Fountain) threw a record from one end of the Dalton Street factory to the other. It was Billy Cotton playing 'Alexander's Ragtime Band'. You came out of your inner office, slammed the doors, hard, and 'Bang', straight across the floor it went. Everybody stopped and looked; it went right to the other end of the room and smashed in pieces on the wall and poor Mr. Pithers just stood there and stamped his foot, trying to say something."

Bill Penny recalled that many years earlier Guy Fountain had given instructions about what wording was to be used in the factory when making announcements to test amplifers etc. These announcements could often be heard in much of the factory and, if they were testing a particularly powerful amplifier, even in adjacent streets. Among these set pieces was, 'Tannoy Products Limited, Guy R. Fountain Limited, Canterbury Grove, West Norwood. Tannoy sound equipment is not mass produced but is individually built and is used by most important undertakings in the country.' Guy Fountain replied to this, "I remember choosing several short strips of varying times, 2 or 3 seconds, one of 5 seconds and one of 10 seconds. I don't know what happened to them." Jim Whiting then commented. "I think they are a very good thing to have. I used to say, 'The word possesses possesses more s's than any other word possesses', or, "Sister Susie's sewing socks for soldiers'."

At the same meeting Norman Robottom told the story of his return from an event in the small hours of the morning. He does not record who was with him but they still had all the equipment set up in the van with the loudspeakers on the roof. As they came through the Blackwall tunnel there was no other traffic in sight except one poor solitary gentleman on a bicycle, pedalling his way wearily home so, just for fun, Norman clipped on the batteries and said, "You have been warned, your days are numbered". This announcement reverberated through the length of the tunnel and the man ended up in a heap in the middle of the road.

Guy Fountain recounted his favourite anecdote of the occasion when George Wheeler was trying to check the speed of a gramophone turntable. The turntable was rather a long way from the light and he had difficulty in seeing the stroboscope so he produced a torch and, completely forgetting the fact that a stroboscope only functions under a light which is operating on an alternating current supply, he shone it on the stroboscope!

Guy also admitted that on his voyages along the river Thames he used to retrieve useful looking pieces of wood, floating on the water, and he would later send a van to collect these and bring them to the factory. He insisted that these were used to build partitions and other structures in the factory to save money although, having been in water for some time, they were possibly useless and certainly difficult to work. These scraps of wood were always known in the factory as Guy's 'river wood'.

Bill Preedy remembered that Guy also commissioned the casting of two bronze busts of himself. One of these was taken to grace his home in Majorca but he insisted that the other was to be exhibited in the showroom whenever Guy was at the factory, rather in the manner of the Royal Standard over Buckinham Palace. Bill Preedy last saw this when it was in use as a doorstop in the showroom.

The TANNOY Story

Private "Ampli Hire" Trailer

RECOMMENDED CABINETS FOR DUAL CONCENTRIC LOUDSPEAKERS

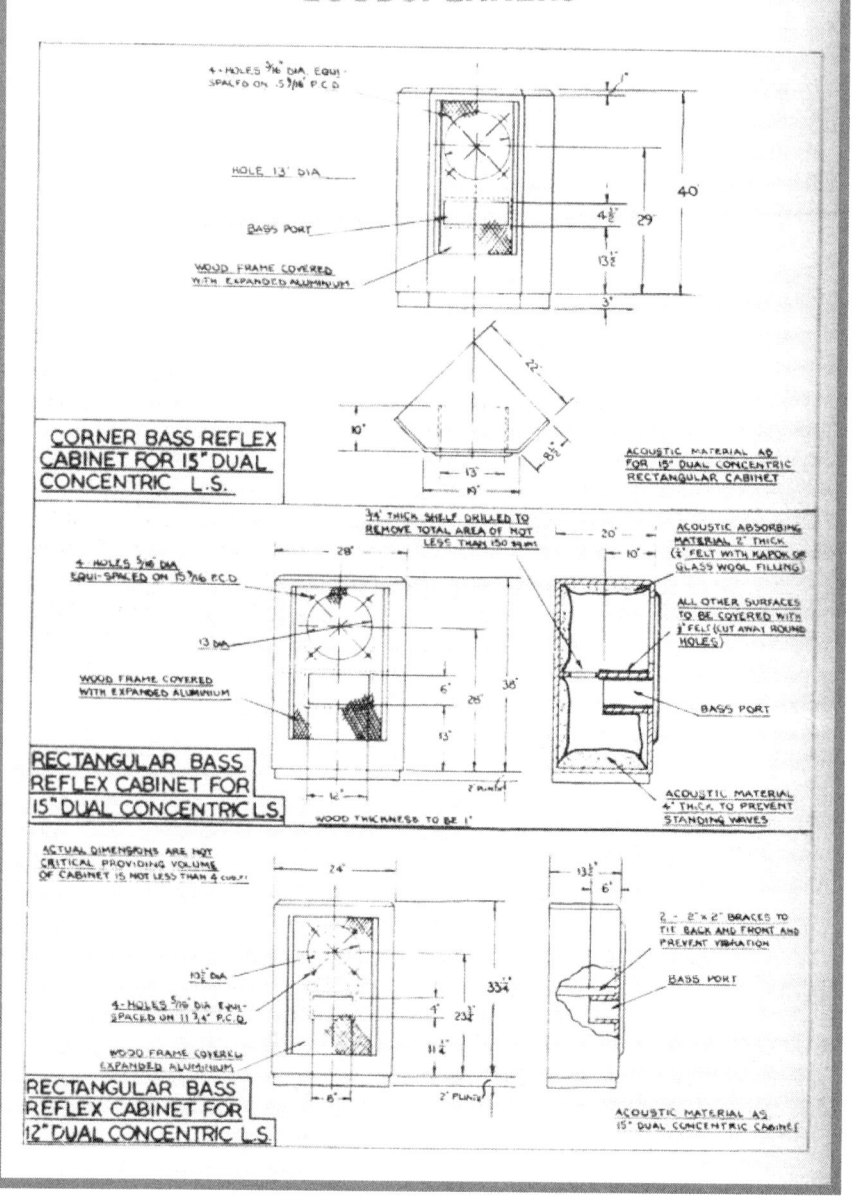

CHAPTER FIFTEEN

THE HARMAN YEARS

To recount the beginning of the Harman story we must go back to 1970 when Sandford Berlin arrived quite unexpectedly in London, booked into the Dorchester Hotel, and telephoned Tannoy asking to speak to Guy. The call was taken by Denis Blackmore. Sandford Berlin was the front man for Sydney Harman, his speech writer and, in effect, heir to *Harman International Inc.,* Sydney Harman's 'Empire'. Guy was under the misguided impression that he had come to poach some of 'his boys' and he therefore decided that Berlin was to be kept out of Norwood at all costs. Being the most dispensible of 'his boys', Bill Preedy was detailed to meet Berlin, entertain him and keep him under constant surveillance. Faced with this problem Preedy decided, rather in the manner of keeping a child amused, that he would take Berlin on a conducted tour of prestige Tannoy systems, with which London then abounded. After three days of this routine as a tour guide, finishing each day with English tea and cucumber sandwiches at the Dorchester Hotel, Preedy made arrangements for *la piece de resistance*; a tour of the Palace of Westminster to see the Tannoy sound reinforcement systems.

This visit was highly successful; too highly successful as it happened. Bill Preedy enjoyed very good relations with the Palace Resident Engineer, Colonel Harris, who gave Sandy Berlin the royal treatment, which he concluded by inviting him to sit on the Lord Chancellor's woolsack and experience for himself the performance of the miniature loudspeakers which had been fitted into the woolsack to allow the Lord Chancellor to derive the maximum benefit from the sound reinforcement scheme. Apparently he used to place his wig around one of the loudspeakers to benefit from the resulting extremely good signal-to-noise ratio of speech reproduction.

When they eventually left the Palace, Preedy realised that he had somewhat overstated the sales presentation with the result that Berlin was more than ever anxious to speak to Guy, which was not at all what had been planned; he said that he had a million dollars burning a hole in his pocket with which to buy Tannoy and he was anxious to clinch a deal. They hurried to the nearest telephone which was opposite Westminster Abbey where, viewed by Preedy from the outside, he soon appeared to be in a state of apoplexy. After a while he banged the receiver down and came out, apparently having been given the brush-off by Guy and having had a rather acrimonious conversation with Denis Blackmore. He cooled down enough to say, "Bill, you've got the greatest public address firm in the world – but you're all stark, raving mad". He then jumped into a cab and disappeared down Victoria Street and went home to America and to Lake Success. Looking back, Preedy felt that he and his colleagues should have been more adequately pre-warned of the intensity of the interest of their potential new bosses. These warnings should, of course have come initially from Freddie and Mary Towler in America, who had been given the responsibility of finding an American buyer for the company, but also from Guy and from Denis Blackmore. However, by that time, Guy was trying hard to dissociate himself from the negotiations, leaving the details, and the responsibility, to Blackmore.

It later transpired, and this was revealed to Bill Preedy when he visited the City Business Library to give the Harman organisation the 'once-over', that on his return to America Berlin must have gone directly to *J.B. Lansing*, in Los Angeles and bought that company for the million dollars which had been burning the hole in his pocket.

It was not until 1974 that the Harman empire started taking an interest again. One Friday evening in July, when Tannoy was shutting down for the weekend, Sandford Berlin reappeared, this time as the advance party for the remaining three Directors and, eventually, Sydney Harman himself, to carry out the final negotiations for the acquisition of Tannoy. Once again Sandy Berlin was put into the care of Bill Preedy for the week-end pending a Monday meeting.

Bill Preedy spent that Saturday with Sandford Berlin and it transpired that Berlin had already decided to buy the company and he was determined to do this for one reason and for one reason only; that reason being that when he had previously visited London and tried to negotiate the purchase of the company, Guy Fountain had refused even to see him, using Bill Preedy to keep him at a safe distance. Now Sandford Berlin was of Russian Jewish descent and it is said he had adopted the surname Berlin because that was where he was born, soon after which event his parents had fled to America. Berlin was an extremely sensitive man and he was deeply affronted by the manner in which Guy Fountain

The TANNOY Story

had so rudely refused even to see him and so, on this occasion, he decided to buy the company without even consulting Sydney Harman, and that is just what he did, for $722,000, the principal beneficiaries being the family Trusts. On the following Friday afternoon, at about 4 o'clock, a taxi arrived at the factory and the scene that followed was described by Livingstone as being just like an old fashioned comedy film. It was a black London cab and people just kept on coming out; Livingstone counted seven men out of the cab. This was a top level team from *Harman International* which included Walter Goodman, Sandford Berlin, Jim Barthell and others but it was significant that Sydney Harman was not among them.

Then, when Harman came over three days later from America he took a very careful look around Tannoy but he was still not told that he had become the proud owner of the company. To gain time, Sandy Berlin booked Harman a passage on board the *France* for his return to America because that gave him three more days to think of a story. It was also said that Harman was under the impression he was travelling on the *Q.E.2* but never noticed the difference. The story that Berlin eventually devised and told Harman is not, regrettably, known but another Harman director, Walter Goodman, had latched on quite quickly to the situation which Berlin had created. He had come to the conclusion that Tannoy looked like 'a sick company in a sick country', but by then it was too late to take any rearguard action; Tannoy had become a subsidiary company of *Harman International*. Sandford Berlin had made a big success of another company which they had bought and, when referring to his acquisition of Tannoy he used to say to Harman, 'Don't worry about this, I'll make both our fortunes again'. So he installed Jim Barthell as production engineer and he and Berlin ran the business but, in the event, they achieved nothing that would turn it from loss into profit.

On take-over day, 13th September, 1974, Bill Preedy and Ron Rackham flew to America and met Freddie Towler in New York. Fred was in charge of Tannoy America and Tannoy Canada and he was as bitter as hell because he was required to act as chauffeur to Preedy and Rackham having been told that Tannoy Canada and Tannoy America were up for grabs. It was Preedy's understanding at the time that the American premises had already been sold to another company for storage purposes. After the weekend they visited *Harman International* at Lake Success and, on the following day, flew to Los Angeles to the other half of *Harman International* at *J.B.Lansing*. There followed a four-day, all-American meeting and Preedy recalled that there was more 'language' difficulty than if he'd been in China, one constant niggle to them both being the repeated reference to any fine piece of Tannoy engineering as 'merchandise'.

There was a somewhat amusing, typically American incident towards the

The Harman Years

end of the meeting when an iced cake was presented to Jim Barthell as a going away gesture before going to West Norwood to be 'plugged in' to Tannoy. The icing on the cake was blue, representing the Atlantic Ocean with East Coast America in the West and the British Isles in the East, but on the East side of Great Britain was Ireland, in the North Sea! Rackham and Preedy returned to the U.K. the following day with Jim Barthell but, because the Harman management seemed to regard their people as Royalty, Jim flew by *Pan Am* leaving at 12 noon, while Preedy and Rackham were obliged to travel on *T.W.A.* leaving at 12.05 p.m.

For a time, Bill Preedy was unaware of the real situation in which Sandy Berlin was Harman's 'front man' and the propagator of 'Worker Participation' under the heading of 'Harmanisation', nor was he aware that he was a very long way to the left of centre in his political persuasion. When Berlin asked Preedy to accept the appointment of General Manager, with a seat on the Board – the only Englishman apart from the company Lawyer, Barry Moughton – and with stock options on offer, he qualified the offer by saying, "If you don't accept, nobody else will be considered and Sydney Harman will appoint 'headhunters' to fill the post".

Now Preedy's interest had always been closely allied to the 'systems' side of Tannoy, viewing 'product' production as merely supplying the bricks for more grandiose projects and, at the time, the systems division had a full order book. However, it became apparent that there were many within the Harman organisation who had a keen interest in Hi-fi and they were very enthusiastic about Tannoy, and Preedy felt that their purchase of Tannoy was closely linked to Tannoy's very strong position in the Canadian and American Hi-fi markets resulting from the huge successes of the Dual Concentric loudspeaker and the Variluctance stereo pick-up cartridge. Preedy was also aware that Fred and Mary Towler, who had managed Tannoy America and Tannoy Canada, had aspirations of securing their own places within the U.K. management. Towler had bought the land in America when considerable expansion there was anticipated and, having done all the work in seeking out Harman as a buyer for the companies, he and Mary were also looking forward to receiving the 10% 'finders fee' applicable under U.S. law to the sale of the businesses on the American Continent, but Guy refused to authorise payment of this fee. As a result of this decision by Guy, the trustees of the family Trusts did not consider it was their responsibility to make a one-sided gesture from the Trust's funds without Guy's participation, so the Towlers received nothing, neither from Guy nor from the trusts.

Preedy's reasoning about Harman's motives for buying Tannoy was, as it turned out, only partly true, since Harman's acquisition of Tannoy was related

500 watt co-axcial horn P.A. speaker incorporating 4 x drive units.

The Fog signal loudspeaker installation on Dungeness Lighthouse. There are ten columns, each of 6 x 100 watt loudpeakers, with the remaining dummy columns incorporated into the design to maintain symmetry of structure.

Above:
Tannoy Marine

Right: Two of Guy's nautical novelties'. The masthead equipment for the wind direction indicator and the anemometer.

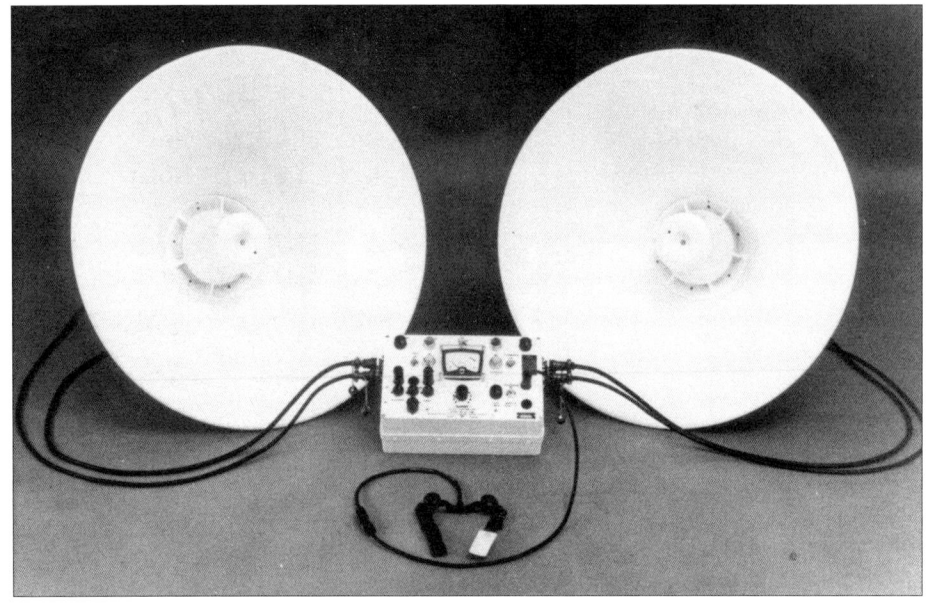

Above: 200 watt transistorised lightwieght, airborne P.A. system. The weight – $^1/_2$ lb per watt – was a record for the time (1965).

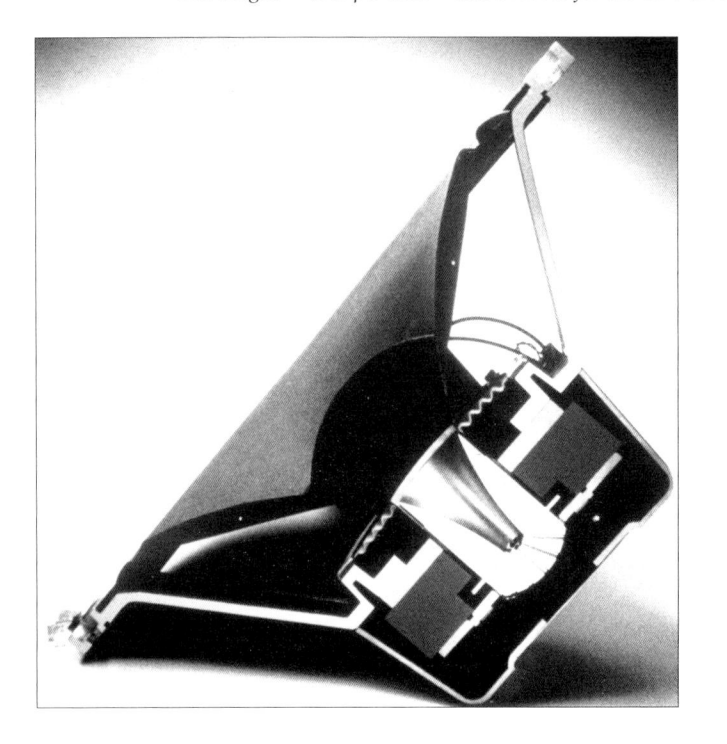

Left: 12 inch Dual Concentric (cut-away)

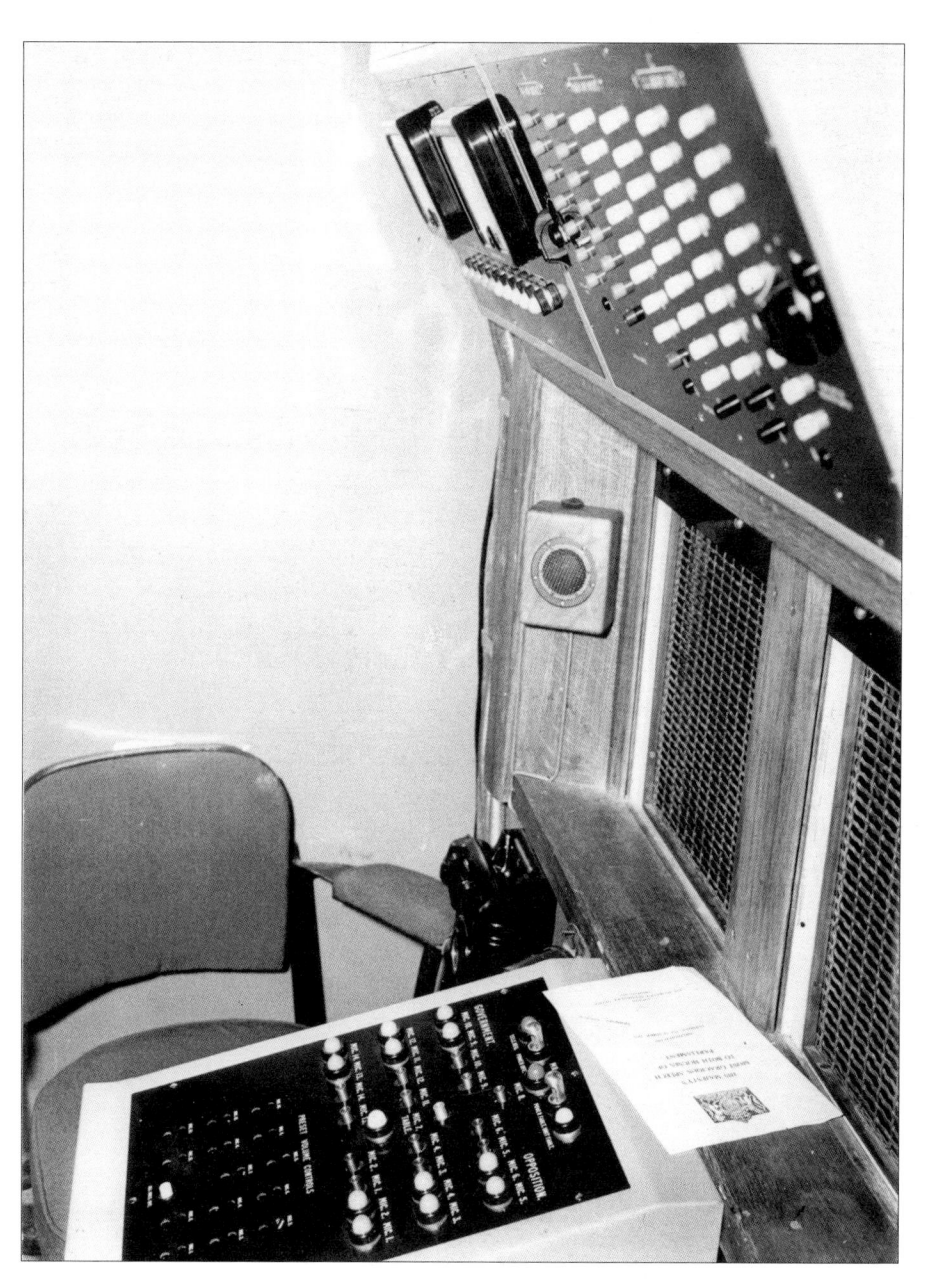

The first Tannoy control panel in the House of Commons photographed 31st October 1950. This installation comprised six microphones for the Government; six for the Opposition; one for Mr Speaker; and one at the despatch box.

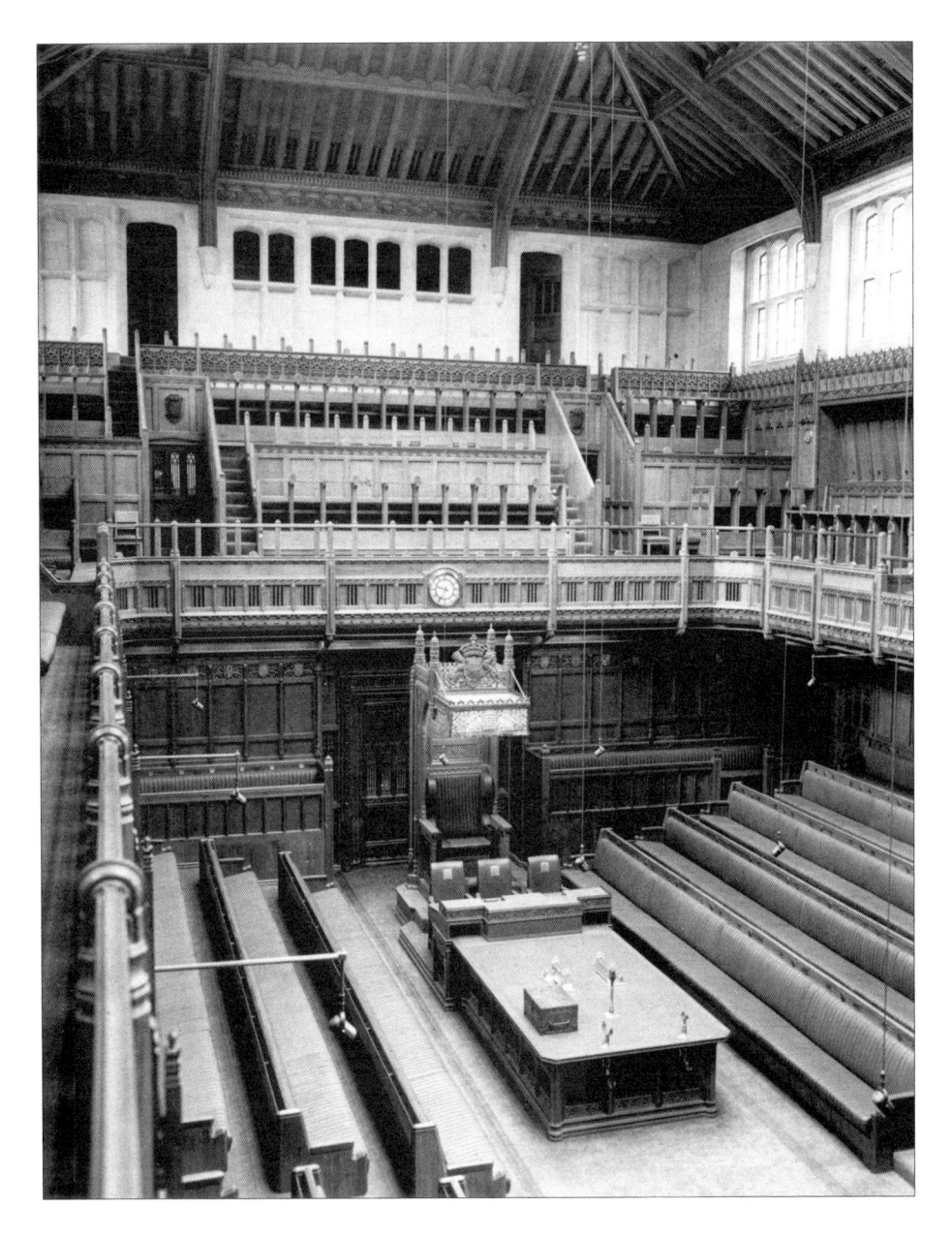

General view of the original Tannoy installation showing some microphones mounted on brackets and others suspended from the roof.

View from the Tannoy 'Cabin' showing a later control console.

Above: Details of the Tannoy Loudspeakers in the backs of the House of Commons benches

Right: View of the alternative Control Panel for use with the periscope during 'Secret Sessions' in the House of Commons

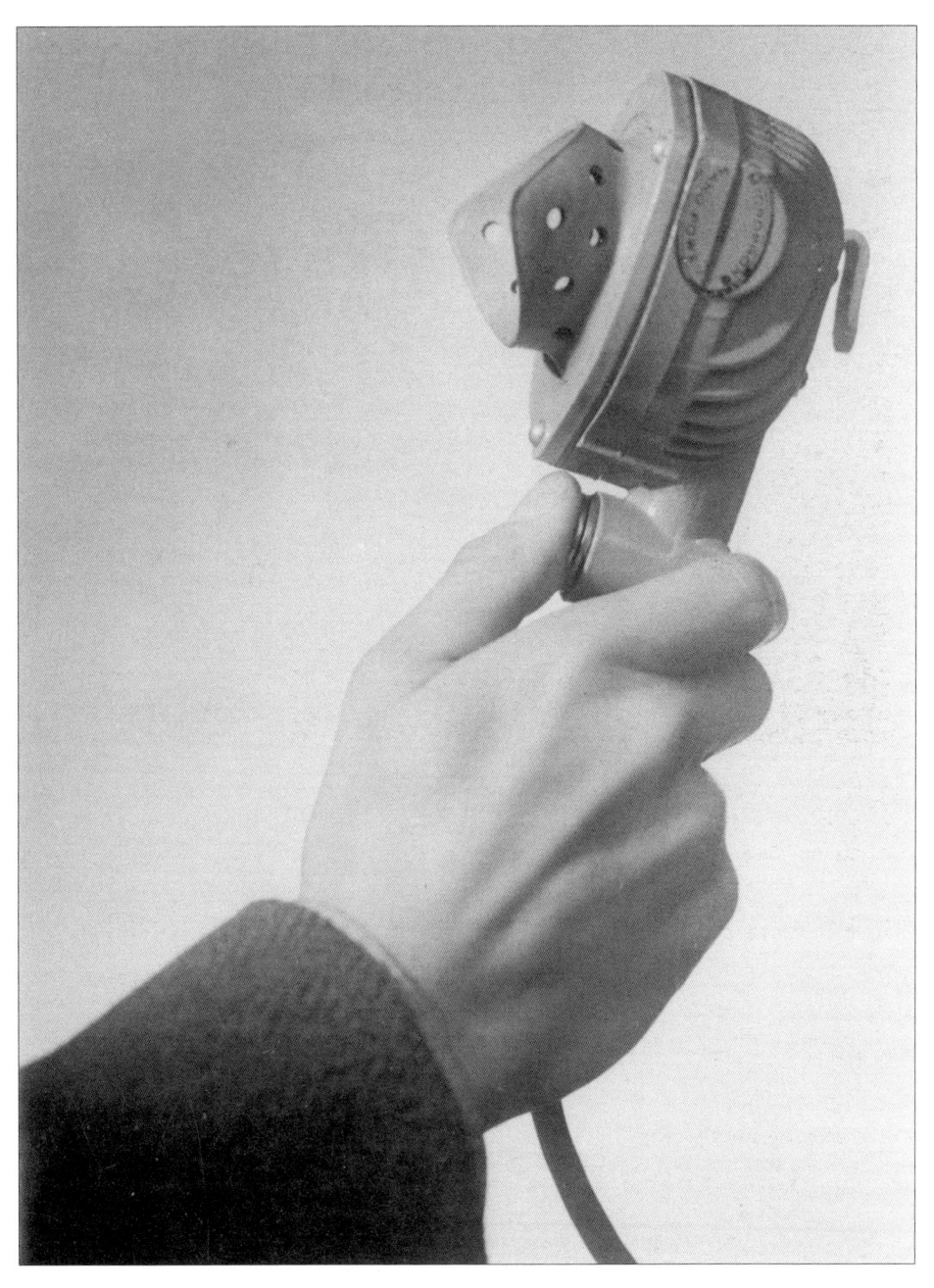

*The Tannoy Power Microphone in its final form.
Stamped on the side of the case is 'Microphone Hand Power', suggesting a military purpose.*

Right : On the right-hand wall is a typical Tannoy Loudspeaker in the Air Traffic Control Tower at RAF Bassingbourn in October 1945. It was at Bassingbourn that the author, then a newly qualified pilot, did a conversion course in 1952 on deHavilland Mosquito Aircraft.

Above: The Army's 'Telephone Loudspeaking, No. 2' – as used by Artillery Batteries during the Second World War.
(from the author's collection)

Right: A demonstration of the 'Tank Emergency Crew Control No. 1'. The Tannoy Power Microphone's control unit is balanced on the Klaxon by the Corporal's right knee.

Left: The first use of Public Address equipment at Buckingham Palace for the Victory in Europe' celebrations 1945. Supplied and installed by Tannoy.

Right: The 'Victory Bowl' Loudspeaker. These were installed in front of Buckingham Palace on 8th June 1946. They contained a CD4 Cone Lodspeaker

Above: The Power Microphone Assembly workshop at No 3 Dene Street, Dorking. Note the Tannoy 'music while you work' loudspeaker in the corner (see Chapter 8). A long shift on these wooden stools must have been very tiring.

Below: Valveless 'Power Microphone battery P.A. System 1942

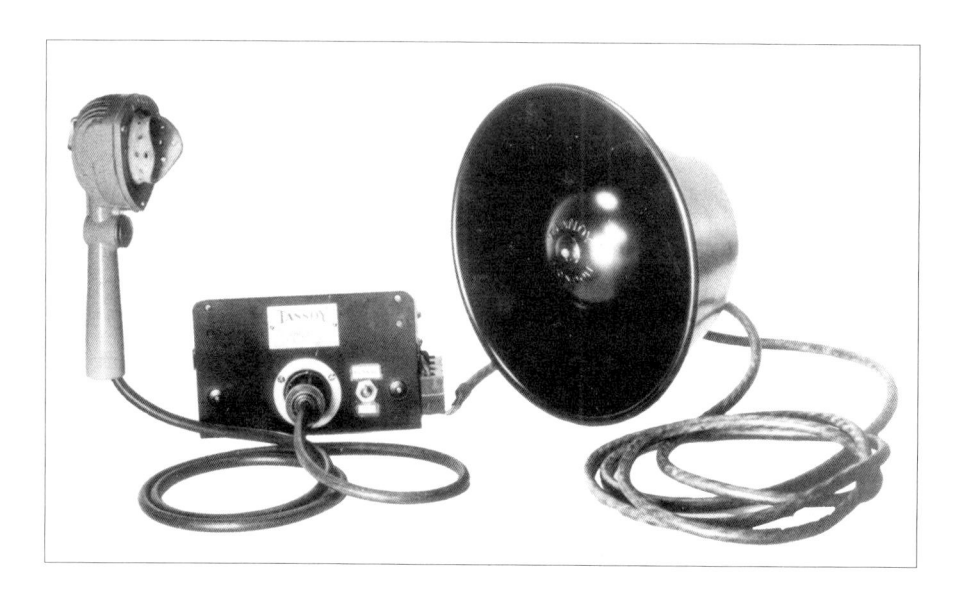

Above: A later view of Canterbury Grove Factory with both vertical and horizontal extensions.

*Below: 348-352 Norwood Road, 'Waylett Place'
Waylett Place is actually the street to the right of these premises.*

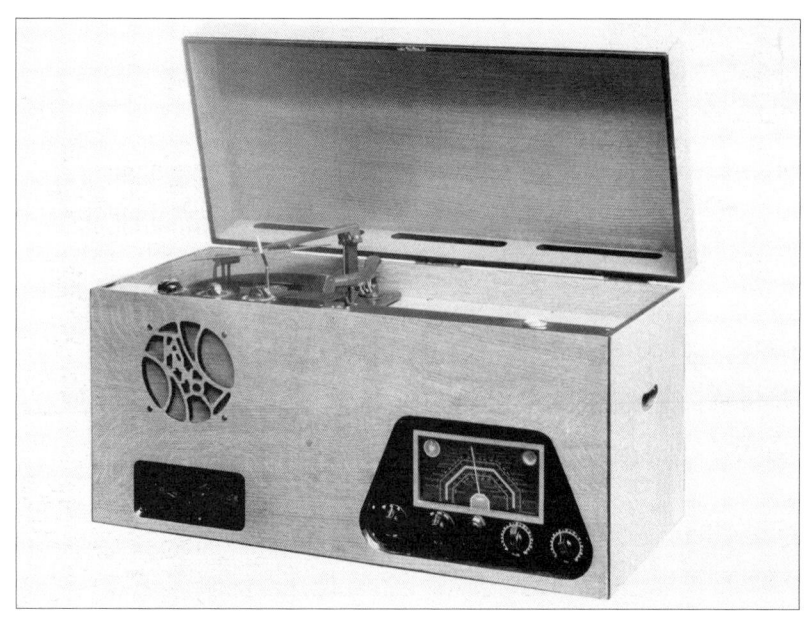

Above: In the early post-war years Tannoy were still producing radiograms specifically for use in schools. This model dates from 1946 and still features 'Mr Tannoy' on the tuning dial to balance the 'Magic Eye' tuning indicator.

Below: 1947 console from Butlins Holiday Camp in Filey, borrowed for Bertram Mills Circus at Olympia. Features the Tannoy Disc Recorder(extreme right).

Above: Again, Olympia 1947. Original dual Concentric Loudspeaker is in the foreground.

*Below: The 'Butlins' console at Clacton-on-Sea.
Mr Tannoy is still prominent and only 78rpm records are yet in use.*

Tannoy Luxury Radiogram c1948

Above: The House of Lords during experimental video recordings. Ron Rackham is seen seated while Dennis Terret makes a speech at the Table to check the correct functioning of the equipment.

Below: The House of Lords showing the Tannoy microphones and the early loudspeaker installation in the Order Paper racks

Above: Church House, Westminster. Table mounted loudspeakers with language selectors.

Below: Headphones and six language selectors installed at the Palais de Chaillot, Paris for the United Nations Conference in 1953.

*The Tannoy Loudspeaker installation devised by Ron Rackham for the
Coronation of Queen Elizabeth the Second.
The installation is in the centre of the picture on the roof of Malaya House.*

Tannoy 'Coronation Bowl' Loudspeakers which were made for the Coronation on 2nd June 1953, seen here at the Henley Royal Regatta a few weeks later.

Tannoy Today

Below: The magnificent Westminster Royal HE
the crowning glory of the current Tannoy Prestige loudspeaker range

Right:

Tannoy 2003

"The GRF Memory HE is a tribute to the founder of Tannoy, Guy R Fountain. This a design of which we feel sure he would have approved."

So reads the brochure advertising Tannoy's Prestige Range of Loudspeakers.

Not only would Guy Fountain have approved of the latest generation of Sound Equipment from Tannoy but he would have beamed with pride to see the Company he founded more than 70 years ago leading the world in the reproduction of sound.

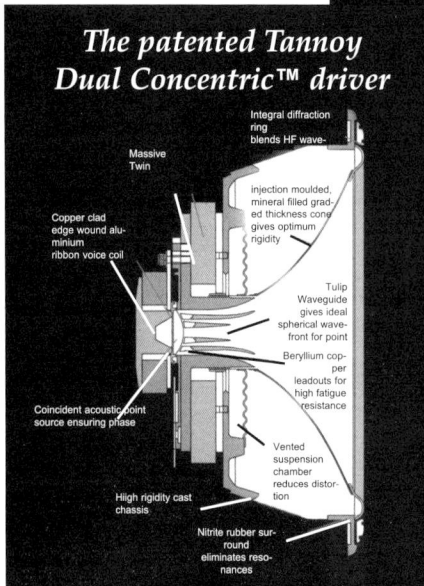

The patented Tannoy Dual Concentric™ driver

Left:

Ronald H Rackham's brain child: the Dual Concentric Loudspeaker – still the jewel in Tannoy's Crown.

Tannoy's D300, D500, D700 & D900 Flagship of the Definition Range
'What Video & TV' January 1999 described the D500/D750 Home Cinema set up as
"Leagues Ahead in both price and performance."

*Left:
The Tannoy
Dimension TD12*

Revolution R3

'What Hi-Fi?' in August 1999:
"Massive orchestral slam, luminous vocals, grumbling bass line, airy and unrestrained atmospherics, and simply, musical enjoyment: the Tannoys deliver them all with consumate ease."

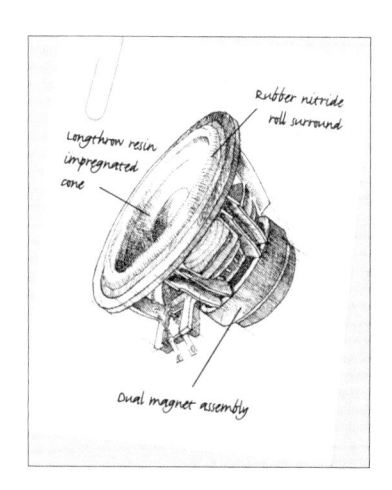

Rubber nitride roll surround
Longthrow resin impregnated cone
Dual magnet assembly

The TANNOY Story

not only to the removal of serious American and European competition in the Hi fi market; but also as preparation for Sydney Harman's political activities for the Democratic Party in the coming elections. However, taking all things into consideration, Preedy accepted the post which was offered to him and his assistant, Dennis Terrett, formerly the Senior Development Engineer who had designed most of Guy's nautical novelties, was transferred from Research and Development to take over Preedy's post with the title, 'Systems Engineering Manager'. Dennis Terrett later became the company's Chief Engineer.

The sale of Tannoy America's property assets, which Freddie Towler and Michael Fountain had bought for the company, also put Sydney Harman's nose out of joint because this was an asset which he understood; almost within spitting distance of his office, and it had been sold to a charitable organisation for rather less than its true value.

Not long after Harman International assumed control of Tannoy, still in 1974, Guy Fountain finally retired and he went to live in his Majorca home with Maureen.

Back in West Norwood, the 'Harmanisation' of Tannoy was progressing and one day Sandy Berlin asked, "Where is Tannoy's Personnel Manager?" All the old hands asked, "Personnel Manager? What the hell is a personnel manager?" Sandford was amazed at this lack of communication between the management and the workforce so he and Jim Barthell took it upon themselves to go headhunting to appoint a Personnel Manager in order to end Tannoy's abysmal lack of democratic relations with the workers, from the very lowest up to the top executives. A week or two later Berlin spoke to Bill Preedy and told him of the 'wonderful success' they had enjoyed interviewing a top-rate man for the post who was duly appointed as the new Personnel Manager. This man very soon had an elaborate Personnel Relations management office built around him.

Things appeared to go well until some three weeks later when Phyllis Jefferson, formerly Guy's and Michael's Secretary and by then Preedy's, told Preedy that a rather agitated Personnel Manager wanted to see him urgently. Suspecting that he may have been told of a terminal illness, Bill Preedy arranged an immediate meeting. The Personnel Manager handed him a brief personal memo stating that as from 4 p.m. the previous day he had become a paid up member of an appropriate union which, quite by chance, was due to enter into negotiations with Tannoy that week, with a view to ensuring a closed shop. As so often happened, Berlin was back in America, having 'unplugged' himself that week. Jim Barthell's immediate advice was, "Hang the bastard", but sanity prevailed when the matter was discussed with Barry Moughton, the English Director and Lawyer, and a settlement was negotiated. The so-called

The Harman Years

'top rate man', the much heralded, most recent recruit to 'Harmanisation' had lasted for just one month.

In the days following the transfer to Harman of the control of Tannoy, Berlin started setting up committees, each with the full paraphernalia of office and so-called democratic ways which had been quite unheard of under the rule of 'The Tyrant Fountain', as he described him. He also realised that Brixton, just a couple of miles away, was a large catchment area for immigrant black labour and, possibly in an attempt to broaden democracy, the company quickly acquired a much larger, but cheaper workforce than previously. In the first year the increase was from about 300 to 470 employees. Sandford Berlin was also keen to be rid of everything except for the loudspeaker business because he believed that once he had reduced it to that core, he was bound to succeed.

At about this time the theft of products, mainly Hi-fi components and equipment, burgeoned – although for some unknown reason the appropriate action of informing the police was frowned upon. At one time, consignments of dual concentric loudspeakers destined for Italy had the contents of the cartons removed and replaced by brick rubble. On another occasion, the railway footbridge in Canterbury Grove was found to be an excellent path for ex-works products which were carried quickly over the bridge to a van on the other side which was strategically parked for a quick get-away. It was not long before equipment started disappearing from the showroom, access being gained through Phyllis Jefferson's and Bill Preedy's offices and they were both asked to go to Gypsy Hill Police Station for finger printing to ensure exclusion from suspicion in a number of repeat burglaries.

Jim Barthell could be said to be the chosen disciple of Berlin in presenting to the Tannoy workforce the 'Harmanising' element of labour control. His previous position in the Harman empire had been that of managing a small factory making wing mirrors in Bolivar, Tennessee, with a religious and obedient staff, who were easy to brainwash into accepting the doctrine that work is beautiful and should be given freely. The challenge was to spread this ethic among a mixture of old Tannoy people and multi-ethnic new workers and one could gauge Jim's state of mental agitation when attending the never-ending 'Harmanising' meetings by the number of times he walked his boots up the side of Guy's magnificent desk.[1]

Under the Harman regime, it was not company policy to supply equipment to Arab countries but, within a short time of the Harman take-over an enquiry was received from the Iraq Ministry of Supply for 'Telephone, Loudspeaking, No. 2' sets with a value of £500,000. Bill Preedy telephoned Harman as Sandy Berlin was 'unplugged' at the time and, after a brief period of conscience squaring, Harman said, "Bill, we will never second-guess

The TANNOY Story

you." The contract was successfully negotiated together with a repeat order.

Dennis Terrett recalled that Derek Pipe, the Contracts Manager, was unwell at the time and was not fit enough to travel to Iraq in response to their request to finalise the contract. Terrett was 'volunteered' to go in his stead but there was no time to obtain a visa for him. He was told to go in any case as there would be 'someone' to meet him on his arrival at Baghdad airport. When he checked in at Heathrow he was told that he would not be permitted to travel without a visa but after showing his instruction to go there, an airline official appeared with a disclaimer for him to sign. This stated that in the event that he was refused entry, he accepted full responsibility for being there and for his consequential return to the United Kingdom.

On arrival at Baghdad that evening there was a large crowd of people around the Immigration desk, like bees around a queen, but there was nobody there with a card bearing his name. The crowd gradually diminished but Dennis was still hopeful that someone would appear before they all left. When the crowd had nearly all dispersed, there was one very official looking gentleman left there who looked as if he was a one man army, able to deal with any security matter that might arise, so Dennis approached him and asked if he spoke English. He did, so Dennis told him that he was told that he would be met but that he could not see the person concerned. The official asked for Dennis's name and then said that it was he who was meeting him. With that he took Dennis's passport from him and took him straight through Immigration and Customs without a pause, having collected his case which was the only one left. Dennis was then handed over to another gentleman, an Army officer, as the contract to be negotiated was for the supply of military equipment to the Iraqi Army and this officer was charged with finding an hotel room for him. Dennis then asked for the return of his passport but he was told quite bluntly that they were looking after it.

There was a very large international conference in progress in Baghdad at the time and all the hotels were full to capacity but a room was eventually found and, quite by chance, Dennis learned that the room had been made available by the army officer giving the previous occupants their marching orders. With this event, and with no passport, the feeling of relaxation was never present.

The following meetings with the Army contracts officers went very well, so much so that as each clause was read through, where Dennis considered that the wording was unacceptable to Tannoy, he said so, whereupon they asked him what the wording should be. By this means he was able to write everything into the contract to suit Tannoy, with no tricky clauses to make things difficult. During the negotiations it transpired that Dennis's hotel was in some difficulty due to the conference and it was necessary for him to move to another hotel. Once again, the might of the military was brought to bear and another hotel was quickly found, adding considerably to Dennis's feeling of unease but, with the contract signed, his passport was returned and he breathed a deep sigh of relief. On the return journey the aircraft made an unscheduled stop at Prague where he learned that there had been a warning of a bomb on board and a search was made. This revealed nothing and the flight continued to London. Such was the excitement of travelling for Tannoy.

It was not long before Sandy Berlin became involved with Lambeth Borough Council over the possibility of locating suitable new premises for the company, he was also busy negotiating with the *Scottish Development Board* in Edinburgh and Bill Preedy accompanied him to these meetings. On one occasion they found a particularly suitable factory of some 47,000 sq.ft. which had previously been used by an electronics company which had then ceased trading. It was an ideal situation for relocation and, at a 'wining-and-dining' session that evening given by the Provost, there were Labour members of the Board present who were very interested in the possibility of employment for the many unemployed skilled people in the area. Among them was a leader of the *National Union of Mineworkers* and he and Berlin got on famously; a relationship which may well have been engineered by Berlin with an eye to the main chance. Such was the success of this relationship that Berlin was, then and there, made an honorary member of the *N.U.M.*, an honour which he treasured greatly.

In December, 1974, there was a Stockholders' Meeting in New York, the first since Harman's acquisition of Tannoy. On his way to this meeting, Bill Preedy, who was by then the company's general manager, called in at Ottawa with Fred Towler and Ted Slater, a former Tannoy Research and Development man who had emigrated to Gananoque, near Kingston, Ontario, the location of Tannoy Canada. The visit was to tie up the ends of Ted's survey of Canada's lower Parliament building. The existing sound reinforcement system had been installed by the American *Marbel Company* to replace the original Tannoy scheme, and it was proving inefficient; the *Marbel* system had fallen far short of expectations. The contract was successfully negotiated for Tannoy and it included English/French simultaneous translation facilities.

At the meeting of the stockholders Berlin proudly showed off his membership of the *N.U.M.* and introduced Preedy from the body of the hall. The announcement to the stockholders' meeting of Tannoy's successes went down almost as well as Berlin's announcement that he had been elected an honorary member of the *National Union of Mineworkers*.

When, upon returning to London, Berlin contacted the *Scottish Development Board* to finalise the deal, he was told that the factory had been sold following a

The TANNOY Story

better offer and, upon demanding to know who it was, he was told that it was a Texas Oil exploration company who would use the premises for the storage of drilling equipment with a staff requirement of less than 20 workers. The air turned blue but the *Scottish Development Board* would not be budged, not even with a high powered 'Harmanising' lecture. In the meantime the hunt for more local premises continued.

At about 4 p.m. one Friday in late 1975, Dennis Terrett was asked by Sandy Berlin to produce a five-year sales forecast for Systems Engineering and to give it to him the next morning. He was only able to complete this by working late into the night and it was a very comprehensive document, including qualifying factors such as the availability of products, both existing and new developments. Early the next morning Dennis saw Barthell and he was told that Berlin was busy just then and he would like Dennis to join him and the others to continue the discussions at the Harley Street flat which he borrowed. Dennis told him that he was packing to go to Ottawa the next day to sort out some problems for Tannoy Canada but he would go to Harley Street that evening.

He was taken there by car with Sandy Berlin, Bill Preedy, Jim Barthell and Tony Roberson. Roberson had started work with the company in the Service Department but, by then, he had been elevated by the Harman heirachy to a position of some authority in the Production Department although he was not the Production Manager, but he was very involved with the negotiations for the relocation of the factory to Scotland. Terrett remembers that they had to call at a delicatessen on the way to Harley Street. The topic was whether to move the manufacturing facilities to Scotland or not and the three British members said that they considered that it would be an unwise move and they gave several reasons for not wanting this to happen. The two American views were completely the opposite and it became clear that they wanted the British three to agree with them to give them the opportunity, in the event that the move did not work, to say that the British members had made the decision. It was then abundantly clear that they had decided, before the meeting, to move the factory to Scotland.

The atmosphere was electric. Sandy Berlin had not taken too well to Terrett's sales forecast although some of the qualifying conditions, which resulted in hostilities towards Terrett, were adopted some time later. The next day, Terrett flew to Canada not knowing whether he would still have a job to return to but, as it happened, he did. It was at this point that Dennis realised that they had exchanged Guy and his pattern of management for another but, apart from a higher salary, was this any better?

Bill Preedy recalled that he had also been summoned to that meeting to discuss the engagement of a possible Managing Director and, as Berlin put it, 'to leave you free to develop Systems Engineering world wide'. Bill Preedy was shown the C.V. of a gentleman called Norman Crocker which showed that he had apparently spent some time closing down factories for *Plessey*. Preedy left after a lot more waffle to which he was, by that time, immune. The first positive indication of the appointment of Crocker was signalled by an instruction to order a Jaguar in the new man's favourite colour. When Crocker arrived he took an instant dislike to Guy's old office, possibly fearing that it was in enemy territory, and arrangements were made for a custom built office to be provided, rather like the cabinet office of No. 10, Downing Street, and this was located in Knight's Hill.

Shortly after Crocker's arrival Berlin disappeared from West Norwood leaving no forwarding address and remained incognito for three weeks. During this time a new man, Herb Horowitz, arrived from America as Crocker's deputy, unannounced and without a work permit. Following his arrival, Sandy Berlin, by then in New York, demanded Preedy's resignation from the Board, a demand which was accompanied by threats. As a sop, he offered him the position of 'Director of International Systems Engineering'.

It was not long before Sandy Berlin was able to make the move to Scotland, to Coatbridge, near Glasgow and this move took place in 1975. Now, notwithstanding any support which the company received from the Scottish Development Board, there is a golden rule that before a factory is moved to a new location, there must be six months revenue in the kitty to survive on because it is probable that no money will be made for those first six months and, of course, there was no such 'kitty'. Sydney Harman did not understand too much about the likely consequences of the move although he was prepared to fund it for a while but the situation soon deteriorated. There were many difficulties with the early products from Coatbridge, probably due to the fact that many skilled workers did not wish to be re-located there and they could not be replaced with equivalent skills, so quality left much to be desired and the failure rate of products was high.

Livingstone was unaware of much of this because he had been sent all over the World by Sandy Berlin, who referred to him as his 'Evangelist', to pump up the sales and he was doing this with considerable success. He said that he only had to tell his customers that this rather old-fashioned company was now part of a large international group and out came the order book; this is perhaps something of an exaggeration but that is how Livingstone explained it. He also visited Harman local agents and got them keyed up but, in the event, there was not a great deal of action at Coatbridge and little in the way of products to sell.

There was, of course, a time when both the West Norwood and Coatbridge factories and offices were working but late in 1976, the Norwood factory was

The TANNOY Story

finally closed and the administration of the company moved to a newly established Head Office at High Wycombe, creating yet more difficulties.

Harman soon saw the writing on the wall and he probably assumed that Norman Crocker would be the fall-guy, but Crocker had never been a fall-guy to anyone. So, after a year or so had gone past, Harman took stock of the situation and wondered what, if anything, he had acquired. He had spent a lot of money; a man in Timbuctoo or somewhere equally unknown to him was sending in orders; the people in Scotland were apparently not doing very much except buying a lot of materials; and, overall, his new company seemed to be achieving very little. Bill Preedy, in recounting the event, said that a tear-stained letter was sent to all executives announcing Berlin's retirement and giving the reason as poor health.

Sidney Harman did not really understand the electronics business but he very soon realised that Tannoy had fallen a long way behind in technology and he tried hard to get it going but, in the event, it was found that they had fallen too far behind and other companies had secured much of their traditional business. The next development was that Sydney Harman, who was a very wealthy man, is reported to have donated a considerable sum of money to support Jimmy Carter's presidential election campaign. Following Carter's election to the Presidency, Harman was appointed as an Under Secretary of State for Commerce in the new administration.

As a result of this appointment Harman had to divest himself of his business interests and he put together a superb portfolio of his companies, one of which had been under the control of Jim Barthell and which enjoyed a monopoly of rear view mirrors which could be operated from inside a car. Another made, and monopolised, the rubber magnetic seal for refrigerators following legisla-tion in America which made mechanical locks on refrigerator doors illegal and, in the U.K., there was Tannoy. Apart from the odd lame duck he had some very sound businesses and *Beatrice Foods Inc.* heard about this portfolio and literally leaped at it, with the result that Harman and Berlin, who still held Harman shares, became millionaires overnight because *Beatrice Foods* paid them in their shares which were then worth a lot of money.

Beatrice Foods were mainly makers of fruit drinks, dairy products, yoghurt etc. and in order to avoid being regarded as a monopoly they diversified their business interests with totally different industries such as *Samsonite Suitcases, Airstream Caravans, Morgan Yachts, Homepack Furniture* and, in 1977, *Harman*, which included Tannoy, and they tried to run them all like a yoghurt factory. *Beatrice Foods* also distributed electric warm air hand dryers and these are still, occasionally, to be seen in public toilets throughout the British Isles marked, 'Supplied by Beatrice Foods Inc.'. The most recently observed example was found by the author in April, 2002, in the gentlemen's toilet at Bletchley Park, the famous 'Station X' of W.W.2.

By this time Bill Preedy had severed his connections with Tannoy, having left in November, 1976, up to which time Tannoy had only two General Managers, George Wheeler and Bill Preedy. George Wheeler was the midwife at the birth of Tannoy: Bill Preedy, however unwittingly, came close to being the undertaker at its demise. Almost, but not quite, as, under the guidance of Norman Crocker the company rose once again, like the Phoenix.

A representative of *Beatrice* came over from America and saw Livingstone and Crocker and said that he felt that he did not really understand the working of the business. Livingstone told him that he had to focus his mind on the fact that if you make yoghurt on a Monday and you have not sold it by the following Monday, all you have is a lot of yoghurt which can't be sold. With capital equipment such as Tannoy's you get an order in January and, with a bit of luck, you complete the order within a year and collect the final payment the following January. Similarly, *Morgan Yachts* would build a yacht to order worth a million or more but might take two years to build it.

The only acquisition which made ready money for them was *Samsonite* but then *Beatrice* made the mistake of moving the factory to Belgium where it made a loss. This led to a boardroom upheaval and all those who had made *Beatrice Foods* into such a conglomerate were fired, after which they decided to concentrate their efforts on making milk products and milk product machinery, which they understood.

Following the sale of Tannoy to *Beatrice Foods*, Norman Crocker waited for the right moment and started negotiating the re-purchase of Tannoy. He achieved this in late 1981 for about the same sum as Sydney Harman had paid the Fountains, and the final completion of the deal took place in January, 1982. So, under the leadership of Norman Crocker, the company was re-purchased by the management team, the other principal members being Stanley Livingstone, Ron Rackham, Peter Russell, (Finance Director), Ian Dunn, (Production Director), Alex Garner, and David Bissett-Powell. They had to mortgage their houses to impress the bank but the company had then successfully negotiated an enormous contract with Iraq for which, while under *Beatrice Foods*, the necessary materials had been purchased and paid for. So Tannoy then built the equipment and invoiced the Iraqis, Livingstone collected the cheque and that paid off the bank. There was then a Board meeting at which the directors all gave themselves rises which were calculated to pay back both their capital outlay, and the interest on the money they had borrowed, in two years. From then on they forged ahead.

However, the new Tannoy structure in Coatbridge was not able to devote sufficient attention to the hire and rentals division, which continued to operate at a loss from West Norwood and, three years later this, too, was the object of a management buy-out. Three executives, under the leadership of Jim MacLennan, the Managing Director, bought the division for £175,000, with Midland Bank venture capital providing £120,000 plus the necessary working capital and the three executives putting up the remainder. This company was given a new name, *Westminster Audio Communications*, and continued to operate, as the mainstay of its business, the sound reinforcement systems in the Palace of Westminster and, at the time of writing, early 2002, this work still continues. Some time later, *Westminster Audio Communications* finally quit the original, purpose-built Tannoy factory in Canterbury Grove, and moved to new premises at High Wycombe.

Mention has been made of Edmund Newton in earlier chapters andhis situation deserves some comment for, when *Westminster Audio Communications* was created, Eddie Newton remained in the Palace of Westminster to manage the sound reinforcement systems under the umbrella of this new company. At the time of writing, 2003, he is still there. His responsibilities include the management of the many sound reinforcement schemes in the Palace including those in both chambers and in the many committee rooms and, of course, the recording systems for the Hansard writers. Bill Preedy has said, "He has made a first class job of this with the result that these systems became an impeccable example of speech reinforcement at its reliable best. Those of us who know the complexities involved were gratified to hear that he received the M.B.E. in the 2002 Birthday Honours List – this is greatly deserved."

Norman Crocker then involved Tannoy with *Goodmans Industries* which was also, at that time, in dire straits and he negotiated a merger of Tannoy and Goodmans to form *Tannoy Goodmans Industries, T.G.I. Ltd*. This also included *Martin Audio Ltd*. of which David Bissett-Powell became Managing Director. By negotiating such a successful management buy-out of the company from *Beatrice Foods*, followed by the Tannoy-Goodmans merger, Norman Crocker demonstrated clearly his outstanding business acumen; he was unboubtedly a very clever man and it was he who saved the Tannoy name from evanescing into total obscurity, although Stan Livingstone once said that he was the most ruthless man he ever met. Perhaps that was the secret of his undoubted success.

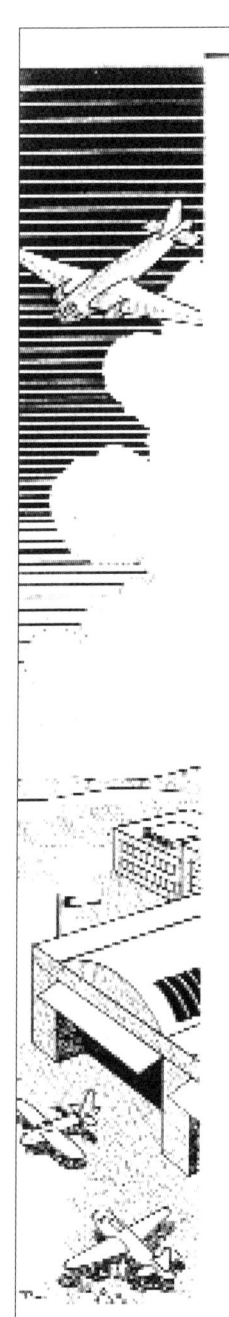

THE VOICE OF
'TANNOY'

The highly robust construction of TANNOY SOUND EQUIPMENT makes it particularly suitable for large permanent installations such as Aerodromes, Factories, etc.

The design of the Tannoy Loudspeakers, coupled with the amplifier circuit arrangement, is such that the very highest degree of speech intelligibility is obtained.

Expert assistance is available for the planning and maintenance of every type of Sound Installation.

Remember, you can BUY, HIRE, or RENT Tannoy Sound Equipment.

TANNOY
THE SOUND PEOPLE
GUY R. FOUNTAIN, LTD.

'TANNOY' is the registered trade mark of equipment manufactured by
GUY R. FOUNTAIN, LTD.
West Norwood, S.E.27, and Hounslow.
Phone: Gipsy 1131-1137

THE LARGEST ORGANISATION IN GREAT BRITAIN SPECIALISING SOLELY IN SOUND EQUIPMENT

TANNOY TODAY

Over the years, Tannoy has continued to develop its expertise wherever there is a requirement for high quality sound; most notably in broadcasting and professional recording (both audio and film sound track). The company is, of course, famous throughout the world primarily for its hi-fi loudspeakers and to this day Tannoy remains active in several key audio sectors: Residential Audio, Installation Speakers and Studio Monitors.

In all market sectors, Tannoy continues to incorporate highly developed derivatives of the Dual Concentric™ loudspeaker into its products. This unique technology, the brainchild of Ronnie Rackham, utilises a centrally mounted HF unit behind the Tulip WaveGuide™ which maintains the sound principles behind the original design concept in that it combines transparent, fluid performance with true, point source symmetrical sound dispersion.

More and more Tannoy products include a very high frequency driver, or SuperTweeter™ first designed for the 1996 Golden Sound Award winning 'Kingdom' model. By covering frequency ranges up to and beyond 50kHz, WideBand™ technology effectively enhances the listening experience even at lower frequencies, making music more natural and true to life.

Within the Residential Audio sector Tannoy is moving strongly into the growing home entertainment market offering home theatre packages, satellite/subwoofer systems and various models designed to be built in to the structure of the home.

In the commercial sector, Tannoy is the brand name on many prestigious sound installations throughout the world and examples include the Hong Kong Convention Centre, the Sydney Opera House, the London Palladium theatre, the Coca Cola Headquarters in Atlanta, the Hard Rock Hotel and Casino and the Bellagio Hotel in Las Vegas, the Dolce & Gabbana headquarters in Milan and the Finnish National Theatre. Tannoy has been particularly active in the Studio Monitor market for more than 15 years; in recent years with the immensely popular 'Reveal' monitors, in both their passive and active forms. Recently released is the top of the range 'Ellipse' monitor with cutting edge design that incorporates both Tannoy WideBand™ and Dual Concentric™ technology. The Tannoy Group's Scottish headquarters are located in Coatbridge, near Glasgow with another facility, Tannoy North America, based in Kitchener, Ontario, Canada. Other world markets are covered through a large network of distributors. Manufacturing is divided between the facility in Coatbridge and a range of sub-suppliers, with some assembly carried out in Kitchener for products specific to the North American markets.

In January 2002 Tgi plc (Tannoy Goodmans Industries), merged its entire portfolio of companies with the TC Group, forming a holding company of several individual companies: Tannoy, Lab Gruppen, TC Electronic, TC Helicon, TC Works and GLL, to which TC Applied Technologies has recently been added, and in 2003 was able to present the first fruits of the combined technological expertise within the TC Group. **iDP**™ Technology (Interactive Digital Programming) provides a powerful digital solution to precision defined acoustics and ultimate audio system flexibility.

Optimising the performance of loudspeakers within the perfect environment is one thing but the listening environment always affects the performance of loudspeakers – often to their detriment. Now, working with the very latest in digital technology, Tannoy is able to provide premium audio solutions with the flexibility to adapt to the environment.

iDPT™ was first exhibited at the 2003 Consumer Electronics Show in Las Vegas. The system had been engineered into the 'Eyris' loudspeaker range to produce a home theatre system of immense flexibility and quality. Following that, at the Frankfurt Musik Messe in Germany, the company unveiled the new 'Ellipse' studio monitor which is also fully equipped with **iDP**™ Technology. It is Tannoy's vision to continue down the path of providing cutting edge audio solutions into all markets in which they are active.

Despite being steeped in history, the company has never dwelt on its past. Proud of its heritage, Tannoy has always been an innovator where quality sound reproduction is concerned. That said, many parallels exist with the period when the company was first established. There is creative, imaginative and energetic management, a supremely talented design team, and a dedicated workforce. All are focussed on the principal objectives of the growth and development of Tannoy as a global brand, using cutting edge technology to design and manufacture innovative consumer electronics and loudspeaker products of indisputable performance.

A rich heritage, combined with a classic brand name, ensures that the company will continue to make history by living up to its mission statement:
'*Tannoy is a leading innovator of premium audio solutions utilising cutting edge acoustic, electronic and digital expertise.*i

In 2015 Tannoy Ltd. was acquired by Music Group.

EPILOGUE

Guy Fountain retired in 1974 and lived his last years in Majorca with Maureen. When he was finally, seriously ill he came home and was taken to Epsom Hospital but would not let anyone tell the family about it; he would not even let Denis Blackmore tell them in spite of the fact that Denis was regarded as a good friend of the family. Such was his determination in this matter, and such was Guy's control over Denis, that Denis did not even tell Michael when, on 10th December, 1977, Guy died. However, Michael was the first member of the family to know of Guy's death having heard the news, eventually, from Denis and from Guy's solicitor two days after the event.

John Gilbert took Maureen to Guy's funeral and she was livid that none of the family attended, largely, John thought, because she did not know anyone else there. Michael said that members of the family, whom Guy had so alienated in his later years, discussed whether to attend the funeral or not but individually they came to the conclusion that it would have been hypocrisy to have done so. Before the funeral Norman Crocker said to Stan Livingstone, "I should like to meet the family; Michael, Jeanne and David."

"No chance," replied Stan.

"You've got Fountain on the brain," said Crocker, "of course they will be there, there's a pound on it."

Crocker was amazed, he thought it was all hearsay, but Stan won the bet.

About two years before Guy Fountain died, he expressed a wish for the Tannoy story to be recorded and he asked John Gilbert if he would be the 'ghost' writer and he invited John to spend a month or two with him in Majorca preparing the text. However, this never came about and, in any case, it would have had to be done in Guy's way, probably with little freedom to record many of the essential facts and opinions, even if they did turn out to be somewhat unsavoury.

The fact that the name 'TANNOY' has become such a household word, even being listed in dictionaries, has been, of course, tremendous publicity for the company for well over fifty years. However, there have been occasions when the popular use of the name has worked very much to the detriment of the company.

The TANNOY Story

Michael Fountain recalled that a few years after the war there was a feature in the *Sunday Express* newspaper about the sinking of the *Bismark* and there was a reference in the article to the crew being alerted over the 'Tannoy'. The company immediately objected as they had not, of course, installed Tannoy equipment on the *Bismark* nor, for that matter, on any German warship and the newspaper was obliged to print a correction. Later, when a cruise ship, the *Lakonia*, sank in the Mediterranean Sea there was another reference to the 'Tannoy', which Denis Blackmore's wife heard on the radio. The reference implied that the 'Tannoy' had not functioned properly with resulting loss of life and she immediately telephoned Denis at the factory. Denis, in turn, telephoned the B.B.C. and a correction was broadcast before the conclusion of the programme.

On one occasion a B.P. oil platform lost a day's production because, it was alleged, the 'Tannoy' system failed and neither the Security officers nor the Safety officers would allow work to continue. This was reported in the *Sun* newspaper and Tannoy established that it had been a *Philips* system which had failed. They offered the *Sun* a choice of a full retraction and a good article for Tannoy or be taken to court. In the end, the *Sun* agreed to a full retraction and gave the company a fair article.

On the occasion of the capsizing of the *Herald of Free Enterprise* off Zeebrugge, it was reported in a leading newspaper that instructions had not been heard by key members of the crew because the 'Tannoy' system was not working. It was not, of course, Tannoy equipment but it was not until much later, and after a good deal of difficulty, that the company received an apology but this was published in such a way that it left Tannoy in a very bad light. The newspaper in question had asked Tannoy to write to them following which small parts of the letter were picked out and published out of context in an apparent attempt to show that Tannoy was trying to make money out of the disaster. The company wrote back and told the newspaper that, based on what had been printed, they would take the matter to court. At the last minute the newspaper apologised and gave the company a full retraction.

Today, at the beginning of the twenty-first century, there are frequent references to Tannoy. In the Spring of 2001 Tina Brown, a personality within the entertainment industry, was heard to say of another television personality during a 'Desert Island Discs' programme on B.B.C. Radio 4, "Janet Street-Porter dresses like a traffic light and sounds like a Tannoy". Bearing in mind Janet Street-Porter's remarkably elegant costumes during her television series on 'Ecclesiastical Architecture', the first criticism seems particularly unfair.

On 23rd. October, 2001 there was a question on Channel Four's 'Fifteen-to-One' programme which asked, 'Which trade name of a public address system that originated in 1922 is now used generally for any make of loudspeaker relay

Epilogue

system?' The answer was, of course, 'Tannoy' although the name was not devised until a few years later than stated.

David Bissett-Powell, who was at the time Export Director of the company, recalled in 1991 that twice in the previous few years, the company had taken the press to task. Once each year, the company advertises in a journal relating to the press; a magazine which is read by journalists. The advertisement reads:

CAPITAL OFFENCE

The word Tannoy must be written with a capital 'T'.
It is a proprietory name.
It must NOT be used as a verb.

However, in conversation, Tannoy frequently is used as a verb. David also recalled that they still then received frequent calls asking them to come and look at a 'Tannoy' system. They have to ask if the caller is quite sure that it is Tannoy equipment and one frequent answer is that, "It must be, because there are lots of loudspeakers."

Norman Robottom recounted a couple of interesting little stories about Stan Livingstone during his consultancy career after leaving Tannoy. Stan used to travel extensively all over the world and apparently he developed the habit of always asking for the same seat in the aircraft with which he was most familiar. When asked why, he said that he had learned that the Black box flight recorder was situated under that seat. There was also the almost unbelievable occasion when he was in Taiwan and one of the factory managers he was visiting invited him to his home where he had two Tannoy 'G.R.F. Autograph' loudspeakers in his sitting room, the largest and the most luxurious of Tannoy loudspeakers. To have a couple of Tannoy loudspeakers is one thing, but to have two G.R.F. 'Autograph' loudspeakers is unparalleled luxury. He asked Stan if he could obtain a photograph of Guy for him. Stan arranged to send him a photograph and at a later visit he found these two enormous Tannoy loudspeaker enclosures with a small table between them with Guy's photograph and with a single rose in front of it, illuminated by a spotlight mounted on the ceiling. Apparently his wife's first duty every morning, before cooking his breakfast, was to place a fresh rose before Guy's photograph. Stan said that he never thought he would live to see the day when he saw Guy's photograph in a shrine!

In about, 1981, Livingstone went to the Korean T.V. studios and was shown a couple of *Pye* studio loudspeakers which had failed. The technicians were not too concerned about it because they'd had them for more than 15 years. They

The TANNOY Story

were somewhat similar to the Tannoy 'York' enclosures, with little amplifiers on shelves near the bottom. This led to a contract to re-equip the two Korean T.V. studios throughout with Tannoy monitor loudspeakers, a business which continued for some 20 years.

In 1967, Michael completed his 21st year with his father's company having started in May, 1946 and, as was the custom, an engraved gold watch was prepared for him. These '21 Year' watches were always presented with some ceremony, usually during a luncheon of the '21 Club' at the Mixing Bowl restaurant and they were attended only by employees who had served 21 years or more with Tannoy. Not long before Michael's presentation he learned that his father had invited Maureen to the lunch which had, of course, always been an 'employees only' occasion. Not unnaturally, Michael was very upset about this and, leaving it until as late as possible, he told his father that he would not be attending the lunch. On 11th December, 1991 the author attended a meeting at Michael's house to discuss the preparation of this book at which David Bissett-Powell was present. He told Michael that his '21 Year' watch had been found in the company safe and he had brought it to the meeting. He then presented it to Michael – 24 years late!

As this narrative nears completion – it is now June, 2003, – the Tannoy company still thrives and continues to progress from strength to strength. The company still occupies the premises at Coatbridge, near Glasgow, where they concentrate their production on high fidelity loudspeakers and enclosures. The loudspeaker systems which they now produce there are said to be the most perfect loudspeakers available anywhere in the world and they are all based on Ronnie Rackham's dual concentric loudspeaker design, with practically no modification. When the author visited the factory with Michael Fountain in February 2002, a demonstration of some of the present range of Tannoy loudspeakers was arranged by the Director of Engineering, Dr. Paul Mills, and it is difficult to find adequate superlatives with which to describe their performance. Of course money is not the only yardstick of achievement but it is interesting to observe that the least expensive of Tannoy's present loudspeaker systems retails at a little under £1,000 per pair and the top-of-the-range models are priced at about £25,000 per pair.

As has already been recorded, during Norman Crocker's most successful period of leadership Tannoy was again brought out of the doldrums and merged with *Goodmans Industries* to become Tannoy Goodmans Industries. Within the last year T.G.I. plc has merged with a manufacturer of particularly fine high fidelity equipment and a leader in the field of digital audio processing, *T.C. Electronic* of Denmark, to become a member of the *T.C.*

Epilogue

Group. This has opened the doors to new opportunities and more advanced developments in audio technology and the future of the name of Tannoy seems brighter than ever.

However, none of this would ever have happened without the intervention of other factors such as luck, coincidence, genius and skill. The luck arose from the inadequacies of the *Southern Railway Company*'s time tables in creating the turning point in the young George Wheeler's career, guiding him back to the *Tulsemere Manufacturing Company*'s offices, to his interview with Guy Fountain and to his subsequent experiments with sound amplifiers. The coincidence, however fragile this may seem, led to the involuntary demonstration of sound amplification to the landlord of the Thurlow Arms and to the first ever sale of a Tannoy amplifier. The genius was that of men like Jack Houlgate and, more particularly, Ronald Rackham in designing and developing the incomparable Dual Concentric Loudspeaker but, above all, the real success is due entirely to the consummate skills of Tannoy's creator, the archetypal entrepreneur, Guy R. Fountain.

Archbishop of Caterbury, Geoffrey Fisher, introducing Guy Fountain to Queen Mary at Church House, Westminster

BIBLIOGRAPHY.

Air Transport Before the Second World War	John W.R. Taylor & Kenneth Munson.
Broadcasting in Britain	Keith Geddes.
A History of Broadcasting in Britain	Asa Briggs.
The BBC; The First Fifty Years	Asa Briggs.
The Cat's Whisker	Jonathan Hill.
The 'Cello and The Nightingale	Beatrice Harrison.
The Power Behind the Microphone	Capt. P.P. Eckersley.
The Setmakers	Keith Geddes and Gordon Bussey.
The Story of Norwood	J.B. Wilson, prepared by H.A. Wilson.
Radio! Radio!	Jonathan Hill.
The R.A.F., A Pictorial History	Bruce Robertson.
The Valetta, Vickers' Last Piston Transport	Bill Overton.
Car Numbers	Noel Woodall.
Radio Times, Special Christmas Edition, 1930	
Wireless World, Various Issues	
Music Trades Review, incorporating *The Talking Machine* and *Wireless Trade News*, Various issues.	

INDEX

21 Club, the   227-228, 233, 254
750 Club, the   121

A

A.C. Cars (*see also Auto Carrier; and Weller Cars*)   17, 137
Abrahams, Mr (accountant)   71
Admiralty, the   101, 110, 125
Admiralty Research Establishment   110
Ahmad, Sheikh (of Barzan)   94
Ajax, HMS   73-74
Air Ministry   83, 85-86, 88-91, 118, 160
Albert, Mrs (café owner; see also Mrs Russell)   131
Albaquila, the   212, 216-217
Alderton, Douglas   5, 26-27, 101, 156
Alderton, Julian   1-2, 5, 11-13, 156
Alderton, Kathleen   5, 26-27, 101, 156
Altec Lansing Inc.   186-187
American Electic Company   35
Anselm, Tony   101, 112
Aragon M.S.   211
Argentine Navy   74, 79, 181, 187
Arlanza M.S.   211
Amazon M.S.   211
Armor   151
Armor Corporation   151
Army (British)   11, 16, 69, 98, 101, 103, 105, 107, 114-115, 118, 141-143, 154
Army (Iraqi)   243
Army (Salvation)   194
Army (USA)   83
Astell, Harry   107
Auster (Taylor Craft Auster)   93
Auto Carrier   17
Avro Anson   111
Avro Lancaster   124

B

B.B.C. (*British Broadcasting Corporation – see also British Broadcasting Company*)   20-21, 33, 39-40, 56, 74, 78, 90, 118, 135, 145-146, 151-152, 166, 169, 171, 175, 182, 187-188, 209, 231, 252, 256
B.B.C. Empire Service   21, 74
B.B.C. Television Engineering   74
B.S.R. Ltd. (*British Sound Reproducers*)   76, 150
B.T-H. (*see also British Thompson-Houston*)   21, 76, 147, 186, 207
Bachelor, Victor   172
Baird Television Co. (*see also Scophony-Baird* and *John Logie Baird*)   23, 50, 190
Barclays Bank Ltd.   91, 160, 164, 186
Barry, Ernie   227, 240-241
Barthell, Jim   239-242, 245, 247
Barzan, Sheikh Ahmad of   94
Battle of Britain   82, 89, 111, 118, 125
Battle of the River Plate   74
Beatrice Foods Inc.   247-249
Belfast   165, 208, 211

Belfast University   165
Belge, *Banque pour l'Etranger (Overseas) Ltd.*   44, 99, 101, 117, 127
Bentley Priory, R.A.F.   89
Berlin, Sandford   237-239, 241-242
Bertram Mills Circus (*see also Mills, Bertram*) 59-61, 67, 208
Bex Electric   120-122, 124, 139
Biggin Hill, R.A.F.   89-90
Birchington, Kent   26, 83
Birmingham, HMS   73
Bisaillion, Chris   105
Bissett-Powell, David   13, 144, 248-249, 253-255
Blackpool   48, 198
Blackpool Station   48
Bloom Grove   132, 134, 136
Boosey & Hawkes Ltd.   152
Boult, Sir Adrian   78
Brake, Westinghouse and Saxby Signal Co. Ltd   23, 40
Bray, Peter   50
Bray, Sam   154
British Acoustic Films Ltd.   153-154
British Broadcasting Company   20
British Relay Ltd.   49
British Thompson-Houston   21, 76, 147, 186, 207
Brush Corporation   188
Bucharest Opera House   226
Buckingham Palace   47, 141, 230
Burndept Ltd.   26, 30, 32
Burnham, Alfred   30
Burnham, Witt   26, 30
Butlin, Billy (*see also Butlin's Holiday Camps*)   64, 142-143, 155, 174
Butterfly brand (recording tape, see also *Samuel Jones & Co.*)   188
Butterfly Centre, Camberwell   188

C

Camco (see also *Carrington Manufacturing Company*) 42, 49, 51, 54, 81, 125-126
Campbell, Shirreff (*Squadron Leader*)   143
Canberra, M.S.   204, 208, 211-212
Canterbury, Archbishop of   47
Canterbury Cathedral   47
Canterbury Grove   51-53, 60, 129-133, 135, 163, 191, 228, 234, 242, 249
Carrington Manufacturing Co. Ltd (*see also Camco*)   42, 49, 51, 54, 81, 125-126
Carson, Violet   119
Carter, Jimmy (*President of the United States*)   247
Carter Patterson Ltd.   158
Carter-Pedlar, Robert (*see also Magnaphone*)   69-71
Carter's Seeds Ltd.   156
Celestion Ltd.   71, 76, 185
Central Electricity Generating Board   213

259

The TANNOY Story

Chalkpits Museum, Amberley 11, 195
Changi, R.A.F. 92
Chapel Royal (*St James Palace*) 46
Charlton Cricket Club 33
Chatham 73
Chelmsford 19-20, 31
Churchill, Rt. Hon. Sir Winston 78, 105, 110, 169
Chusan, SS 225
Clark, Allen (*see also Plessey Ltd.*) 113, 120, 124, 139, 195, 218
Clarke, Lester (*see also Lester Clarke Garages and Bex Electric Ltd.*) 120, 124, 139, 218
Clarke Pickering & Partners 218
Clifford & Snell Ltd. 97-98, 101
Cliftonville, Kent 57, 90, 151, 156-157, 193, 216, 225
Clinker, RC (*see also British Thompson-Houston*) 21
Coatbridge, Scotland 11, 246-247, 249, 252, 256
Cole, EK and Co. Ltd. (see also EKCO) 153
Coleman, Eric 204
Colley, Colonel (*see also Thermionic Products Ltd., and the Soundmirror*) 156, 188-190, 195
Collins, Peter 222-223
Compigne, George 83, 234
Constable, Dr. 87
Cooper, Freddy 59-60
Cossor Radar Ltd. 133, 135, 163
Courtenay-Snell, Alfred 97-103, 110, 117
Cowling, Tom 140
Cox, Mr 131
Cox's Yard 131-133, 163
Cranwell, R.A.F. 90
Crocker, Norman 246-249, 251, 255
Crofthill Investment Trust 44, 56
Crowhurst, Norman 49, 79-80, 87
Cullis, Fred 133, 135
Cunard Ltd 210-211
Cunningham, Dennis 13

D

Dagenham Motors 154
Daily Herald 52
Daily Mail 19
Daily Mirror 44-46, 48, 52, 74, 82, 212
Daily Mirror Eight, the 44-48, 74, 82, 212
Daily Sketch 45, 48
Dakota (aircraft) 92-93
Dalton Street 23-25, 31-34, 193, 234
Davey, Alfred 50
Davis, Dr 87
Davis, Edie 132
Decca 80, 183-187
Decca/Brunswick 80
de Forest, Lee 21
Dene Street 112
Devonport 73
Dixon, Leslie 163

Dorking 26, 37, 111-113, 118, 137
Douglas Dakota 92-93
Douglas, Sir James Scott 222
Dowding, AVM Sir Hugh 89-90
Dowty Ltd 203
Draddy, Thomas 136
Duke of Richmond and Gordon 52, 68, 81
Dungeness Head 204-205
Dunn, Ian 248
Dust C. Eric 9
Dutton, Dr 187
Duxford, R.A.F. 85
Dyson family 15
Dysons Jewellers, of Leeds 15

E

East Wretham USAAF Station, East Anglia 107
Eckersley, Capt. PP (*see also Marconi, BBC Co. & Rediffusion*) 19-20, 27, 39, 55, 90, 258
Eden, Sir Anthony 176
Edwards, Freddy 125-127
EKCO 26, 38, 153, 166
Electradix Ltd. 163
Elizabeth, HM the Queen 173, 201, 210
Empire Electric Co. Ltd. 98
Empire Exhibition 43, 77
Empire Service, BBC 21, 74, 84
Erie Ltd. 153
Euston Station 198

F

F.H. Wheeler Ltd 90, 107, 160
F.I.D.O. (*Fog Intensive Dispersal Operations*) 110
F.W. Lucas 74, 154
Fairbrother, Joe L 195, 197
Fairley, Alan 142
Fangio, Juan Manuel 222
Farnborough RAE 178
Feisal, HM King 114
Fisher, Rt Reverend 47
Fleming, Dr JA 21, 27
Flying Scotsman 55
Forest de, Lee 21
Fountain, David 25, 29-30, 101, 111, 143, 156-157, 216, 251
Fountain, Dylis 11, 13
Fountain, Elsie (nèe Portwine) 13, 17-18, 23, 25-26, 74, 85, 90, 101, 156, 161, 163, 192-193, 210, 214-216, 219-220, 225
Fountain, Guy 5-18, 21--35, 38-41, 44-45, 47-54, 56-57, 59-61, 63-70, 74-75, 78-79, 81-83, 85-86, 89-92, 100-101, 111-114, 117, 119-122, 124-127, 129-132, 134-137, 139-143, 148-151, 153-161, 163 165, 168-169, 172-173, 178-179, 185-186, 188-189, 191-195, 197, 199-205, 207-225, 227-229, 231-235, 237-242, 245-247, 250-251, 253-255
Fountain, Jean 25, 101, 143, 156, 251

INDEX

Fountain, Mary (nèe Oldcorn) 15, 16
Fountain, Michael 5-13, 25-30, 83, 101, 110-112, 133, 141-147, 156, 160, 168, 191-193, 198, 204, 208, 211-225, 231-233, 241, 251-254
Fountain, Richard 11, 13, 16
Foyle Riding, near Oxted 20
Frew, Group Captain 82

G
G.E.C. 26, 59, 72, 76, 227-228
Garner, Alex 248
Garner Motors 44-45
Garrard Ltd 33, 42, 54, 150
Gatwick 199
George V 16, 21, 43, 77, 81, 85-87, 141
George VI 81, 141
Gilbert, John C.G. 11, 195, 219-224, 251
Gilbert, Marion 219-224
Gilbert, R.C. 13, 104
Gilbert Scott, Sir Giles 179
Glendenning, Raymond 146-147
Gloster Gladiator 88
Gold, Solomon (Solly) 119
Goodmans Ltd (see also *Martin Audio Ltd* and *Tannoy Goodmans Industries, T.G.I. Ltd.* 76, 91, 184-185, 249, 255
Granada 188
Gregory, Ken 107
Greyhound Racing Association 66, 142-143, 174, 197
Guy R. Fountain Ltd. 23, 25, 44, 165, 197, 234

H
H.M.V. (*His Master's Voice*) 51, 188
H.J. Leak & Co. Ltd. 76
Haines, W. (Bill) 13, 41, 49-53, 99-100, 110, 121-122, 130, 158, 185, 192-193, 202-203, 227, 231-232, 244
Hall, Willy 210
Handley Page 90
Hansard 170-171, 249
Harland & Wolff Ltd 208, 211
Harman, Sydney 237-249
Harman Industries (*International*) 50, 171, 228-249
Harris, Colonel 171, 237
Harrison, Beatrice (*cellist*) 20-21, 27, 256
Healey, Pat (*see also* Telephone Manufacturing Co) 74
Hendon, R.A.F. 86-87
Henley 144, 146, 148, 182, 212
Henley Royal Regatta 144, 146, 148, 182
Herald of Free Enterprise, the 252
Higgins, Margaret 112
High Wycombe 11, 228, 247, 249
Hill, Jonathan 13, 256
Hill, Keith 74, 81 117
Hinaidi, R.A.F. 94
Hindle, Ross 161
His Master's Voice (H.M.V.) 51, 98

Horowitz, Herb 246
Houlgate, Jack 62, 75, 79, 81, 87-88, 99-103, 105, 108-110, 124-125, 134-135, 143, 165, 181-182, 186-188, 255
House of Commons 165, 168, 171, 173
House of Lords 166, 168, 171, 230
Hudson, Jack 113, 117, 132
Hyams, Mr (accountant) 71
Hyman, Carl 142

I
Ice Rinks 52
Idzerda, Hans 31
Indian Railways 49
Ingram, Alan 203
International Broadcasting 80, 82
Iraq 113-114, 242-243, 248
Irish Broadcasting System 153

J
Jefferson, Phyllis 241-242
John Brown (*Shipbuilders*) 209, 211
John Logie Baird 23, 50
Johnson Matthey 100
Johnstone, Trevor 189
Jones, Samuel & Co. 188-189

K
Kelf-Cohen 102, 113
Kellog, Edward (*see also* Rice-Kellog) 35
Kenfig Hill & District Radio Relays, Porthcawl 39
Kenley, R.A.F. 82, 149
Kent 25-26, 39, 57, 204
Keston Manufacturing Co. Ltd. 41, 60, 130
Kingsway 20
Kingsway Hall, London 174, 176-177
Kirsting, Bill (*see also* Keston Manufacturing Co. Ltd.) 41
Kirsting, 'Chum' 41
Knight's Hill 129-130, 246
Krapoweickei, Madame 78
Kurt Muller 227

L
l'Enfant, Wally 154
Lake Success 238-239
Lambeth 130, 188, 244
Lambeth Borough Council 130, 244
Lancaster Avenue, West Norwood 17, 23, 25, 29, 34, 51, 112, 119, 216
Lancaster House 175-176
Lancaster Motors 17-18
Lancaster Road, West Norwood 17
Langdon, Claude 142
Langmuir, Irving 21
Lansdowne Hill 129-131, 136, 228
Leach, Jimmy 227

The TANNOY Story

Leander, HMS 73
Leeds 15, 158
Lester Clarke Garages 120
Liverpool 48, 210
Liverpool Street Station 48
Livingstone, Joan 153, 215
Livingstone, T.B. (Stan) 54, 65, 71, 75, 78-79, 101, 110, 122, 132, 137, 148, 155, 157-158, 163-164, 168, 173, 182, 184, 190, 194, 204, 207-208, 214-216, 220, 251, 253
Lockwood & Co. 127, 187
London County Council 62
London, Midland & Scottish Railway Co. 48, 53
London & North Eastern Railway Co. 48
Lord Chamberlain 47
Lucas (F.W.) Ltd 74, 154

M
M.B.E. 249
McDonald, Maureen 155
McDonald's Restaurants 9
McIntosh 'Mac' 126
MacKintosh, Charles 9
McLachlan, Dr Neil 33, 35
MacLennan, Jim 249
MacNamara, Terry 189
MacRobertson Air Race 85
MacRobertson, Sir William 95
Magnaphone Ltd. 69-71
Major, Bert 130
Majorca 225, 232, 235, 241, 251
Malaya, HMS 73
March, Freddie (*see also* Richmond and Gordon, Duke of 52, 68, 81 52
Marconi 19-20, 26-27, 31, 35, 76, 86, 187-188, 206
Marconi House 19-20
Margaret, H.R.H. Princess 47
Marks, Philip 49, 109
Marsden, Ernest 13, 158, 168
Martin Audio Ltd (see also *Goodmans Ltd* and *Tannoy Goodmans Industries, T.G.I. Ltd*)
Mason, Patrick 202-203
Melba, Dame Nellie 19-20, 31
Mercers of Sydenham 100
Merrick, Dick see also *Ferrograph Company* and *Wright and Weare Ltd.* 109
Metcalfe, Violet 50, 100
Metropolitan-Vickers Ltd 24
Microphone Bar Amplifier 97-98, 115
Mildenhall, R.A.F. 85
Mills, Bertram (*see also Bertram Mills Circus*) 67-68, 72, 142, 206, 208, 218, 254
Mills, Cyril 67-68, 72
Mills, Dr Paul 254
Ministry of (*Various*: Defence, Transport, Supply & Aircraft Production 16, 83-91, 102-103, 113, 118, 148, 159-160, 229

Ministry of Supply (Iraq) 242
Minnickfold, near Beare Green 111-112, 137
Mordaunt, Norman 184-185
Moughton, Barry 240-241
Mullard Ltd 124
Murkham, Leonard 79
Musa Ali 114

N
N.P.L. (*National Physical Laboratories*) 87-88
Naiad (Motor Cruiser) 83
Navy (Argentinian) 63, 74, 79, 181, 187
Navy (Royal) 63, 73-74, 79, 108-109, 118, 124-125, 131, 133, 181, 187
Navy (Royal Norwegian) 131-132
Navy Week, Chatham 73
Navy Week, Devonport 73
Nettlefold Place, West Norwood 49, 52, 129-136
New Wilson Electrical Manufacturing Ltd 98
Newark Air Museum 11, 13, 110
Newman, Tommy 70
News of the World 188
Newton, Edmund MBE 13, 104, 115, 216-217, 249
North Weald, R.A.F. 82
Norwood Road, West Norwood 17, 23, 27, 34, 129 134, 136

O
Odell, Leslie 49, 57, 158, 189
Oldcorn, Henry 16
Oldfield, Jack 156
Olympia 23, 38, 40, 49-54, 59-60, 62-65, 72, 78, 100, 152, 163, 210
Oxted 20

P
P.C.G.G., Radio (*see also* Idzerda, Hanz) 19, 31
P.L.U.T.O. (*Pipeline Under the Ocean*) 107
Paillard Ltd. 42-43
Palace of Westminster 11, 141, 143, 155, 165-176, 197-198, 219, 229-230, 235, 237-238, 249
Paramount Pictures Inc. 80
Parsons, Sir Charles 10
Pennefather, Capt. 73-74
Philips Ltd. 26, 76, 166, 187, 190, 227, 252
Pickering, Ronald 68, 207-208, 218, 229
Pickles, Wilfred 119
Pipe, Derek 13, 61, 243
Plessey Ltd (*Plessey Telecom*) 79, 81, 91, 113, 126, 137, 194-195, 246
Pontin's Holiday Camps 174
Porthcawl 39
Portwine, Constance 17-18
Portwine, Doris 17-18
Portwine, Elsie 17-18, 26
Portwine, Emma 17-18
Portwine, John 17-18, 25-26, 154

INDEX

Portwine, Joyce 17-18
Portwine, Marjorie 17-18
Portwine, Walter 16-18, 23
Post Office 18-20, 183
Preedy, E.A.H.W. (Bill) 11-13, 80-83, 107, 144, 158, 171-178, 193-194, 208, 213-214, 227-250
Prime Minister 169, 174
Princess Margaret 47
Public Services Agency 229
Pye Ltd 26, 224, 227, 254

Q

Queen Elizabeth II (Queen of England) 56, 172, 201
Queen Elizabeth Hall 201
QE2, M.V. 201, 208-210, 229
Queen Elizabeth, R.M.S. 210
Queen Mary, HRH 86
Queen Mary, R.M.S. 209
Quick, Michael (Mickey) 48, 74

R

R & A Sound 76
Rackham, Mollie 144
Rackham, Ronald H, 47, 57, 65, 83, 115, 134, 143 144, 146-147, 165, 167-168, 172, 182, 184-188, 194, 200-203, 205-206, 213-214, 216, 226-227, 239-240, 248, 254-255
Radio Exhibition 23, 37, 40-42, 60, 77
Radio Industries Club 157-158
Radio Luxembourg 40
Radio P.C.G.G. 19, 31
Ranmore Common 112, 118
Rediffusion Ltd. (also see Eckersley, Capt. P.P.) 39, 53, 157
Reith, John (*later Sir and Lord; see also BBC*) 20
Reslo Ltd (*see also* Murkham, Leonard) 76, 79, 91
Rice, Chester 35
Rice-Kellog (*see also* Rice, Chester; Kellog, Edward; and *American Electic Company*) 32, 35
Richmond and Gordon, Duke of 52, 68, 81
River Plate 74
Roberson, Tony 245
Roberts, Harry 30, 85, 95, 256
Robinson, E. Yeoman 24
Robottom, Norman 11-13, 46-47, 66-67, 70, 82, 112, 121, 145, 147, 168, 175, 177, 192, 194, 212, 217-218, 234, 253
Rocola Ltd 150
Rola Ltd 71, 76, 79, 91
Roper, Stanley 9, 26, 46, 64, 71, 98, 126, 129, 131, 134, 139, 144-145, 154, 177, 197, 213, 241, 252
Rosendale Road, West Dulwich 134
Round, HJ 21
Royal Albert Hall 81
Royal Observatory
Royal Train 55-56

Russell, Mrs (café owner, see also Mrs Albert) 131
Russell, Peter (finance director) 248

S

St. Athan, R.A.F. 92-93
S.G. Brown & Co. 31, 98, 109
Samuel Jones & Co. 188-189
Saunders, Roy 228
Savoy Hill 20
Saxby Signal Co. Ltd. (Westinghouse Brake) 23, 40
Scophony-Baird (see also Baird) 190
Scott Douglas, Sir James 222
Scottish Development Board 244-246
Selby, Yorks 15, 197
Selfridges 23
Shirreff, A. Campbell 143
Short Stirling 120, 124
Siemens Bros. 107
Simon Sound Ltd. 151
Simon, Reginald 151-153
Singfield, Thomas 13
Sizer, Group Captain 86-87, 89
Slater, Ted 244
Snagge, John 145
Sound Plastings Ltd. 155, 165, 197
Sound Rentals Ltd. 71, 161, 165, 197
Sound Systems Ltd. 153-154
Soundmirror, the (see also *Thermionic Products Ltd*) 188-189, 195
Southampton University 171, 199
St Margaret's Church 47
St James's Palace 46-47
St. Lawrence River 205
Standard Telephone & Cable Co. Ltd. 77
Street-Porter, Janet 253
Sun, The 252
Sunday Express 188, 252
Surrey 5, 11, 111
Sutherland, James 88
Swimming Pools 52
Sydenham Place, West Norwood 131, 136

T

T.C.C. Ltd. 79
T.G.I. Ltd (*see also* Tannoy Goodmans Industries) 249, 254
Tannoy Canada 197, 207, 239-240, 244-245
Tannoy Goodmans Industries 249, 255
Tannoy Ireland 154, 197
Tannoy Marine Ltd. 133, 155-159, 197, 201, 204-205, 211-212
Tannoy Motor Company 74, 132, 154
Tannoy Products Ltd. (*see also* Tulsemere Mfg. Co.; *and also* Sound Rentals Ltd.) 38, 42, 54, 76, 140, 159, 188, 197, 203-204, 211-212
Tannoy Rentals Ltd. 37, 197
Tannoy, 'The Sound People' 45, 61

263

The **TANNOY** Story

Tantalum Alloy 22-24, 26, 40
Taylor, John W.R. 256
Taylor, W.F. 81
Telephone Manufacturing Co. 31,42, 74, 85
Terrett, Dennis 11-13, 115, 119, 134, 158, 161, 167, 169-172, 192, 199-200, 202-203, 205, 213-214, 217 218, 231, 241-243, 245
Thermionic Products Ltd 188-189
Thomas Place, off Norwood Road, West Norwood 17, 27, 137
Thompson, Diamond, Butcher, Radio and Record Distributors (see also *Decca*) 184
Thompson, E.C. 76
Thompson-Houston, British 21, 76-77, 147, 186, 207
Thorneycroft Ltd. 210
Thumbwoood, Tom 131
Thurlow Arms 34-35, 37, 42, 136, 255
Thurlow, Lord Edward 136
Timms, Mr (see also *Lockwood & Co.*) 126-127, 187
Towler, Freddie 207, 239, 241 207-208, 238-241, 244
Towler, Mary 207, 238-240
Trinity House 13, 79, 204-205
Triotron 57
Truby, W (Bill) 50
Truscott, Bert 130
Tulsemere Manufacturing Co. 23-26, 38, 41-42, 255
Tulsemere Road 23-24, 26
Twentyman, Mr (see also Bex Electric) 120-121
Twiss, Admiral Sir Frank 230

U
U.S.A.A.F. East Wretham 107
Ultra Ltd. 38
United Nations 141, 173, 198, 207, 232

V
V.E. Day 141
V.J. Day 144
Venables, Frank 133-134, 215
Vickers 24, 92, 94-95, 256
Vickers Valentia 94
Vickers Valetta 92
Vickers Victoria 94
Victory Parade 141-144
Voigt, Paul 39, 60, 63, 68, 72, 76

W
Waples, Philip 165, 172, 193, 200
Warner's Holiday Camps 174
Warners 142
Watts, Cecil 152-153
Waylett Place
Weller Cars 137
Weller, John 15, 17, 137

Wells, Gerald
Western Electric Ltd. 35, 43, 75, 77, 146, 181-182, 186-187
Westinghouse Brake and Saxby Signal Co. Ltd 23, 40
Westminster Audio Communications Ltd 249
Wheeler, Frank (*see also FH Wheeler Ltd. and Bex Electric*) 90-92, 111, 120, 133, 156, 160-161
Wheeler, George 11-13, 30-37, 40-42, 47-49, 51, 53, 55, 62, 65, 68, 71-72, 74-75, 80-81, 85-87, 90-91, 95, 97, 100, 105, 110, 122, 124-126, 139-140, 148-149, 156, 159-161, 164-166, 179, 181, 187, 191-193, 233-234, 248, 255
Wheeler family (George) 31
Wheeler, Phyllis 90, 111
White City Stadium, Shepherd's Bush 145
White, David 145
Whiteley, Dick 224-225
Whiteley Electrical and Radio Company 224
Whiting, Jim 137, 176, 193-194, 234
Wild, Norman 133, 160, 163-165, 184-186, 190, 195, 197, 207
Wilson, Harold 174
Wilson, J.B. 256
Wireless World 9, 24-25, 30, 32, 40-43, 49-50, 54, 76 77, 95, 152, 183, 214, 256
Woolwich 33, 35, 37, 42, 87, 122
Woolwich Town Hall 33, 35, 37, 42
Worters, Paul 203, 216-217
Writtle, Nr Chelmsford 19

Y
Yates, Claude 13, 121-122